Digital Currencies in The New Global World Order

Ranjan Aneja · Robert Dygas
Editors

Digital Currencies in The New Global World Order

palgrave
macmillan

Editors
Ranjan Aneja
Department of Economics
Central University of Haryana
Mahendragarh, Haryana, India

Robert Dygas
SGH Warsaw School of Economics
Warsaw, Poland

ISBN 978-981-97-4809-9 ISBN 978-981-97-4810-5 (eBook)
https://doi.org/10.1007/978-981-97-4810-5

This Palgrave Macmillan imprint is published by the registered company Springer Nature Singapore Pte Ltd.
The registered company address is: 152 Beach Road, #21-01/04 Gateway East, Singapore 189721, Singapore

We Dedicate this Book

to

Late Mrs. Veena Aneja
(Mother of Prof. Ranjan Aneja)

Preface

The Digital Currencies in the new Global world order define a new era of the digital transformation of the world economy which is getting more dependent on blockchain technology and the systems are controlled by the central banks, which want to establish their digital currencies (CBDC). The new world order is in progress as more military conflicts such as in Ukraine, the Middle East, Africa, and Central Asia stream to set up the conditions where trade is from one side more global but from the other more controlled by the systems. There is no definite answer regarding how the central banks by establishing their digital currencies will impact the world order and global trade. At the moment, the economy is in the transition stage where several new features of the international financial settlement systems are tested. It seems that CDBC is not an accidental event but rather the set of opportunities created by large financial asset management companies like Black Rock and Vanguard. Data transmission and accuracy play an important role in global trade which is an important part of the global financial system. As there is the point of the creation of the new world order related to the global economy and trade there is the challenge of control and financial system management. CBDCs seem to be the option but there is a need also for the existence of cryptocurrencies which can be also effectively used for the settlement among the business.

IMF tries to find a way to regulate the coexistence of such digital currencies in different economies depending on their level of economic development are not even ready to start the transformation process to replace their fiat currencies with digital ones. The book gives a current overview of digital currencies and how they are in line with the trade activities in the chosen countries in Asia, Europe, and other parts of the world. The feedback is not clear as there are no agreed standards in global trade and even international institutions like the World Trade Organization (WTO) are not able to give the proof of concept (PoC) of the digital currency tools, which can be used in global trade. Besides the problems related to scalability, and security the authors believe that one of the important and positive aspects of digital currencies in global trade is the cost reduction of the transactions. The countries, which are the engines of global trade like China, India, Japan, the US, and South Korea are trying to use that opportunity with their partners. In the case of China, it is quite often done on the level of the FTAs or multilateral trade agreements such as RCEP (Regional Comprehensive Economic Partnership Agreement). This is also the process of dethroning the US dollar by China in the new world order trade era, where the global trade strength is supported by military readiness and the capacity in case of war. Furthermore, considering the context of the uncertain international political and economic environment, which is under the RCEP a sovereign digital currency could improve the effectiveness of monetary policy and supervision capacity, and thus improve the financial risk prevention and control system of regional countries. Consequently, Chinese sovereign digital currency based on blockchain technology could become an effective path for the internationalization of e-CNY under the RCEP framework. There could be a concern if China monopolizes the digital currency system in global trade and makes the countries, which are members of the Belt and Road Initiative (BRI) more dependent on China. Even though logically it seems that this scenario is possible, there is no stated evidence by the scientists that it is going to happen shortly. The aim of the book is also to keep the problem clean of the unpredictable politics and bias which make the entire problem difficult to size and evaluate from the economic perspective. The effort made by the authors is significant and huge regarding the complex topic and strongly relates to undefined standards in the implementation of digital currencies in global trade. The complexity of the topic is the challenge but it needs to be tackled and analysed from different angles and perspectives. That is the way that this book gathered so many scientists and enthusiasts of digital currencies in global trade from different countries. The future of the technology standards in global trade is created now by the countries with the biggest share in international trade such as the US, China, India, and Japan. The role of the EU is weakening now due to the very rapid “green transformation”, which does not give the business an alternative and imposes severe restrictions and reporting obligations such as ESG reports. It creates further problems in the global trade cooperation between the EU and MERCOSUR countries, which are not as advanced in sustainability approach in the global trade as the EU.

In an era defined by rapid technological advancements and an increasingly interconnected global economy, digital currencies have emerged as a transformative force with the potential to redefine the foundations of international trade. More than 130 countries (98% of the global economy) are exploring the possibility of introducing digital currencies to their economies, especially in global trade. The war in Ukraine and Israel accelerated the process of changing the current world order. This book gives a broad spectrum of the problem, especially in China, India, Germany, and Iceland. It is a joint effort of Indian, Polish, and Icelandic academic scientists to make this book up-to-date with the problem analysis. **The main research question of the book is how digital currencies impact global trade in the new global economic world order**. There are also other questions, which relate to this main one raised in the other chapters. As traditional financial systems grapple with challenges ranging from cross-border payment inefficiencies to complex currency exchange processes, the advent of digital currencies promises to streamline transactions, enhance security, and facilitate more efficient cross-border trade. The introduction and widespread adoption of the digital yuan in China exemplify the evolving landscape of global trade, where nations are exploring digital currencies as tools to enhance efficiency, reduce costs, and exert greater control over their financial systems. As other countries and regions observe and respond to these developments, the digital yuan serves as a notable case study in the application of digital currencies in the context of international trade especially in India.

The book consists of 18 chapters. Chapter 1 analyses the most relevant literature on the topic of the book giving the different views on the subject. The main tool for literature review is the Mendelay.com platform. The period of the literature review covers 2010–2023. The topic regarding implementation of the digital currencies in international trade evolved dynamically in the literature recently. As an outcome, 332 relevant publications were found on the Mendeley platform in 2014–2023, but 290 were published after 2019 and 206 in 2020. That is why the authors decided to focus on the period 2019–2023.

Chapters 2 and 3 focus on The Eurosystem and assess the possible issuance of digital central bank money for the digital euro area. These chapters analyse the economic potentials of the future Digital European Central Bank Currency, the Digital Euro, against the background of the current global trade position, European finance system, regulatory environment, and tech-innovation ecosystem and ask for the risks accompanied by the ongoing race for the leading international Central Bank Digital Currency between US, EU, and China as well as the competition with private digital currencies in the form of stablecoins. A digital euro would provide another payment method to choose from in the euro area. Therefore, a digital euro should be designed to meet the needs of the population. This raises a whole series of interesting questions, not least given the current investigation phase: How do private individuals currently assess a possible digital euro? What needs could it satisfy? Could it be designed as a kind of digital cash? Or, could it conceivably compete with traditional non-cash payment instruments? And what factors could ultimately influence its acceptance and use by consumers? According to the author, German society must ultimately decide for itself, through trust, acceptance, and use, whether the introduction of a digital euro is ultimately a curse or a blessing. If the financial system is based on the Digital Euro, an innovative ecosystem of competitive new solutions and services ECB should develop with traditional and new finance actors a masterplan for future development. Without a promising business model, the Digital Euro constitutes only a relatively weak line of defence for the ECB.

Chapter 4 identified the questions of distances and culture when doing international trade. Therefore, the well-known and classical SWOT analysis allows us to shed light on the pros and cons of digital currencies. The authors of the chapter conclude that, while CBDCs hold considerable promise, their implementation must be carefully managed to preserve financial stability and complement existing monetary mechanisms.

Chapter 5 shows that the economic factors are not the only aspects in the debate about the implementation of the CBDCs. The public debate neglects the fact that particular features of CBDCs have incredible political potential. The chapter lists the most important political opportunities and dangers that relate to CBDCs based on the author's critical review of the projects. For each opportunity, the probability and significance were evaluated based on the questionnaire among experts. The results of the survey are then analysed in the context of international trade. Especially, political risks and their impact on international trade will be considered. The authors of the chapter concluded that CDBC is rather a political project which is influential on international trade.

Chapter 6 investigates how the distribution of monitoring assets is impacted not only by the choice of digital currencies but also by several hypothetical situations, such as those relating to the introduction of digital currencies by central banks (CBDCs). Digital currencies, which have recently witnessed a proliferation of design options, are considered to be a factor challenging established financial systems and may affect the way these systems are now regulated. Recently, there has been a proliferation of design options for digital currencies. One of the most notable developments in the realm of digital currencies is the proliferation of Central Bank Digital Currencies (CBDCs). Governments around the world are exploring and, in some cases, actively developing their digital currencies to modernize payment systems, reduce transaction costs, and gain better control over monetary policy. The rise of CBDCs holds significant implications for global trade, as these state-backed digital currencies have the potential to simplify cross-border transactions, mitigate exchange rate volatility, and improve financial inclusion on a global scale.

Chapter 7 highlights the swift expansion of digital payments, with China leading in cumulative transaction value and India's Unified Payment Interface (UPI) changing the nation's payment landscape. Besides that, the digital currency stands balanced to appear as an invigorating tool for enhancing the current stability of the financial system. In addition to this it plays an important role in promoting the adoption of green finance practices, and thus contributing towards achieving sustainable development goals.

Chapter 8 deals with various aspects of digital currencies including their evolution, types, and positive and negative dimensions. This is a descriptive study, which aims to discuss the potential benefits of digital currencies and their impact on international trade and the economic growth of the Indian economy. Although there are potential benefits that can be drained out, the implementation of digital currency is accompanied by several challenges, such as those related to wallet security and privacy of the consumers, data management, irreversibility of transactions, price volatility, lack of availability of infrastructure facilities, awareness and acceptability among the public. Such concerns need to be addressed efficiently.

Chapter 9 clarifies the concept of digital money, its differences with "cryptocurrencies", the reason behind the recently experienced boom in acceptance theoretically and its importance in international trade. It concludes that the digital rupee can be utilized by financial institutions for quicker lending and payments in the global economy, as well as for programmed payments for subsidies. In the foreseeable future, a cashless economy may become more widespread (Bender, 2022). This might help the government achieve its goal of cashless transactions and benefit the banking sector.

Chapter 10 attempted to test the influence of attitudes regarding the e-Rupee towards the intention of adopting the e-Rupee among the traders. 327 traders have expressed their opinions through a structured questionnaire. The result indicates a profound connection between attitude and intention of adopting e-Rupee. The chapter suggests the two most important factors involved in the judgement of people regarding the e-Rupee, and the Government of India may focus on promoting the same. An awareness campaign regarding the usefulness of the e-Rupee for its successful adoption of usage among traders is needed. The Government shall also take necessary steps to convince the traders to use the e-Rupee.

Chapter 11 investigates the transformative landscape of Central Bank Digital Currencies (CBDCs) and their profound impact on global trade. The overarching aim is to comprehensively analyse the significance of CBDCs in fostering financial inclusion, driving economic growth, and reshaping international trade dynamics. The central focus of the chapter is to assess how CBDCs might positively or negatively impact a nation's monetary policies, financial stability, and overall economic landscape. This includes evaluating the potential to enhance payment systems, foster financial inclusion, and streamline cross-border transactions while also considering the implications for traditional banking institutions.

Chapter 12 analyses the potential of currency system shifts from historic Dollar dominance towards a new multipolar regime in the digital age. Based on trade and currency theory as well as current empirical research chances and risks associated with digital currency competition among leading central bank currencies but also with private digital currency forms are considered and prospective development paths in global trade with them are outlined. Digital currencies may have the potential to break up existing path dependencies and rearrange international finance orders. CBDC can take a pacemaker role in shaping new global financial architecture that brings innovative solutions for urgent global issues. However, at this point, and concerning currency competition, the current status of CBDC projects does not allow for concrete projections of future contributions to international financial systems advancement.

Chapter 13 examines the significant effects that digital currencies will have on the development of international trade and economic growth. These cutting-edge financial instruments are reshaping the traditional dynamics of global trade and fostering economic growth as they gain increasing popularity. The study begins by elucidating the foundational concepts underlying digital currencies, with a specific focus on their impact on international trade and economic growth. It concludes that digital currencies can ease cross-border payments and lower the expenses associated with currency translation, which can help with global trade. They also cast doubt on the stability of currency rates and the coordination of monetary policy. The long-term impact of digital currencies depends heavily on how widely they are adopted by businesses and consumers.

Chapter 14 examines the relationship between digital payments and economic growth in India using the ARDL cointegration-bound testing approach. It has been found that the use of card payments and retail electronic payments has a favourable effect on India's economic growth. Prepaid payment methods and Retail electronic payments, however, have less of an impact on India's economic progress. Consequently, this chapter underscores the significance of card payment and retail electronic payment as a catalyst for economic expansion in India.

Chapter 15 unveils the significance of The Reserve Bank of India's Digital Currency and answers the question of how it reshapes and impacts the landscape of international trade. Establishing CBDC is an essential step towards modernizing financial institutions, promoting inclusive economic growth, and establishing India as a leader in the digital economy. RBI can navigate the changing global finance landscape and support a more effective, equitable, and robust international commerce ecosystem by using the potential of CBDCs while resolving issues.

Chapter 16 focusses on understanding the significance and impact of CBDCs in the world of banking, particularly in the context of fostering financial inclusion, economic growth, and global trade. It was stated in this chapter that RBI's digital currency, if introduced, can play a prominent role in global trading, potentially simplifying cross-border transactions and reducing costs, enhancing financial inclusion, and improving transparency. The methodological approach involves an in-depth examination of existing CBDC initiatives worldwide, with a focus on case studies such as China's e-CNY, The Bahamas' Sand Dollar, and Nigeria's e-Naira. A significant revelation is the multifaceted role of CBDCs beyond mere transactional efficiency. The chapter identifies an often-overlooked aspect—their potential to revolutionize credit information for trade finance. By providing a transparent and traceable platform, CBDCs have the capacity to offer a robust foundation for evaluating the creditworthiness of businesses engaged in international transactions.

Chapter 17 examines the complex relationship between digital currencies and international trade, investigating the various opportunities along with the obstacles. A comprehensive analysis of empirical evidence and case studies have been included to demonstrate the positive impact of digital currencies on cross-border transactions. Specifically, the chapter's findings highlight the enhanced efficiency, cost reduction, promotion of financial inclusion, and facilitation of transparency and traceability in trade that digital currencies offer. Digital currencies have the potential to transform global trade, offering both opportunities and challenges. Due to the landscape's dynamic character, stakeholders must be adaptable and proactive to maximize benefits and minimize the risks.

Chapter 18 explores the benefits of CBDC to enhance cross-border payment processes. Implementing CBDCs in cross-border payment systems can alleviate privacy, data safeguards, transparency, and security concerns. Key insights and lessons from various cross-border projects are elaborated, providing future directions for the cross-border CBDC projects. This study also discusses policy recommendations that can be implemented to make the most of CBDCs' benefits in cross-border payment systems.

Simultaneously, the decentralized nature of cryptocurrencies, exemplified by the pioneering Bitcoin and the multitude of alternative coins, has garnered considerable attention in the international trade arena. These digital assets, operating on blockchain technology, offer an alternative to traditional fiat currencies and present new opportunities for borderless commerce. While cryptocurrencies pose challenges related to regulatory concerns and market volatility, they also provide a decentralized, transparent, and immutable ledger that has the potential to revolutionize supply chain finance, reduce fraud, and increase overall trade efficiency.

In this exploration of the impact of digital currencies on global trade, it is crucial to examine the multifaceted aspects of this technological shift. Beyond the financial benefits, the integration of digital currencies necessitates a comprehensive understanding of regulatory frameworks, cybersecurity considerations, and the potential social and economic ramifications. As the world moves towards a more digitized and interconnected future, stakeholders in global trade, including governments, financial institutions, businesses, and consumers, must navigate the evolving landscape of digital currencies to harness their benefits while addressing challenges and ensuring the stability of the international financial system. This comprehensive analysis aims to provide insights into the intricate dynamics that shape the future of global trade in the digital age.

We hope that this book will help professionals and academic researchers to better understand Digital Currencies in the new Global world order and their application in global trade.

Mahendragarh, India — Ranjan Aneja
Warsaw, Poland — Robert Dygas

Contents

Editors and Contributors

About the Editors

Ranjan Aneja, Ph.D., is a Professor in Economics at the Central University of Haryana, India. He completed his Master's Degree in economics from Kurukshetra University, Kurukshetra, India, and his Ph.D. from Guru Jambheshwar University of Science and Technology, Hisar, India. He has 18 years of teaching and research experience. His areas of interest are Economic Modelling and Policy Analysis and Macroeconomic stability. He has published several research papers in premium journals. He serves as a reviewer to multiple journals of international repute indexed in Scopus and Web of Science and listed in ABDC. He has also served/serving on the editorial board of several journals such as the Journal of Public Affairs, Wiley, SN Business & Economics, Springer-Nature and Cognet Economics & Finance, Taylor & Francis.

Robert Dygas, Ph.D., is an Assistant Professor at SGH Warsaw School of Economics at the East Asian Economic Studies Department of The World Economy Research Institute. He completed his master's studies at the Warsaw School of Economics, majoring in Finance and Banking, and at the University of Aarhus in Denmark, majoring in Management. He received his Ph.D. in Economics from the Warsaw School of Economics in 2003 (dissertation: "Strategic Management in the Mobile Telephony Industry in Poland in 1995–2001"). In 2011, he was awarded the Executive Master of Business Administration degree by the Warsaw University of Technology, Business School. He has 23 years of professional experience in multinational corporations in IT, telecommunications, and the public sector. From 2015 to 2020, he worked also as the external expert for the evaluation of Horizon2020-ECI-FTI proposals (Research Executive Agency EASME under the power delegated by the European Commission).

Academic interests: geoeconomics, economies of Asian countries.

Contributors

Anjali Ahuja School of Commerce and Finance, Geeta University, Panipat, Haryana, India

Ranjan Aneja Department of Economics, Central University of Haryana, Mahendragarh, Haryana, India

Andreas Bielig SGH Warsaw School of Economics, Warsaw, Poland

Suman Dahiya Department of Commerce, Central University of Haryana, Mahendragarh, Haryana, India

Aryan Deb Institute of Engineering & Management (UEM-K), Kolkata, India

Saptaparni Dhol Institute of Engineering & Management (UEM-K), Kolkata, India

Robert Dygas SGH Warsaw School of Economics, World Economy Research Institute, Warsaw, Poland

Gretar Thor Eythorsson Faculty of Business, University of Akureyri, Akureyri, Iceland

Mohit Fogaat Department of Commerce, Central University of Haryana, Mahendragarh, Haryana, India

Soumik Gangopadhyay Institute of Engineering & Management (UEM-K), Kolkata, India

Saugat Ghosh XBS, St. Xavier's University, Kolkata, India

Rajender S. Godara Department of Economics Mittal School of Business, Phagwara, Punjab, India

Sanjeev Gupta Central University of Himachal Pradesh, Dharamshala, Himachal Pradesh, India

Anuj Jatav Shri Ram College of Commerce, University of Delhi, Delhi, India

Magdalena Kozińska Department of Banking Safety Net, SGH Warsaw School of Economics, Collegium of Socio-Economics, Institute of Banking, Warsaw, Poland

Helga Kristjansdottir Faculty of Business, University of Akureyri, Akureyri, Iceland

Jitender Kumar Department of Management Studies, Deenbandhu Chhotu Ram University of Science and Technology, Murthal, Haryana, India;
Department of Management Studies, Deenbandhu Chhotu Ram University of Science and Technology, Murthal, Haryana, India

Krishan Kumar Department of Commerce, Central University of Haryana, Mahendragarh, Haryana, India

Sunil Kumar Department of Economics Mittal School of Business, Phagwara, Punjab, India

Vikas Kumar Central University of Haryana, Mahendragarh, India

Madan Lal Department of Commerce, University of Delhi, Delhi, India

Sonu Madan Department of Economics, Ch. Bansi Lal University, Bhiwani, India

Rajendra Prasad Meena Department of Commerce, Central University of Haryana, Mahendragarh, Haryana, India

Waldemar Milewicz SGH Warsaw School of Economics, Warsaw, Poland

Gabriel A. Ogunmola Faculty of Management, Sharda University, Andijan, Uzbekistan

Manas Roy Department of Economics, Faculty of Management Studies, Marwadi University Rajkot, Rajkot, Gujarat, India

Suchana Roy Institute of Engineering & Management (UEM-K), Kolkata, India

B. Sangeetha Department of Commerce, Central University of Haryana, Mahendragarh, Haryana, India

N. Savitha Department of Social Sciences, School of Social Sciences and Languages, Vellore Institute of Technology, Vellore, Tamil Nadu, India

Krati Sethi Department of Economics, School of Humanities and Social Sciences, Manipal University Jaipur, Jaipur, Rajasthan, India

Rajni Sharma Department of Economics, Arya P.G. College, Panipat, India

Kjartan Sigurdsson Faculty of Business, University of Akureyri, Akureyri, Iceland

Bhushan Singh Department of Commerce, Central University of Haryana, Mahendragarh, Haryana, India

Gurjinder Singh Department of Commerce, PGGCG Sector 42, Chandigarh, India

Geethu Rachel Stephen Department of Social Sciences, School of Social Sciences and Languages, Vellore Institute of Technology, Vellore, Tamil Nadu, India

Tanvi Central University of Himachal Pradesh, Dharamshala, Himachal Pradesh, India

Pankaj Tiwari Faculty of Management, Sharda University, Andijan, Uzbekistan

Amandeep Verma Department of Economics, Central University of Haryana, Mahendragarh, India

List of Figures

List of Tables

CHAPTER 1

Literature Review: The Digital Currencies in the New Global World Order

Robert Dygas and Ranjan Aneja

The Literature Review

Even though the period before 2019 can be treated rather as the historic which supports the current state of literature development in the aspect of implementing digital currencies in the global trade, two positions from 2015 require the attention. The most cited article (113 citations) was the Ripple payment system and digital currency as it was developed independently of Bitcoin. An interesting fact is that, although this system attracted many businesses having the second highest markup after Bitcoin, it has no scientific studies of the provision of Ripple and it did not become a popular trade platform (Armknecht et al., 2015).

R. Dygas (✉)
SGH Warsaw School of Economics, World Economy Research Institute, Warsaw, Poland
e-mail: rdygas1@sgh.waw.pl

R. Aneja
Department of Economics, Central University of Haryana, Mahendragarh, Haryana, India

R. Aneja and R. Dygas (eds.), *Digital Currencies in The New Global World Order*, https://doi.org/10.1007/978-981-97-4810-5_1

In the second example from 2015, one of the authors described the model, which pilots to use of digital currencies for climate change transactions known as Complementary Currencies for Climate Change (4C) or Global 4C Mitigation (G4CM), but it was not the case with the application of digital currencies in international trade but rather the market and monetary instrument as the part of the financial architecture of climate change regulations in European Union (Chen, 2015). Those two examples confirmed in some sense the statement of the author that the relevant literature describes in more depth the application of digital currencies in global trade can be found after 2019. Of course, it cannot be generalised, but this can be treated as the starting point for further analysis. Additionally, important events such as technology development for global trade, artificial intelligence (AI) and automation studies and applications, the global trade digitalisation process, COVID-19, and the war in Ukraine and Israel impacted the application process of digital currencies in international trade. Most of those events started after 2019.

The authors used mainly articles as a form of writing published by different 242 journals. Interestingly, only 20 relevant books were indicated in the analysed period. It shows that the topic of the application of digital currencies in international trade is still not fully analysed and is quite complex to measure and evaluate not only from the perspective of the global trading companies but also the governments especially central banks and International Monetary Fund (IMF).

As of now, digital currency is not a fact yet on the global scale in trade, but some authors indicate that is unavoidable (Hachim, 2022; Kadoo & Sodi, 2023; Manjula et al., 2022; Shkodina et al., 2019; Sigurðsson et al., 2023; Singh et al., 2019; van der Linden & Łasak, 2023) and can lead even to the global digital currency (Bhaskar et al., 2022). The majority of the authors are positive about the implementation of digital currency in trade, but some authors still have doubts regarding the existence of one global financial system due to the expansion of the Belt and Road Initiative and its financial system (Maddox et al., 2021; Ricoy-Casas, 2022). That is why some of the authors recommend the need for global regulations by the United Nations in the aspect of the governance of the digital economy (Shelepov, 2022) and also implementing the standards in the national regulations (Arunda, 2021; Kochergin, 2022). According to the World Bank Group, the G20 has made enhancing cross-border payments a priority and endorsed a comprehensive programme to address the key challenges (World Bank Group, 2021). Also, the need for establishing the Multilateral Committee on Financial Instruments (MultiCoFI) to work out the fine details to innovate financial instruments (such as The New World Trading Currency) facilitating trade for development was underlined by some authors (Adeshile, 2021).

China is a leader of the e-CNY as the real money for trade transactions and it gives directions to the entire financial world, but the problem is that China would like to frame the global financial system for trade transactions, especially under the global trade agreements, especially The Regional Comprehensive Economic Partnership Agreement (RCEP) where China is the leader and controller of the trade transactions. So far, the literature on this topic is rather limited and some authors tried to find the implementation of digital currencies in trade as the model for integration of the Asian countries (New Asian Regionalism) participating in such agreements using the soft law. This type of thought in literature underlines the New Regional Economic Order (NREO) (Mishra & Valencia, 2023) or Bilateral Currency Swap Agreement (Yao & Wang, 2023), which can be part of the New Global World Order which intakes the entire financial system used in the global trade. These aspects of the global financial system and the role of digital currencies were discussed by the authors Ranjan and Robert Dygas. The authors also studied the International Monetary Fund's documents, the European Commission's directives and recommendations regarding international settlements and the new global financial system design. Besides that, the summary of published quantitative approaches/models and results of the research were a starting point for the further investigation of a design of The New Global Financial System (NGFS) and how it can be implemented globally (Aneja & Dygas, 2022).

An interesting approach besides the application of digital currencies in the global free trade agreements (GFTAs) is the analysis of the implementation of digital currencies and electronic payments in global investment initiatives such as the Belt and Road Initiative (BRI) funded and managed by the Chinese government in 2013. The authors used the systematic fit index to show the reasoning for using digital currencies for electronic payments between China and the countries involved in BRI (more than 100 countries in 2022). This reasoning showed that bilateral agreements, bilateral trade, level of financial development, geopolitics, economic foundation and infrastructure development had a relevant impact on the implementation of the Chinese payment system in such countries as

Malaysia, Singapore, Thailand, Russia, UAE (Li et al., 2023). Chinese authors rather show positive aspects of the Chinese financial e-payment system used in The Belt and Road Initiative so that can be misleading that such a system is applicable on a global scale and has a positive impact on international finance (Li et al., 2021).

There is also described in literature an interesting example of a BRICS case regarding the use of the electronic settlement platform for the transactions between Russia (due to the sanctions for war in Ukraine) and other BRICS countries. This payment mechanism was originated by Russia as the pilot project for BRICS countries and others, which wanted to join the new settlement system (Asish & Swarupa, 2022; Balyuk & Balyuk, 2023).

The digital currencies in global trade are also treated by some authors as "the third form of money", which will change the existing economic, financial and trade relations both within individual states and in the global space (Kuznetsova & Larina, 2023). Some authors believe that the blockchain will be the main technology for the use of digital currencies in global trade because the blockchain has the potential to minimise the cost and time required to facilitate transactions that rely on third-party loans or insurance (Mukherjee, 2023). The other authors believe that the Bitcoin infrastructure is the prerequisite for the implementation of the digital currency in the trade (Saiedi et al., 2021). According to recent studies, international financial messaging systems play a significant role as part of the global financial infrastructure, because they secure the legitimacy of the transactions before they are settled (Wong & Nelson, 2021). It is also important for building a national monetary system on national digital currencies and their further integration into the global digital currency which can be used in trade (Panova, 2020). From the perspective of the time line digital currencies will have to go through a long evolution before they might have a chance to become an integral part of the monetary systems instead of being purely speculative assets (Sławiński, 2019).

Other authors try to analyse which technology will last and support the future global financial system in trade. For some authors, technical factors are the most important criteria for accepting digital currencies in trade transactions compared to the goal (Tavasoli, 2020). There is no clear answer as it is quite difficult to predict the future technology game changer in international trade (Wandhöfer, 2022).

References

Adeshile, A. R. (2021). The Imperatives of Financial Instruments to Addressing the Working Capital Challenges of Businesses in the Global Value Chains Trades: The New World Trading Currency. *International Journal of Applied Research in Management and Economics, 4*(1), 50–59. https://doi.org/10.33422/ijarme.v4i1.618

Aneja, R., & Dygas, R. (Eds.). (2022). *Digital Currencies and the New Global Financial System* (1st ed., pp. 1–16). Routledge. https://doi.org/10.4324/9781003310365

Armknecht, F., Karame, G. O., Mandal, A., Youssef, F., & Zenner, E. (2015). Ripple: Overview and Outlook. In M. Conti, M. Schunter & I. Askoxylakis (Eds.), *Trust and Trustworthy Computing: 8th International Conference, TRUST 2015, Heraklion, Greece, August 24–26, 2015, Proceedings 8* (pp. 163–180). Springer. https://doi.org/10.1007/978-3-319-22846-4_10

Arunda, B. B. (2021). Transmutation of Central Banking Policies and the Legal Implications of Adopting Central Bank Digital Currencies (CBDCs). *Journal of Cmsd, 6*(4), 143–171.

Asish, D., & Swarupa, C. K. (2022). De-centralized Cross-border Payments for Global Economic Status Quo. *i-Manager's Journal on Management, 16*(4), 1. https://doi.org/10.26634/jmgt.16.4.18899

Balyuk, I. A., & Balyuk, M. A. (2023). Digitalization of International Settlements: Tradecoin VS US Dollar. *World Economy and International Relations, 67*(7), 33–43. https://doi.org/10.20542/0131-2227-2023-67-7-33-43

Bhaskar, R., Hunjra, A. I., Bansal, S., & Pandey, D. K. (2022). Central Bank Digital Currencies: Agendas for future research. *Research in International Business and Finance, 62*. https://doi.org/10.1016/j.ribaf.2022.101737

Chen, D. B. (2015). World Currencies for Sustainability. In *World Economics Association (WEA) Conferences* (Vol. 1, pp. 1–26).

Hachim, B. A. (2022). Mechanism of Transition of the Digital Economy in Developing Countries/reality and Challenges (The Experience of Singapore as a Model). *International Journal of Humanities and Educational Research, 4*(2). https://doi.org/10.47832/2757-5403.13.12

Kadoo, S., & Sodi, K. (2023). An Analysis of Cryptocurrency, Bitcoin and the Future. *International Journal of Advanced Research in Science, Communication and Technology*, pp. 287–292. https://doi.org/10.48175/ijarsct-8157

Kochergin, D. (2022). Crypto-assets: Economic Nature, Classification and Regulation Turnover. *International Organisations Research Journal, 17*(3). https://doi.org/10.17323/1996-7845-2022-03-04

Kuznetsova, V. V., & Larina, O. I. (2023). Implications of the Introduction of Retail Digital Currencies by Central Banks for Economic Relations. *International Trade and Trade Policy, 9*(2), 85–99. https://doi.org/10.21686/2410-7395-2023-2-85-99

Li, T. Y., Min D., & Miao, H. (2023). The Development Fit Index of Digital Currency Electronic Payment Between China and the One Belt One Road Countries. *Research in International Business and Finance, 64*. https://doi.org/10.1016/j.ribaf.2022.101838

Li, Y., Guo, S., Yang, T., & Tang, L. (2021). Forecast on the Impact of Chinese New Digital Currency on the Whole International Finance. In *ACM International Conference Proceeding Series* (pp. 318–322). Association for Computing Machinery. https://doi.org/10.1145/3450148.3450185

Maddox, A., & Heemsbergen, L. J. (2021). Digging in Crypto-Communities' Future-Making. *M/C Journal, 24*(2). https://doi.org/10.5204/mcj.2755

Manjula, B. C., Shilpa, B. S., & Sundaresh, M. (2022). Analysis of Cryptocurrency, Bitcoin and the Future. *East Asian Journal of Multidisciplinary Research, 1*(7), 1293–1302. https://doi.org/10.55927/eajmr.v1i7.803

Mishra, N., & Valencia, A. M. (2023). Digital Services and Digital Trade in the Asia Pacific: An Alternative Model for Digital Integration? *Asia Pacific Law Review, 31*(2), 489–513. https://doi.org/10.1080/10192557.2023.2216058

Mukherjee, B. N. (2023). Blockchain: Contemporary Challenges and Future Application in International Trade. *Manchester Journal of International Economic Law, 20*(1), 12–33.

Panova, G. S. (2020). Cryptocurrency–Money of the Digital Economy. In *Lecture Notes in Networks and Systems* (Vol. 84, pp. 604–612). Springer. https://doi.org/10.1007/978-3-030-27015-5_72

Ricoy-Casas, R. M. (2022). Digital Currencies: Challenges Between the United States, the European Union and Asia Pacific. *Cuadernos Europeos de Deusto,* (3), 95–114. https://doi.org/10.18543/CED-03-2022PP95-114

Saiedi, E., Broström, A., & Ruiz, F. (2021). Global Drivers of Cryptocurrency Infrastructure Adoption. *Small Business Economics, 57*(1), 353–406. https://doi.org/10.1007/s11187-019-00309-8

Shelepov, A. (2022). The Influence of the G20's Digitalization Leadership on Development Conditions and Governance of the Digital Economy. *International Organisations Research Journal, 17*(1). https://doi.org/10.17323/1996-7845-2022-01-04

Shkodina, I., & Derid, O. Z. (2019). Digital Transformation of Global Banking: Challenges and Prospects. *Financial and Credit Activity: Problems of Theory and Practice, 3*(30), 45–51.

Singh, Er. B. P., & Faisal, Ar. Mohd. (2019). Cryptocurrency: An Analysis of the Growth of Bitcoin and its Future. *International Journal of Innovative Science and Research Technology, 4*(6), 221–224. https://ijisrt.com/wp-content/uploads/2019/06/IJISRT19JU44.pdf

Sigurðsson, K., Þór Eyþórsson, G., & Kristjánsdóttir, H. (2023). Digital Currencies, Swot Analysis. *Baltic Journal of Economic Studies, 9*(3), 1–9. https://doi.org/10.30525/2256-0742/2023-9-3-1-9

Sławiński, A. (2019). Will IT Technologies and Globalisation Change the Mechanism of Money Creation? *Zarządzanie Publiczne, 4*(50), 5–14. https://doi.org/10.15678/zp.2019.50.4.01

Tavasoli, A. (2020). Investigating, Choosing and Prioritizing the Challenges of Using Crypto Currencies in Global Transactions. *Agricultural Marketing and Commercialization Journal, 4*(1), 13–24.

Van der Linden, R. W. H., & Łasak, P. (2023). The Digitalization of Cross-Border Payment Systems and the Introduction of the CBDC. In *Financial Interdependence, Digitalization and Technological Rivalries* (pp. 75–92). Springer Nature. https://doi.org/10.1007/978-3-031-27845-7_7

Wandhöfer, R. (2022). The Future of Cross-border Wholesale Payments: Mobilising Central Bank Money Across Borders. *Journal of Payments Strategy and Systems, 16*(4), 389–398.

World Bank Group. (2021, November). Central Bank Digital Currencies for Cross-border Payments: A Review of Current Experiments and Ideas. World Bank. https://openknowledge.worldbank.org/handle/10986/36764

Wong, L., & Nelson, R. M. (2021). International Financial Messaging Systems. *Congressional Research Service* (pp. 1–17). https://sgp.fas.org/crs/row/R46843.pdf

Yao, J., & Wang, S. (2023). A Study on the Integration Path of China-ASEAN Digital RMB Cross-border E-commerce in the Context of Big Data. *Journal of Education, Humanities and Social Sciences, 16*, 295–301. https://doi.org/10.54097/ehss.v16i.9773

CHAPTER 2

The Introduction of the Digital Euro from a German Perspective

Waldemar Milewicz

Introduction

In the course of digitalisation, more and more areas of our lives are taking place online, including the way we pay. People's payment behaviour is changing at an unprecedented rate. The share of cash payments in the euro area has declined from 72 to 59% over the last three years. At the same time, digital payments have become increasingly popular (ECB, 2022). In the Netherlands and Finland, for example, cash is now used in only one-fifth of transactions. At the same time, people appreciate the possibility of paying with public money. For most, it is important or very important to have this choice at all times.

However, as shown above, the changes in payment methods in recent years are unquestionable. Indeed, a digital euro would be the answer to this ever-increasing preference for electronic payments, because it would make public money available in digital form. In addition to cash, people in Europe would be able to use the digital euro to pay anywhere in the

W. Milewicz (✉)
SGH Warsaw School of Economics, Warsaw, Poland
e-mail: wmilew@sgh.waw.pl

R. Aneja and R. Dygas (eds.), *Digital Currencies in The New Global World Order*, https://doi.org/10.1007/978-981-97-4810-5_2

euro area without incurring any costs. In other words, this is not intended to replace conventional cash, but merely to serve as an additional, generally accepted and secure alternative. Ease of access and usability would support its adoption and financial inclusion (Panetta, 2023). Not only governments and financial institutions but also private individuals would have the option of a central bank account (Lutz et al., 2020).

Central Bank Digital Currencies—The New Face of Financial Digitisation

Worldwide, 114 countries representing more than 95% of the world's gross domestic product are currently working on the development of Central Bank Digital Currencies (CBDCs), some within their jurisdictions. Some of these countries are in advanced pilot phases for their CBDC projects. The Chinese digital renminbi (e-CNY), for example, already had over 260 million users by the end of 2021 (Kosse & Mattei, 2022). Eleven countries, including Nigeria and Jamaica, had also hitherto widely introduced digital central bank money in March 2023 (Atlantic Council, 2023).

In July 2021, the Governing Council of the ECB decided to intensify work on possible concepts for digital central bank money—specifically: a digital euro. Within the framework of a two-year study phase, the possible design and effects of a digital euro are to be examined in more detail. The German Bundesbank and the other central banks of the Eurosystem are also participating in the analyses (Balz, 2022b).

As the central banking work in the Eurosystem progresses, the finance ministers of the euro area are also increasingly concerned with the ideas for a possible digital euro. In their statement of 16 January 2023, they affirmed that the introduction and design of a digital euro would require political decisions to be discussed and taken at the political level (Eurogroup, 2023). The Federal Ministry of Finance in Germany welcomed the European Commission's announcement that it will submit a legislative proposal in the second quarter of 2023 that would define the legal framework conditions for a digital euro. At the same time, the legislative procedure would offer the space to discuss important design issues between the European co-legislators (Council and European Parliament) in a democratically established procedure (Bundesfinanzministerium, 2023).

Attitudes of Private Households in Germany Towards the Introduction of the Digital Euro

What benefits and costs would be associated with a digital euro from the consumer's point of view? How would the cost–benefit balance of a possible digital euro compare with cash and fiat money? Is the concept of a digital euro already known in parts of the population? To find answers to these questions, a representative opinion poll was first conducted in April 2021 as part of the "Bundesbank Online Panel Households". In the Bundesbank Online Panel Households (BOP-HH), private individuals in Germany are surveyed monthly about their economic expectations and behaviour. The participants are 16 years old or older, live in Germany and have internet access. In the period from 16 to 27 April 2021, the panel dealt, among other things, with the topic of the "digital euro". The 2718 respondents were first shown the following explanatory text:

> A digital euro would be an electronic form of central bank money. Central bank money is money that can only be created by the central bank. Nowadays, central bank money exists mainly in the form of cash that the central bank puts into circulation. A digital euro would enable everyone to pay with central bank money in non-cash form. A digital euro is not the same as crypto assets, such as bitcoin. A digital euro would be protected and regulated by the European Central Bank. It would also be fail-safe, as a central bank cannot go bankrupt. Crypto assets are issued and traded without any state control. This means that no institution ensures value stability and, as a result, crypto-assets, unlike a digital euro, are sometimes subject to large and inexplicable fluctuations in value.

Afterwards, the participants were asked questions about their previous knowledge and insights into the digital euro. It turned out that the digital euro was still largely unknown to the public at the time of the survey. Only 23% of respondents said they had already heard or read something about the digital euro before the survey. Sixty per cent said they had not yet heard or read anything about the digital euro but had heard or read about crypto tokens. Seventeen per cent on the other hand, did not know either of the two terms. Surveys on the digital euro are therefore still made difficult at this point by the fact that, against the background of comparatively little prior knowledge, the formation of opinion in the population has probably not yet been completed. The survey provides a representative picture of the digital euro at the time of the survey. Over time and as the level of information in the population increases, there could still be shifts in attitudes and perceptions of the digital euro.

Assuming they were familiar with the introductory explanatory text, the study participants were next asked for their opinion on the digital euro. Around 13% of the respondents were in favour of issuing a digital euro (the results are shown in Fig. 2.1—*"strongly support"* and *"strongly agree"*). Among respondents with prior knowledge of the digital euro, however, the approval rate was almost twice as high at 22%. More than half (56%), however, said they were not in favour of the introduction of a digital euro ("*rather not support*" and "*not at all in favour*"). About one-third were undecided. In a repeat survey at the end of July 2021, 44% had already heard or read about a digital euro. Awareness seems to have increased in the wake of the Governing Council's decision to launch the digital euro project (Fig. 2.1).

Of those in favour of a digital euro, 65% saw it as a good alternative to cash and 63% as a good alternative to private means of payment.[1] Around 61% of those in favour also thought that a digital euro was part of a digitised society. Those respondents who rejected the introduction of a digital euro, on the other hand, thought that the existing payment instruments were sufficient. In addition, around 61% of those opposed feared that a digital euro would lead to the abolition of cash. Assurances that a digital euro would only be considered as a supplement to cash, but

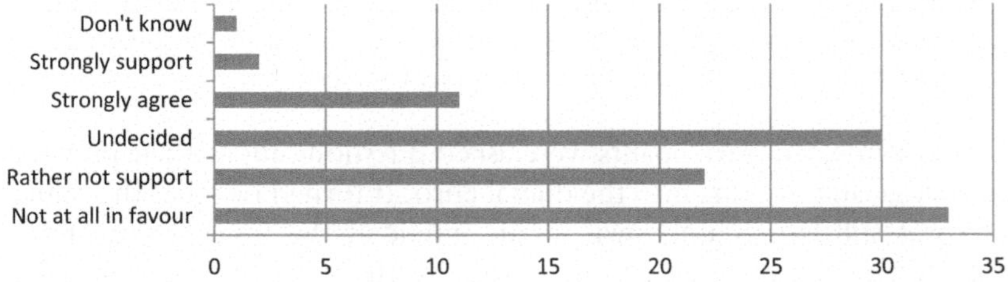

Fig. 2.1 Attitude towards the digital euro (in %) *Question: To what extent would you support the introduction of a digital euro?* (*Source* https://www.bundesbank.de/resource/blob/878744/c7a08ef9bec6d0e00aa2ae15d7aa596a/mL/2021-10-monatsbericht-data.pdf, p. 72)

[1] For a successful introduction, the added value of a digital euro compared to the existing means of payment should be clearly communicated.

not as a replacement for it, were therefore not yet firmly anchored among the general population.

The 40% of all respondents could imagine using a digital euro in the future. Here too, the proportion in the group of people who had already heard of a digital euro is somewhat higher (47%). Finally, the respondents gave information on the importance of possible features of a digital euro. From the participants' point of view, free use, the privacy of payments and data protection were particularly important (Deutsche Bundesbank, 2021).

The findings presented above are only partly consistent with the findings of the European Central Bank's (ECB) non-representative public consultation on the digital euro. The consultation was launched on 12 October 2020 and ended on 12 January 2021. In total, around 8,200 responses were received, with the majority of respondents being private individuals (94%) and the remaining respondents being professionals, including banks, payment service providers, merchants and technology companies. According to the ECB's public consultation, data protection (43%) is the most important issue for both the public and professionals when it comes to the digital euro. This is followed by security (18%), the possibility of paying with the digital euro throughout the euro area (11%), no additional costs (9%) and offline usability (8%). (European Central Bank, 2021) (Figs. 2.2, 2.3 and 2.4).

Attitudes of Enterprises in Germany Towards the Introduction of the Digital Euro

Another important issue from the point of view of the German economy is the attitude of entrepreneurs themselves towards the introduction of the digital euro. A survey on this topic was undertaken by the digital association Bitkom. In the process, 652 people responsible for digital technologies or blockchain in companies with 50 or more employees in Germany (101 banks and financial service providers) were interviewed by telephone. The questions were: "In your opinion, should politicians or the European Central Bank issue a digital euro?" "In your opinion, what are the reasons in favour of a digital euro?" and "In your opinion, what are the reasons against a digital euro?".

Based on the interviews conducted, it can be concluded that three-quarters (78%) of all companies in Germany want the ECB to introduce a digital euro. Only one in five (20%) think nothing of such plans. This is the result of a representative survey of 652 companies from all sectors in Germany commissioned by the digital association Bitkom. "Other nations are already further ahead with digital central bank money and have already launched pilot projects. We need to increase our speed to catch up", says Bitkom CEO Dr Bernhard Rohleder. "Europe should aim to be a global leader in digital central bank money. The digital euro is a very central element of a digitally sovereign EU".

The main argument in favour of a digital euro, in the view of businesses, is that otherwise, other state or private digital currencies would be used, which could undermine European values (78%). Two-thirds (69%) argue in favour of the digital euro so that seamless payment and settlement processes are possible on the future capital market with tokenised securities. A similar number (64%) see an advantage in the fact that even with the declining importance of cash in the digital age, citizens will still have direct access to the central bank. Six out of 10 (60%) expect that a digital euro will enable the ECB to implement new monetary policy

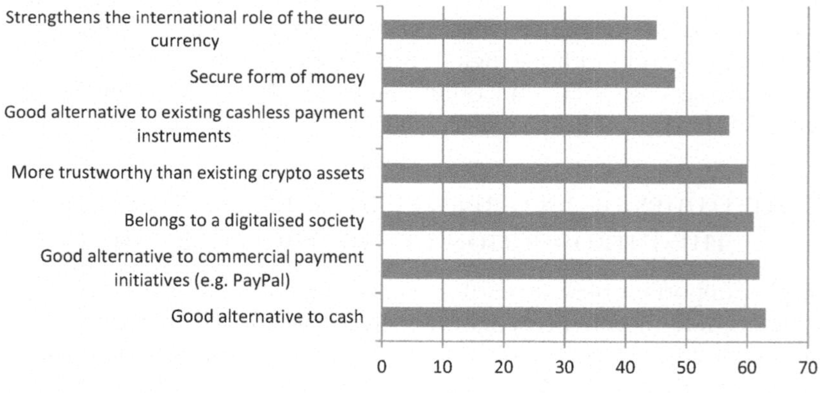

Fig. 2.2 Advantages of the digital euro (in %)[2] (*Source* https://www.bundesbank.de/resource/blob/878744/c7a08ef9bec6d0e00aa2ae15d7aa596a/mL/2021-10-monatsbericht-data.pdf, p. 71)

[2] This graphic and the next two are based on research conducted by the German Bundesbank. The data comes from a study carried out on 364 people who would tend to support or strongly support the introduction of the digital euro. Question posed: "For what reasons would you support the introduction of the digital euro?" Multiple answers possible.

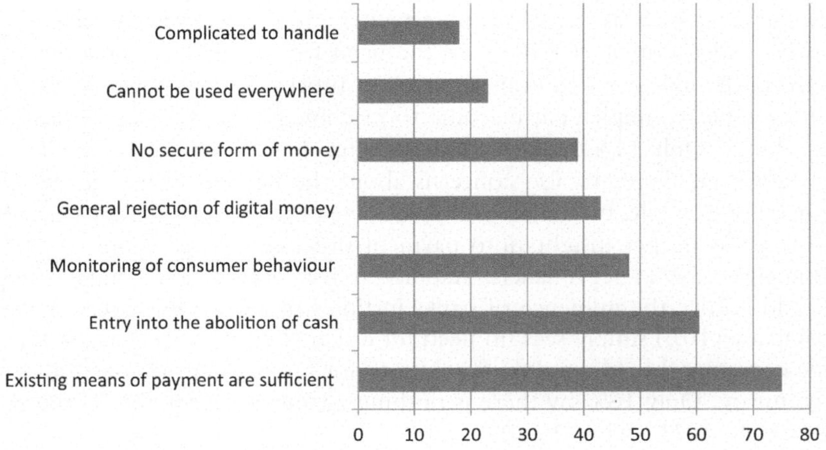

Fig. 2.3 Disadvantages of the digital euro (in %) (*Source* https://www.bundesbank.de/resource/blob/878744/c7a08ef9bec6d0e00aa2ae15d7aa596a/mL/2021-10-monatsbericht-data.pdf, p. 72)

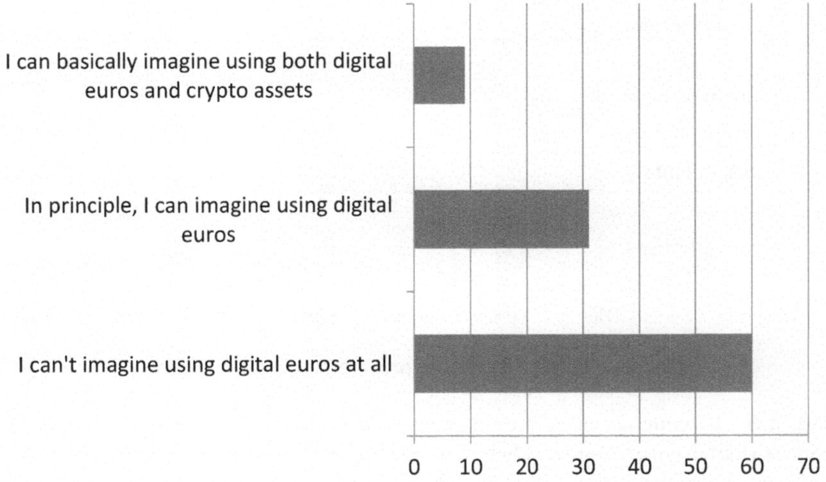

Fig. 2.4 Use of the digital euro *Question: Which of the following statements regarding the use of a digital euro apply to you personally?* (*Source* https://www.bundesbank.de/resource/blob/878744/c7a08ef9bec6d0e00aa2ae15d7aa596a/mL/2021-10-monatsbericht-data.pdf, p. 73)

instruments such as negative interest rates more effectively in times of crisis. And 4 out of 10 (40%) see the need for a digital, programmable euro in the industry to automate payment processes. This could be used, for example, to implement machine-to-machine payments in the Internet of Things. Only 11% think that a digital euro has no advantages at all.

However, there are also concerns about the introduction of a digital euro. For example, two-thirds (65%) see data protection risks if the central bank gains deeper insights into payment processes. Around one in two companies (49%) see financial stability at risk because the digital euro would reduce the influence of banks in times of crisis. Only every tenth company (10%) simply sees no need for a digital euro, and 8% think that the economy should develop its solutions for the payment transactions of the future. Only 13% say there is nothing against a digital euro (Bitkom Research, 2021) (Figs. 2.5, 2.6 and 2.7).

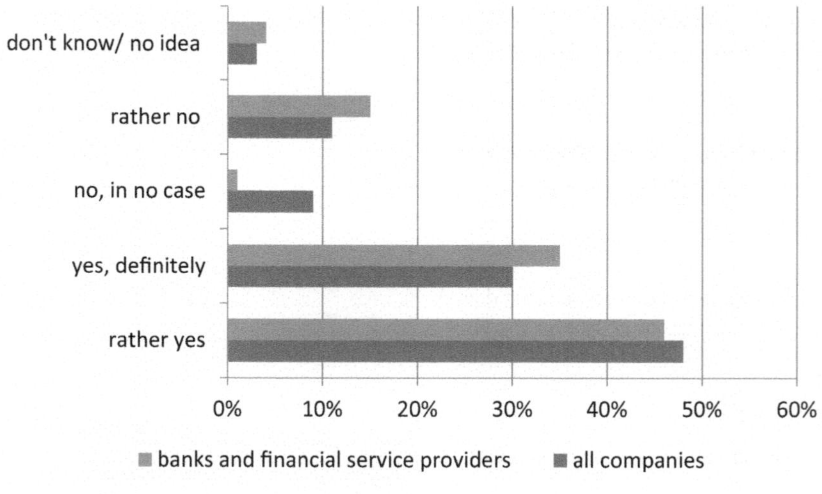

Fig. 2.5 In your opinion, should policymakers or the European Central Bank issue a digital euro? (*Source* Own elaboration on the basis of: https://www.bitkom.org/sites/main/files/2021-07/210708_breite-mehrheit-spricht-sich-fur-einen-digitalen-euro-aus_pg.png)

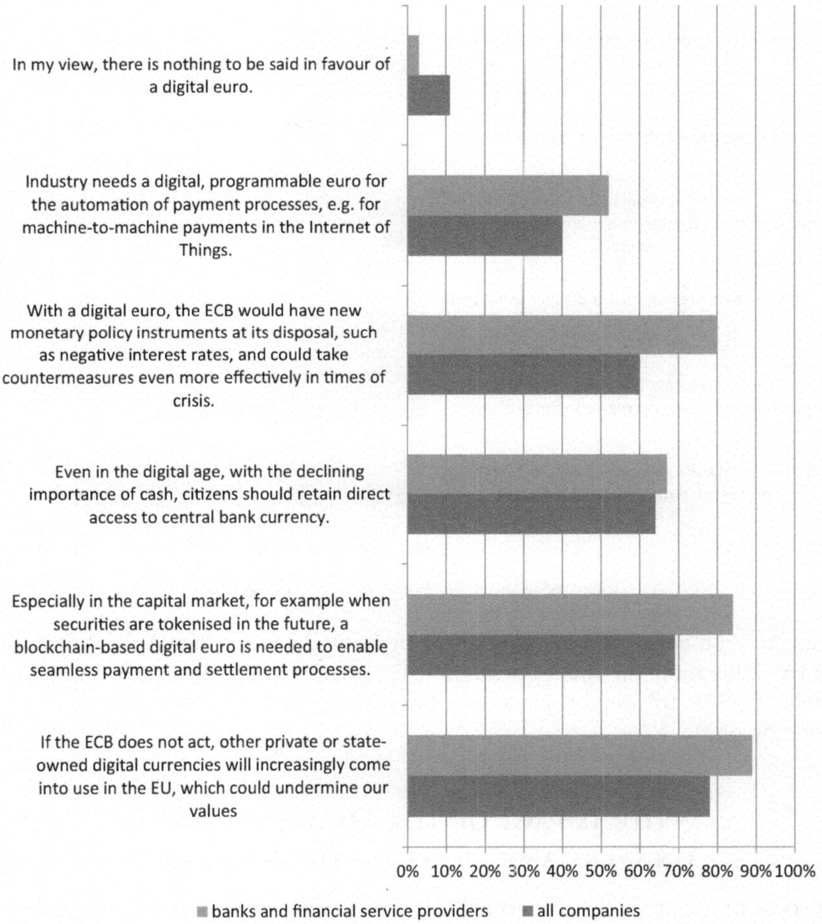

Fig. 2.6 In your opinion, what are the reasons in favour of a digital euro? (*Source* Own elaboration on the basis of: https://www.bitkom.org/sites/main/files/2021-07/210707_digitaler-euro-muss-internationalen-wettbewerb-aufnehmen_pg.png)

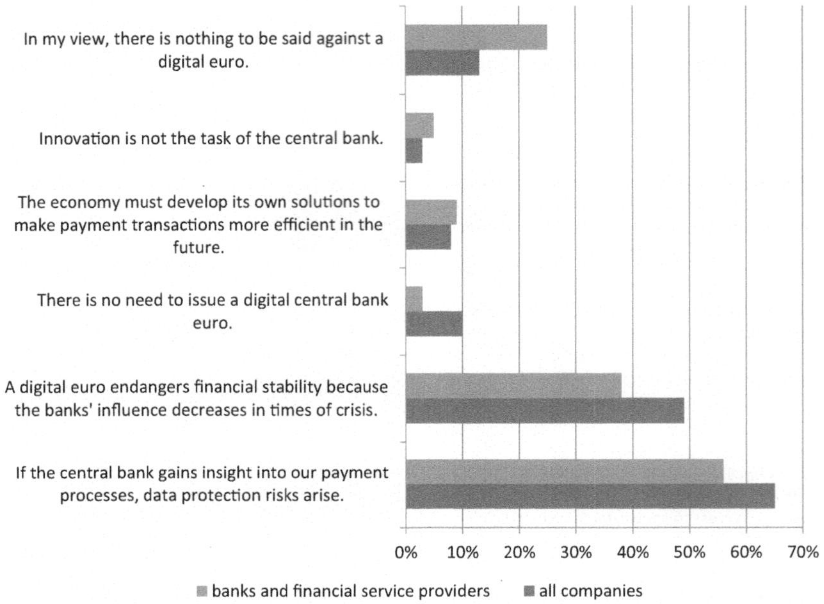

Fig. 2.7 In your opinion, what are the reasons against a digital euro? (*Source* Own elaboration on the basis of: https://www.bitkom.org/sites/main/files/2021-07/210707_es-gibt-nur-wenige-bedenken-gegenuber-einem-digitalen-euro_pg.png)

The Impact of the Digital Euro on Germany's International Trade

Also not insignificant is the impact of the digital euro on Germany's international trade. To test this impact, the DB Research Management team published a report in July 2021 that examines the potential effects of the new currency on Germany's international trade as well. They conclude that the role of the euro in international competition is also unlikely to be strengthened by the issuance of a digital euro. The use of a currency in international payments is mainly determined by the importance of the respective economy in global trade and the liquidity and size of the financial market, as well as the reliability of economic policy.

Furthermore, it is questionable whether the digital euro is at all suitable for international payments if the amount per user (private individuals as well as companies) and probably also the access of foreigners are restricted. This makes the digital euro uninteresting for payments in global trade compared to bank deposits. The digital euro also remains unattractive to euro cash, an estimated 30–50% of which is used outside the euro area, and which is not subject to any access or quantity restrictions. However, it could be used for migrants' remittances to their home countries if an international infrastructure for the transfer of digital central bank money were to exist in the future (Deutsche Bank Research, 2021).

The possible implications of the introduction of the euro for Germany's international trade have become part of a document published by The Federal Association of German Cooperative Banks (BVR—Der Bundesverband der Deutschen Volksbanken und Raiffeisenbanken). This organization refers to a study "Digital Euro—The Perspective of the German Economy". It underlines that a digital euro for the everyday payments of citizens cannot meet the requirements of corporate customers in the same way. After all, a large proportion of companies in Germany would like to see payment transactions integrated more closely into their business processes. Furthermore, the report notes that the processing of international payments would be much simpler based on digital euro—including the important documentary payment transactions in import and export (Paul et al., 2021).

The Federation of German Industries (The Bundesverband der Deutschen Industrie e.V.—BDI) also commented on the anticipated facilitation of international trade through the introduction of the digital euro. The organisation highlights in its report that in the global exchange of goods and services, German and European companies benefit greatly from the strong and globally accepted European common currency. This strength and the confidence associated with it should be maintained or expanded by keeping the euro in step with international technological developments. In BDI's view, the rapid establishment of a digital euro with attractive performance features is the logical consequence (Schönborn & Rudelt, 2022).

In turn, the authors of the report "The Digital Euro Influence on the German Economy" show examples of the potential benefits of the digital euro for German industry, which could be a potential spearhead for improving Germany's international trade. In their view, besides private end customers, the German industry could also benefit from a digital euro, especially if the digital euro were programmable. Specifically, the digital euro could be implemented on a distributed ledger technology

(DLT). Therefore, such a DLT-based digital euro could be linked to smart contracts. Put simply, smart contracts are coded, DLT-based "if–then conditions" that can trigger payments automatically. High-efficiency gains can be achieved through this automation of transactions, as DLT-based business transactions can be directly linked to payments. The increasing digitalisation of business processes already has the potential to fundamentally transform many industries. A DLT-based, digital and programmable euro would also lead to the emergence of entirely new business models in addition to the transformation itself. The areas of Industry 4.0, logistics, mobility, energy, the machine economy and the Internet of Things (IoT) could benefit from this in particular.

Opinions of the Scientific Community in Germany on the Digital Euro

In addition to showing what effects the introduction of the digital euro will have on trade relations in Germany it is also worth researching how the scientific community approaches this topic—not from the emotional side, but from a purely evidential point of view, based on a simple profit and loss account. Among others, the President of the Bundesbank, Joachim Nagel, took a stand in this area, referring to the opportunities and risks involved.

In his view, one of the risks is the bank run. With the digital euro, citizens would in future be able to convert their daily bank deposits into central bank money in a matter of seconds with a few mouse clicks or "touches" in the event of tensions in the financial system. In an extreme case, this could lead to the collapse of many banks if they run into liquidity problems due to the fast-flowing deposits. The American economist, Perry Mehrling, once put it somewhat martially: "Liquidity kills you quick", and by this, he of course means a lack of liquidity at banks (Pardee, 2019).

The other risk, as perceived by the Governor of the German Central Bank, is called structural disintermediation: It is that bank customers could shift a significant proportion of their bank deposits from their current or other deposit accounts into digital central bank money. For commercial banks, this would mean losing a cheap and stable source of funding. If commercial banks were to lose a significant part of these deposits because citizens use the digital euro as a store of value, the supply of credit by banks could decrease and the financing conditions for the real economy could deteriorate.

There are also positive aspects to this innovative venture. From a monetary policy perspective, the introduction of a digital euro is a measure that secures the anchor function of central bank money even in an increasingly digitalised world. Furthermore, the introduction of a digital euro could support progress in the field of payments and increase European sovereignty (Nagel, 2022).

Arguments of a similar type are referred to by Burkhard Balz, a Member of the Executive Board of the Deutsche Bundesbank. He points out that the first reason concerns strategic sovereignty in European payments. In this context, he recalls the opinion of ECB President, Christine Lagarde who rightly observed that "in a more digital economy, we also need to ensure the strength and autonomy of European payment systems." (Lagarde, 2020). The second reason in his view is summarised in the statement that people are paying less often with cash. Currently, in stationary trade in Germany, 36% of sales are made with coins and banknotes. In 2017, however, cash still accounted for almost half of everyday spending (Bundesbank, 2023). Added to this is the growing online trade, which is penetrating more and more areas—the share of online trade in the turnover of recorded payments quadrupled from 2017 to 2021. Shoppers now spend almost every fourth euro online. As a result, a digital euro could largely support digital processes. This would possibly make automated payments possible in the future within the framework of smart contracts (Balz, 2022a).

Two German academics, Jonas Groß and Philipp Sandner, also addressed the question of the anticipated advantages of the new form of the euro currency. They mention in this context 4 benefits:

1. Security: in the classic financial system, data is typically stored centrally on the servers of one party, for example, the servers of a (central) bank. By using DLT,[3] on the other hand, transaction data is stored simultaneously on a large number of computers. This

[3] Distributed ledger technology (DLT) is a digital transaction recording system in which transactions and their details are recorded in multiple places simultaneously. The Eurosystem is experimenting with different approaches and technologies to making a digital euro available. This includes both centralised and decentralised solutions such as DLT. https://www.computerweekly.com/de/definition/Distributed-Ledger-Technologie-DLT, https://www.ecb.europa.eu/paym/digital_euro/faqs/html/ecb.faq_digital_euro.en.html.

would make the system more resistant to hacker attacks, as there would no longer be a single point of failure.

2. Tamper resistance: since transactions are stored simultaneously on several computers, it is not possible to manipulate transaction data or change it afterwards. Especially in applications where all participants must have the same level of knowledge, but do not necessarily know and trust each other, such resistance to manipulation offers considerable advantages.
3. Automation: technological innovations such as smart contracts and peer-to-peer (micro) payments, e.g. between machines, can be realised in euros and do not have to be settled in volatile and unregulated crypto values, as has been the case so far. Smart contracts would enable devices connected to the DLT, such as machines, cars and sensors, to offer services on a pay-per-use basis or even leasing or factoring. The impact of a DLT-based payment method is therefore particularly promising in the context of the Machine Economy. IoT Analytics estimates that by 2025, more than 20 billion devices will be connected to the internet—three times as many devices as there are currently people on Earth. Many of these devices will also be integrated into a payment network so that in a few years, this network will comprise hundreds of millions of devices. DLT is best suited for equipping millions of devices with a computer chip and thus also with their digital wallet and transferring the digital euro directly from wallet to wallet. Then a device will be able to receive payments and transfer money autonomously.
4. Efficiency gains: In addition, significant efficiency gains could be achieved in the case of a peer-to-peer DLT euro system. The payment system could be enormously simplified, and many middlemen would no longer be needed (e.g. clearing houses). This would significantly reduce the costs of the payment system and make transactions faster. Especially for cross-border payments, considerable efficiency gains are possible. Today, international transfers, for example, from Germany to Argentina, take up to ten days and often cost up to 10% of the transfer amount in fees. The use of DLT systems could enable immediate processing at very low transaction costs (Klein et al., 2020).

The same German authors point out in another report the effects of the digital euro on Germany's financial system. In their perception, the introduction of a CBDC tends to entail risks for the financial stability and business model of banks. The digital euro offers another means of payment besides cash and scriptural money that can be used for everyday transactions. First, the possibility of investing savings risk-free at the central bank in the form of the digital euro could lead to a shift from bank deposits to the digital euro. In times of crisis, customers might decide to deposit a large part of their savings risk-free at the central bank. If banks were to lose large parts of their customers' deposits, this could lead to a disintermediation of the banking sector. The consequence would be liquidity shortages and higher refinancing costs for banks (Sandner et al., 2021).

Finally, it is worth taking a look at how the subject is approached by various organisations and associations in the economically strongest country in the European Union. The digital association Bitkom fears that Europe could be left behind internationally in the realisation of a digital currency and calls for a significant increase in the pace of testing a digital euro. For instance, China already issued its digital renminbi—also known as e-yuan—to selected employees of state-owned companies in the summer of 2020. The chief economists of the Savings Banks Finance Group (Sparkassen-Finanzgruppe) advocate in turn careful consideration and emphasise the still unresolved risks regarding the digital euro. The Federal Association of German Cooperative Banks (BVR—Der Bundesverband der Deutschen Volksbanken und Raiffeisenbanken) sees no added value at all in electronic central bank money. The "Deutsche Kreditwirtschaft" (German Banking Industry) also currently sees no need to tackle the introduction of CBDC in the euro area as a matter of priority; its member Bundesverband deutscher Banken (BdB), on the other hand, pleads for a quick introduction to secure digital sovereignty (Bundesdruckerei, 2023).

Conclusion

Due to globalisation and digitalisation, the world of payment transactions is in a constantly changing, dynamic process. Payment habits are changing, and new forms of money are emerging. Changes in needs and technological innovations promote competition and challenge traditional financial institutions, above all the central banks (Lutz et al., 2020).

Central banks, too, are setting up their offerings in line with the future to offer the accustomed level of security and stability in the digital age. For the ECB, this is not only an opportunity to make the digital euro competitive, but also to strengthen its financial market stability and keep welfare in focus. A digital euro could also significantly contribute to sovereignty in European payment transactions. Political sovereignty and the highest security standards can in turn create resilience to external influences. Although the pandemic acted as a catalyst for digitalisation, German society must ultimately decide for itself, through trust, acceptance and use, whether the introduction of a digital euro is ultimately a curse or a blessing. The investigation phase in the digital euro project will run until October 2023, by which time the German society wants to have a good initial idea of the digital future of its money (Balz, 2022c).

References

Atlantic Council. (2023). Central Bank Digital Currency Tracker. https://www.atlanticcouncil.org/cbdctracker/

Balz, B. (2022a). *The Digital Euro—An Opportunity for Europe*. Speech at CashCon. https://www.bundesbank.de/de/presse/reden/der-digitale-euro-eine-chance-fuer-europa-896806

Balz, B. (2022b, March). Digitales Zentralbankgeld: Währungen zukunftsgerecht gestalten. *BaFinJournal*. https://www.bundesbank.de/en/presse/gastbeitraege/digitales-zentralbankgeld-waehrungen-zukunftsgerecht-gestal ten-889912

Balz, B. (2022c, July 18). *The Digital Euro—The Future of Digital Payment?* Speech at the “Liberal Round Table”. Frankfurt am Main. https://www.bun desbank.de/de/presse/reden/der-digitale-euro-die-zukunft-des-digitalen-bez ahlens--894494

Bitkom Research. (2021). *Three Out of Four Companies Want the Digital Euro*. https://www.bitkom.org/Presse/Presseinformation/Drei-von-vier-Unt ernehmen-wollen-den-digitalen-Euro#_

Bundesbank. (2023, July). *Payment Behaviour in Germany 2021*. www.bundes bank.de/zahlungsverhalten

Bundesdruckerei. (2023). *Der digitale Euro—brauchen wir ihn?* https://www.bundesdruckerei.de/de/innovation-hub/der-digitale-euro-brauchen-wir-ihn

Bundesfinanzministerium. (2023, April). *Digital Central Bank Money and the Digital Euro*. Monthly Report of the Finance Ministry (p. 23). https://www.bundesfinanzministerium.de/Monatsberichte/2023/04/Inhalte/Kapitel-3-Analysen/3-1-digitales-zentralbankgeld-und-digitaler-euro-pdf.pdf?__blob=publicationFile&v=5

Deutsche Bank Research. (2021). *The Digital Euro, Political Ambitions Meet Economic Realities* (p. 3). https://www.dbresearch.de/PROD/RPS_DE-PROD/PROD0000000000519087/Der_digitale_Euro%3A_Politische_Ambitionen_treffen_a.pdf?undefined&realload=nqG3poVygRgYbTd1R96Pkp98rrrmqahg4pwTXu78ym4Pabr~O/yS~y767xPbEx9K

Deutsche Bundesbank. (2021). *Monatsbericht Oktober 2021* (pp. 65–73). https://www.bundesbank.de/resource/blob/878744/c7a08ef9bec6d0e00aa2ae15d7aa596a/mL/2021-10-monatsbericht-data.pdfEurogroup

Eurogroup. (2023, January 16). *Eurogroup Statement on the Digital Euro Project*. https://www.consilium.Europa.eu/en/press/press-releases/2023/01/16/eurogroup-statement-on-the-digital-euro-project-16-january-2023/

European Central Bank. (2021). Eurosystem Report on the Public Consultation on a Digital Euro (p. 10). https://www.ecb.europa.eu/pub/pdf/other/Eurosystem_report_on_the_public_consultation_on_a_digital_euro~539fa8cd8d.en.pdf

European Central Bank. (2022, December). *Study on the Payment Attitudes of Consumers in the Euro Area (SPACE)*. https://www.ecb.europa.eu/stats/ecb_surveys/space/shared/pdf/ecb.spacereport202212~783ffdf46e.de.pdf; https://www.ecb.europa.eu/paym/digital_euro/investigation/governance/shared/files/ecb.degov230116_eurogroupstocktake.de.pdf?55d13366cc74303c85f996ec9f60ab47

Klein, M., Groß, J., & Sandner, P. (2020). Der digitale Blockchain-Euro: Sind Central Bank Digital Currencies die Zukunft? *ifo Schnelldienst, ifo Institut, München, 73*(03), 39–47. https://www.ifo.de/DocDL/sd-2020-03-sandner-gross-klein-blockchain-euro-2020-03-11.pdf

Kosse A., & Mattei I. (2022, May). *BIS Papers No 125, Gaining Momentum—Results of the 2021 BIS Survey on Central Bank Digital Currencies* (p. 1). Monetary and Economic Department.

Lagarde, Ch. (2020, September 21). *Introductory Remarks by Christine Lagarde, President of the ECB, at the Franco-German Parliamentary Assembly*. https://www.ecb.europa.eu/press/key/date/2020/html/ecb.sp200921~5a30d9013b.en.html

Lutz, J., Geering, S., & Lambertz, A., (2020). *Der digitale Euro—Fluch oder Segen für unsere Gesellschaft ?* (p. 2) Heinrich-Heine-Universität Düsseldorf. https://www.wiwi.hhu.de/fileadmin/redaktion/Oeffentliche_Medien/Fakultaeten/Wirtschaftswissenschaftliche_Fakultaet/Ressourcen/HHU_Whitepaper_Der_digitale_Euro_Lehrstuhl_Finanzdienstleistungen.pdf

Nagel, J. (2022). *Digital Euro—Opportunities and Risks*. CFS-IMFS Special Lecture Goethe-Universität. https://www.bundesbank.de/de/presse/reden/digitaler-euro-chancen-und-risiken-894264

Panetta, F. (2023, January 23). *The Digital Euro: Our Money, Wherever and Whenever We Need It*. Introductory remarks by Fabio Panetta, Member of the Executive Board of the ECB, before the Committee on Economic and Monetary Affairs of the European Parliament. https://www.ecb.europa.eu/press/key/date/2023/html/ecb.sp230123~2f8271ed76.de.html

Pardee, F. S. (2019). *Mehrling Interviewed in Bloomberg on Repo Market*. https://www.bu.edu/pardeeschool/2019/12/23/mehrling-interviewed-in-bloomberg-on-repo-market/

Paul S., et al. (2021, November). *Digitaler Euro—Die Perspektive der deutschen Wirtschaft*—Ein Kooperationsprojekt des Bundesverbandes der Deutschen Volksbanken und Raiffeisen- banken (BVR) und des Lehrstuhls für Finanzierung und Kreditwirtschaft, Ruhr-Universität Bochum.

Sandner, P., Groß, J., & Grale, L. (2021). *Digitaler Euro Einfluss auf die deutsche Wirtschaft*, Konrad-Adenauer-Stiftung e. V. 2021 (p. 5). https://www.kas.de/documents/252038/11055681/Der+digitale+Euro+-+Einfluss+auf+die+deutsche+Wirtschaft.pdf/f06d51c7-cb78-911f-a37c-cb3849a61e81

Schönborn, S., &Rudelt, Ch. (2022, September 28). *Digitaler Euro. Industriebedarfe bei Etablierung nicht vernachlässigen*, Bundesverband der Deutschen Industrie e.V. (BDI). https://bdi.eu/publikation/news/digitaler-euro-innovation-digitalisierung-waehrung

Internet

https://www.computerweekly.com/de/definition/Distributed-Ledger-Technologie-DLT

https://www.ecb.europa.eu/paym/digital_euro/faqs/html/ecb.faq_digital_euro.en.html

CHAPTER 3

The Digital Euro—Just a Digital Form of Cash?

Andreas Bielig

Introduction

Since 2020, the European Central Bank has discussed and analysed the potential of broadening its scope of Euro central bank money in European economies and financial systems. It responds to challenges deriving from the current emergence of private blockchain-based cryptocurrencies like Bitcoin or Ethereum, private stable coins projects like Diem/ Libra of Facebook and foreign public Central Bank Digital Currencies, like Chinese pilot project Digital Yuan or of other economies (see, for central banks project status, CBDC Tracker, 2023). European Central Bank regards the Digital version of the Euro also as a countermeasure against declining public demand for cash in the form of banknotes and coins in most Euro area countries that impedes transmission of monetary policy and has the potential to harm financial system stability. The article provides a brief overview of the historic Digital Euro project development, introduces the current project status and European directive draft

A. Bielig (✉)
SGH Warsaw School of Economics, Warsaw, Poland
e-mail: abielig@sgh.waw.pl

R. Aneja and R. Dygas (eds.), *Digital Currencies in The New Global World Order*, https://doi.org/10.1007/978-981-97-4810-5_3

on the Digital Euro and evaluates project results made from an economic perspective.

Historical Summary of the Digital Euro Project

The idea of a Digital Euro began to gain attention as the advent of Digital currencies like Bitcoin and central bank Digital currencies (CBDCs) in other parts of the world started to gain popularity. As a result, the European Central Bank (ECB) began preliminary internal discussions on the potential benefits and challenges of a Digital Euro. In January 2020, the ECB established a high-level task force to advance work on its own central bank Digital currency (CBDC) in the Euro area and to study the possibility of launching a Digital Euro (ECB, 2020a, p. 6). They conducted a comprehensive analysis of the basic technical, economic and legal aspects of issuing a European CBDC. In October 2020, ECB published a report on the Digital Euro, outlining the key considerations and potential features of a Digital Euro (ECB, 2020a). This marked the beginning of more public and official discussions on the topic. In the same month, the ECB launched a public consultation on the Digital Euro to gather feedback from the public and various stakeholders (ECB, 2020b). The consultation aimed to understand the potential demand for a Digital Euro and its possible design. In April 2021, the ECB published its report on the results of public consultation, which served as input for the concretization of further investigations on potential features of the future Digital Euro (ECB, 2021a). As a main finding, it underlines privacy to be the most important aspect of Digital Central Bank Currency for both public audiences and professionals. The next desired features followed security, usability across the Euro area, no additional costs of payment and offline usability (ECB, 2021b). Based on these previous steps, ECB announced in July 2021 the launch of an experimental project known as "Investigating the Digital Euro" (IDEA) to further explore the technical feasibility of a Digital Euro (ECB, 2021c). This project involved experimenting with various aspects of a Digital currency. Throughout the next 24 months, the ECB continued its research and analysis, aiming to make informed decisions about whether to proceed with the development of a Digital Euro. The central bank was considering factors like privacy, security and the potential impact on the financial sector. In October 2023, the ECB concluded the investigation phase of the Digital Euro by publishing a final report on results (ECB, 2023a) and decided to proceed with project work starting a preparation period of initially two years to make way for future political decisions on the Digital Euro introduction (ECB, 2023b). In the following, a brief description of the current Digital Euro project status in October 2023 is given.

Current Digital Euro Project Status

On 18th October 2023, ECB finished with the investigation phase the second main step of its Digital Euro project and published preliminary results in above-mentioned report (ECB, 2023a). Simultaneously, it announced the start of a new two-year preparation phase beginning in November 2023. According to the ECB, the initiation of preparations for a Digital Euro represents a further step of project development aiming at consent about the form and technical details of the Digital Euro as well as on shaping a rulebook for the Digital Euro scheme (Balz, 2023). Nevertheless, it doesn't imply at this stage a decision for the future introduction of a European CBDC. This is solely, as of other political decisions in the EU, in the competence of European Union legislators, thus the European Council and European Union Parliament. Positive decision process provided; ECB would decide later on about a future CBDC introduction based on actual project outcomes. To initiate the political decision process, the EU Commission prepared in June 2023, an EU directive draft for discussion by and decision of the European Parliament and European Council for the introduction of Digital Euro (EU Kommission, 2023a). Together with the discussion document about CBDC introduction, EU Commission presented a draft on the Euro cash role with banknotes and coins as legal tender in the Euro area to care for future cash provision and usage in times of increasing Digital payments (EU Kommission, 2023b). Both forms of Central Bank Money are regarded by the ECB as necessary means of payment also in the future to provide individual freedom of choice in payment instruments and achieve high financial stability in European Banking and Finance Architecture (Panetta, 2023a). During political decision processes, the ECB intends to forward clarifications of many open technical CBDC details and as well as to shape framework issues in the CBDC rulebook in the coming years of preparation. Further unclear issues are among others related to stability risks deriving from bank deposit interdependencies with future Digital Euro holdings (Balz, 2023). Initial assumptions about prospective Digital Euro launch dates just in 2026 were rejected by ECB officials hinting at lengthy political decision processes in the EU (Balz, 2023). Given the possible ECB decision about future CBDC introduction only after positive votes of both mentioned EU legislators and a European policy calendar with EU parliament elections in 2024, subsequent EU Council decisions could take place in late 2024. Provided the fact that substantial reforms of EU monetary policy like the introduction of a common CBDC require also ratifications by national parliaments of the 20 Euro members undergoing several elections in coming years (Europe elects, 2023) perhaps an ECB decision could be expected not before 2027. Consequently, after final preparation, the introduction of the Digital Euro may be postponed to 2029/30. The lengthy political process brings advantages in the form of extensive tests applicable to the new Digital currency design, i.e. in cooperation with professional key stakeholders like banks, savings banks and payment service providers, and learning benefits from pilot lessons of other economies experimenting with their own CBDC but increases also political risks of project rejection and discretionary blockades. In 2025 sovereigns of two members of the Euro area will elect new national parliaments, in 2026 four members and in 2027, eight states, hence, the political landscape in Europe is likely to change during this time.

ECB Expectations about the Digital Euro as a New Means of Payment

According to the ECB introduction, Digital Euro is a response to declining cash shares in Euro payments (Balz, 2023; Panetta, 2020). The COVID-19 pandemic accelerated by increasing digitalization is also the trend towards electronic payments and online transactions worldwide thereby reducing the attractivity of cash payments. Also, if cash affinity in payment patterns shows huge variety among Euro member states (ECB, 2020c, p. 57– 60), the ongoing trend persists (ECB, 2022) and raises doubts if available public means of payment still meet the needs of most people in Digital age (Panetta, 2020). For Digital payment environments, the ECB like other major Central Banks still doesn't provide an adequate alternative to increasingly used private means of payment in the form of fail-safe central bank money in the Digital sphere (Balz, 2023). However, the provision of widely publicly available access to fail-proof central bank money in Digital transactions may rather be regarded as an argument of defence in light of shrinking cash use, consequently, 93 per cent of central banks run their own CBDC projects but seems not sufficient to serve as the profound basis for a business model for the future Digital Euro. Hence, the ECB argues for the Digital Euro as the first Pan-European means of payment with an application scope covering nearly all payment situations (Balz, 2023) that requires CBDC status as legal tender as claimed by above mentioned EU directive draft initiative for the Digital Euro (EU Kommission, 2023a). With the introduction of the Digital Euro ECB intends also to challenge the dominance of foreign internationally active providers in areas such as card schemes and online transactions to reduce dependencies on large market dominant players and build more internal resilience in the European finance sector (Panetta, 2020) to prevent negative consequences, like harm of competition, limited consumer choices or non-competitive pricing patterns. According to the ECB, the Digital Euro could serve inclusively as a financial and open technological basis for new innovative private solutions also of European suppliers and technology of the Pan-European range. However, if this vision comes true the Digital Euro is very arguably concerned past development of the European payment system. With the establishment of the Single European Payment Area (SEPA) the European finance system made a huge leap forward to better system integration, faster service, improved quality, higher capacity and lower costs of transactions, hence towards efficiency. But despite successfully establishing Pan-European payment infrastructure available at the back-end level of the finance industry many national payment systems in Europe remained fragmented at the front end with customer interface and payment solutions (Panetta, 2023b) thereby hampering the usability of customer payment solutions in other European countries, reducing transaction speed or increasing final customer costs for payments. Considering the current ECB motivation to leverage the SEPA system and infrastructure also to new payment solutions based on the Digital Euro, the question arises how these current challenges can be met in case of a future European CBDC? According to the ECB summary report of the investigation phase of the CBDC project the Digital Euro would be a liability of the central bank in analogy to cash as claimed on the bank sheet but its distribution should be in the competence of private Payment Service Providers (PSP) who function as entry points to access Digital Euro services (ECB, 2023a, p. 18). However, in this perspective, the Eurosystem shall not take the liabilities of other stakeholders and be a party in commercial disputes (ECB, 2023a, p. 27). Consequently, the

ECB intends to provide for payment processes mainly back-end infrastructure for settlement and some additional related supporting services for PSPs, like CBDC scheme provision, onboarding checks and portability support, alias lookups, a platform for dispute management, central fraud and risk management system, a Digital Euro app with basic functionality, a funding enabler for credit institutions and a system for offline Digital Euro provision (ECB, 2023a, pp. 27– 30). Hence, most activities, functions and processes in payment services remain also in the case of Digital Euro a domain of private PSPs, like user onboarding, servicing, payment initiation and validation, post settlement and finally offboarding to provide for maximum freedom of dispositions for private finance industry. If this provides sufficient economic incentives to tackle current market fragmentation with a Pan-European payment instrument as intended by the ECB (ECB, 2023a, p. 8) will show future development after the CBDC introduction. The Digital Euro should be available for users in two forms: online and offline (ECB, 2023a, p. 13). The use of Digital central bank money in online mode with the condition of an internet connection would allow for most payment situations with remote function and discharge users from reliance on bearer payment instruments that are subject to specific risks of loss, theft or destruction. In contrast, the offline Digital Euro emulates some cash-like characteristics of bearer instruments, like independent use of the online connection, thereby preserving the highest possible level of privacy for transaction partners involved (Balz, 2023). For offline use, the bearer instrument is needed in advance and is limited to proximity payments under direct contact of payment instruments, like for NFC technology used in many payment cards. However, in the case of offline Digital Euro payments full anonymity is hard to achieve for technical reasons but also legal issues of regulation and compliance. From a technical perspective, reachable levels of privacy depend mainly on choices of technical security solutions applied for services made by suppliers (Security Insider, 2019). Considering technological races between security solution developers and hackers and concerning evident cost aspects, there is no full objective security feasible but only more or less sufficient levels of relative privacy. Hence, many deficits in data security and privacy result from suppliers' choices in terms of solution design, development process and finally targeted cost level. For future offline Digital Euro development ECB is mainly in charge, of pursuing a model of tamper-proof chip usage with pre-installed secure software to avoid external manipulation where confidential and cryptographic data can be stored and secure applications can be run (ECB, 2023a, p. 13). Against the background that transactions always leave information traces in Digital bearer instruments there are by nature also potential points of attack, which is recognized also by the ECB that must balance the benefits and risks of the future Digital Euro. But the ECB hints also at potential legal restrictions for the privacy scope of the offline version of the Digital Euro that come from the political decision in Europe and final legislation. As offline transactions are provided for low-value payments with supposed low-risk profiles their politically desired privacy level depends on the preferences of policy decision-makers in the EU to apply accordingly for these payments exemptions from Anti-Money Laundering/Combating Financing of Terrorism (AML/CFT) obligations (IMF, 2023) with compliance of finance industry (ECB, 2023a, p. 38). If the underlying usual risk-based approach of this concept is rejected by EU policy and legislators envisaged privacy level of offline payments will be substantially lower. Anyway, in terms of achievable privacy level cash is still king and far to be surpassed even by modern up-to-date Digital forms of money, hence, for users seeking the highest level of privacy this traditional and somehow outdated bearer instrument remains the first choice considering also negative aspects like forgery, lacking comfort, or risks of loss. In comparison with offline-mode privacy of online payments with Digital Euro will be much more limited as it is treated in terms of data protection, privacy and AML/CFT compliance equivalent to private Digital payment instruments with regulations of electronic payments in place (ECB, 2023a, p. 38), like General Data Protection Regulation (GDPR) (GDPR info, 2023). Data on Digital Euro payments available for PSPs should be limited to provide basic Digital Euro services at a necessary minimum. If EU legislators would opt for such compliance exemption, some low-value transactions could provide for certain higher privacy levels by reducing information requirements according to Transfer of Funds regulation (TFR) for transactions up to € 1000 (EU, 2023). However, TFR regulation still requires also in this case comprehensive information collection about transaction partners by PSPs as well as transmission of sensitive data to other involved PSPs even beyond the EU. If this future scenario applies to the online version of the Digital Euro privacy issues will stand back far behind regulators' motivation to detect and prevent criminal activity in the finance sector. Seen from a dynamic perspective, however, huge PSP loads of information requirements may have also the potential to harm innovation progress in some parts of the fintech sector, as the case of unhosted wallets shows (Krück, 2022). For the Eurosystem foreseen data requirements limit data collection, storage and processing to purposes of critical Digital Euro back-end functions fulfilment mentioned above, in particular for settlement tasks (ECB, 2023a, 2023b, p. 38). Personal data will be pseudonymized, which allows in general an ex-post restoring of individual profiles with identification specifics (Otterbach, 2023; Weiss & Strauß, 2020) in contrast to anonymization techniques. Nevertheless, the ECB expects from the envisaged privacy model of the online Digital Euro a sufficient user privacy sphere achieved by personal data segregation among PSP, support service providers and Eurosystem and the use of privacy-enhancing data techniques. In concrete terms, the privacy of the future online Digital Euro will mainly depend on legislators, applied privacy schemes and chosen security technology. Facts that may improve privacy situation in comparison with most common private Digital means of payment but depart far from cash as a traditional form of central bank money. The promise of the ECB as an operator of settlement infrastructure not to allow for tracing transaction information back to specific users (ECB, 2023a, p. 39) is a relative one that is endowed with many technical but especially political gateways to principles of the compromise. The introduction of Markets in Crypto-Assets Regulation MICA (Bafin, 2023; Bundesbank, 2023) and the currently amended TFR (EU, 2023) shows EU legislator's willingness to close privacy doors by AML/CFT measures, for example, cryptocurrencies. For online Digital Euro future EU reassessments of payment risk profiles may induce substantial reductions of privacy levels of new CBDC by regulation. ECB associates online CBDC transactions with higher risks concerning AML/CFT than offline CBDC payments being subject to explicit payment restrictions in analogy to cash use (EU Kommission, 2023a, p. 45). However, in the EU, cash payments still do not exist with unified limits for cash payments, hence national regulations vary substantially. Therefore, the EU Commission intends to introduce mandatory limits of € 10,000 in the future whereas the EU Parliament votes for an even reduced level of € 7,000 (EVZ, 2023) to close doors for abuse of finance channels for organized crime. In comparison with transactions for cash holdings whether limits are in place or intended. Cash is therefore almost provided a price stability-focused monetary policy of CB, a suitable store of value for users and a relatively safe form of investment. In contrast, the use of the Digital Euro as a store of value will be restricted by narrow holding limits to prevent dangers to the stability of the financial system, e.g. in case of bank runs (Balz, 2023). Holding caps of € 3,000 for private persons are discussed, whereas future limits for business users would be zero (ECB, 2023a, p. 23). To provide for constantl0,y sufficient user liquidity despite tight holding limits set future Digital Euro comes with basic liquidity management features of automatic waterfall and reverse waterfall functions as user options (ECB, 2023a, p. 23). For this, user may link their Digital Euro account (DEA) after onboarding with commercial bank accounts of PSPs. In other cases, they have options to fund or defund accounts manually at PSPs, other institutions, or Automated Teller Machines (ATMs). Offline-holdings management is restricted to manual funding or defunding only. The definition of CBDC holding caps by the ECB is related also to privacy schemes applied for the Digital Euro. At the onboarding process, prospective users must identify themselves to PSPs or other institutions entitled to distribute Digital Euro as prerequisites to limit CBDC use as a store of value (ECB, 2023a, p. 37). First registration in line with information requirements compliance allows for enforcing individual holding limits, hence, the ECB tries to balance privacy and data protection issues also with aspects of financial stability. But for the Digital Euro also the balance with other public objectives is at issue, e.g. the innovation-related area of open banking and open finance both with comprehensive sharing of private data under the consent of users (ECB, 2023a, p. 37, Bafin, 2022). Here, the ECB opts for a conservative approach limiting information flows by data sharing and processing to the extent necessary for fulfilling functional tasks of basic Digital Euro services. Besides outstanding security and the highest possible privacy level among available digital payments ECB expects further user benefits substantial increases in comfort, reductions of costs and increases in the speed of transactions (Balz, 2023). With claimed legal tender status for Digital Euro a necessary precondition is laid down by the EU Commission draft for CBDC introduction (EU Kommission, 2023a) to provide for seamless Euro area-wide distribution and acceptance for transactions to enhance users' comfort. Considering decreasing cash use in Europe and to avoid further crowding out effects by the Digital Euro ECB also made efforts to strengthen the legal tender status of traditional central bank money in the form of banknotes and coins (EU Kommission, 2023b). Focussed on future domestic use of the Digital Euro in the Euro area, the ECB still restrains itself in terms of exploration and definition of ways of international use of the new

CBDC. In its project report under the multi-currency enabling features chapter ECB addresses requirements to prior currency agreements with central banks of other EU states and third countries as future agenda for external Digital Euro use after successful implementation and rollout of CBDC in Euro members (ECB, 2023a, p. 30). This proprietary approach follows the principle of a multi-currency enabling features integration at a later stage in established back-end infrastructure to ease interoperability with working functionalities. ECB underlines the prior necessity to accept legal, economic and technical back-end requirements of the Euro system by agreeing on other European Union and European Economic Area central banks. ECB expects from the prospective external rollout of the Digital Euro positive effects on the international position of the Euro in foreign trade and international capital and finance markets (EU Kommission, 2023a, p. 35 f.) by easing border-crossing payments but sees also potential risks in unintended effects on consolidated ECB balance sheet by excessive Digital Euro supply outside of Euro area (EU Kommission, 2023a, p. 34). This may also lead to negative consequences on the monetary sovereignty and financial stability of countries outside of the Euro area, especially in cases where the Digital Euro would substitute large shares of domestic transactions in specific countries or even substitute national currency. Also, in the case of the future limited Digital Euro's external role the dominance of the US dollar in global trade and invoicing patterns is expected to remain in economic literature (see for instance ECB, 2020d, Gopinath & Stein, 2018, IMF, 2020). The Digital Euro may have the potential to support a visible rise in the Euro's prominence throughout neighbourhood economies as well as in some African countries that are intensively linked to Euro states (ECB, 2020d, p. 18). However, economic findings indicate that the dominance of a global currency is based on economic fundamentals that support the continuation of the US dollar as an anchor currency also in the future (ECB, 2020d; Gopinath & Stein, 2018; IMF, 2020).

Conclusion

About present forms of central bank money, the ECB regards the medium Digital Euro as an outcome of natural evolution into digital currency forms (ECB, 2023a, p. 30). The underlying approach of refining cash with digital features can be regarded as of an almost conservative nature in terms of many aspects. It seems questionable if pure development and distribution of cash-like digital lookalikes are sufficient to attract users against the background of a strongly increasing variety of private payment instruments available on the market. That applies especially if the additional benefits of CBDC in comparison to competing private means of payments remain still widely unclear. According to ECB, users' fees for transactions with Digital Euro services should not exceed competitive levels of private means of payment. For this reason, for instance, merchant fees should be limited and transaction costs of involved parties recompensated in line with a specific Digital Euro compensation model (ECB, 2023a, p. 30 f.). Here, distribution fees follow mainly those also applied for private digital payment services, which raises doubts if there are significant cost advantages of the new CBDC system if the ECB's costs of infrastructure and settlement services are considered. Even more, to achieve a close digital companion of cash (ECB, 2023a, p. 32) in times of cash's phasing out is lacking forward-looking towards more innovative market guidance in terms of new and attractive solutions. However, ECB expectations concerning these aspects remain vague and short-kept. If the financial system is based on the Digital Euro, an innovative ecosystem of competitive new solutions and services ECB should develop with traditional and new finance actors a masterplan for future development. Without a promising business model, the Digital Euro constitutes only a relatively weak line of defense for the ECB.

References

Bafin. (2022, September 1). *Open Banking und Open Finance*. Bundesanstalt für Finanzdienstleistungs-aufsicht. https://www.bafin.de/DE/Aufsicht/FinTech/Geschaeftsmodelle/OpenBanking_OpenFinance/OpenBanking_OpenFinance_node.html (accessed 13 November 2023).

Bafin. (2023, May 17). *Europäische MiCA-Verordnung: Regel-Fundament für Kryptowerte*. Bundes-anstalt für Finanzdienstleistungsaufsicht. https://www.bafin.de/SharedDocs/Veroeffentlichungen/DE/Fachartikel/2023/fa_bj_2305_Mica.html (accessed 13 November 2023).

Balz, B. (2023, October 19). Was der Digitale Euro für die Bürger bringt, Interview mit der FAZ, im Gespräch mit Christian Siedenbiedel. *Frankfurter Allgemeine Zeitung*. https://www.bundesbank.de/de/presse/interviews/was-der-Digitale-euro-fuer-die-buerger-bringt-917460 (accessed 13 November 2023).

Bundesbank. (2023). *MiCAR—Markets in Crypto-Assets Regulation: Dienstleistungen und Tätigkeiten im Zusammenhang mit Kryptowerten*. Deutsche Bundesbank. https://www.bundesbank.de/de/aufgaben/bankenaufsicht/einzelaspekte/micar-markets-in-crypto-assets-regulation-799398 (accessed 13 November 2023).

CBDC Tracker. (2023, October). *Today's Central Bank Digital Currencies Status*. https://cbdctracker.org/ (accessed 13 November 2023).

ECB. (2020a, October). *Report on a Digital Euro*. European Central Bank. https://www.ecb.europa.eu/pub/pdf/other/Report_on_a_Digital_euro~4d7268b458.en.pdf (accessed 13 November 2023).

ECB. (2020b). *Digital Euro: Listening to the Public*. European Central Bank. https://www.ecb.europa.eu/paym/Digital_euro/html/pubcon.en.html (accessed 13 November 2023).

ECB. (2020c, December). *Study on the Payment Attitudes of Consumers in the Euro Area (SPACE)*. European Central Bank. https://www.ecb.europa.eu/pub/pdf/other/ecb.spacereport202012~bb2038bbb6.en.pdf (accessed 13 November 2023).

ECB. (2020d, August). *Patterns in Invoicing Currency in Global Trade*, Working Paper Series, no. 2456. European Central Bank. https://www.ecb.europa.eu/pub/pdf/scpwps/ecb.wp2456~540fd64604.en.pdf (accessed 13 November 2023).

ECB. (2021a, April). *Eurosystem Report on the Public Consultation on a Digital Euro*. European Central Bank. https://www.ecb.europa.eu/pub/pdf/other/Eurosystem_report_on_the_public_consultation_on_a_Digital_euro~539fa8cd8d.en.pdf (accessed 13 November 2023).

ECB. (2021b, April 14). *ECB Publishes the Results of the Public Consultation on a Digital Euro*. European Central Bank. https://www.ecb.europa.eu/press/pr/date/2021/html/ecb.pr210414~ca3013c852.en.html (accessed 13 November 2023).

ECB. (2021c, July 14). *Eurosystem Launches Digital Euro Project*. European Central Bank. https://www.ecb.europa.eu/press/pr/date/2021/html/ecb.pr210714~d99198ea23.en.html (accessed 13 November 2023).

ECB. (2022, December). *Study on the Payment Attitudes of Consumers in the Euro Area (SPACE)—2022*. European Central Bank. https://www.ecb.europa.eu/stats/ecb_surveys/space/shared/pdf/ecb.spacereport202212~783ffdf46e.en.pdf (accessed 13 November 2023).

ECB. (2023a). *A Stocktake on the Digital Euro: Summary Report on the Investigation Phase and Outlook on the Next Phase*. European Central Bank. https://www.ecb.europa.eu/paym/Digital_euro/investigation/profuse/shared/files/dedocs/ecb.dedocs231018.en.pdf (accessed 13 November 2023).

ECB. (2023b, October 18). *Eurosystem Proceeds to Next Phase of Digital Euro Project*. European Central Bank. https://www.ecb.europa.eu/press/pr/date/2023/html/ecb.pr231018~111a014ae7.en.html (accessed 13 November 2023).

EU. (2023). *Regulation (EU) 2023/1113 of the European Parliament and of the Council of 31 May 2023 on information accompanying transfers of funds and certain crypto-assets and amending Directive (EU) 2015/849 (Text with EEA relevance)*. European Union. https://eur-lex.europa.eu/legal-content/EN/TXT/?uri=CELEX%3A32023R1113 (accessed 13 November 2023).

EU Kommission. (2023a, June 28). *Vorschlag für eine Verordnung des Europäischen Parlaments und des Rates zur Einführung des Digitalen Euro*, COM(2023] 369 final, 2023/0212 (COD). Europäische Kommission. https://eur-lex.europa.eu/legal-content/DE/TXT/?uri=CELEX:52023PC0369 (accessed 13 November 2023).

EU Kommission. (2023b, June 28). *Vorschlag für eine Verordnung des Europäischen Parlaments und des Rates über Euro-Banknoten und Euro-Münzen als gesetzliches Zahlungsmittel*, COM(2023) 364 final, 2023/0208 (COD), Europäische Kommission. https://eur-lex.europa.eu/legal-content/DE/TXT/?uri=CELEX:52023PC0364 (accessed 13 November 2023).

Europe elects. (2023). *Europe Elects: Calendar*. https://europeelects.eu/calendar/ (accessed 13 November 2023).

EVZ. (2023, October 19). *Barzahlung: Bargeld-Obergrenzen in Deutschland und Europa*. Europäisches Verbraucherzentrum Deutschland. https://www.evz.de/finanzen-versicherungen/bargeld-obergrenze-in-der-eu.html (accessed 13 November 2023).

GDPR info. (2023). *General Data Protection Regulation GDPR*. https://gdpr-info.eu/ (accessed 13 November 2023).

Gopinath, G., & Stein, J. C. (2018). *Banking, Trade, and the Making of a Dominant Currency*, Working Paper 24485. National Bureau of Economic Research. http://www.nber.org/papers/w24485 (accessed 13 November 2023).

IMF. (2020, October). *Digital Money Across Borders: Macro-financial Implications*. IMF Policy Papers. https://www.imf.org/en/Publications/Policy-Papers/Issues/2020/10/17/Digital-Money-Across-Borders-Macro-Financial-Implications-49823 (accessed 13 November 2023).

IMF. (2023). *Anti-Money Laundering/Combating the Financing of Terrorism (AML/CFT)*. https://www.imf.org/external/np/leg/amlcft/eng/ (accessed 13 November 2023).

Krück, C. (2022, May 21). Kryptoregulierung: Was bedeutet die „Transfer of Funds Regulation" wirklich? *Finanz Magazin*. https://www.it-finanzmagazin.de/kryptoregulierung-was-bedeutet-die-transfer-of-funds-regulation-wirklich-141388/ (accessed 13 November 2023).

Otterbach, B. (2023). *Beispiele für die Pseudonymisierung & Anonymisierung von Daten*. https://www.dataguard.de/blog/pseudonymisierung-und-anonymisierung-in-dsgvo-und-datenschutz (accessed 13 November 2023).

Panetta, F. (2020, November 27). *From the payments revolution to the reinvention of money*. Speech by Fabio Panetta, Member of the Executive Board of the ECB, at the Deutsche Bundesbank conference on the "Future of Payments in Europe", Frankfurt am Main. European Central Bank. https://www.ecb.europa.eu/press/key/date/2020/html/ecb.sp201127~a781c4e0fc.en.html (accessed 13 November 2023).

Panetta, F. (2023a, September 4). *Die Digitale Zukunft Europas gestalten: Auf dem Weg zu einem Digitalen Euro*. Einleitende Bemerkungen von Fabio Panetta, Mitglied des EZB-Direktoriums, vor dem Ausschuss für Wirtschaft und Währung des Europäischen Parlaments. Europäische Zentralbank. https://www.ecb.europa.eu/press/key/date/2023/html/ecb.sp230904~8f5dff1e57.de.html (accessed 13 November 2023).

Panetta, Fabio. (2023b, June 16). *Bringing European payments to the next stage: a public-private endeavour*. Keynote speech by Fabio Panetta, Member of the Executive Board of the ECB, at the European Payments Council's 20th anniversary conference. Europäische Zentralbank. https://www.ecb.europa.eu/press/key/date/2022/html/ecb.sp220616~9f8d1e277b.en.html (accessed 13 November 2023).

Security Insider. (2019). *Grundsätze für sichere Softwareentwicklung*. https://www.security-insider.de/grundsaetze-fuer-sichere-softwareentwicklung-a-856585/ (accessed 13 November 2023).

Weiss, M., & Strauß, K. (2020). *Pseudonymisierung vs. Anonymisierung: Was ist der Unterschied?*. https://www.datenschutzexperte.de/blog/datenschutz-und-eu-dsgvo/pseudonymisierung-und-anonymisierung/ (accessed 13 November 2023).

CHAPTER 4

CBDCs at the Crossroads: Seizing Opportunities and Confronting Threats in the Financial Frontier

Kjartan Sigurdsson, *Gretar Thor Eythorsson*, *and Helga Kristjansdottir*

Introduction

In the face of rapidly evolving financial technologies, central banks worldwide are conducting an intensive analysis of Central Bank Digital Currencies (CBDCs) as the potential future standard for legal tender, which could fundamentally alter the fabric of monetary exchange. Morales-Resendiz et al. (2021) note that this heightened scrutiny is a response to the technological advancements that promise to streamline payment

K. Sigurdsson · G. T. Eythorsson · H. Kristjansdottir (✉)
Faculty of Business, University of Akureyri, Akureyri, Iceland
e-mail: helga@unak.is

K. Sigurdsson
e-mail: kjartansig@unak.is

G. T. Eythorsson
e-mail: gretar@unak.is

R. Aneja and R. Dygas (eds.), *Digital Currencies in The New Global World Order*, https://doi.org/10.1007/978-981-97-4810-5_4

processing and the observed decline in traditional cash usage, marking a pivotal shift in the global financial architecture.

The transformative impact of the digital revolution, compounded by the forces of globalization, has extended beyond economic transactions, reshaping social relationships, labour markets, and the valuation of human and intangible capital (Wilkins, 2016). This change in basic assumptions, which emphasizes scalable returns and the obsolescence and emergence of professions, is increasingly reflected in the academic discourse (Kristjánsdóttir, 2010; Krugman, 1991). The corporate sector innovations that have successfully met the challenges of this digital era are now permeating educational institutions, signifying a reorientation towards a knowledge-based economy.

The systemic implications of integrating CBDCs into national economies are profound, necessitating the development of strategic frameworks to manage the potential threats and leverage opportunities (Brunnermeier & Niepelt, 2019; Fernández-Villaverde et al., 2020; Kwon et al., 2022). Scholars and policymakers are thus engaged in formulating policy design frameworks that consider the implications for cross-country payments, the international role of currencies, and the legal considerations surrounding the issuance of such digital currencies (Auer, 2020; Davoodalhosseini & Rivadeneyra, 2020; Duque, 2022). Nevertheless, as of now, no primary district among the world's largest economies has fully embraced a retail CBDC as the standard legal tender, highlighting the novelty and cautious approach being undertaken in these complex financial systems.

While several sovereign states, including the Bahamas, Jamaica, and Nigeria, have already introduced CBDCs for retail payments, the global landscape remains a patchwork of developmental stages, with many countries still in the exploratory phase of adopting such digital currencies (Adrian et al., 2023; Noll, 2023). This situation leaves numerous unresolved questions, including how central banks should create money and whether CBDCs are a prudent step forward (Armelius et al., 2020; Jackson & Pennacchi, 2021; Keister & Sanches, 2023). Consequently, this study is guided by the overarching question: What are the anticipated impacts of CBDC introduction on the mechanisms of payment processing, the formulation of monetary policy, and the preservation of financial stability against the backdrop of progressive technology and diminishing cash usage? This question underpins the research, providing a foundation for a comprehensive exploration of CBDCs and their potential to redefine the global financial landscape (Sigurdsson et al., 2023).

Before the advent of CBDCs by central banks, particularly in developed economies, it is paramount to assess their anticipated effects on monetary policy and overall financial stability. The notion that "***distance is dead***" in digital finance (Smith, 1996; Todri et al., 2022) prompts a closer examination of this assertion and its implications for the future of monetary exchange and policy. Thus, this research delves into the profound impacts digital currencies may have on international trade, opportunities, and threats, contributing to a comprehensive assessment of their anticipated effects on monetary policy and overall financial stability in the context of central bank adoption, particularly in developed economies.

Literature Review

Rapid technological advancements have brought about a transformative shift in the payment service market in recent years. Today, a considerable portion of the population engages in transactions utilizing various forms of electronic money, often without full awareness of the extent of this change in thinking. Common practices such as using credit cards, making phone payments, and managing transactions through bank accounts exemplify the pervasive influence of electronic money in our daily lives (Sorensen, 2022).

The imperative for diverse payment solutions becomes increasingly evident in the unfolding landscape of financial uncertainties, exemplified by events like the COVID-19 pandemic and an inherently volatile financial environment. As underscored by Auer et al. (2020), the resilience and inclusivity exhibited by traditional cash highlight the essential attributes sought in any payment method. Looking ahead, the course of challenges remains unpredictable, prompting central banks to adopt a forward-thinking stance. In navigating an array of potential future scenarios, careful consideration is bestowed upon the role of CBDCs. These considerations align with a commitment to cultivating enduring financial systems capable of withstanding a broad spectrum of threats.

Digital Currencies Definition and Characteristics

CBDCs are electronic claims against a central bank, expressed in the nation's unit of account, serving as state-sanctioned digital tokens equivalent to paper currency, and acting as both a means of payment and a store of value, underpinned by the trust and authority of the issuing central bank (Carapella & Flemming, 2020). Unlike decentralized cryptocurrencies like Bitcoin, which operate independently of a central authority, CBDCs are centrally issued and regulated, ensuring their legitimacy and acceptance as a medium of exchange and store of value (Carstens, 2021). CBDCs mark an important evolution in monetary policy, integrating the established role of central bank-issued money with digital innovation (Löber & Houben, 2018).

The Central Bank of Iceland has been at the forefront, defining CBDC as a digital claim on the central bank owned by the currency bearer (Seðlabanki Íslands, 2018a). This claim is not merely conceptual but is vested with the full faith and credit of the nation's monetary authority. The International Monetary Fund (IMF) expands upon this characterization, positioning a CBDC as a multifaceted financial instrument that functions as a unit of account and a store of value, framed within the sovereign currency's nominal unit (Mancini-Griffoli et al., 2018). Such definitions are crucial in distinguishing CBDCs from other forms of digital assets and in emphasizing their potential role within the broader economic framework.

CBDCs represent a centralized alternative to cryptocurrencies, known for their decentralized nature and reliance on blockchain technology. The centralization of CBDCs is crucial, as the central bank issues and regulates them, thus providing a stable and universally accepted currency for payments and savings. This centralized approach seeks to ensure the integrity of the national payment system and maintain public trust in the currency (Auer et al., 2020). In contrast to the reserves held by commercial banks at central banks, which are digital but not publicly accessible, CBDCs democratize access to central bank money. By extending the reach of central bank liabilities to the public, CBDCs can enhance the efficiency of payment systems and promote financial inclusion, which is increasingly seen as a public good.

The Evolution and Integration of Central Bank Digital Currencies

Drawing keen interest from global financial institutions, the introduction of CBDCs marks an important shift in the monetary paradigm (Sigurdsson et al., 2023). The journey began in 2012 with the nascent idea of a digitized currency issued by central banks. This concept quickly gained traction, leading to intense research and development from 2015 to 2018, during which the foundational principles of CBDCs were rigorously analysed and debated (Opare & Kim, 2020). A comprehensive survey conducted in 2021, encompassing sixty central banks, unveiled that an overwhelming 86% are actively investigating the potential and intricacies of CBDCs (Boar & Wehrli, 2021). Graphical depictions, often used in economic literature, place CBDCs on the same continuum as physical cash and commercial bank money yet highlight the distinctive nature of CBDCs—their valuation is pegged directly to the national currency. Emulating the characteristics of traditional currency, CBDCs bear no counterparty risk, they are underwritten by the central bank, ensuring their inherent value and security, backed by the institution's assets (Riksbank, 2017).

Integrating CBDCs into the existing payment systems represents a pivotal technological advancement. Central banks aim to design CBDCs to operate within, yet independently from, current financial infrastructures, offering a seamless transition for users wishing to exchange bank deposits or cash for CBDCs. This approach demands agility from banking institutions to meet the evolving demands of consumers and the strategic direction of monetary policy (Riksbank, 2018), thus, CBDCs are anticipated to enable transactions in physical marketplaces, mirroring the tangible nature of cash. Furthermore, the inherent digital nature of CBDCs has the potential to transform online payment methods, offering a secure and direct mechanism for internet-based transactions, which supports continuous innovation in the digital payments landscape (Fung & Halaburda, 2016; Riksbank, 2018).

Digital Currency Transformation

The financial discourse has undergone a significant transformation with the introduction of digital currencies, a movement pioneered by Nakamoto's (2008) groundbreaking whitepaper on Bitcoin. This innovation heralded digital tokens, founded on the principles of blockchain technology, with an original vision of creating decentralized alternatives to government-issued currencies. These digital tokens were crafted to function autonomously, free from central banking authorities' traditional confines and oversight. However, as noted by Swan (2015), these digital assets have struggled to penetrate the mainstream market despite their pioneering beginnings, finding traction primarily within specialized sectors.

According to Cheah et al. (2015), Bitcoin and its digital counterparts are not anchored in intrinsic value, nor do government guarantees underwrite them. Blundell-Wignall (2014) suggests that their valuation is a product of scarcity and the collective willingness of a niche market to pay, thereby creating a speculative market. This speculation-driven valuation leads to volatility that Yermack (2015) and Ciaian et al. (2016) argue diminishes these digital assets' effectiveness as mediums of exchange or stores of value, thereby hindering their potential role in investment portfolios. The tendency of these markets to experience bubble-like conditions, where price movements are disconnected from historical data, is highlighted by Bouoiyour and Selmi (2015) and Cheah et al. (2015), making these currencies unreliable for conventional financial application. Despite these challenges, (Seðlabanki Íslands, 2022) notes a surge in public interest, predominantly driven by the lure of profits, overshadowing a genuine engagement with the technology itself or its intended purpose as a functional currency.

Addressing the volatility inherent in digital tokens, stablecoins were introduced and anchored by more stable financial entities such as national currencies, a concept explored by Fantacci and Gobbi (2021). However, the uptake of these blockchain-based stablecoins has not matched that of their more volatile digital counterparts, a trend noted by the Central Bank of Iceland (2022), which indicates that the market is still driven by speculative interests rather than the utilitarian use of these tokens. The advent of stablecoins issued by prominent technology companies could herald a significant shift in the economic landscape, potentially challenging the current monetary order, as suggested by OMFIF (2018).

Additionally, the emergence of corporate-led electronic currency initiatives, which mirror the stability of coins, has drawn the focus of regulatory bodies. The Central Bank of Iceland acknowledges that these entities are subject to rigorous financial regulation to ensure the backing of their value by substantial assets, positioning them primarily as mechanisms for electronic payments rather than as investment opportunities (Seðlabanki Íslands, 2018b). Within this evolving context, the concept of CBDCs has gained clarity. CBDCs, while analogous to stablecoins instability, are underwritten by the full faith and credit of a nation's assets, presenting a digital alternative to the traditional currency that central banks can manipulate to steer economic policy akin to their interventions in fiat currency markets.

Digital Currencies and the Future of Money

CBDCs represent a transformative development in the economic landscape, poised to revolutionize financial transactions for households and businesses. This novel iteration of currency, as envisioned by Mancini-Griffoli et al. (2018) and supported by Löber and Houben (2018), allows direct electronic transactions through central bank funds, seemingly a subtle change but one with profound implications for financial management and the pursuit of central bank's objectives, including price stability and the stability of financial markets.

However, the impact and progress of CBDCs may vary significantly depending on the specific implementation details. Factors such as interest rates, deposit restrictions, and the design choices outlined by Kumhof and Noone (2018), Riksbank (2017), all play a pivotal role in shaping the outcomes of CBDC adoption. These considerations underscore the importance of carefully structuring CBDCs to strike a balance between facilitating electronic transactions and ensuring compatibility with existing central bank initiatives and financial systems, as emphasized by Bindseil (2020).

To fully comprehend the implications, it is essential to consider the multifaceted aspects of CBDCs and their potential effects on financial stability. The introduction of CBDCs may introduce intermediation within banking systems, raising concerns about increased central bank liquidity management risks, as noted by Kumhof and Noone (2018). As such, meticulous deliberation is imperative to ensure that CBDCs fulfil their intended role as a means of payment without undermining ongoing central bank endeavours. This necessitates a comprehensive examination of CBDC design and deployment strategies, considering the delicate balance between innovation and financial stability.

Impact of CBDCs on Financial Stability: Opportunities and Threats

Introducing a paradigm shift in the financial sector, the advent of CBDC presents an influential opportunity to enhance systemic stability and resilience. This innovation, as examined by authorities such as (Seðlabanki Íslands, 2018a), the Central Bank of Sweden (Riksbank, 2018), and the European Central Bank (Bindseil, 2020), could mitigate the systemic importance of traditional financial institutions by providing an alternative payment mechanism capable of operating seamlessly, even amid disruptions affecting conventional systems (Bindseil, 2020). In doing so, CBDCs also offer the potential to alleviate temptation problems that often manifest in the risk profiles of commercial banks (Morrison, 2011).

The potential for CBDCs to disrupt the established financial order should not be underestimated, particularly concerning commercial banking, a sector Diamond and Dybvig (1983) identified as inherently susceptible to mismatches between the maturities of assets and liabilities—a condition that can precipitate liquidity crises during economic turmoil. Nevertheless, despite these potential threats, the indispensable function of commercial banks persists; their role in converting savings into productive investments and extending long-term financing is irreplaceable (Fabozzi et al., 2014). Their unique capability to generate liquid capital from the aggregated savings of individuals remains a cornerstone of economic growth and stability. Therefore, the advent of CBDCs casts a spotlight on both the innovative prospects they offer and the challenges they may pose to established liquidity protocols. This dichotomy emphasizes the critical need for a considered approach in weaving CBDCs into the financial fabric—one that not only capitalizes on their capacity to bolster systemic stability but also judiciously accounts for the enduring roles and inherent fragilities of traditional banking institutions.

The introduction of CBDC poses specific threats, particularly for households and businesses that adopt it as a means of payment, thus transferring a portion of their deposits and cash to the central bank. Such transfers could particularly impact the current structure of the banking system, potentially destabilizing the financing that relies heavily on deposits from households and businesses (Riksbank, 2018). Consequently, banks would need to strategize how to adapt to changing funding dynamics, possibly resorting to increasing interest rates on deposit accounts to reduce expected outflows or relying more on wholesale funding and central bank financing, which could elevate their funding costs (Bindseil, 2020). This shift in financing costs could result in higher lending rates and reduced commercial bank lending, impacting economic growth. Furthermore, central banks must manage their response on the asset side of their balance sheets to prevent increased central bank activity in bond markets, which could disrupt market information and pricing, and this shift in the banking system's dynamics, known as intermediation, must be cautiously addressed in the context of CBDC (Löber & Houben, 2018).

While the European Central Bank believes that reasonable implementation can minimize the threat of these challenges, they caution against electronic bank runs during times of banking system uncertainty, where individuals may swiftly migrate to CBDCs in large numbers. Under normal circumstances, central banks would provide liquidity support to commercial banks through collateralized loans and may continue to do so. Additionally, central banks are exploring mechanisms such as interest rates and deposit limits to influence the demand side and mitigate the potential rush and arbitrage of the banking system heavily dependent on CBDC demand (Bindseil, 2020; Löber & Houben, 2018).

CBDCs and the Dual Edges of Opportunity and Threat in Monetary Policy

The concept of an interest-free CBDC may exert a nuanced impact on executing monetary policy, particularly in the context of the central bank's balance sheet management and its influence on short-term market interest rates through policy rates. This assertion, which represents both an opportunity and a potential threat, finds support in the analysis conducted by Riksbank (2017). However, a significant threat associated with CBDCs, irrespective of their form of issuance, warrants attention. A notable concern is the substantial funds shift from commercial to central bank balance sheets, triggered by high CBDC demand. This scenario could significantly deplete the commercial bank's deposits at central banks, thereby escalating liquidity risks and intensifying the challenges of credit transformation. However, the magnitude and manifestation of these threats vary among central banks due to differences in monetary policy implementation (Engleske, 2021; Löber & Houben, 2018).

Despite these identified threats, CBDCs present several monetary policy opportunities. Central banks traditionally employ interest rate reductions as a stimulus measure during economic downturns. In the financial landscape, interest rates may encounter a lower bound, marginally below zero, primarily due to the costs of maintaining physical banknotes (Alsterlind et al., 2015). Dyson and Hodgson (2016) propose that interest-bearing CBDCs could disrupt this lower bound, especially if CBDCs replace banknotes, presenting a significant opportunity. This capability of central banks to lower interest rates as needed, particularly in severe economic contractions, could fortify their arsenal against deflation. Conversely, non-interest-bearing CBDCs would reinforce this lower bound, given the lower costs of holding CBDCs compared to cash.

Barrdear and Kumhof (2016) and Kumhof and Noone (2018) suggest that the variable interest rates on CBDCs could enhance not only monetary policy efficiency and emerge as a novel tool but also their effectiveness is underscored by the direct correlation between interest rate decisions and the savings behaviours of households and businesses, creating both opportunities and threats. Barrdear and Kumhof (2016) further assert that CBDCs could enable central banks to better navigate economic cycles by providing a new countercyclical instrument. This opportunity allows for manipulating CBDC quantity or price to mitigate economic fluctuations. Meaning et al. (2018) concur that CBDCs might amplify monetary policy transmission, contingent upon their implementation. Mancini-Griffoli et al. (2018) emphasize the pronounced opportunities for this strengthening in countries with lower financial inclusion.

Bindseil (2020), however, views the interest rate not as a direct monetary policy instrument but as a mechanism to incentivize specific behaviours, thereby influencing the mediation process indirectly and presenting a subtle threat to traditional policy tools. Utilizing CBDCs for a novel form of quantitative easing is also explored (Dyson & Hodgson, 2016). This approach could circumvent the traditional banking system, implementing direct "helicopter drops" of CBDC to individuals, potentially stimulating the economy more effectively than conventional quantitative interventions and presenting an equitable opportunity. Dyson and Hodgson (2016) argue that such a method would be more equitable than traditional quantitative easing, which disproportionately benefits asset owners. Engert and Fung acknowledge the opportunity of this approach, given the existing infrastructures in most countries.

While the Committee on Payments and Market Infrastructures (Löber & Houben, 2018) acknowledges the diverse opportunities that CBDCs could offer for monetary policy, it simultaneously cautions against an overreliance on these digital instruments, emphasizing that CBDCs should serve to complement, rather than replace, the extensive and proven tools already possessed by most central banks for managing price stability. This perspective highlights the delicate balance between embracing CBDC's opportunities and mitigating the threats they pose to the existing financial ecosystem.

Findings and Discussions

A crucial debate has been ignited on the potential impacts of CBDC across various dimensions of the financial system. The findings of this study reveal that the inception of CBDCs is poised to have far-reaching consequences for payment processing, monetary policy, and financial stability due to progressive technological advancements and decreasing reliance on cash.

Our findings suggest that CBDCs are likely to revolutionize current mechanisms significantly in the payment processing realm. Consistent with the observations of Sorensen (2022), the transition towards a digital-centric approach is expected to permeate daily transactions further, offering enhanced efficiency, reduced transaction costs, and improved accessibility. This shift aligns with the broader movement towards electronic forms of money and encapsulates the transformative nature of financial technologies that have become increasingly prominent in contemporary society.

Concerning monetary policy formulation, the study underscores a pivotal opportunity for central banks to recalibrate their policy tools. As Carapella and Flemming (2020) noted and supported by the principles outlined by the Central Bank of Iceland (Seðlabanki Íslands, 2018a), CBDCs represent a new frontier for conducting monetary policy. Their potential to act as both a means of payment and a store of value allows for innovative approaches to managing economic cycles, particularly in developed economies at the forefront of this digital transition. The variable interest rate feature of CBDCs, highlighted by Barrdear and Kumhof (2016), could offer central banks unprecedented control over their monetary policy levers, thus presenting both an opportunity for enhanced efficiency and a threat if not managed with prudence.

The preservation of financial stability, a cornerstone of central banking, emerges as a complex challenge in the face of CBDC adoption. The findings draw attention to the threats identified by Diamond and Dybvig (1983) concerning liquidity risks stemming from mismatches in the maturities of assets and liabilities. The shift in funds from commercial to central bank balance sheets, as CBDC demand increases, could exacerbate these risks, necessitating a strategic response from financial institutions to adapt to the evolving dynamics.

Moreover, the study highlights the dual-edged nature of CBDCs in monetary policy. While they can potentially break through the lower bound of interest rates, as posited by Dyson and Hodgson (2016), and offer a new countercyclical tool, as suggested by Barrdear and Kumhof (2016), they also solidify the lower bound if non-interest-bearing. This duality underscores the need for a delicate balance in integrating CBDCs into existing financial frameworks, as echoed by the Committee on Payments and Market Infrastructures (Löber & Houben, 2018).

Our findings suggest that while CBDCs are agents of substantial change, offering opportunities for a more efficient financial system, they also carry threats that require careful consideration. The study highlights the importance of a balanced strategy in adopting CBDCs, ensuring financial stability and the continued efficacy of monetary policy.

Figure 4.1 proposes a model of the dual impact of CBDCs on the financial system. It highlights CBDCs as a central innovation that offers opportunities to enhance efficiency in payment processing, refine monetary policy tools, and promote financial inclusion. Conversely, the model illustrates potential threats, indicating that CBDCs could challenge systemic financial stability, risk disintermediation of traditional banks, and create regulatory complexities. Black arrows denote positive influences, while red arrows signify potential risks, encapsulating the complex interplay between CBDCs and the economic landscape.

The model illustrated in Fig. 4.1 can also be expressed more formally with the following propositions:

P1: Efficiency in payment processing.

CBDCs are posited to significantly increase the efficiency of payment processing systems, reducing transaction times and costs and fostering an economic environment conducive to rapid and cost-effective financial exchanges.

P2: Monetary policy influence and financial inclusion.

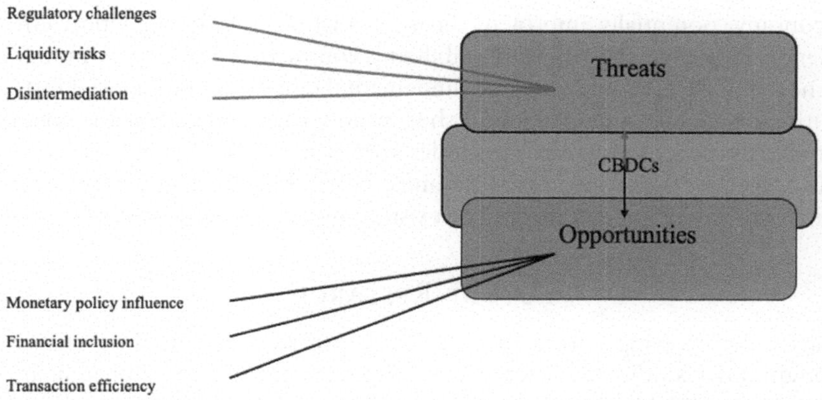

Fig. 4.1 Proposed a model of CBDC's opportunities and threats (*Source* The authors' concept)

The introduction of CBDCs provides central banks with novel, direct monetary policy tools that could enhance their influence over the economy and contribute to greater financial inclusion, particularly by offering banking services to unbanked populations.

P3: Systemic financial stability and banking disintermediation.

While CBDCs may improve systemic efficiency, they threaten traditional banking models through disintermediation, potentially destabilizing existing financial institutions by shifting deposits from commercial banks to the central bank.

P4: Regulatory challenges.

The emergence of CBDCs necessitates the development of new regulatory frameworks to address the complexities introduced by digital currencies, ensuring that financial systems can adapt to and integrate these innovations without compromising the stability and security of the economic infrastructure.

Conclusion

The research findings indicate that CBDCs present both opportunities and threats to the current financial system. As a tool for monetary policy, they could enable central banks to exert more direct influence on the economy, potentially improving financial inclusion and transaction efficiency. However, the risk of destabilizing commercial banking cannot be ignored. CBDCs could alter the fundamental operations of financial institutions, necessitating a paradigm shift in how banks interact with money and customers. This study concludes that while CBDCs hold considerable promise, their implementation must be carefully managed to preserve financial stability and complement existing monetary mechanisms.

Future Research

Given the evolving nature of CBDCs, future research should focus on longitudinal studies to assess their long-term impact on global financial markets. Additional research is needed to explore the international implications of CBDCs, particularly how they might affect cross-border payments, currency exchange rates, and international trade. There is also a need to understand better how CBDCs could integrate with emerging technologies such as blockchain and their potential role in combating financial crimes. As countries move from exploration to implementation, empirical data will become available, offering a rich ground for analyzing the actual, as opposed to anticipated, effects of CBDCs on the financial ecosystem.

References

Adrian, T., He, D., Mancini-Griffoli, T., & Sun, T. (2023, November 20). Central Bank Digital Currency Development Enters the Next Phase. IMF Blog.

Alsterlind, J., Armelius, H., Forsman, D., Jönsson, B., & Wretman, A. L. (2015). How Far Can the Repo Rate be Cut? *Economic Commentaries, 11.*

Armelius, H., Claussen, C. A., & Hendry, S. (2020). *Is Central Bank Currency Fundamental to the Monetary System?* (No. 2020–2). Bank of Canada Staff Discussion Paper.

Auer, R., Cornelli, G., & Frost, J. (2020). *Rise of the Central Bank Digital Currencies: Drivers, Approaches, and Technologies.*

Barrdear, J., & Kumhof, M. (2016). *The Macroeconomics of Central Bank-issued Digital Currencies.*

Bindseil, U. (2020). Tiered CBDC and the Financial System. *Available at SSRN 3513422.*

Blundell-Wignall, A. (2014). *The Bitcoin Question: Currency versus Trust-less Transfer Technology.*

Boar, C., & Wehrli, A. (2021). Ready, Steady, Go?-Results of the Third BIS Survey on Central Bank Digital Currency. *BIS papers*.

Bouoiyour, J., & Selmi, R. (2015). What Does Bitcoin Look Like? *Annals of Economics & Finance, 16*(2).

Brunnermeier, M. K., & Niepelt, D. (2019). On the Equivalence of Private and Public Money. *Journal of Monetary Economics, 106*, 27–41.

Carapella, F., & Flemming, J. (2020). *Central Bank Digital Currency: A Literature Review*.

Carstens, A. (2021). *Digital Currencies and the Future of the Monetary System*.

Cheah, E. T., & Fry, J. (2015). Speculative Bubbles in Bitcoin Markets? An Empirical Investigation into the Fundamental Value of Bitcoin. *Economics letters, 130*, 32–36.

Ciaian, P., Rajcaniova, M., & Kancs, D. A. (2016). The Digital Agenda of Virtual Currencies: Can BitCoin Become a Global Currency? *Information Systems and e-Business Management, 14*, 883–919.

Davoodalhosseini, S. M., & Rivadeneyra, F. (2020). A Policy Framework for e-money. *Canadian Public Policy, 46*(1), 94–106.

Diamond, D. W., & Dybvig, P. H. (1983). Bank Runs, Deposit Insurance, and Liquidity. *Journal of Political Economy, 91*(3), 401–419.

Duque, J. J. (2022). State Involvement in Cryptocurrencies. A Potential World Money? In *Money, Finance, and Capitalist Crisis* (pp. 104–121). Routledge.

Dyson, B., & Hodgson, G. (2016). Digital Cash: Why Central Banks Should Start Issuing Electronic Money. *Positive money*, 6–14.

Engleske, B. B. (2021, July 5). *Central Bank Digital Currency: Opportunities, Challenges and Design*. Pristupljeno.

Fabozzi, F. J., Modigliani, F. P., & Jones, F. J. (2014). *Foundations of Financial Markets and Institutions: Pearson New International Edition*. Pearson.

Fantacci, L., & Gobbi, L. (2021). Stablecoins, Central Bank digital Currencies and US Dollar Hegemony: The Geopolitical Stake of Innovations in Money and Payments. *Accounting, Economics, and Law: A Convivium*, (0), 20200053.

Fernández-Villaverde, J., Schilling, L., & Uhlig, H. (2020). Central Bank Digital Currency: When Price and Bank Stability Collide. CEPR Discussion Paper No. DP15555.

Fung, B. S., & Halaburda, H. (2016). Central Bank Digital Currencies: A Framework for Assessing Why and How. *Available at SSRN 2994052*.

Jackson, T., & Pennacchi, G. (2021). How Should Governments Create Liquidity? *Journal of Monetary Economics, 118*, 281–295.

Keister, T., & Sanches, D. (2023). Should Central Banks Issue Digital Currency? *The Review of Economic Studies, 90*(1), 404–431.

Kristjánsdóttir, H. (2010). Foreign Direct Investment: The Knowledge-capital Model and a Small Country Case. *Scottish Journal of Political Economy, 57*(5), 591–614.

Krugman, P. (1991). Increasing Returns and Economic Geography. *Journal of Political Economy, 99*(3), 483–499.

Kumhof, M., & Noone, C. (2018). *Central Bank Digital Currencies-design Principles and Balance Sheet Implications.*

Kwon, O., Lee, S., & Park, J. (2022). Central Bank Digital Currency, Tax Evasion, and Inflation Tax. *Economic Inquiry, 60*(4), 1497–1519.

Löber, K., & Houben, A. (2018). Committee on Payments and Market Infrastructures Markets Committee. *Bank for International Settlements: Basel, Switzerland.*

Mancini-Griffoli, T., Peria, M. S. M., Agur, I., Ari, A., Kiff, J., Popescu, A., & Rochon, C. (2018). Casting Light on Central Bank Digital Currency. *IMF staff discussion note, 8*(18), 1–39.

Meaning, J., Dyson, B., Barker, J., & Clayton, E. (2018). *Broadening Narrow Money: Monetary Policy with a Central Bank Digital Currency.*

Morales-Resendiz, R., Ponce, J., Picardo, P., Velasco, A., Chen, B., Sanz, L., Guiborg, G., Segendorff, B., Vasquez, J. L., Arroyo, J., & Aguirre, I. (2021). Implementing a Retail CBDC: Lessons Learned and Key Insights. *Latin American Journal of Central Banking, 2*(1), 100022.

Morrison, A. D. (2011). Systemic Risks and the 'Too-big-to-fail' Problem. *Oxford Review of Economic Policy, 27*(3), 498–516.

Nakamoto, S. (2008). Bitcoin: A Peer-to-peer Electronic Cash System. *Decentralized business review.*

Noll, F. (2023). What Consumer Surveys Say about the Design of a US CBDC for Retail Payments. *Payments System Research Briefing,* 1–5.

OMFIF. (2018). Retail CBDCs the next payment frontier.

Opare, E. A., & Kim, K. (2020). A Compendium of Practices for Central Bank Digital Currencies for Multinational Financial Infrastructures. *IEEE Access, 8*, 110810–110847.

Riksbank, S. (2017). *The Riksbank's e-krona Project*. Sveriges Riskbank.

Riksbank, S. (2018). *The Riksbank's E-Krona Project Report 2.* Sveriges Riskbank.

Seðlabanki Íslands, S. (2018a). Sérrit Seðlabanka Íslands nr. 12-Rafkróna. *Seðlabanki Íslands.* https://www.sedlabanki.is/library/Skraarsafn/Serrit/Serrit_nr_12

Seðlabanki Íslands, S. (2018b). Sérrit nr. 13: Smágreiðslumiðlun frá sjónarhóli viðbúnaðar og fjármálastöðugleika: Neytendur og atvinnulíf reiða sig á virkni rafrænnar greiðslumiðlunar. *Seðlabanki Íslands.*

Seðlabanki Íslands, S (2022). Fjármálastöðugleiki 2022/2. *Seðlabanki Íslands.*

Sigurdsson, K., Eyþórsson, G. Þ., & Kristjánsdóttir, H. (2023). Digital Currencies, SWOT Analysis. *Baltic Journal of Economic Studies, 9*(3), 1–9. https://doi.org/10.30525/2256-0742/2023-9-3-1-9

Smith, R. (1996). Distance is Dead: The World Will Change. *BMJ, 313*(7072), 1572.

Sorensen, E. (2022, October 7). What is Digital Money? Definition and Types Explained. Mobile Transaction. https://www.mobiletransaction.org/what-is-digital-money/

Sveriges Riksbank. (2018). *The Riksbank's e-krona project. Report 2.*

Sverges Riksbank. (2022). *E- krona report. pilot phase 2.*

Swan, M. (2015). *Blockchain: Blueprint for a new economy.* O'Reilly Media, Inc.

Todri, V., Adamopoulos, P., & Andrews, M. (2022). Is Distance Dead in the Online World? The Moderating Role of Geographical Distance on the Effectiveness of Electronic Word of Mouth. *Journal of Marketing, 86*(4), 118–140.

Wilkins, C. (2016). Fintech and the Financial Ecosystem: Evolution or Revolution? *Remarks to Payments Canada, Calgary, Alberta, 17.*

Yermack, D. (2015). Is Bitcoin a Real Currency? An Economic Appraisal. In *Handbook of Digital Currency* (pp. 31–43). Academic Press.

CHAPTER 5

Central Bank Digital Currency—Political Risks and the Implications for International Trade

Magdalena Kozińska

Introduction

Currencies and their systems were always seen as one of the determinants that define the place of a given country in the international economy, especially in trade. The stronger and the more universal, as well as the more prevailing role of a national currency in terms of international economic connections, the higher the impact of the country on the global economy. Leaders in terms of the development of currency systems are usually seen also as one of the most essential economic powers, which translates into their position in international trade.

The national currencies started to change their character, as society became more and more used to cutting-edge solutions including new, electronic, and often remote channels for contact with institutions,

M. Kozińska (✉)
Department of Banking Safety Net, SGH Warsaw School of Economics, Collegium of Socio-Economics, Institute of Banking, Warsaw, Poland
e-mail: magdalena.kozinska@sgh.waw.pl

R. Aneja and R. Dygas (eds.), *Digital Currencies in The New Global World Order*, https://doi.org/10.1007/978-981-97-4810-5_5

including financial ones. This ramps up the pressure on all players in the financial system, including central banks and other public authorities that try to catch up and be as digital as possible (He, 2021, pp. 353–354, 357, 359). One of the results of such an environment is the idea of central bank digital currencies (CBDCs), which are planned to be a digital equivalent of cash (ECB, 2020, p. 11). It should be highlighted that their design options carry influential powers over the economies, being the next possible tool for stimulating them and shaping their role in international trade.

This chapter aims to show that non-economic issues are of significant importance in the global project of launching CBDCs. These non-economic, political opportunities will however create the future world of digital currencies. The intention is to identify the potential non-economic, and political issues that should be taken into consideration when analyzing the economic consequences of CBDCs (they are called "political opportunities"), also in terms of global trade.

The chapter is structured as follows. The first part is devoted to the presentation of the CBDC in general and the state of play in the world. The second part contains an analysis of the identified, most important political risks that are associated with the CBDCs. The analysis of each political opportunity for exploiting CBDCs is summarized with the presentation of the results of the questionnaire among CBDC's experts. The article ends with the conclusions, where implementations for global trade are indicated.

CBDCs—Notion and State of Play

CBDC is usually described as a digital equivalent of cash (ECB, 2020, p. 11), but does not necessarily aim to replace coins and banknotes. Therefore, it would be an additional, digital form of central bank money (along with cash and central bank deposits/reserves) (Bank of England, 2020, p. 7; ECB, 2020, p. 6) serving as its next natural development phase. Most central banks working on CBDCs assume that they should be widely accessible to the general public. The reasons for their introduction are multiple, but mostly, they are concentrated on the desire to maintain viable control and impact on the financial system in the face of the growing relevance of the tech giants (so-called BigTech, Big Four, or Big Five referring to Amazon, Apple, Facebook (Meta), Google, and sometimes Microsoft; more and more frequently Asian companies are also enumerated, e.g., Alibaba, Samsung or Tencent) for its functioning and rising popularity of crypto assets, especially stablecoins (e.g., Tether or earlier planned Meta's Diem). Although the number of countries that implemented CBDCs is low,[1] the idea attracts the attention of more and more entities, not only central banks but also other stakeholders. The pioneers in this area are e.g., Canada, Netherlands, Singapore, and Great Britain, where in-depth analyses and experiments have been running since 2015 (Auer et al., 2021, p. 4). Skandinavian countries are also well-advanced. Even the US Federal Reserve, which initially kept its distance towards the idea of CBDCs, has finally joined the group of central banks analyzing the case (Board of Governors of the Federal Reserve System, 2022, p. 1). There are also central banks that are even more advanced in the works on CBDCs. In October 2020 the Central Bank of the Bahamas issued a Sand Dollar. In March 2021, the Eastern Caribbean Central Bank launched DCash (Auer et al., 2021, p. 5) and in October 2021 the eNaira was introduced by the Central Bank of Nigeria (but described as a pilot project) (IMF, 2021). In January 2022 People's Bank of China announced the next phase of the implementation of its e-CNY—the extension for the use of individual citizens (Feng, 2022)—and then launched a dedicated application in September 2022 (even though it is still described as a pilot project). A similar project was introduced in India. It should be noted that some retail CBDC projects have already been rejected by a few countries like Denmark, Ecuador, Finland (project Avant that is assessed as the first launched project on CBDC), Haiti, Philippines, Singapore (project Orchid, other projects are continued) (CBDC Tracker, 2022).

The three basic forms of CBDC might be enumerated:

- CBDC for interbank settlements (so-called wholesale CBDC),
- CBDC with features ideally equivalent to cash (might be counted toward so-called retail CBDC),
- CBDC with features that are specifically appealing as a new public policy tool (might also be counted towards so-called retail CBDC, but as a more advanced/broadened type).

[1] As of August 2024.

The specific characteristics connected with the mentioned forms of CBDCs are presented in Table 5.1.

The presented forms of CBDCs might also be seen as potential stages of their development. Interbank settlements are organized in a way that is analogous to the idea of CBDCs. Therefore, it might be judged that this first phase of the CBDCs' evolution (CBDCs for interbank transactions, i.e., wholesale CBDCs) has already been implemented. Central banks are now analyzing especially the technology that backs such primitive CBDCs (restricted in terms of entities that have access to them), which might increase the efficiency of the settlement systems (costs and speed of transactions).

Nowadays, central banks are facing the debate whether this type of innovation could be commonly introduced, for a broader scope of entities (potentially whole societies—not only interbank market participants, but also other financial institutions, non-financial companies, and households). Such an expansion of the CBDCs might take a more or less advanced form. The less developed form of the next phase of the CBDCs' evolution might be a CBDC available for the whole society with features that are the same as cash (unrestricted access, anonymous character, no remuneration for holding). Nevertheless, central banks are analyzing many features of CBDCs that are different from cash (user verification, the potential to be remunerated for holding CBDCs, expiration date, etc.).

Political Opportunities of CBDCs

Multiple researches suggest that the economic benefits of implementing CBDCs seem to be uncertain. Nevertheless, the list of non-economic (usually political) opportunities that might be accomplished thanks to CBDCs seems to be open-ended. The most important issues identified by the author are raised below.

Opportunity 1: Access to Very Broad Data that Might be Monetized

CBDCs, due to their power to track all the transactions, have the potential to be the source of up-to-date data about people's and companies' spending habits, current market trends, emerging points of stress, and the condition of the economy. Such data might be easily used to properly plan the activities of public authorities (especially those connected

Table 5.1 Potential features of CBDCs

General form of CBDC	*Type of the CBDC*	*Scope of entities with access to CBDC*	*Anonymity*	*Remuneration*	*Expiry time*	*Engagement of the central bank*	*CBDC delivery tool*	*Technology*	*Centralization*
CBDC for interbank settlements	Wholesale CBDC	Restricted (usually to banks, sometimes other financial institutions)	No (all entities taking part in the system assuring the CBDC are identified)	No remuneration	No	Rather direct (but it is possible to imagine indirect)	Account-based as well as Token-based the technology of delivering the CBDC might be used	Central ledger or distributed ledger is possible to apply	Centralized and decentralized control over the C BDC's system might be designed

(continued)

Table 5.1 (continued)

General form of CBDC	*Type of the CBDC*	*Scope of entities with access to CBDC*	*Anonymity*	*Remuneration*	*Expiry time*	*Engagement of the central bank*	*CBDC delivery tool*	*Technology*	*Centralization*
CBDC with features ideally equivalent to cash	Retail CBDC	Open and broad (unlimited)	Yes			Direct (so-called one-tier system) or indirect (within the so-called two-tier system)			
CBDC with features that are specifically appealing as a new policy tool	Retail CBDC		Not necessary (anonymity might be assured, but no anonymity broadens the scope of the application)	Might be applicable, especially for monetary policy purposes	Might be appli-cable				

Source Own elaboration based on Kozińska (2022) and Zaleska (2022) with the changes in the legislation enabling to address novelties in the economy, e.g., to tax the new, so-far unidentified types of businesses). It might also change the perspective of the public institutions and their approaches. It is now the rule that the authorities and the legislation follow the institutions in the economy (public authorities usually depend on the data reported by the entities, which are by nature always reported after a while). CBDCs might allow keeping a close eye on all capital flows in the economy enabling the authorities to react immediately.

It should also be noted that access to such broad, current, and valued data might be a source of income. Most companies in the economy develop their strategies based on market research. Its preparation requires granular and current data. Such data would be at the disposal of central banks[2] (or other public authorities managing the data on behalf of the central bank) and could be monetized. The problem is, however, to ensure proper privacy protection for the parties of the transactions.

Opportunity 2: Disintermediation as a Mean for Limiting the Influence of International Banks

Firstly, in the opinion of many commentators on the CBDCs, their introduction (especially if CBDC would be directly issued by the central bank to the public and be remunerated) might lead to the situation that part of the bank deposits is converted into CBDCs and is no longer robust/stable and cheap source of financing for banks. This means that the traditional connection of lending and deposit activity of banks might be split (since banks will no longer be accumulating deposits).[3] Moreover, part of the transaction business might be shifted towards direct usage of CBDCs for

[2] It should be emphasized that as a rule central banks are non-commercial entities. Therefore, they should not be interested in making deals on public data. However, one should take into consideration that there are central banks that contribute to the state budget (by transferring the agreed and fixed percentage of its profit). Under such circumstances and where central bankers might be dependent on the policymakers, central banks might be prone to such actions.

[3] Such a situation when the cash is distributed to the entities without intermediaries (banks) is called disintermediation. CBDC might cause disintermediation, but there are preliminary analysis that suggest that this might not be true if banks have market power in the deposit market. Nevertheless, the introduction of CBDC will certainly impact the banks' business models (Chiu, Davoodalhosseini, Jiang, and Zhu 2019, p. 31; Chiu, Rivadeneyra 2021, p. 14).

debt settlement. These two trends may result in the loss of two important businesses waning the position of banks in the economy. This also means the diminishing position of banks as lobbyists when governments try to implement reforms that are inconvenient for the banking sector (but may bring additional income for the state budget or some benefits for the society).

Secondly, because of disintermediation, the growing diversification of the financial system (increasing number of types of institutions offering financial services)[4] may reduce the market power of financial giants also lowering the impact of their business strategies and plans on the economy. This paves the way for public authorities to employ tools enabling non-market control over the economy.

Consequently, CBDCs might enable public authorities to suppress big banks in the financial market, whose current market power might limit the achievement of the goal of public authorities (including getting cheap financing on the markets that might be easily influenced by monopolistic companies).

Opportunity 3: Capturing the Tentacles of BigTech Companies

The Big Tech companies have an insight into the broad set of data about the clients, and their businesses through the e-commerce, messaging, social media, or search queries. The next reason for their competitive edge over other companies are very strong network effects they generate, since they gather on their platforms vast amounts of people from all over the world (and the bigger the number of users of such a platform the more attractive it is for the next ones—which is called "data-network-activities" or "DNA" loop) (BIS, 2021, p. 67). This makes them currently the most powerful companies in the world with exclusive access to their unique and broad data. This data is frequently not accessible to public authorities due to the data protection legal frameworks (such frameworks usually foresee that the data might be made available for public authorities only in limited scope and under specified circumstances). CBDCs (as potentially more

[4] Currently banks offer a wide range of financial services. Disintermediation means that the idea of "narrow banking" might be the dominant form of banking business, where banks concentrate on the lending activity (with excellent expertise, since it might be the main area of activity). The provision of tools for CBDC holdings as well as investment for people's savings might be taken over by other, emerging new ecosystem, institutions.

reliable option of electronic money than private currencies and therefore preferred over the latter ones), which would be used to settle the bills on the platforms of BigTech could immediately open the knowledge about all transactions for the public authorities. Under such circumstances, the databases of BigTech companies would probably be not so interesting as a potential product to be bought by public authorities (since they will already possess such data). Also, the market power of BigTech companies as the sellers of aggregated and usually anonymized databases would be hindered, as similar databases could offer also public authorities (but for more competitive prices since they are non-profit organizations).

Opportunity 4: Reduction of Illegal Events (e.g., Tax Evasion, Money Laundering)

CBDCs might improve the tracking of transactions, both domestically and internationally (Cecchetti & Schoenholtz, 2021, p. 59). The ability to track every capital flow allows the public authority to control quicker whether it relates to real transactions (not aimed at laundering dirty money), as well as control its taxation. CBDCs might therefore tremendously boost the efficiency of AML/CFT and tax authorities. The condition is however that the holder of CBDC can be easily identified (is tracked) what is currently controversial. The research shows that CBDC with a cash feature (anonymity) would even sharpen tax evasion (Wang, 2021, pp. 34–35).

Opportunity 5: Possibility for State Surveillance and Increased Influence Over the Economy

Firstly, CBDCs might be easy to track. As mentioned above, this gives the opportunity to meticulously control all capital flows in the economy. Consequently, increased public surveillance opens the door for more stringent tax controls and money laundering/financing terrorism policies. Looking at the whole financial system and the economy, state surveillance creates an incentive to try to include all the transactions and entities within the regulatory perimeter (Brunnermeier & Payne, 2021, p. 67), since it is relatively easier to identify them.

If central banks introduced remunerated CBDCs, they could be easily used to impact the level of consumption. In an economy where all money holdings take the form of CBDC and bank deposits, setting negative interest rates would have stronger effects (than in the situation when people can store the value in cash) and stimulate spending, since otherwise all savings would lose their value. In a situation where people can store a value in cash the possible reaction to maintain the value of savings is to convert to cash (since cash is not negatively renumerated).

Under the condition that the payments in the economy might be made only via CBDCs, they could be an option to influence the peoples' spending, by preventing them from buying particular types of goods (as it would be impossible to pay for them with CBDCs thanks to used technical solutions), e.g., alcohol or drugs. Opposite, setting the expiry date of CBDCs might have tremendous power to boost people's consumption.

Opportunity 6: Tool for the Government Propaganda

The introduction of CBDC might be the way the countries (mainly governments) could enhance the level of digitalization. In most countries, one of the goals of currently implemented programs and reforms is to increase the presence of new (digital) technologies in the public services for citizens. The wide array of already available services often includes remote submission of various forms and official documents. Also, private entities frequently offer digitalized services. The CBDCs could be seen by society as a natural supplement to already completed actions. This could increase the evaluation of the governing party by the citizens (by realizing the digitalization programs supporting the communities).

Looking at the payment habits in most economies, the introduction of a CBDC might be then marketed as a way the government tries to shape its administration and the way the public authorities work in the whole country that is convergent with the expectations of the society. This might be a good supporting tool in the race for voters.

Opportunity 7: Tool for Money Redistribution Policy

As mentioned above, CBDCs might enable stark state surveillance meaning that the public authorities will ultimately have access to all data about every person in the country. That means that it will be easy to determine and control the level of wealth for every citizen. For that reason, it will be easier to select only those residents who genuinely deserve public support (e.g., benefits or privileges). Also, as the circulation of CBDCs would relate to the necessity to have an account or device (registering the amount of CBDCs) for which it will be relatively easy to implement the obligation of verification of the beneficiary's identity, the transfer of benefits or monetary support will be easier, since it could be transferred by the public authorities directly to the beneficiary.

However, central bankers should beware of potential further "politicization" of their activity. The direct connections between the central bank and the economy (through direct exposures via CBDCs) may result in the outflow of funds from banks which means that central banks will probably have to help banks by providing them with liquidity through open market operations and the lender of last resort (LoLR) function (opposite would mean systemic liquidity problems of banks). This may be an opportunity for the banking sector to exert higher pressure on the central bank making it more politicized. Being politicized means being targeted for asking for more and more financing (Niepelt, 2021, p. 42).

Opportunity 8: Security Considerations

It is predicted that CBDCs will not squeeze out traditional payment systems. However, in case of payment systems' unavailability (e.g., system breakdown), CBDCs and their system could play the role of additional, backup solutions, that might be used by people to settle their bills (ECB, 2020, pp. 13–14). In such a dimension, the introduction of the whole CBDC framework might be seen as an activity aimed at enhancing the security and stability of the whole national financial system. This is naturally true provided that the CBDCs will be operable under every circumstance (i.e., also offline), which is not so obvious and easy to implement (but not impossible).

Nevertheless, making the payment system dependent on the digital form of cash might lure hackers who gain additional targets to attack. It is impossible to hack the physical holdings of cash, but it is possible to hack the holdings of virtual cash. The increased danger to the security of society's financial means might be seen by politicians as an argument against the introduction of CBDCs. Such cyberattacks on publicly provided digital cash might suggest that the governing authorities did not ensure a proper level of security resulting thus in the decline of their public evaluation.

The possibility of being exposed to the cyberattacks might however also be seen as an opportunity. Usually, it is possible to establish the source of the cyberattack (including the geographical origins and the type of attacking entity). This facilitates the identification of allies and enemies which takes on great importance in today's uncertain world.

Opportunity 9: Effective Tool to Compete with Private Currencies (Especially Stablecoins)

So far, the most popular private digital currency (Bitcoin) has not become the most commonly used means of payments due to its high volatility.[5] Nevertheless, its biggest drawback is reduced (but not eliminated) in the case of digital currencies whose worth is bundled with the fiat currency (or the basket of currencies)—stablecoins. The stablecoins have therefore the potential to grow to the role of credible means of payment. Since they will be delivered by the technological giants with access to a tremendously broad network of users, the stablecoins might pose a threat to central banks' currencies. Central banks that do not want to lose their power may see CBDCs as a potential method of counteraction. Their advantage is greater stability and even global financial stress does not translate into fear about the CBDC (Stolbov et al., 2022), contrary to private digital currencies. The condition is here however the appropriate design of CBDCs that will offer advantages at least the same as stablecoins. Consequently, CBDCs should be anonymous which thwarts other potential political benefits that could be achieved by them (under the option that the CBDC is not anonymous).

Moreover, stablecoins are growing to be a potential threat to governments. Generally, the (especially tax) status of private currencies is undefined in many countries. The very modest legislation concerning private currencies varies widely across the world. The transactions that are settled using private currencies are difficult to track (DLT technology based on accounts without verification of the identity) and, consequently, control and tax. The growing power of especially stablecoins poses a real threat to the budgetary incomes. CBDCs could surpass their development and enhance budgetary profits.

Wide-spread usage of private currencies might also lead to the effect of currency substitution similar to dollarization. Consequently, the growing

[5] Companies that initially accepted payments in Bitcoin often withdrew from that solution, e.g., car manufacturer Tesla.

impact on the monetary conditions in the economy would have technological companies. This threatens the country's financial and political sovereignty.

Opportunity 10: International Aspects

It might be true that the country that will first enable the CBDCs to be used in the international settlements (i.e., also by non-residents) will gain a leading position in the international financial system. Such a position will facilitate the efforts to become a leading currency also in international trade.

The ECB rightly emphasizes that the widespread usage of non-ECB CBDCs made available for EU citizens might lead to currency substitution that increases the foreign exchange risk for the eurozone. The growing influence of other CBDCs in the euro area might threaten the financial, economic, and political sovereignty (ECB, 2020, pp. 11–12). Moreover, CBDCs (especially those from stable jurisdictions) might be an interesting goal of investments abroad. Assuming the unhindered ability to exchange the CBDCs as well as CBDCs and cash, there is a risk, that national CBDCs would be spread around the world. Also, the national economy would be flooded with foreign currencies. This phenomenon might occur since it would be very easy to exchange currencies—it is possible to do it even from home due to technical solutions. Such a national currency spread around the world and national "currency mismatch" would weaken the effectiveness of monetary policy aimed at targeting the national economy.

Opportunity 11: Tool for the Circumvention of International Sanctions

It is foreseen that CBCDs might weaken the position of main currencies (e.g., dollar, euro) in the economy exacerbating the shift away from the SWIFT-dominated banking system that is subject to US influence. They would also mean greater control and autonomy of domestic or regional financial systems that are subject to sanctions (Davis, 2021). It should be noted that there are already countries that introduced CBDCs or announced plans to introduce CBCDs mainly to lower the impact of sanctions, e.g., Venezuela, North Korea, and Iran (National Bank of Poland, 2021, pp. 32–33).

Opportunity 12: Central Banks and Government Authorities Fight for Primacy

In an ideal world central bank is an independent institution, whose responsibility is to run monetary policy (aimed usually at price stabilization and supporting economic growth) taking care of financial stability at the same time. In practice, the central bank and its monetary policy contribute to the optimal policy mix where fiscal policy is also crucial. There are multiple interdependencies between the central bank and the government, which expects the central bank to boost the national economy (since it raises the sentiment of citizens) by employing monetary policy tools (shouldering the standing of the state budget). Central banks know however that expansionary policy has its price (e.g., higher future inflation). Therefore, there is sometimes quite a visible conflict of interest (at least a conflict of goals) between the central banks and the government. CBDCs might be an opportunity (as an additional and quite powerful tool) for central banks to enhance their power and thus the independence from the government.

Central banks must however be aware that CBDCs carry significant risks that might be used against them (possibly forcing them to be more prone to political influence). One such risk might be a reputational one. Implementation of CBDCs entails the necessity to build as well as ensure the ultra-resilience of the whole framework and infrastructure. Any glitches or irresistibility to cyber-attacks[6] might be a "hook point" for undermining the position of the central bank and be the starting point for exercising pressures on its policy (as irresponsible where the evidence is that it was not able to ensure the security of the CBDC's system).

Summary

To preliminarily assess the probability and the significance of the identified political opportunities, experts on CBDCs were asked for their opinions. The results of their evaluations are provided below in Table 5.2.

[6] The practice shows that such a possibility should not be excluded. In January 2022, the DCash (the Eastern Caribbean Central Bank's digital currency faced "technical issue" and was unavailable for the holders. In its statement central bank admitted that the CBDC will need some "upgrades" to function properly (Margulies 2022).

Table 5.2 Number of respondents assessing the level of probability and significance for each identified political opportunity

	Probability			*Significance*		
	High	*Medium*	*Low*	*High*	*Medium*	*Low*
Opportunity 1	12	22	12	22	16	8
Opportunity 2	9	23	14	21	16	9
Opportunity 3	16	17	13	19	19	8
Opportunity 4	**22**	14	10	**29**	11	6
Opportunity 5	17	19	10	25	15	6
Opportunity 6	18	16	12	18	10	**18**
Opportunity 7	19	19	8	25	15	6
Opportunity 8	20	16	9	25	13	8
Opportunity 9	16	20	10	20	20	6
Opportunity 10	12	22	12	15	21	10
Opportunity 11	12	19	15	14	19	13
Opportunity 12	12	14	**20**	16	14	16
Maximum	*22*	*23*	*20*	*29*	*21*	*18*
Minimum	*9*	*14*	*8*	*14*	*10*	*6*
Average	*15,42*	*18,42*	*12,08*	*20,75*	*15,75*	*9,50*

Source Own elaboration based on the results of the questionnaire

According to experts' evaluation the most probable and at the same time the most influential political opportunity is the possibility to use CBDCs to reduce illegal events like tax evasion, money laundering, or terrorist financing. Specialists evaluated most frequently that there is a low probability that the political fallout of CBDCs will be a fight between central banks and government authorities for primacy. Also, most often it was assessed that there is a low significance of using CBDCs as government propaganda.

In general, experts usually assessed the importance of identified political opportunities than their probability (on average more people assessed significance as high than probabilities as high). When it comes to probabilities of opportunities, experts were quite conservative in the assessments. Their assessment was frequently dispersed (not allowing for the identification of the dominant group/assessment) and various groups of assessments (high, medium, low) were often similar in terms of number. Experts were braver when assessing the significance of provided political flip sides of CBDCs. Here, on average, the highest number of people assessed them as high and the average number of low assessments was more than two times lower.

Conclusion

As noted above, CBDCs should be a digital equivalent of cash. Nevertheless, cash features do not offer such influential benefits. Therefore, features other than those of cash are strongly analyzed by central banks and sometimes even implemented. This however means that the CBDCs are becoming increasingly political projects.

As indicated in this chapter, there are multiple ways of using CBDCs' projects for political purposes. Most of the identified political opportunities are assessed by the experts as of medium or high importance. The probability was usually assessed to be a little bit lower (compared to importance), but still most often scored medium or high assessments. There is no doubt that the political opportunities should not be neglected.

From the point of view of global trade, it should be emphasized that some political opportunities are directly connected to it. Issues connected with international sanctions, international security, and ways of stimulating the national economies will undoubtedly define the role of a given country in international trade.

References

Auer, R., Frost, J., Gambacorta, L., Monnet, C., Rice, T., & Shin, H. S. (2021). *Central Bank Digital Currencies: Motives, Economic Implications and the Research Frontier*. BIS Working Papers No. 976.

Aneja, R., & Dygas, R. (Eds.). (2022). *Digital Currencies and the New Global Financial System* (1st ed., pp. 1–16). Routledge. https://doi.org/10.4324/9781003310365

Bank of England. (2020). *Central Bank Digital Currency: Opportunities, Challenges and Design. A Discussion Paper*. https://www.bankofengland.co.uk/-/media/boe/files/paper/2020/central-bank-digital-currency-opportunities-challenges-and-design.pdf (accessed 12 December 2023).

BIS. (2021). *CBDCs: An Opportunity for the Monetary System*. BIS Annual Economic Report.

Board of Governors of Federal Reserve System. (2022). *Money and Payments: The U.S. Dollar in the Age of Digital Transformation*.

Brunnermeier, M., & Payne, J., 2021. *Central Bank Digital Currency, FinTech and Private Money Creation*. In D. Niepelt (Ed.), *Central Bank Digital Currency: Considerations, Projects, Outlook*. Centre for Economic Policy Research.

CBDC Tracker. (2022). https://cbdctracker.org/ (accessed 12 December 2023).

Cecchetti, S.G., & Schoenholtz, K.L. (2021). *Central Bank Digital Currency: Is It Worth the Risk?* In D. Niepelt (Ed.), *Central Bank Digital Currency: Considerations, Projects, Outlook*. Centre for Economic Policy Research.

Chiu, J. (2021). *Central Bank Digital Currency, Bank Intermediation and Payments*. In: Niepelt D. *Central Bank Digital Currency: Considerations, Projects, Outlook*, Centre for Economic Policy Research

Chiu, J., Davoodalhosseini, S. M., Jiang, J., & Zhu, Y. (2019). *Bank Market Power and Central Bank Digital Currency: Theory and Quantitative Assessment*. Bank of Canada Staff Working Paper No. 2019–20.

Davis J. (2021). *International Security Implications of Central Bank Digital Currencies*. https://www.lawfaremedia.org/article/international-security-implications-central-bank-digital-currencies (accessed 01 August 2024).

ECB. (2020). *Report on a Digital Euro*. https://www.ecb.europa.eu/pub/pdf/other/Report_on_a_digital_euro~4d7268b458.en.pdf (accessed 12 December 2023).

Feng, C. (2022). *China Digital Currency: e-CNY Wallet Lands in App Stores Ahead of Winter Olympics 2022*. https://www.scmp.com/tech/policy/article/3162094/china-digital-currency-e-cny-wallet-lands-app-stores-ahead-winter (accessed 12 December 2023).

He, D. (2021). Monetary Effects of Global Stablecoins. *Cato Journal*, *41*(2).

IMF. (2021). *Five Observations on Nigeria's Central Bank Digital Currency*. IMF Country Focus. https://www.imf.org/en/News/Articles/2021/11/15/na111621-five-observations-on-nigerias-central-bank-digital-currency (accessed 12 December 2023).

Kozińska, M. (2022). *Issue of Central Bank Digital Currencies—Potential Consequences for the Shape of the Financial System*. In R. Aneja & R. Dygas (Eds.), *Digital Currencies and the New Global Financial System*. Routledge.

Margulies, B. (2022). *ECCB Digital Currency Suffers Outage*. CentralBanking.com (accessed 12 December 2023).

National Bank of Poland. (2021). *Central Bank Digital Currency*. https://www.nbp.pl/systemplatniczy/cbdc/raport-cbdc.pdf (accessed 12 December 2023).

Niepelt, D. (2021). *Reserves for All: Political Rather than Macroeconomic Risks*. In D. Niepelt (Ed.), *Central Bank Digital Currency: Considerations, Projects, Outlook*. Centre for Economic Policy Research.

Stolbov, M., Shchepeleva, M., & Karminsky, A. (2022). *When Central Bank Research Meets Google Search: A Sentiment Index of Global Financial Stress. Journal of International Financial Markets, Institutions and Money, 81*.

Wang, Z. (2021). *Tax Compliance, Payment Choice, and Central Bank Digital Currency*.

Zaleska, M. (2022). Wybrane trendy w bankowości centralnej [Selected Trends of Central Bank]. *Bank i Kredyt, 53*(3).

CHAPTER 6

Investigations of Digital Currencies by Central Banks Throughout the World – Challenges and Opportunities

Mohit Fogaat, B. Sangeetha, and Rajendra Prasad Meena

Introduction

Banks have been maintaining virtual books and records that record transactions in digital currency for several years now. This has enabled clients to electronically transfer money across accounts held at different banks without ever having to deal with physical documents. The digital storing of financial value in a single accounting unit like the euro, dollar, or renminbi, or a group of currencies, is still the predominant definition for digital currencies (Rahman, 2019). However, compared to what they were twenty years ago, the potential possibilities for design aspects have significantly diversified at this point. People had a choice in 2009, when Bitcoin's path first began, between traditional fiat currencies that had recently been ravaged by the global economic crisis and a digital ledger

M. Fogaat (✉) · B. Sangeetha · R. P. Meena
Department of Commerce, Central University of Haryana, Mahendragarh, Haryana, India
e-mail: mohit201008@cuh.ac.in

R. Aneja and R. Dygas (eds.), *Digital Currencies in The New Global World Order*, https://doi.org/10.1007/978-981-97-4810-5_6

entrance defined as a cryptocurrency that was supported solely by a mathematical algorithm but could be transmitted on a peer-to-peer basis. Bitcoin was defined as a cryptocurrency that was supported solely by a mathematical algorithm but could be transmitted on a peer-to-peer basis. After a few years, there was an even wider variety of options, including fiat currencies on one side and swarms of cryptocurrencies competing with not only public money but also the new options that were emerging in the private sector (Yuneline, 2019). These options included fiat currencies on the one side and swarms of cryptocurrencies on the other side. Consumers have access to a wider variety of options than they ever have before, ranging from Bitcoin and other cryptocurrencies to stable coins with a variety of features and the highly anticipated digital currencies issued by central banks, each of which is available in several different iterations. These options are all available to consumers today.

There are a lot of doors that may be opened for us, but the challenges that we will face in the future are going to be directly related to the choices that we make right now. The ability to maintain people's faith in the monetary system will be the fundamentally most critical challenge, which will have implications for both central banks and other actors, such as regulators in the financial industry (Leuprecht et al., 2022).

Because very few people even spread stronger trust in social media networks than they do in financial platforms, the arguments surrounding confidence in the financial system need to be addressed in their entirety. It has been shown via experience in a few countries, like Kenya's M-Pesa, that one does not need to have bank goods and services to meet at least a fraction of the characteristics of money, such as exchange mediums across networks. Simply put, this proposition is a significant roadblock for the banking sector as it exists in its current iteration at this point. The features of new monetary systems are connected to a degree of risk that falls somewhere in the middle. Administrative considerations must also be taken into account regarding the paths. Production of "inside money" via the use of payment systems has traditionally been a carefully regulated process. This was done to ensure that the financial system could continue to be relied upon while also serving as an effective means of resource distribution (Ozili, 2022). The manner that financial regulators take to their work has to evolve to accommodate new means of transmitting money.

The decline of traditional credit financial intermediaries' systems that are centered on direct financing, the rise of massive venues that capitalize on connectivity, and the spread of personal digital currencies across countries will all have a profound impact on how we assess potential threats to economic stability.

To put it mildly, new players such as crypto-assets have not yet presented any substantial risks to the existing monetary system or the regulatory supervision of the financial markets. This is true at most for the time being. Although the market valuation of digital currencies surpassed a record high of $ 800 billion in January 2018, also with the largest of them (bitcoin) achieving approximately $ 320 billion, their magnitude is still relatively small in comparison to the resources of the top 20 financial institutions, which have investments totaling trillions of dollars collectively. Bitcoin's current market price of over $150 billion makes it impossible to compare it to any of the top 100 worldwide bankers. Nevertheless, the sheer scale of crypto assets continues to be relevant for a diverse range of authorities. Because its operation does not involve the creation of new money but rather the construction of a new trading platform, Reliable, for example, cannot rightfully be called a current kind of electronic currency. However, when taking into account the impact that a variety of actions might have on one's trust in the financial markets, this aspect must also be thoroughly discussed. It is impossible to ignore the fact that major technologies, which erase national borders and capital constraints, provide the promise of a sustainable income basis. The expansion of tokenized financial markets occurring simultaneously with one another gives additional touch points for the analysis of the development of new types of market effects. The current paper may be broken down into the following sections: The second section provides an in-depth discussion of the numerous alternatives that are available for virtual currencies, as well as the limitations that each of these alternatives faces on the regulatory machinery in general (Ekong & Ekong, 2022). The third section presents several scenarios, as well as the purported advantages of using virtual currencies. While Sect. 6.4 analyzes the significant challenges those digital currencies provide to the existing control structure of economic institutions and monetary systems, Sect. 6.5 presents some potential answers to the challenges that have been identified. The vast majority of the discussions that are brought up in this article are now being had in a variety of online communities, even though a great number of the issues that are brought up here are not resolved and need more discussion. At the end of the report, various courses of action are analyzed, and a few points are brought up for further discussion.

The Overview of Recently Proposed Research Regarding Digital Currencies

We uncovered specific significant points linked to digital currencies based on our past study, and we incorporated those points in this article so that readers may better comprehend the notion of digital currencies.

1. **Central Bank Digital Currencies (CBDCs):** Many central banks around the world have been exploring or experimenting with CBDCs. These digital currencies are issued by central banks and aim to provide a digital equivalent of a country's national currency. Research has focused on the design, implementation, and potential impacts of CBDCs on the financial system.
2. **Cryptocurrency Regulation:** Governments and regulatory bodies have been actively considering and developing regulations for cryptocurrencies. Research in this area often examines the legal and regulatory frameworks needed to govern digital currencies, addressing issues like consumer protection, anti-money laundering (AML), and counter-terrorism financing (CTF).
3. **Blockchain Technology:** Beyond cryptocurrencies, research continues to explore the underlying blockchain technology. This includes advancements in consensus algorithms, scalability solutions, and interoperability between different blockchain networks.
4. **Privacy and Security:** Privacy concerns related to digital currencies have led to research on enhancing privacy features in transactions. Additionally, security issues, such as the risk of hacking and fraud, remain a focus of ongoing research to improve the robustness of digital currency systems.
5. **Smart Contracts and Decentralized Finance (DeFi):** Smart contracts, self-executing contracts with the terms of the agreement directly written into code, have gained attention. DeFi, which leverages blockchain and smart contract technology to recreate traditional financial systems, has been a significant area of research and development.
6. **Cross-Border Payments:** Digital currencies are seen as a potential solution for improving cross-border payments. Research explores the use of blockchain and digital assets to streamline and make cross-border transactions more efficient and cost-effective.

7. **Environmental Impact:** The environmental impact of proof-of-work consensus mechanisms, as seen in popular cryptocurrencies like Bitcoin, has spurred research into more environmentally friendly alternatives, such as proof-of-stake.
8. **Stable coins:** Stable coins, which are pegged to the value of a fiat currency or another stable asset, have been the subject of research. This includes their potential role in the financial system, stability mechanisms, and regulatory considerations.

The Theoretical Framework of Digital Currencies

Technological advancements in recent years have resulted in an increasing array of rapid, electronic payment options available to consumers for their everyday transactions. This trend has prompted policymakers to grapple with the appropriate role of the public sector in furnishing a digital payment instrument for the contemporary economy. From a theoretical perspective, the introduction of a central bank digital currency (CBDC) brings forth enduring inquiries regarding the provision of both public and private money. It also raises considerations about the central bank's capacity to utilize CBDC as a direct conduit for transmitting monetary policy to households.

The theoretical literature on CBDC has thus far addressed these questions by concentrating on the impact of CBDC introduction on (i) commercial banks and (ii) monetary policy and financial stability, subsequently evaluating the associated welfare implications. Policymakers have demonstrated a keen interest in these issues and others. In a general sense, the body of literature examining CBDC views it as a form of payment capable of earning interest, not necessarily confined to holding an account at a commercial bank. While there is no universally agreed-upon definition of CBDC among policymakers or academics, the existing literature has predominantly examined the ramifications of a central bank liability directly held by the public. The models and assumptions in the current body of literature offer streamlined frameworks for addressing questions regarding the impacts of CBDC at both micro- and macro-levels. Notably, these frameworks abstract from numerous intricate design issues pertinent to policymakers, providing a foundation for further exploration and analysis.

Various Choices in Digital Currencies

The term "digital currency" does not refer to a specific form of virtual money but rather to a broader category that encompasses a wide range of financial instruments, from the reserves of a central bank, which are represented by book entries, to the units of the account used by third parties on decentralized applications, which are represented by virtual currency. The term "digital currency" is used in both of these contexts. That is the definition of currency: anything that can be used as a means of exchange, a store of value, a monetary unit of account, and a deferred standard of repayment all at the same time. In days gone by, something as simple as a clam could be considered wealth.

These days, however, money only exists in the form of physical cash (also known as "Fiat Currency") in most sovereign governments. This is because physical cash is the only kind of exchange rate that is officially recognized by the government as valid for paying bills and fees. The legal tender may, in addition to being used to settle debts, be used to generate new sorts of private debts and assets that will need to be monitored by the government. This will need the usage of even more legal currency.

The probability of the aforementioned qualities may be varied to provide a variety of different designs for currencies; however, each of these currencies requires its specific kind of regulation. For instance, a virtual currency that is produced independently, enables settling between peers, is available to everyone, and can be redeemed at its face value might have a lot in common with traditional currency and would need to be regulated in a manner that is analogous to how traditional currency is. However since it is so convenient to execute purchases, this kind of virtual coin would also interact with account-based virtual currency alternatives, which would call for a similar monitoring system to be implemented (Khan & Hakami, 2022). The two primary types of currencies that are created by central banks and are accepted as legal tender in countries all over the world are finance inflow and reserve balances in the accounts of commercial banks that are kept with central banks. The latter type of currency is also sometimes referred to as "external currency."

Because these reserve levels are kept digitally and may be transferred digitally from one account to another, they can be regarded as a kind of virtual money that is maintained in the ledgers of central banks. Through the production of new money from the outside, central banks can earn "Seigniorage," which is, in a nutshell, the difference between the cost of producing liabilities and the income received on assets. Because all of its commitments would be guaranteed by the promise of a sovereign entity, narrow banking, often known as a monetary system that exclusively depends on money from outside the country, would need very little monitoring (Ramassa & Leoni, 2022).

In the meanwhile, the currency that is produced by the central banks is converted into deposit accounts at the high school level. Of these deposit accounts, a part is kept as a reserve, and the remaining is lent to customers, which results in an increase in the money supply (also known as "internal" generated by the financial system). It is reasonable to assume that the various methods of payment used by commercial banks should provide a money multiplier of 20 times with 5% bank reserves. A commercial bank can create new cash in the form of ledger entries, which can then be recorded and stored digitally. Because of this, one can consider these ledger entries to be a different kind of cryptocurrency, even though the bank does not have to physically produce any paper cash. Internal money is only as good as the organization that issues it; hence, it is necessary to have a solid supervision structure in place to avoid abuses and sustain public confidence in financial companies (Malladi, 2022). Virtual currency or even funds placed to financial institutions can now be converted into various kinds of electronic funds such as e-wallets, subscription bill payments, and other types of electronic funds to serve as a comfortable exchange method for the same store-of-value and unit of financial reporting as that of an official currency. This was made possible by the development of new technologies. As long as virtual money used in the business sector may be converted into legal tender in whichever form it takes, not much has changed; all of these currencies continue to operate within the same ecosystem that is composed of external and internal currencies. However, when new news networks arise as a direct consequence of the development of new technologies, things need to be seen from a different perspective. Both the present financial system and the mechanism of monitoring that has been effective up until this point are susceptible to any changes that may occur in the environment in which they operate (Ozili, 2023). The status quo is being challenged both from inside and outside of the surroundings of the financial system, as shown by two events of a significant magnitude.

Cryptocurrencies: Cryptocurrencies emerged as an initial external rival and are now largely recognized entirely as crypto-assets by significant international norm-creating authorities. This recognition comes even though cryptocurrencies were first developed as an external competitor. To record transactions in an immutable ledger that could not be changed after being verified by the program's majority of users, these cryptocurrencies made use of a technique known as distributed ledger technology (DLT), which is sometimes referred to as blockchain. In contrast to the conventional dual accounting practice, the ledger entry on the distributed ledger technology (such as Bitcoin) is not the responsibility of any one source or organization (assets with matching liabilities).

Only when it exists independently can it be considered a resource (similar to a shell), capable of still being relocated from one respondent to some other, of income generated out of faith that the stock of these kinds of investments based on an electronic journal entry is limited and that nobody will create dubious chapter because of complicated technique and high correlation operating expenses? In other words, a shell. The idea that cryptocurrencies can be traded for established regulatory bids has been viewed as exceptionally risky (A. A. Rahman, 2020). This has led to the development of a successor of virtual currencies known as secure, which suggests steadying the international currency with both legal tenders. This can be accomplished by either maintaining legal currency as a resource or by employing a fiscal and monetary algorithm that takes into account buyers and sellers of banknotes to maintain liquidity.

As time has progressed, several other types of virtual money have emerged, the majority of which assume the characteristics of either equity tokens (as in Initial Coin Offerings, or ICOs) or utilitarian coins. Throughout, different types of virtual currency have popped up into existence. In a word, the development of new crypto-assets that can jeopardize the stability of the existing economic system is now taking place. The emergence of new markets for tokenized assets, in which these currencies can find their ideal home, has the potential to have a considerable impact on all current marketplaces, such as the financial and foreign exchange markets.

Central Bank Digital Currencies: Even the world's central banks are trying to shake things up by making new adjustments, and a number of these changes are already in the process of being validated. Central banks can issue virtual currencies by shifting their responsibilities, which now come in the form of paper currency banknotes, onto a digital platform. This would allow for more legitimate uses of legal tender. A form of such a monetary use scenario that involves the use of general products, with each variant having various design components and, as a result, varied repercussions on the existing monetary system. In contrast, the CBDC retailing version would be open to consumers of all ages and backgrounds, while the CBDC commercial version would be accessible exclusively to a limited number of buyers. e-Krona, an effort of the Bank of Sweden, is an example of a retail variation, while Ubin, an initiative of the Monetary Authority of Singapore (MAS Project), and Project Jasper, an initiative of the Bank of Canada, are examples of commercial variants. The retail version of CBDCs may take one of two primary architectural forms; the first is based on accounts, while the second is based on transactions. In the retail version of CBDC, consumers would have accounts that were comparable to those that customers of the banking sector keep, and they would have direct linkages to the central financial statement. The independence of a man, together with the ability to verify their financial situation and make payments, need to be the major drivers behind account-based systems. Coin On the other hand, CBDC envisions a central bank producing electronic tokens that closely resemble cash. These tokens will be used by the general public regardless of whether or not the public utilizes CBDC's proposed arrangement with the central bank. Virtual coin exchanges, in contrast to those that use fiat money, are driven by the digital reality of the tokens themselves.

Without directly interacting with the general public, central banks can issue CBDCs that are based on tokens. In practice, it is possible for a monetary authority to issue virtual currencies to state institutions, which would then disperse them to the general public, imitating the two-tier approach that is used in the transmission of physical currencies. This would be similar to how the transmission of physical currencies currently works. On a distributed ledger technology (DLT) network, account-based CBDC might be used by various public organizations as a component of commercial multi-dimensional and multi-financial transactions. Central banks think that wholesale CBDCs may have the potential to increase the efficiency of resolution procedures; nevertheless, more testing and practice are required before their broad use. BDCs may be utilized by central banks both at the level of speciality stores for a variety of reasons, some of which include, but are not limited to the following: enhancing the efficacy with which monetary policy is transmitted; expanding access to banking services; encouraging greater competition in the payments industry; safeguarding the status quo economic model; and ensuring the continued primacy of sound financial sense. How a CBDC is designed will fully determine the effect that it has on the economy as it exists at present.

A CBDC that is based on accounts rather than tokens would compete with savings accounts, while a CBDC that takes the form of tokens and has general-use and privacy features would seem to directly compete with money in the system. Every modification that is made to the manner that banks are overseen has to take into consideration the influence that it will have on the credit-intermediation process to guarantee economic autonomy. As a result, determining whether CBDC design is superior will be challenging owing to the various factors that compete with one another.

Identification of new pathways via which hazards could be transmitted to current institutions of banking and finance is a significant problem for regulators of emerging economic structures that include CBDCs and digital currencies. Presently, the region of contact among the personal funds and digital currencies could be quite tiny moving ahead the rising existence of prudent macroeconomic pathways, may require\supervisory participation with intensification. Emerging economic structures like CBDCs and digital currencies provide regulators with a big challenge in terms of the identification of new routes via which risks might be passed to existing banking and financial institutions. This is a serious dilemma for regulators. At the moment, the area of interaction between personal finances and digital currencies might be fairly small. Moving forward, the increasing availability of cautious macroeconomic routes may necessitate the intervention of supervisors in an intensified manner.

Digital Currencies Scenarios

The shifting competition in the financial sector is expanding beyond the digital vs. non-digital segment as a result of the proliferation of several forms of electronic money and online transactions. Specifically, this shift is because digital money and online transactions have made it easier to conduct business. Even in the virtual world, competition will be strong, and it's possible that certain choices could become unusable due to flaws or because they will no longer be relevant. Because of how rapidly things may change, it might be difficult to gain a clear image at any one time, but the following are some aspects that can be taken as signs of where we are right now:

Cash Scenario: Since there is a potential for cash to provide revenue, either as a kind of financial asset or as a means of conducting financial transactions, it may not be prudent to actively strive toward the goal of eliminating cash from the economy. Even if the use of virtual currencies is becoming more widespread, many areas still have a significant need for conventional cash. However, the BIS emphasizes that one of the key reasons for central banks to embrace CBDCs is to replace cash as a medium of exchange. Even on the most basic level, having a variety of options available to choose from in economic models would be of great assistance in maintaining stability if one of the alternatives were to fail. Guaranteeing an equitable distribution of public and private finances requires keeping an adequate cash reserve at all times. In addition, the employment of new supervisory components is bound to come with a cost if private capital development is pushed too aggressively, whether freely or involuntarily.

This is the case whether the development of private capital is undertaken voluntarily or involuntarily. Because some countries have outlawed the use of cash, their respective central banks are investigating CBDC as a potential replacement. When there is a limited amount of cash available, whether by choice or out of need, having access to a CBDC might be advantageous. However, it would be irresponsible to establish CBDC to forcefully correct the issue. The choice of the preferred payment method and the preferred medium of holding wealth should be left up to the economic participants in the market.

Although a CBDC may be something to think about, its use may be limited if there are already or soon will be speedy (even instantaneous) and successful alternatives to payment that may be used. Does the use of non-anonymous CBDC have the capability of completely replacing cash? It is very improbable that this is the case given that there has not been a significant reduction in the need for cash despite the rise in popularity of digital payment methods. It would be prudent to keep money as a viable mode of payment anywhere in the globe, both for the benefit of the market as a whole and, more specifically, the groups of individuals who are digitally marginalized.

Domestic retail payment scenarios: Traditional retail transactions are already being served by technologies like electronic wallets, digital cash, and others. However, virtual currencies, such as account-to-account cash transmissions through 24/7 modes of payment, were introduced before these tools. It is important to research the potential additional benefits that might accrue from giving users access to a wider variety of alternatives, such as CBDC or steady. As long as there are many viable alternatives, there will be intense competition in the market, and the less appealing options will ultimately be forced out of business. This will continue as long as there are many viable options. The preferences of a variety of individuals have a significant role in deciding the types of payment methods that are put into practice.

Therefore, domestic retail payments are already extremely efficient in many countries, suggesting that boosting the economy for payment systems is not a significant motivator for adopting new forms of electronic money. This is because, in many countries, domestic retail payments are already extremely efficient. As a consequence of the monopolistic concentration of payment infrastructures in the hands of a few numbers of corporations, certain governments could be driven to experiment with the design of electronic money as a way to combat this problem. A probable illustration of this phenomenon may be seen in the People's Republic of China (PRC), where the whole Internet payment sector is controlled by only two corporations. When paired with the right protections, the capacity of the financial system to absorb shocks will be improved by the use of virtual currencies for as long as they continue to promote a broad array of different possibilities. This, of course, does not eliminate the need for stringent inspection in the areas where unlawful behavior in the market and regulatory systems is concerned.

Domestic wholesale payments scenario: Frequently, the infrastructures supporting local commercial financial transactions are on par with those supporting international money transfers spanning numerous countries. While the commercial financial transactions used by many central banks are getting close to reaching the end of their technical lifetime, there are new technological possibilities that need to be researched to construct the economic framework of the future. Additionally, when new markets develop, such as tokenized commodities, a variety of central banks have been conducting experiments to assess the usefulness of application operations like DLT in boosting the efficiency of transactions as well as clearing and settlement. It is envisaged that efficiency would improve in areas such as the transfer of payments, verification, document administration, and database management, amongst others.

Cryptocurrency assets and virtual currencies are two examples of newly developing businesses that need to be closely watched because of the risks they bring to the larger financial industry. This is because these new industries pose several unique challenges.

Scenarios Affecting Cross-Border Flows: The area of international money transfers, which is now beset with challenges due to market flaws, is the one in which contemporary forms of electronic currency are most likely to make an impact. More than at any other point in human history, the contemporary global economy is based not just on international trade but also on personal connections between individuals. The average dividend from overseas transactions is equivalent to about 1.8 times the gross domestic product of the whole planet. Transactions between businesses and individuals, as well as those involving big amounts of money, will have a significant impact on the development of the market in the years to come. It is expected that peer-to-peer transactions, often known as remittances, would have a significant impact on virtual currencies. It is becoming more important for people to send and receive money across international borders. In 2018, remittances were three times as big as government aid, and they are on track to become larger than FDIs to low- and middle-income countries this year. The existing money transfer idea of payment transactions, which depends on several layers of financial intermediary, is in urgent need of change as a result of the advent of non-bank services such as steady.

This concept is in dire need of reform. The characteristics of Steady, such as their outward nature, their ability to remove boundaries, their processing and communication architecture, etc., make them an appealing choice for conducting transactions, at least in the P2P categorization. Even so, it is important to keep in mind that the framework of global virtual currencies like steady does not yet have enough information to accurately evaluate a large number of the differences that exist in currency transactions. These differences include differences in legislation and requirements, payment every month facilities, and costs of certifications, among other things. Given those existing initiatives (such as the program) are mostly focused on large value transfers between central banks, it appears doubtful that CBDCs will play a substantial role in facilitating P2P international transactions any time soon. It would be necessary to harmonies capital countermeasures along with managerial tracking at the worldwide platform if central banks were to give foreign citizens equal access to CBDC for P2P exchanges across all boundaries. This would also present issues in terms of regulation over macroeconomic policy, stable growth, and the transfer of funds between central banks, among other issues.

Cost scenario: Remittance-Prices According to research conducted in 2019, the average cost of a transfer across borders is estimated to be 6.82%, with banks continuing to charge the highest rate of 10.46%. When all fees are included, the total cost of transferring money via Smart Corridor comes to 4.37 percent of the amount being sent.

The Sustainable Development Goal (SDG) aim of decreasing costs for international money transfers to 3% by the year 2030 is much more than what is being paid at this time. The entire cost of sending money internationally is comprised of many components, two of which are money transfer costs and currency conversion expenses. The prevalence of intermediaries in the corresponding monetary system results in an accumulation of expenses at each of the system's layers.

In addition, it is anticipated that the widespread usage of electronic money will stimulate competition on global trade platforms, which will result in a pricing structure that is more favorable to clients and improved outcomes overall. In this context, what is required is a valuation of cryptocurrency that takes a more comprehensive approach. The number of intermediaries may decrease with the use of fair access cryptocurrencies; nevertheless, the participants will still be responsible for covering the expenses of regulation. In addition, there would be an increase in the cost of control if there was a separate monitoring structure for P2P international remittances that were located outside of the relevant banking sector.

Transaction Ease: Virtual currencies excel in their capacity to make business transactions easier. Due to the one-of-a-kind architectural features of many cryptographic currencies, cash-like transactions using these digital assets could one day be possible. To put the finishing touches on a business transaction, all that is required is an easy technical method for communications and, thereafter, an update to the ledger. When dealing with digital money, the trader's location and other factors that may potentially impede the transaction are irrelevant.

Because of the emergence of decentralized business networks and systems that remove the need for conventional payment providers, end-to-end payments are now conceivable. This was previously impossible. As transactional efficiency increases, it is becoming more difficult to differentiate between monetary and non-monetary forms of payment. It is too early to make any educated guesses about the impact that a global event will have on the way that market volatility will spread from one nation to the next. However, to avoid having a detrimental influence on the oversight systems, the monitoring procedures will need to be simplified.

Financial Inclusion: The broad use of electronic currency has huge ramifications for the creation of an enabling environment, particularly in countries that are lagging in the invention of local transaction methods. To provide customers, access to various types of financial assets, the banking intermediary system is going to undergo significant transformations as a result of the implementation of CBDC. Even though some technological barriers to entry will still need to be eliminated at the grassroots level, one of the key reasons why numerous central banks promote electronic money is the prospect of making a huge leap in digital payments. For this reason, maintaining protection for consumers and combatting such misconduct must be regarded with the objective of greater participation. Since certain distinct classes may be more prone to engaging in unethical behavior in the marketplace.

Changes in the World of Financial Regulation and the Money System: How these potential replacements are being disseminated, in addition to the material that is being proposed as a replacement, is something that poses a risk to the current setup. The particular form in which some challenges present themselves is highly dependent on the design elements that have been selected.

Challenges for financial supervision: The advent of digital money is expected to influence the strategy for supervising, which will need a reassessment of the constraints placed on monitoring resources and the allocation of those resources. Due to the inherent qualities of the designs of electronic currencies, it may be required to consider the potential danger to the financial system from the following fresh vantage point:

Disintermediation of banks and other financial intermediaries: The current system of regulation is dependent on the ability of banks and other financial institutions to function as intermediaries between savers and borrowers. This is a process that involves maturations and transformations of liquidity, as well as widespread exposure to loans, marketplace, liquidity, and moral hazard. If greater access to CBDC was implemented at wholesale outlets, this would result in the loss of retail financing, which would have a detrimental influence on the liquidity profiles of banks as well as the cost of doing business. Any change to the level of risk tolerance that their firm is willing to accept would need to be coordinated with this adjustment. There is a possibility that the aircraft phenomena may become systematically directed, which will have implications for adequate capitalization.

This strategy necessitates the creation of novel approaches to economic surveillance and regulation on the part of central banks. Networks for virtual currencies have the potential to bridge the informational divide that exists between lenders and borrowers in the future, which would make bilateral lending more accessible. It is necessary to investigate whether or if this mechanism enhances the efficiency of the financial system by providing a more equal distribution of loans and a firmer financial footing using transitioning between maturities. As early experiences have demonstrated, in particular about peer-to-peer lending in a small number of countries, decentralization of the mortgage market may make it even more difficult to make precise assessments of credit risk to differentiate valuable assets from less desirable ones.

Technology Risk: When supervising, it is desirable to have a proactive approach as opposed to a "tech-neutral" one. This is because different types of technology systems transmit different components of technical risk, some of which are not even completely recognized. It is possible that the slight but important differences in the development characteristics of distinct digital solutions were the root cause of the significantly different risk profiles that structured finance exhibited during the global economic crisis. In this context, regulators need to assess whether the idea of risk is to be regarded as a separate category of corporate risk or if, rather, it should be considered a subset of business hazards. To carry out an efficient supervised review, there has to be some kind of concept of the corporations that are related to the new technological technologies in terms of the inherent risks they pose and the management flaws they have. When attempting to discern signals of business hazards, some of the factors that may be considered include processing capabilities, network structure, and even recognized technological impact, such as the use of frameworks that are built on top of other technologies. To get a unified opinion about all of the inherent and controllable components of mismatch indicators, the industry of supervision has to have more conversations about these topics.

Cyber-risk challenge: Since the software solutions for virtual currencies have not yet been subjected to exhaustive testing, there are additional concerns that need to be answered about the building and optimization of the networks from a technological risk perspective. The administration of network security becomes more challenging each time a new layer is added on top of the one that serves as the basis for online media. The available evidence implies that encrypting may not be the most advantageous choice. If the attackers are unable to get into the blockchain system, they will look for other ways to undermine the network, such as the payment mechanism or the transaction itself. There is a possibility that either the user's identity or the data that has been stored on the device might be compromised. In the sphere of preventing or mitigating cyber risks, everything should be left up to random chance. In addition, computer hackers shouldn't only be thought of as a small group of thieves working alone; the virtual realm may also be actively used as part of political strife to destroy particular networks. Because of this, it will be difficult for any organization to successfully safeguard digital currency.

Liquidity Challenges: One of the most important functions of constant financing markets is to meet day-to-day demands for availability, and this capacity is still one of its most important capabilities. As a direct consequence of this, market authorities are often forced to keep a more vigilant lookout for any indications of unease. The popular wisdom is that only financial systems have the necessary capacity to move enormous sums of money in several nations across a variety of states, which helps to mitigate worries about volatility on both the national and the provincial scale. It is vital to evaluate the degree to which several different Bitcoin transactions can accomplish the goal at hand. The creditworthiness and liquidity risk profiles of the various virtual currencies would be quite different from one another. To provide just one illustration, the liquidity and trustworthiness profiles of a virtual coin that was issued independently would be substantially different from those of a CBDC that was authorized by a national currency. This is just one example. In a manner somewhat dissimilar to the previous example, the components of virtual currencies can likewise provide a challenge when it comes to the preservation of their liquidity. For instance, putting in place a liquidity-saving mechanism (also known as LSM) using distributed ledger technology (also known as DLT) would be difficult due to the nature of the system itself, which would need effective labor to solve.

KYC-AML Challenges: For the present financial system to comply with KYC and AML standards, it would result in significant additional costs. In addition, the regulatory agencies that are assigned with the responsibility of ensuring such conformance have enormous powers at their disposal. According to one piece of data, even though non-banks have to spend just 3%–5% of sales on adherence in comparison to banks'

10%, the gap between the two is projected to close as the mounting pressure on both sectors intensifies. Any digital currency that aspires to compete with conventional banking systems or alternative deposit options must be resilient enough to resist the inherent instability of the system. Know Your Customer and Anti-Money Laundering rules seem to be a barrier to providing general-use electronic money, such as general-use CBDCs. These regulations aim to combat money laundering.

In light of these concerns, it is difficult to imagine a scenario in which a CBDC could ever be employed for any purpose and yet provide perfect anonymity. A quasi-CBDC is one option that seems to be available; however, this solution throws significant operational obligations on national banks in terms of Know Your Customer and Anti-Money Laundering legislation. In terms of shifting the KYC-AML criteria to the intermediate, the two distinct structures of CBDC, one of which involves monetary authorities issuing CBDC via the mediation of a corporate third party, appear to be the most practically applicable option. Even more significantly, the decentralized nature of development stage systems like DLT makes it hard to delegate the responsibility of ensuring that transactions conform with KYC and AML rules. When autonomous transactional authentication is utilized, a considerable number of organizations are brought into question. These companies include those who deal in bitcoin trading as well as those who provide wallets, which makes KYC/AML management challenging.

The ease with which we overcome obstacles posed by KYC and AML regulations will significantly impact the pace at which new digital currencies are introduced in the future. It is not yet known to what degree technologically autonomous systems can be maintained by their inherent intelligent qualities and without human supervision. Because the majority of technological skills have not been exhaustively evaluated, it is necessary to address them from the outside to guarantee even the most fundamental level of safety.

Cross-border challenges: According to their definition, cryptocurrencies can transcend national boundaries, which may generate issues in the enforcement of laws and rules on a global scale. These challenges may make it impossible to regulate cryptocurrencies. It is too soon to make a prediction as to what impact the adoption of a CBDC within one authority would have on another, but given the existing condition of international trade, it seems normal to anticipate that the result would not necessarily be harmonized. Another thing that cannot be predicted is how the wider trading system made up of CBDCs will evolve when there is no global central bank. To add more complication to the situation, it is not apparent how swings in currency exchange rates and the prices of other assets would be affected when international transactions are conducted using virtual money. There is a chance that the distinctions between activities that take place inside the country and those that take place internationally, as well as between residents and non-residents, might become just academic. In some nations, the launch of a CBDC that provides access to cross-border trade may stimulate a move away from the nation's primary currency, which may result in a turbulent money market and a change in consumers' preferences about economic instruments.

Big tech Challenges: Even though the engagement of big tech companies in financial intermediaries is developing as a risk due to the tendency of technology overlaying, virtual currencies get a perfect place in the big tech environment. This is even though virtual currencies have a perfect place in the big tech environment. The multiplying effect of their linked networks and the ease of access provided by the internet contribute to the effectiveness of their methods.

The implications of the combination of big data and cryptocurrencies must be included in assessments of the general state of the economic system, and the regulatory community is just now starting to give this aspect of the situation the attention it deserves. Anecdotal data suggests that the majority of huge internet companies would start their operations in the transaction industry utilizing their already established clientele before branching out into other financial services such as credit, insurance, savings, and so on. According to the findings of certain studies, large technology companies lend more in countries where the banking system is less developed. Because of this, nations are exposed to a greater risk of economic instability. Even though large tech enterprises have a deeper grasp of credit assessment than traditional credit agencies, it would be premature to make judgments about the overall effectiveness of big tech credit rating systems without first progressing through the whole financial sector. The impact of larger networks in the market might be a double-edged sword, enhancing efficiency on the one hand but also raising the risks on the other.

Consumer protection: There aren't that many primary challenges that need to be tackled head-on, and those that do exist are quite a few. The issue of who is liable for the administration of electronic currencies arises because these currencies are not backed by any government and are not the responsibility of any one individual. It is also uncertain how authorities will deal with issues such as shifting asset values, crises in asset prices, and market manipulations such as circular trading that may cause prices to soar. There are several obstacles to overcome in terms of design when attempting to integrate surveillance capabilities into a decentralized market. Putting restrictions on the power that dominant corporations have in the market is one of the most important things that can be done to protect consumers.

Problems confronting the monetary system: Any plan to implement a new financial system must first be examined in the context of the framework that is already in place. In this particular setting, the fundamental components of the economic system are of utmost significance.

Monetary policy: The first findings of this study imply that the issuance of CBDCs would not fundamentally alter the method in which financial institutions conduct monetary and fiscal policy or the instruments that they have available to them. However, several studies have demonstrated that the presence of CBDC may help cope with the zero lower limit (or even the lower, effective limitation) on lending rates. This is something that has been proven to be the case. As a consequence of this, the efficiency of fiscal policy may very well be improved. In addition, a CBDC that offered interest and was organized more similarly to banking services would be in direct competition with bank deposits. This would have a significant impact on the pricing system and call for a transfer of monetary policies that was both swifter and more immediate. Although the effects of CBDC on financial regulation are readily apparent, it is more difficult to quantify the effects of other virtual currencies and digital products. This is especially true for the effects of virtual currencies and digital products that do not exist within the environment of central banks.

However, it is impossible to rule out the possibility of difficulties in interpreting the position of macroeconomic factors when they become more evident in a particular region. In addition, the environment of tokenized booms and busts that is far outside the environment of the central bank means that any simplicity in the procedures of macroeconomic policy may not ensure the delivery of a considerably more consistent financing system.

Inter-operability: Given the prevalence of digital currencies that make use of a variety of system implementations, the most significant obstacle is achieving interoperability across hundreds of different categories to boost economic efficiency. The convergence of links will result in an increase in production as a result of seamless interactions across ecosystems; nevertheless, this will also result in the opening of new channels via which risk might spread. The fact that there are significant profits to be made by keeping access restricted, on the other hand, means that it is not proving to be that straightforward to break the authoritarian grip that has been placed on the systems.

The resolution of a few operational problems is also necessary for the interoperability of the many different types of systems. For instance, shifting money from one system to another requires transferring funds from one lender's trustee to another, which seems to go counter to the concept of a fragmented market as a whole. Furthermore, the environment of digital currencies requires the implementation of compatible quality standards for all digital assets. Before it is possible to build interoperability across various kinds of systems, several challenges need to be conquered first.

How Do We Come Up with Solutions?

Level of governance: Because of the interconnected nature of the issues at hand, the establishment of a global system of governance for virtual currencies would need considerable effort. To solve common challenges and concerns in areas such as data security and know-your-customer/anti-money-laundering legislation, this is what is required. However, because there is already a significant amount of disagreement in global monetary networks, it would be challenging to construct a shared vision in many different areas. This includes the free flow of information as well as the transfer of monetary value that is independent of payment systems. Even if there is only a minimal degree of unanimity on the matter, this would be an appropriate starting point for the development of a framework that may be used to develop global monitoring norms. Although the emergence of a single worldwide framework for management is unlikely, this would be an appropriate starting point for the development of a framework. To comply with the most fundamental requirements for effective administration, central banks that have the mission to encourage private industry within their borders need to maintain a clear separation between the responsibility they have to regulate various commodities and the responsibility they have to promote private industry. The supervisors' ability to use discretion and remain impartial should under no circumstances be put in jeopardy.

Synthetic CBDC: The search for a settlement that results in the least amount of disruption feasible is yet another potential approach. The issuance of a "central bank digital currency" (also known as a "central bank digital currency" or "CBDC") by central banks in collaboration with certain issuers of e-money is one of the potential options available. This digital currency could serve as an alternative to conventional forms of monetary exchange. If central banks make it possible for digital currencies to access their reserve funds, then this becomes a prospect that can be taken seriously. An artificial CBDC could be able to undertake many of the technology operations connected to investigative work in client enrollment, monitoring and reporting, and other activities like these, which would reduce the moral hazard for central banks. E-money issuers have access to supported services and, if required, reserve funds via this configuration of the banking sector's role in the financial system. The CBDC version that has been synthesized might become an alternative to the existing financial systems, which would cause less disruption and be subject to fewer regulations.

Increasing the effectiveness of the regulatory and supervisory structures: In the realm of threat monitoring, one of the most important tenets is that the level of oversight that is offered ought to be proportional to the nature and degree of the threat that is posed by a certain service or group of services. There has been some discussion over the possibility of using the same risk-based approach that is used for controlling and supervising the operations of vitally important financial institutions to the operations of enormous digital firms. The BCBS approach to virtual money, which is "similar vulnerability, identical exercise, identical cure," would begin the process of building universal regulatory environments and supervisory organizations. However, the question of whether the corporate governance strategy must also be compatible with the new remains open for discussion. This is because disparities in the architectural component of innovation can be a source of unbiased risk (kind of look at any other business risk).

Open Challenges: The choices that we make today will have a direct bearing on the path that lies ahead. The spread of different types of virtual currency is an example of an internal challenge to the existing monetary system, while the growth of CBDCs is an example of an external threat. Finding, quantifying, and managing the underlying vulnerability may be challenging for managers. This vulnerability may be concealed under numerous layers of technical development or may have its origins in the disruption of the existing market system. The performance of exotic financial products during the global economic crisis of 2008 proved that risks cannot be avoided by repackaging them in a new form and selling them to investors. To maintain the confidence of customers in the market, there must be a modification in the manner in which regulation is carried out to keep up with the development of even the most essential business plans.

The Current Gaps in Supervision May be Broken Down into Three Groups

Risk Governance: Given the many different approaches that have been taken to the creation of virtual currencies, what type of institutional structure would be commensurate to the dangers that are involved? How do we make sure that technological advancements may proceed without compromising the safety of the monetary system?

Risk identification and assessment: In the securities markets, new types of business risk have evolved; how can we recognize and analyze the risk that is present in evolving technological frameworks that function on several levels?

Risk Mitigation and Control: What steps can we take to mitigate or control the risks connected with the emergence of virtual currencies? Will the active participation of reserve banks, through their CBDCs, help to alleviate the risks associated with private virtual money, or will it disrupt the existing system from inside it, therefore adding a layer of complexity?

New Capital, Liquidity, and Other Supervisory Standards: The question then is how we would control decentralized networks that develop new currencies or systems of trading value that are independent of the conventional banking system.

There is a need for additional discussion on several of the ideas presented in the article, such as the necessity for a shift in supervision posture toward digital supervision and the potential use of CBDCs in the promotion of economic security. This discussion should take place after the publication of the article. However, none of these problems can be handled by individual states, and a significant portion of them may need discussion on the international stage.

Conclusion

In this article, we have discussed how the distribution of monitoring assets is affected not only by the selection of digital currencies but also by a variety of hypothetical circumstances, such as those connected to the introduction of digital currencies by central banks (CBDCs). For example, the choice of digital currency is just one factor that might affect the distribution of monitoring assets. In this article, we present an outline of research that has been suggested about digital currencies both in the past and more recently. The theoretical framework was utilized for this article to grasp the notion of digital currencies and to make an attempt to explain aspects linked to digital currency. The majority of the research that was done in the past on digital currencies is still applicable to understanding the notion of digital currencies; nevertheless, academics need to be familiar with the research that has been done more recently on digital currencies. It may not be simple to come to a consensus on a specific plan of action because of the frictions that exist in the international monetary systems. If prudential regulation and supervision followed the idea of "same-risk, same activity, same treatment," then they would be entity-neutral.

References

Ekong, U. M., & Ekong, C. N. (2022). Digital Currency and Financial Inclusion in Nigeria: Lessons for Development. *Journal of Internet and Digital Economics, 2*(1), 46–67. https://doi.org/10.1108/jide-11-2021-0018

Khan, R., & Hakami, T. A. (2022). Cryptocurrency: Usability Perspective versus Volatility Threat. *Journal of Money and Business, 2*(1), 16–28. https://doi.org/10.1108/jmb-11-2021-0051

Leuprecht, C., Jenkins, C., & Hamilton, R. (2022). Virtual Money Laundering: Policy Implications of the Proliferation in the Illicit Use of Cryptocurrency. *Journal of Financial Crime, 30*(4), 1036–1054. https://doi.org/10.1108/JFC-07-2022-0161

Malladi, R. K. (2022). Pro Forma Modelling of Cryptocurrency Returns, Volatilities, Linkages and Portfolio Characteristics. *China Accounting and Finance Review, 25*(2), 145–183. https://doi.org/10.1108/cafr-02-2022-0001

Ozili, P. K. (2022). Assessing Global and Local Interest in eNaira CBDC and Cryptocurrency Information: Implications for Financial Stability. *Journal of Internet and Digital Economics, 3*(1/2), 1–17. https://doi.org/10.1108/JIDE-10-2022-0019

Ozili, P. K. (2023). Determinants of Interest in eNaira and Financial Inclusion Information in Nigeria: Role of FinTech, Cryptocurrency and Central Bank Digital Currency. *Digital Transformation and Society, 2*(2), 202–214. https://doi.org/10.1108/dts-08-2022-0040

Rahman, A. A. (2020). Organic Global Cryptocurrency: Towards a Stable International Monetary System that is Closer to Maqāṣid Sharīʿah. *Islamic Economic Studies, 28*(1), 63–82. https://doi.org/10.1108/ies-10-2019-0032

Rahman, S. F. H. S. A. (2019). Regulating Digital Currency: Taming the Unruly. *Emerging Issues in Islamic Finance Law and Practice in Malaysia*, 265–280. https://doi.org/10.1108/978-1-78973-545-120191021

Ramassa, P., & Leoni, G. (2022). Standard Setting in Times of Technological Change: Accounting for Cryptocurrency Holdings. *Accounting, Auditing and Accountability Journal, 35*(7), 1598–1624. https://doi.org/10.1108/AAAJ-10-2020-4968

Yuneline, M. H. (2019). Analysis of Cryptocurrency's Characteristics from Four Perspectives. *Journal of Asian Business and Economic Studies, 26*(2), 206–219. https://doi.org/10.1108/JABES-12-2018-0107

CHAPTER 7

Development and Implications of Digital Currency

Suman Dahiya, Bhushan Singh, and Krishan Kumar

Introduction

During the last decade, the world has witnessed substantial changes in the financial system characterized by many financial innovations. With the development of financial and payment systems, the form of money has also changed over the period from commodity to digital currency (Haque & Shoaib, 2023). The emergence of digital currencies such as Bitcoin, Alipay, Libra, and Libra coins has led to a spur in non-cash transactions. Considering the significant impact of digital currencies on economies, businesses, investors, and consumers, central banks across the world have started working on the launch of their digital currency (Tan & Xue, 2021).

Digital currencies offer a spectrum of benefits facilitating international trade, promoting financial inclusion by providing inexpensive and broad access to financial services, preventing tax evasion and money laundering

S. Dahiya (✉) · B. Singh · K. Kumar
Department of Commerce, Central University of Haryana, Mahendragarh, Haryana, India
e-mail: suman@cuh.ac.in

R. Aneja and R. Dygas (eds.), *Digital Currencies in The New Global World Order*, https://doi.org/10.1007/978-981-97-4810-5_7

cases, simplifying business operations, enabling faster and economical cross-border payment systems, etc. But when opportunities come, the challenges follow. Digital currencies are based on new technology and are relatively new so they require clear guidelines and regulatory framework for their usage at the global level. These currencies have demonstrated inadequacies in meeting the measures of security, stability, and privacy of international payment systems (Kumar & Pawan, 2022). Thus, it is very important to bring a balance between financial innovations, technological advancements, and financial stability. The robust regulatory framework governing digital currency usage will install confidence among the users.

Development of the Digital Currencies

The development of digital currencies on a global scale continues to gain momentum and reshape the financial landscape. In 2023, the Digital Payments market is poised to achieve a remarkable total transaction value of US$9.46tn, with expectations of an annual growth rate (between 2023 – 2027) at 11.80%, driving the total transaction value to a substantial US$14.78tn by 2027. Notably, Digital Commerce emerges as the largest market segment, with a projected total transaction value of US$6.03tn in 2023, underlining the significance of digital currencies in facilitating online transactions and e-commerce. In a broader international context, China leads the way with the highest cumulative transaction value, anticipated to reach US$3,639.00bn in 2023, underscoring the global impact of digital currencies and their increasing role in the world economy (Statista, 2023).

In India, a remarkable transformation in the digital payment landscape is quietly revolutionizing the country's economy. We already have large strata that make regular use of digital payment systems for National Electronic Funds Transfer (NEFT), Real Time Gross Settlement (RTGS), and Immediate Payment Service (IMPS). These methods are considered to be safe, secure, and 24*7 accessible (Haque & Shoaib, 2023).

At the heart of this shift is the Unified Payment Interface (UPI), which facilitated an astonishing eight billion transactions, equivalent to nearly $200 billion, in just the month of January 2023. This surge underscores a substantial move toward digital payments, with 40% of all transactions in India now occurring electronically. This monumental shift was made possible through a homegrown instant payment system, initiated by government agencies and further advanced through a healthy public–private partnership (PPP). Notably, the value of instant digital payments in India now surpasses the combined figures of the United States, Britain, Germany, and France(PIB Research Wing, 2023). Fig7.1 shows a constant rise in the digital transactions in India which were only 14.59 billion in the year 2018 and crossed 100 billion in the current year and continues to grow.

The main goal of all methods of digital payment is to provide customers with an alternative way of paying cash for different purposes. (Reserve Bank of India, 2022c). Cryptocurrency is one such way where transactions are verified and records are kept by a decentralized system employing encryption (Nakamoto, 2008). The development of digital currency, specifically cryptocurrencies like Bitcoin, has been a significant and innovative shift in the financial landscape. It emerged in response to the global financial crisis of 2008– 2010, as central banks' massive monetary base expansion eroded trust in traditional fiat currencies. Bitcoin, introduced in 2008 by an entity known as Satoshi Nakamoto offered a new form of currency that relied on peer-to-peer networks and cryptographic techniques, with a novel consensus mechanism called "Proof of Work." This marked a transition from trust in central banks to trust in technology for financial transactions (Wątorek, M., et al., 2021). The showrunner of cryptocurrency is the blockchain technology or a distributed ledger that keeps a record of payments and distributes access to certified users (Dogra, 2022).

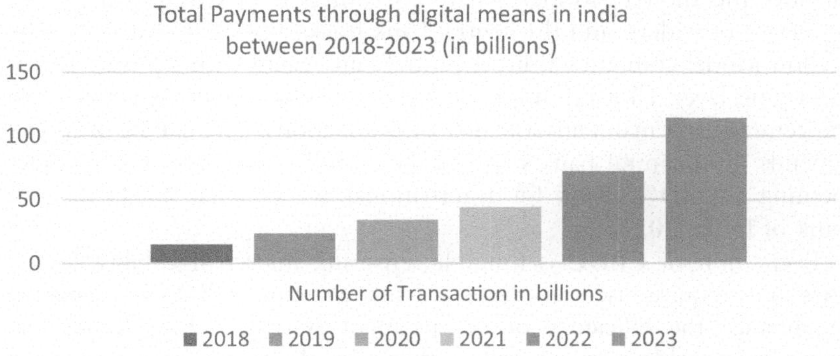

Fig. 7.1 Total volume of digital payments in India from 2018 –023 (in billions) (*Source* Extracted from Statista [2023] report on Digital payments worldwide)

However, the limited supply of these private cryptocurrencies and the growing demand for them led to significant price increases, making them both profitable assets and unreliable mediums of exchange due to their high volatility (Katsiampa et al., 2019). As a result, some countries, like India, China, Bolivia, Indonesia, Turkey, and Egypt, imposed outright bans on cryptocurrencies, while others, such as Singapore, Ireland, Kenya, Nigeria, and the UK, issued warnings to citizens about the risks associated with using cryptocurrencies. Central banks began to recognize the need for a more controlled and regulated digital currency alternative, leading to the development of CBDCs (Reserve Bank of India, 2022b).

Central Bank Digital Currency (CBDC) is issued by the central bank as a country's official currency. It functions as legal tender, equivalent to physical cash, and appears as a liability on the central bank's balance sheet. CBDC is designed to be widely accepted, and usable by individuals, businesses, and government agencies for various transactions. It can be exchanged one-to-one with both commercial bank money and physical cash, making it highly convertible (Reserve Bank of India, 2022b).

There are presently three models for the issuance and management of Central Bank Digital Currencies (CBDCs). The first model is the Single-Tier Model where the central bank is exclusively responsible for all aspects of the CBDCs system, including issuance, transaction verification, and maintaining account balances. It offers resilience but limits private sector involvement and innovation. The second model the Two-Tier Model, recognizes inefficiencies of the single-tier approach. It includes the Indirect Model, where consumers hold CBDC with banks or service providers, and the central bank tracks all CBDC balances. The Hybrid Model combines a direct central bank claim with a private sector messaging layer, allowing intermediaries to handle retail payments while the central bank maintains a ledger of transactions. The choice of model depends on a central bank's specific goals and circumstances for implementing a CBDC (Bank for International Settlements, 2021; Reserve Bank of India, 2022a).

Every unit of CBDC is fungible, ensuring interchangeability, and it does not require users to hold a bank account. CBDC is expected to enhance the efficiency of the payment system, reduce transaction costs, and provide a secure and modern digital alternative to traditional fiat currency, aligning with a country's monetary policy and economic objectives (Johnson, G., & Pomorski, 2014; Reserve Bank of India, 2022c).

In the rapidly evolving landscape of global Central Bank Digital Currency (CBDC) development, a remarkable shift is underway. From just 35 countries exploring CBDCs in May 2020, the number has surged to approximately 130, encompassing 98 percent of the world's GDP. Notably, 64 of these nations have progressed to advanced stages, such as development, pilot programs, or even launch preparations, indicating a significant commitment to digital currency adoption. Among the G20 nations, 19 are at advanced stages, with nine already in pilot phases. Leading the charge, China's extensive CBDC pilot, reaching millions and being tested in various scenarios, is emblematic of this movement. The European Central Bank is gearing up for a digital euro-pilot, while numerous other countries are poised to begin their own CBDC trials. (Atlantic Council, 2023) (Fig. 7.2).

At the heart of this global CBDC surge lies a range of compelling motivations. In Sweden, where traditional paper currency is dwindling, CBDCs are seen as a tool for embracing digital money. Meanwhile, in nations like Denmark, Germany, Japan, and the United States, the optimization of currency issuance aims to reduce the costs associated with printing and managing physical cash. For regions grappling with geographical barriers, such as The Bahamas and the Caribbean islands, CBDCs offer seamless solutions for digital transactions. Private cryptocurrencies are gaining traction, driving central banks worldwide to provide

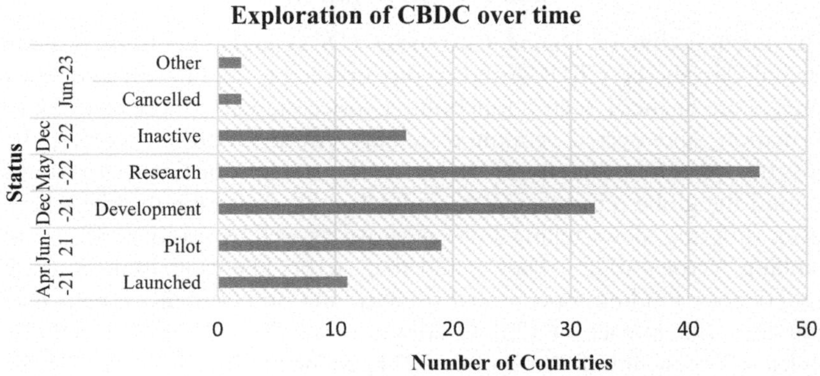

Fig. 7.2 Number of countries and currency unions exploring CBDC over time (*Source* Extracted from www.atlanticcouncil.org)

regulated digital currency options that mitigate the risks of unregulated crypto assets (Reserve Bank of India, 2022a).

These CBDC initiatives aren't just about embracing digital currency; they also serve as a means to bolster financial system efficiency and security. Settlement finality and real-time, cost-effective cross-border transactions are becoming more accessible, enhancing the global financial landscape. In India, a nation where digital payments thrive alongside high cash demand, CBDCs are poised to facilitate a transition to a more cash-efficient economy. They foster innovation and inclusivity in financial services, providing the unbanked with greater access and reinforcing trust in national currencies in the face of proliferating cryptocurrencies. In essence, CBDCs represent a pivotal step in modernizing payments, promoting financial inclusion, and addressing the challenges posed by private crypto assets, ultimately reinforcing trust in national currencies. (Reserve Bank of India, 2022a).

This surge in CBDC development not only reflects the changing global financial landscape but also emphasizes the diverse motivations, challenges, and national security implications at the forefront of the future of global finance.

Impacts and Implications of Digital Currency

Impact of Digital Currency on the Stability of Financial Institutions and Financial Systems

The introduction of Digital Currencies (DCs) including Central Bank Digital Currencies (CBDCs) and cryptocurrencies could have a significant impact on financial sector functioning, price stability, monetary policy formation, and overall economic stability (BOE, 2020). However, the possible impact of digital currencies on the stability of financial systems around the globe remains unclear and debatable. Several researchers have given differing views telling both negative as well as positive effects on banking sector stability. They found that factors like capitalization, bank size, deposit funding, operational strategy, and domestic investment may influence the impact of CBDC adoption on financial system stability (Juks, 2018; Kumhof & Noone, 2021; Mancini-Griffoli et al., 2018). A global study with data from 86 nations suggests that adopting digital currencies including CBDCs can help in stabilizing the financial system by minimizing leverage asset risks and enhancing lending opportunities. Although, there may be a variation in its impact across different economies and bank sizes, while the retail CBDCs normally improve the stability wholesale CBDCs may pose impediments (Luu et al., 2023).

Additionally, Samudrala, and Yerchuru (2021) found that digital currencies and cryptocurrencies can have a positive impact on improving financial inclusion, streamlining transactions, and improving access to financial services. However, they also present some challenges such as regulatory uncertainty, cyber security risks, and possible disruptions to traditional banking models. The stability of financial institutions and systems relies on how efficiently and effectively these challenges are addressed and how digital currencies are impeccably incorporated into existing systems. Hence, to understand the possible implications of digital currencies on financial system stability and inform policy decisions to ease risks and maximize benefits there is a strong need for research in this relevant field.

Impact of Digital Currency on Financial Inclusion

Financial inclusion leads to the creation of employment opportunities, reduction of poverty, income parity, and economic growth at large through the efficient distribution of financial resources. An inclusive financial system can truly improve the financial and living conditions of unprivileged people in society (Dahiya & Kumar, 2020). Financial inclusion has been documented as serving 7 of the 17 SDGs (Sustainable Development Goals) of the United Nations (Lannquist & Tan, 2023).

It is important to learn that in the year 2017, one-third of the world's adult population was financially excluded, they didn't have bank accounts in the formal financial system (World Bank, 2021), and in the year 2021, as per Global Findex survey, 1.4 billion people were outside of the system so it becomes a moral responsibility to make them a part of the proper financial system. To serve the people who are financially excluded and rely on cash, a huge infrastructure has to be developed to store, transport, and process cash. Setting up physical facilities in remote places along with staff involves enormous costs and it results in high operational expenses. In this system, all the transactions are done in cash form and no record of the financial activities of the household restricts the financial service provider from serving the tailored needs. Contrarily, digital financial services for example digital payment-based transactions enable households to keep the history of their financial transactions and they can share it with the financial service providers. Consequently, they can access a wide range of customized financial products and services such as deposits, insurance, and credit (Lannquist & Tan, 2023). So, digital payments made specifically during the COVID-19 time have triggered thoughts toward the introduction of digital currency in developing countries.

Digital currency can be proved a milestone in the larger financial inclusion because it can address all the problems that keep people away from availing of financial services. A new financial system based on digital currency or digital finance will be more inclusive and people-friendly (Ekong & Ekong, 2022). In the next five years, most of the major central banks will either introduce or start the plan to introduce their digital currency (CBDCs) to meet the contemporary requirements and one of them is financial inclusion (Zuluaga, 2021). A retail CBDC is more expected to contribute to financial inclusion than a wholesale CBDC because it can directly be used by the people to store value or to transact through an account or token. Moreover, it is a sovereign legal tender, guaranteed by the central bank and it offers instant settlement so it is more appropriate for end users such as consumers and merchants. CBDC can address demand side as well as supply side barriers to financial inclusion. It can be planned to work in both modes online as well as offline through Bluetooth and NFC technology and multiple servers enable it to operate continually (24*7*365) even if one server is down. It will deepen the trust of the consumer in digital payment transactions as all the transactions are guaranteed by the central bank, and more affordable financial services can be delivered with no requirement of the mediators, able for the people who are not digitally literate and versed with smart technologies. From the suppliers' side, CBDC will enable them to manage their liquidity in a better way, lower their credit risk, and boost immediate settlements and clearing (AFI, 2022). On the other hand, some criticisms are that CBDC will not support financial inclusion because it requires buying digital devices, and special regulatory mechanism, and increases transaction costs. In addition, people like to have cash over digital currency (Ozili, 2022).

Alternatively, cryptocurrencies have the potential to transform the financial system by providing access to financial services such as savings, loans, insurance, etc., in those areas where conventional banking services couldn't reach through the use of decentralized applications that work on blockchain networks. They don't need stringent requirements to meet for entry because these currencies are not controlled by the central banks. People can store and transfer their money using cryptocurrencies without any dependency on traditional financial institutions. Cryptocurrencies also enable to borrow money by keeping them as collateral and earn interest on these holdings. Apart from this, these also offer a store of value in economies where the inflation rate is high and the market is volatile (Patel, 2023). Also, Vincent and Evans (2019) empirically investigated that cryptocurrency, mobile subscription, and internet connectivity have significant positive impacts on financial inclusion and financial sector development in emerging countries like India, Nigeria, China, and South Africa. But these currencies are also criticized due to less consumer protection and more chances of accumulation of black money.

It can be concluded that CBDC and cryptocurrency along with FinTech have the potential to improve financial inclusion by extending financial services to those who have been unbanked so far but at the same time, proper regulations are required to put a check on the threats and risk to financial stability, especially in case of cryptocurrency (Ozili, 2023a).

Impact of Digital Currency on the Global Trade

The global trade is changing due to digital currency, which includes cryptocurrencies and central bank digital currencies (CBDCs). Bitcoin in particular has gained popularity as a potential game-changer for international trade. WTO research indicates that the time and expense involved in transferring money between countries can be significantly reduced by using digital currencies in cross-border transactions. Speedy cross-border transactions can enhance the efficiency of businesses and thereby, the volume of international trade transactions. Apart from this, many digital currencies are working based on blockchain technology that makes business processes easier which earlier used to take many days for example letter of credit issuance and document verification. The traditional overseas payments are subject to exchange rate volatility but the use of digital currency reduces this currency exchange risk (He et al., 2022).

Even though digital currency may gain popularity and give a big boost to international trade, still many challenges need the immediate attention of policymakers at the global level. Using digital currencies in global trade involves many physical, technical, and legal challenges. So, to reap the full advantages of digital currency in international trade, the intervention of policymakers is required to make international payments of cross-border trade transactions safe, hassle-free, and cost-effective. In addition to this, many countries that are still struggling with political instability and poor economic indicators will remain un-benefited from these advancements. However, Chen (2021) found that countries with weak institutions are more likely to adopt cryptocurrencies to promote international trade. But, in many countries, digitalization process is very slow, they lack the minimum infrastructure to settle their international trade transaction using digital currency.

Impact of Digital Currency on Sustainability

CBDC offers opportunities to invest in sustainable activities and projects as it can increase access to finance, make the payment system more efficient, and improve the speed of transactions. CBDC leads to faster distribution of funds among financially excluded sections of society. These people can access CBDC-based loans and credit facilities easily and can use them to improve their standard of living by spending on basic facilities like food, health, education, etc. Thereby, the poor people can bring themselves above the poverty line and come out of the hunger zone. CBDC facilitates fast funding to research in the area of resilient and sustainable health services that everyone can access at affordable prices. The problem of especially concerning to accessibility of digital financial services by women can also be addressed through CBDC. Likewise, CBDC can be an important gateway in the accomplishment of sustainable development goals (Ozili, 2023b).

It is also observed that CBDC promotes the issue of green bonds' contribution in the reduction of toxic gas emissions. Subsequently, it improves the green land ratio, accelerates the use of green finance, and advances sustainable development (Yang et al., 2023). At present, cryptocurrencies are operating based on an energy-intensive mechanism due to their trustless environment. The consumption of energy depends on the type and structure of cryptocurrency. For instance, Ethereum which is the second largest cryptocurrency as per the market capitalization uses proof-of-work for its Sybil resistance mechanism. It is expected to consume 87.97 TWh annually. Now considering the sustainability approach, many cryptocurrencies like Cosmos, Solana, and Polkadot are using proof-of-stake that consumes less energy comparatively. Wendl et al. (2023) also explored that PoW cryptocurrencies, particularly Bitcoin, are linked with growing environmental effects and the researchers have proposed PoS as a sustainable solution to the environmental issue. CBDC will require a different energy consumption structure because it doesn't need to earn trust as it is backed by the central bank (Lee & Park, 2022).

Conclusion

The present chapter provides a basic understanding of the increasing landscape of digital currency within the current financial system and its profound impact on the various facets of business, society, and individuals such as financial stability, financial inclusion, global trade, and sustainability. It is found that digital currency stands balanced to appear as an invigorating tool for enhancing the current stability of the financial system. In addition to this it plays an important role in promoting the adoption of green finance practices, and thus contributing toward achieving Sustainable development goals.

The development of CBDCs has massive scope to provide a good amount of benefits to businesses, individuals, society and nations. Its potential to provide low-cost products/transactions and improve the reach of everyone to the formal financial system makes this a transformative force. Furthermore, it can work as an important deterrent to check the corruption and money laundering cases as it maintains a comprehensive record of all transactions. By keeping a record of all transactions, it institutes a clear and traceable financial ecosystem. These features will not only improve accountability but may also contribute to building trust in the financial system.

To get the full benefit of digital currency, governments, policymakers, and financial institutions have to change and develop adequate infrastructure for the smooth functioning of the digital currency-based financial system. Also, it becomes critical to introduce a detailed and well-considered regulatory structure to competently incorporate digital currencies into the current financial system.

References

AFI. (2022). *Central Bank Digital Currency Opportunity for Financial Inclusion in Developing and Emerging Economies?* https://crimesciencejournal.biomedcentral.com/track/pdf/10.1186/

Aneja, R., & Dygas, R. (Eds.). (2022). *Digital Currencies and the New Global Financial System* (1st ed., pp. 1–16). Routledge. https://doi.org/10.4324/9781003310365

Atlantic Council. (2023). *Central Bank Digital Currency Tracker*. www.atlanticcouncil.org.

Bank for International Settlements. (2021). *Annual Report*.

BOE. (2020). *Central Bank Digital Currency: Opportunities, Challenges and Design*.

Chen, E. R. (2021). Determining the Economic Impact of Cryptocurrency Adoption on International Trade from a Gravity Model Framework. *Research and Reviews: Journal of Social Sciences, 8*(1), 1–11.

Dahiya, S., & Kumar, M. (2020). Linkage Between Financial Inclusion and Economic Growth: An Empirical Study of the Emerging Indian Economy. *Vision, 24*(2), 184–193. https://doi.org/10.1177/0972262920923891

Dogra, S. (2022). What is Digital Rupee and How it is Different from Bitcoin and Other Cryptocurrencies? www.indiatoday.in.

Ekong, U. M., & Ekong, C. N. (2022). Digital Currency and Financial Inclusion in Nigeria: Lessons for Development. *Journal of Internet and Digital Economics, 2*(1), 46–67. https://doi.org/10.1108/jide-11-2021-0018

Haque, M. A., & Shoaib, M. (2023). The Digital Currency in India: Challenges and Prospects. *BenchCouncil Transactions on Benchmarks, Standards & Evaluations, 3*(1).

He, C., Milne, A., & Zachariadis, M. (2022). Central Bank Digital Currencies and International Payments. Swift institute Working Paper 2020–002. https://ssrn.com/abstract=4112382

Johnson, G., & Pomorski, L. (2014). Briefing on Digital Currencies. *Briefing to the Senate of Canada*.

Juks, R. (2018). When a Central Bank Digital Currency Meets Private Money: The Effects of an e-krona on Banks. *Sveriges Riksbank Economic Review, 3*, 79–99.

Katsiampa, P., Corbet, S., & Lucey, B. (2019). High-frequency Volatility Co-movements in Cryptocurrency Markets. *Journal of International Financial Markets, Institutions and Money, 62*, 35–52.

Kumar, D., & Pawan. (2022). Digital Currency: Issues, Opportunities and Challenges. *Shodh Drishti (An International Peer Reviewed Refereed Research Journal), 13*(3), 1–7. https://doi.org/10.13140/RG.2.2.13884.00642

Kumhof, M., & Noone, C. (2021). Central Bank Digital Currencies—Design Principles for Financial Stability. *Economic Analysis and Policy, 71*, 553–572.

Lannquist, A., & Tan, B. (2023). *Central Bank Digital Currency s Role in Promoting Financial Inclusion* (2023rd ed.). International Monetary Fund.

Lee, S., & Park, J. (2022). *Environmental Implications of a Central Bank Digital Currency (CBDC)* (No. 8; World Bank Group Korea Office Innovation and Technology Note Series). https://openknowledge.worldbank.org/handle/10986/37702

Mancini-Griffoli, T., Peria, M. S. M., Agur, I., Ari, A., Kiff, J., Popescu, A., & Rochon, C. (2018). *Casting Light Central Bank Digital Currency IMF Staff Discussion Note 8.*

Nakamoto, S. (2008). Bitcoin: A Peer-to-Peer Electronic Cash System. *Decentralized Business Review.*

Ozili, P. K. (2022). Can Central Bank Digital Currency Increase Financial Inclusion? Arguments for and Against. In K. Sood, B. Balusamy, S. Grima, & P. Marano (Eds.), *Big Data Analytics in the Insurance Market(Emerald Studies in Finance, Insurance, and Risk Management)* (pp. 241–249). Emerald Publishing Limited. https://doi.org/10.1108/978-1-80262-637-720221013

Ozili, P. K. (2023a). CBDC, Fintech and Cryptocurrency for Financial Inclusion and Financial Stability. *Digital Policy, Regulation and Governance, 25*(1), 40–57.

Ozili, P. K. (2023b, February). Using Central Bank Digital Currency to Achieve the Sustainable Development Goals. *SSRN Electronic Journal,* 1–13. https://doi.org/10.2139/ssrn.4370181

Patel, E. (2023). Cryptocurrencies: How Can Cryptocurrencies Play a Role in Promoting Financial Inclusion?—The Economic Times. In *The Economic Times.* https://economictimes.indiatimes.com/markets/cryptocurrency/how-can-cryptocurrencies-play-a-role-in-promoting-financial-inclusion/articleshow/100205450.cms?from=mdr

PIB Research Wing. (2023). *From Local to Global: How India's Digital Payment Revolution is Inspiring the World.* www.pib.gov.in.

Reserve Bank of India. (2022a). *Annual Report.*

Reserve Bank of India. (2022b). *Central Bank Digital Currency—Is This the Future of Money?* www.rbi.org.in.

Reserve Bank of India. (2022c). *Concept Note on Central Bank Digital Currency.* www.rbi.org.in.

Statista. (2023). *Digital Payments—Worldwide.*India: number of digital payments 2023 | Statista.

Samudrala, R. S., & Yerchuru, S. K. (2021). Central Bank Digital Currency: Risks, Challenges and Design Considerations for India. *CSI Transactions on ICT, 9*(4), 245–249.

Tan, L., & Xue, L. (2021). Research on the Development of Digital Currencies under the COVID-19 Epidemic. *Procedia Computer Science, 187*, 89–96.

Vincent, O., & Evans, O. (2019). Can Cryptocurrency, Mobile Phones, and the Internet Herald Sustainable Financial Sector Development in Emerging

Markets? *Journal of Transnational Management, 24*(3), 259–279. https://doi.org/10.1080/15475778.2019.1633170

Wątorek, M., Drożdż, S., Kwapień, J., Minati, L., Oświęcimka, P., & Stanuszek, M. (2021). Multiscale Characteristics of the Emerging Global Cryptocurrency Market. *Physics Reports, 901*, 1–82.

Wendl, M., My Hanh, D., & Remmer, S. (2023). The Environmental Impact of Cryptocurrencies Using Proof of Work and Proof of Stake Consensus Algorithms: A Systematic Review. *The Journal of Environmental Management, 326*. https://doi.org/10.1016/j.jenvman.2022.116530

World Bank. (2021). The Drive for Financial Inclusion: Lessons of World Bank Group Experience. *Independent Evaluation Group,* 1–34. http://www3.weforum.org/docs/WEF_The_Global_Covid19_FinTech_Market_Rapid_Assessment_Study_2020.pdf

Yang, Q., Zheng, M., & Wang, Y. (2023). The Role of CBDC in Green Finance and Sustainable Development. *Emerging Markets Finance and Trade, 59*(15), 4158–4173. https://doi.org/10.1080/1540496X.2023.2185096

Zuluaga, D. (2021). Which Type of Digital Currency for Financial Inclusion? *Cato Journal, 41*(2), 413–421. https://doi.org/10.36009/CJ.41.2.16

CHAPTER 8

The Impact of Digital Currencies on International Trade and Economic Growth in India

Geethu Rachel Stephen and N. Savitha

Introduction

The technological revolution has reshaped the financial system in such a way that innovations in payment in the form of digital currencies have an upper hand over the traditional banking system. With the outbreak of the COVID-19 pandemic, there has been an expansion in the attention gained by digital currencies all around the globe. Reduced exposure to the outside world accelerated the development of these digital forms of currency (Tan & Xue, 2021). The India Digital Payments Annual Report 2022 recorded that transactions through Unified Payment Interface (UPI) were 74.05 billion in terms of volume and 126 trillion Indian Rupee in trade. The innovation of infrastructural developments such as 5G networks and big data also promoted its growth. The application

G. R. Stephen (✉) · N. Savitha
Department of Social Sciences, School of Social Sciences and Languages, Vellore Institute of Technology, Vellore, Tamil Nadu, India
e-mail: geethu.rachel@vit.ac.in

R. Aneja and R. Dygas (eds.), *Digital Currencies in The New Global World Order*, https://doi.org/10.1007/978-981-97-4810-5_8

scenarios of such currencies are widened by the increase in e-commerce activities and the advancement in the online economy. The electronic form of any currency is digital currency which is dominating the financial system of most of the countries these days. With the advancement of technology and the increase in usage of smartphones and digital payments, India introduced the Central Bank Digital Currency (CBDC), which is the e-rupee. The central bank of a country is responsible for the issuance and supervision of CBDCs. This digital token acts as a legal tender and also made a turning point for payments made digitally in the country. According to the United Nations Conference on Trade and Development (UNCTAD) report, in the ownership of digital currency, India occupies the position of seventh highest in 2021 with 7.3% of its population owning assets in the form of digital currency. In that list, Ukraine occupies the highest position with 12.7% ownership followed by Russia (11.9%), Venezuela (10.3%), Singapore (9.4%), Kenya (8.5%), and the U.S. (8.3%). The report also showed that, among the top 20 economies in the list, 15 of them are developing countries.

Review of Literature

Various studies are discussing the revolution happening in the financial system focusing on digital currencies. According to Rose (2015), one of the key features of virtual currencies is their network externalities. It implies that the value of digital currencies increases with their increase in usage. Several studies show that there are both positive and negative impacts on the economy with the introduction of digital currencies.

Naboulsi and Neubert (2018) investigated the impact of digital currency on the economy of Kenya. It aimed to find out the usefulness of Bitcoin in reducing the cost of transfer of international funds. A case study design was used in the research along with the purposive sampling method. The study raised concerns regarding the price volatility and legal framework of bitcoin which was unregulated. On the other hand, the output of the study showed that the cost of transfer of money was reduced while using BitPesa. The study concluded that the use of modern technologies attracts foreign investments into the country and benefits society as a whole.

Abendin and Duan (2021) examined the role of the digital economy in international trade and the economic growth of the African economy using samples of 53 countries during the period 2000 to 2018. The study used methods such as Pooled Ordinary Least Squares (POLS), random and fixed effects, and the Generalised Method of Moments (GMM) model. Cobb–Douglas production function was also employed in this study. The outcomes of the study showed that in the context of the digital economy, there were only positive effects of trade on economic growth. Banerjee and Sinha (2023) highlighted the role of Central Bank Digital Currencies (CBDCs) in promoting financial inclusion. Morbale et al. (2022) stated that cryptocurrencies not only promoted financial inclusion in India but also reduced the cost of transactions.

On the other hand, Haque and Shoaib (2023) discussed the challenges related to digital currencies such as feasibility, scalability, security concerns, etc. Thakur et al. (2022) also examined the issues and challenges related to cryptocurrency and pointed out that, since the proof of ownership was restricted in cryptocurrency, there could be a possibility for hacking. The study also discussed the positive side while mentioning that, the cryptocurrency did not require any middlemen, processing charges were absent unlike debit and credit cards, and also facilitated faster transactions along with promoting economic growth with an increase in its accessibility. According to Heckel and Waldenberger (2022), since the deposits in the Central Bank were already digitalized, the CBDCs did not have any negative influence on the financial stability of the economy.

Thus, studies show that like any other innovation, digital currencies also have their pros and cons.

Research Questions

The study aims to answer the following questions:

- What are the benefits of using digital currencies?
- What are the impacts of digital currencies on international trade and the economic growth of the Indian economy?

Research Objectives

The objectives of the study are:

- To know the potential benefits of using digital currencies.

- To understand the impact of digital currencies on international trade and the economic growth of the nation.

Research Methodology

The study is descriptive and uses secondary data collected from various reliable sources such as the Reserve Bank of India (RBI) official website including RBI press releases 2022–2023, Digidhan Dashboard of Government of India, and Statista Market Insights database. Using secondary data, it shows the growth of digital transactions and their value over the years from 2017 to 2022. The study explains the advantages of using digital currencies and their impact on international trade and economic growth.

Evolution of Digital Currencies

The development of digital currencies can be traced back to the evolution of money in the barter system as a medium of exchange depending upon the double coincidence of wants. The Great Financial Crisis (2007–2008) led to a significant change in the monetary system with the introduction of a virtual currency known as Bitcoin which is independent of any financial intermediation. It has broader application in many areas from the implementation of fiscal policies to the execution of property rights. Due to the systemic initiatives of the Central Bank of India, the last three decades saw significant growth in the payment sector of India. The payment market in India has undergone a digital shift with the increase in the usage of smartphones and the accessibility of the internet. The emergence of payment systems, which are telco-based such as Airtel Money and Vodafone M-Pesa, mobile wallets, and prepaid cards stimulated the shift. The demonetization of the Indian economy in 2016 also forced citizens to choose a digital mode of payment. The outbreak of the COVID-19 pandemic in 2020 also prompted people to switch from the usage of cash to digital payments. In India, the revolution in currencies took another phase with the introduction of Central Bank Digital Currency by the Reserve Bank of India (RBI) on 1st November 2022, which is in line with the objectives of monetary policy to ensure financial stability and currency efficiency. It has a three-stage implementation process including proof of concept, pilots, and finally, among the

Table 8.1 RBI-Digital Payments Index (RBI-DPI). with March 2018 as a base

Period	*RBI-DPI Index*
March 2018	100
March 2019	153.47
September 2019	173.49
March 2020	207.84
September 2020	217.74
March 2021	270.59
September 2021	304.06
March 2022	349.30

Source: RBI Press Releases 2022–2023

public. Thus, the digital mode of payment eased accessibility and facilitated convenient modes of financial transactions, which in turn led to the financial inclusion of all sections of society (Table 8.1).

The Digital Payment Index of RBI shows the level of digitization of payments in the country. The table above shows that the index for March 2018 is 100 and it increased to 153.47 in March 2019. The RBI-DPI Index is 173.49 and 207.84 in September 2019 and March 2020 respectively. Likewise, the index shows an increase in digital payments over the years as the index stands at 349.30 in March 2022 as against 304.06 in September 2021 (Table 8.2).

The table shows that there is a continuous increase in digital transactions both in volume and in value over the financial years from 2017–18 to 2021–22. The digital transaction volume increased from 2,071 in the financial year 2017–18 to 8,840 in 2021–22. On the other hand, a digital transaction in value also shows an increase from 2017–18 to 2021–22

Table 8.2 The digital transactions in volume and value during the financial years 2017–2018 to 2021–2022

Financial Year	*2017–2018*	*2018–2019*	*2019–2020*	*2020–2021*	*2021–2022*
Digital Transaction Volume (in crore)	2071	3134	4572	5554	8840
Digital Transaction Value (in lakh crore)	1962	2482	2953	3000	3021

Source Digidhan Dashboard of Government of India

which is 1,962 and 3,021 respectively. Thus, the last five years have shown a substantial growth of transactions in digital mode. The combined efforts of the government and its stakeholders have played a significant role in this growth.

Types of Digital Currencies

Digital currencies, which are electronically transferred can be broadly divided into two types:

1. Central Bank Digital Currency (CBDC) and
2. Cryptocurrency

Central Bank Digital Currency (CBDC)

The digital versions of the conventionally used fiat currencies are called CBDC. Examples of CBDCs are the Rupee which is the CBDC of India, the Digital Currency Electronic Payment (DCEP) of the People's Bank of China, and the Sand Dollar of the Central Bank of Bahamas. It provides a convenient and secure mode of payment that can be accessed and used by all sections of society including banked and unbanked. Through this payment system, transactions between person-to-person and person-to-merchant are possible. Various technological advancements are used to implement CBDC such as blockchain technology. This technology tracks transactions and acts as a transparent ledger by ensuring currency integrity. Other approaches can also be used to implement CBDC such as a centralized database or a hybrid combination of both centralized and decentralized one. The current financial infrastructural status and the regulatory environment influence the selection of technological approaches.

Cryptocurrency

Cryptocurrencies are virtual forms of currencies that secure transactions using cryptographic techniques. These currencies are decentralized as they are independent of any financial institution or regulatory authority. Such currencies also make use of blockchain technology. The usage of currencies based on the technology of blockchain is a revolutionary shift in the field of finance and technology. The creation and addition of each unit of cryptocurrency to the blockchain is based on a process called mining, in which complex mathematical problems have to be solved to validate the process of transactions. It also requires computational aid with specialized hardware.

Benefits of Digital Currencies

As the digital currencies undergo transactions directly between the parties involved and are undertaken without the intermediaries, the amount of time for transfer is much less. Thus, it is better compared to the traditional payment system involving banks or clearing houses and facilitates faster cross-border transfers and transactions. Global transactions are expensive as people get charged high fees for the transfer of funds between countries, especially in situations of currency conversions. In such cases, digital assets can make global transfers cheaper and more cost-effective (Rodeck, 2023). Accessibility and availability are also important advantages of digital currencies. Transactions can be conducted at any time depending on the needs of the individuals. Since digital currencies are in electronic form, it does not require any manufacturing facilities, which are essential for the physical currency, thereby reducing the cost of operation, printing, distribution, and storage. It is also immune to physical defects and soiling which are concerns related to physical currency. In India, the digital rupee based on blockchain technology increases the transparency and efficiency of the monetary system. It will also allow real-time tracking, ledger maintenance, and account settlements. There is also no concern about volatility as it will be backed by RBI. It also facilitates financial services to both banked and unbanked customers as a bank account is not a requirement to transact with the digital rupee. Thus, the main motive behind the introduction of the digital rupee is to address the problems of physical currency and to make cross-border transactions easier. It also empowered the vision of the government toward a cashless economy by reducing the demand for cash.

Impact of Digital Currencies on International Trade

Global transactions involve human interactions to verify the information of senders and recipients to prevent terrorism and money laundering. As a result, there will be delays in payments. Digital currencies can make global cross-border transactions and payments more efficient with less time (Thakker, 2023) and can thereby address the problem of the global trade financing gap of $1.7 trillion. To trade finance, digital currency also provides alternate information related to credit. The usage of public ledgers of digital currency to share information related to the history of payment and financial transactions helps to underwrite loans for trade including export and import. To achieve this, stringent privacy protocols need to be implemented. Blockchain technology helps to automate trade-related processes such as trade finance, logistics, and trade clearance and thus makes trade more efficient and paperless (Ganne, 2018). The issues related to de-risking can be reduced using digital currencies. Countries having a high risk of anti-money laundering and combatting terrorism financing like Latin America and the islands in the Pacific, face the barrier of de-risking to participate in global transactions. It will increase the transaction cost of buyers and sellers in those countries. With the digital setup, digital currencies can reduce their overall transaction cost. It also provides other channels of payment for merchants and consumers in those countries which in turn allows them to maintain connection with buyers and sellers of other countries (Table 8.3).

The market of digital payment is experiencing an upswing over several years due to an increase in the adoption of mobile payment applications and e-commerce. The table shows that from the year 2017 to 2022,

Table 8.3 The transaction value of digital payments worldwide from 2017 to 2022 in trillion US Dollars

	2017	*2018*	*2019*	*2020*	*2021*	*2022*
Digital Commerce	2.98	3.27	3.53	3.99	4.86	5.42
Digital Remittances	0.06	0.07	0.08	0.09	0.12	0.12
Mobile POS Payments	0.33	0.76	1.19	1.98	2.51	2.82
Total	3.36	4.10	4.80	6.06	7.48	8.35

Source: Statista Market Insights (Digital Payments-Worldwide)

digital commerce increased from 2.98 to 5.42. In the case of digital remittances, the increase is from 0.06 to 0.12. The mobile point of sale (POS) payments which are transactions using mobile devices show a continuous increase from 0.33 to 2.82. Thus, it is evident that the overall transaction value in digital payments over the years has shown an upsurge and the growth is valued at 8.35 in 2022 from 3.36 in the year 2017 in trillion US Dollars (US $).

Although digital currencies can bring potential benefits to international trade, they cannot affect trade depending on comparative advantage. Countries with a lack of economic development and political stability continue to face problems related to foreign trade such as currency conversion and lack of demand globally. There will be challenges to financial inclusion in those areas, which lack access to infrastructure and cannot afford digital devices to support digital currencies (Adrian & Griffoli, 2021). Thus, the digital divide needs to be closed to reap the benefits of digital currency. New trade agreements have to be made such as those in Australia, the UK, Singapore, and New Zealand to enable private issuers of digital currencies to access the market and to allow the free flow of data with security.

Impact of Digital Currencies on Economic Growth

The impact of digital currencies can be seen in various spheres of the economy. The digital rupee launched by the Central Bank forms a part of the total money supply which in turn affects prices and demand in the economy. It will also bring about a change in the velocity of currency in circulation (Gadia, 2022). Digital currencies will bring cost-effectiveness to the economy by reducing the cost of printing and transaction of new currency notes and their storage. It will also prevent the issues and frauds arising out of counterfeit currency notes. It will also accelerate the journey toward a cashless economy by reducing the overall cash dependence in the economy. It will also lead to greater efficiency in government payments by making them faster and easily accessible. It provides services to both banked and unbanked in society as a bank account is not a requirement to use digital currency and thus addresses the problem of financial inclusion and flaws of the traditional banking system in the economy. Since transactions in digital mode are conducted quickly compared to traditional payment systems, it increases the cash flow of small businesses. They can also increase the consumer base all over the world as foreign exchange rates are not required for transactions of digital currencies. According to Morbale et al. (2022), in future, cryptocurrency will be the global currency and countries need not keep their specific currencies. The cryptographic technique used in cryptocurrency transactions ensures protection and security for small businesses against transactions, which are unlawful. Blockchain also helps the producers and micro, small, and medium enterprises (MSMEs) in developing countries to participate in global trade by lowering the cost of trade and enabling easier access to trade finance (Ganne, 2018). Central Bank Digital Currency makes the Direct Benefit Transfer more efficient and helps in better implementation of other government schemes without any leakage. Cryptocurrency also has an impact on the job market as it provides employment opportunities in the blockchain industry, especially to software engineers. It will also allow real-time visibility into the economy for policymakers because of its transparency.

According to the Union Budget (2022–2023), there will be a 30% reduction in tax on income from digital assets and cryptocurrencies. However, the anonymity involved in blockchain transactions could lead to tax avoidance and leakage in the medium and long term. In addition to this, since currency substitution into CBDC is similar to that of dollarization, it can weaken the effectiveness of monetary policy transmission in the economy. In another scenario, if several CBDCs co-exist, then this multipolarity could affect the exchange rate regimes which in turn lead to financial volatility and instability in the country (Zhang, 2020). Production of cryptos also affects the environment badly as its mining requires high consumption of electricity and emits tons of carbon dioxide.

Conclusion

The innovation of digital currency is a giant leap in the transformation of the banking system. This study helps to know about the potential benefits of digital currencies and their impact on international trade and economic growth of the economy. The study found out that, although there are potential benefits that can be drained out, the implementation of digital currency is accompanied by several challenges, such as those related to wallet security and privacy of the consumers, data management, irreversibility of transactions, price volatility, lack of availability of infrastructure facilities, awareness and acceptability among the public. Such concerns need to be addressed efficiently. To maintain price stability, some companies have introduced stablecoins which are pegged against other currencies or another external reference such as a commodity or a financial instrument. There should be better facilities regarding data management and privacy security for broadening the scope of technological innovations. Apart from the concerns, the role of digital currencies in improving the lives of the underprivileged and reducing their poverty through financial inclusion should be highly appreciated. As the G20 members stated, "technological innovation, including that underlying crypto assets, has the potential to improve the efficiency and inclusiveness of the financial system and the economy more broadly." But for the efficient implementation of digital currencies, challenges faced by Indian society such as the digital divide and digital illiteracy should be dealt with properly. A regulatory framework should also be provided to curb the illegal activities associated with digital currencies and to increase the faith of the public in such innovations.

References

Abendin, S., & Duan, P. (2021). International Trade and Economic Growth in Africa: The Role of the Digital Economy. *Cogent Economics & Finance, 9*(1). https://doi.org/10.1080/23322039.2021.1911767

Adrian, T., & Griffoli, M. T. (2021, June). *A New Era of Digital Money*. imf.org. https://www.imf.org/external/pubs/ft/fandd/2021/06/online/digital-money-new-era-adrian-mancini-griffoli.htm

Banerjee, S., & Sinha, M. D. (2023). Promoting Financial Inclusion Through Central Bank Digital Currency: An Evaluation of Payment System Viability in India. *The Australasian Accounting Business and Finance Journal, 17*(1), 176–204. https://doi.org/10.14453/aabfj.v17i1.14

Gadia, P. J. (2022, November 5). Digital Rupee Launched—Its Impact on Indian Economy and Banks. *bfsi.economictimes.indiatimes.com*. https://bfsi.economictimes.indiatimes.com/blog/digital-rupee-launched-its-impact-on-indian-economy-and-banks/95307830

Ganne, E. (2018). *Can Blockchain Revolutionize International Trade?* wto.org. Retrieved September 25, 2023, from https://www.wto.org/english/res_e/publications_e/blockchainrev18_e.htm

Haque, M. A., & Shoaib, M. (2023). *E-rupee—The Digital Currency in India: Challenges and Prospects*. ScienceDirect.

Heckel, M., & Waldenberger, F. (2022). *The Future of Financial Systems in the Digital Age: Perspectives from Europe and Japan*. Springer Nature.

Morbale, R., Patil, B., & Nrip, N. (2022). Effect of Cryptocurrency on Indian Economy—An Overview of Current Status and Prospects. *Zenodo (CERN*

European Organization for Nuclear Research). https://doi.org/10.5281/zenodo.6653926

Naboulsi, N., & Neubert, M. (2018). Impact of Digital Currencies on Economic Development in Kenya. *Proceedings of the ACBSP Region 8 Fall Conference 2018,* 368–387.

Rodeck, D. (2023). Digital Currency: The Future of Your Money. In M. Adams (Ed.), *Forbes.* Retrieved September 25, 2023, from https://www.forbes.com/advisor/in/investing/cryptocurrency/digital-currency/#:~:text=With%20digital%20currency%2C%20transactions%20work,More%20efficient%20government%20payments

Rose, C. (2015). The Evolution of Digital Currencies: Bitcoin, a Cryptocurrency Causing a Monetary Revolution. *International Business & Economics Research Journal, 14*(4), 617. https://doi.org/10.19030/iber.v14i4.9353

Tan, L., & Xue, L. (2021). Research on the Development of Digital Currencies under the COVID-19 Epidemic. *Procedia Computer Science, 187*, 89–96. https://doi.org/10.1016/j.procs.2021.04.037

Thakker, M. (2023, May 2). E-rupee and its Impact on the Indian Economy. *The Times of India.*

Thakur, S. D., Varma, A. R., & Hake, M. D. (2022). Regulation of Cryptocurrency in India: Issues and Challenges. *Journal of Positive School Psychology, 6*(5), 8921–8929. https://journalppw.com/index.php/jpsp/article/download/9707/6356/11347

Zhang, T. (2020, October 30). New Forms of Digital Money: Implications for Monetary and Financial Stability. *"Financial Risks, Innovation and Inclusion in a Post-COVID" World.* CAFIN Webinar Series. https://www.imf.org/en/News/Articles/2020/10/30/sp103020-new-forms-of-digital-money

CHAPTER 9

Digital Currency: The Role of World Trade with Reference to India

Krati Sethi and Manas Roy

Introduction

Due to the recent endemic consequences of "COVID-19", changing trade dynamics, and prevalent industrial improvements, traditional banking and financial systems are undergoing global transformation. The Indian government has emphasised the usage of digital space and digital money since its manifestation in the year 2016 with the introduction of the "Digital India" project. With the launch of "Central Bank Digital

K. Sethi (✉)
Department of Economics, School of Humanities and Social Sciences, Manipal University Jaipur, Jaipur, Rajasthan, India
e-mail: sethikrati16@gmail.com

M. Roy
Department of Economics, Faculty of Management Studies, Marwadi University Rajkot, Rajkot, Gujarat, India
e-mail: manas.roy@marwadieducation.edu.in

R. Aneja and R. Dygas (eds.), *Digital Currencies in The New Global World Order*, https://doi.org/10.1007/978-981-97-4810-5_9

Currency",[1] in this fiscal year, the Central Bank of our country is considering passionately launching the country's own CBDC, which would limited to be used only by wholesale enterprises at first (Kaur, 2023).

The Central Bank of our country is about to implement the country's "central bank digital currency", CBDC, which is categorised as "money in the digital form of legal tender". These currencies will be accepted as payment, can be exchanged with fiat money, and be recognised as a safe place to save money. A different name for CBDC is "digital rupee".

The CBDC introduced by the central bank of our country, sometimes referred to as "the digital" or "e rupee", is a kind of currency in the modern era that isn't all that dissimilar from the banknotes that are now in use. The sole distinction is that more transactions and exchanges for the digital rupee are anticipated (Haque & Shoaib, 2023). As a result, central bank digital money is comparable to a fiat currency; the central bank will issue and govern digital legal tender that is based on blockchain technology.

Key Drivers of CBDC

The drivers for CBDC are aspiration for speedier repayments, accelerated digitisation higher "risk mitigation" for "clearing and settlement" and thus urgency for CBDCs at the universal level. Better domestic and international value transfers as well as financial inclusion are also in demand. In addition, to using CBDC to influence not only monetary but also fiscal policy, four important forces have been classified causing the Central Bank in general to assess CBDC (Deloitte, 2022; Whited et al., 2022).

- Central banks must once again be at the forefront of money creation and trust.
- CBDCs offer tremendous potential to improve the financial system's efficiency.
- Increasing financial inclusion and access.
- The improvement of monetary and fiscal policies.

[1] Commonly acknowledged as CBDC announced by Finance Minister, Nirmala Sitharaman in the Union Budget.

Review of Literature

Kaur (2019) studied the fintech revolution, which will have an impact on many domains, including payment and settlement systems and services, including digital currencies as a key component. Although the idea of digital currency is currently less widespread, it will eventually appear and disrupt the current systems and processes (how). India's attitude towards cryptocurrencies hasn't been positive from the beginning. The adoption of the blockchain is required, either by necessity or choice, and it will dominate economies around the world in the years to come.

Auer et al. (2021) has found that as far as public service is meant for academics, decision-builders as well as the common people, the publication also includes an innovative CBDC "project index, speech, search interest scores", and other relevant data. Several economists were shortly raised the issue of CBDCs due to the growing interest in them. Central banks of different countries also recognise CBDC since it has a "direct cash-like claim on the central bank", but with all customer-facing activities being handled by the private sector.

Das (2022) analysed that as the world develops, technological intervention is causing maintenance and methods of functioning throughout commerce to become digital. With more cutting-edge payment systems being developed, the globe is now on the verge of beginning a unique chapter in investment, which comprises the digitalisation of cash serving as initial steps throughout the transition. These days, central banks are creating their own "digital currencies".[2] The valid digital currency of our country would be the mirror of either current private company-organised "electronic wallets", which is mostly likely to become unveiled by the beginning of 2023.

Ferriare (2021), found that foreign digital money was to largely replace current domestic currency means of payment or to offer a connection with the central bank of money in an increasingly digitalisation of the economy. The main reason for releasing a digital euro is not to support the euro's international function. But if the use of a digital euro in cross-border payments were permitted—a decision that has yet to be made—this would also have effects on the euro's standing internationally.

Bennet et al. (2022) found that the most important national economies are likely to be affected by CBDCs, a quickly evolving and

[2] Often known as CBDCs or central bank digital currencies as already discussed.

inevitable innovation, in the next 12 to 24 months, according to analysis. Depending on how it assesses the objectives of CBDCs, market maturities, and pertinent local factors, each jurisdiction will probably make sovereign decisions about the issuance and design of CBDCs. To provide a safer, "risk-free digital medium of exchange, store of value and unit of account", CBDCs are essential with the progress of digitisation with the invention of globalisation. Monetary authorities, as well as other financial service providers, must develop their strategy to combat the impact of this new kind of "asset class" which will have their "own balance sheets, customer value propositions" to reap the advantages it passes in terms of "atomic transactions" and minimising "settlement risks".

Objectives

- To study the conception of digital currency
- To understand the major drivers of CBDC
- To differentiate between digital and cryptocurrencies
- To analyse the role of CBDC in international trade

Methodology and Data Sources

A review organised by the "Bank for International Settlements" (BIS) in the year 2021 announced that 86 per cent of central banks were actively investigating the possible outcome of CBDC, 60 per cent were testing the technology, and 14 per cent were running leading projects. A centralised digital currency is being developed by more than 91 nations, accounting for more than 90% of global GDP. India is still developing its own digital money.

This study looks into the notion of digital currency and key drivers of central bank digital currency (CBDC). The present study attempts to clarify theoretically what digital money means, its differences with cryptocurrencies the reason behind its recent experience with such a boom in popularity and its importance in international trade.

Benchmarking throughout the globe and advancements in the Asia Pacific markets

The majority of regulators around the world have made steps to start their journey with CBDC by either interacting with commerce and business professionals through investigating various miniatures or already in an investigating state. Few nations in the world[3] have already started operating CBDC.

Some of the active initiatives around the WORLD in terms of CBDC are shown in the graphic below (Fig. 9.1):

The growing number of instances of "retail and wholesale CBDC projects" can be seen from the research work of various researchers. For example, it can be understood that there seems to be a significant improvement as well as growing instances for CBDC throughout the globe from 2016 to 2020. It is also seen that more communications about the implementation procedure of CBDCs from late 2018 (Auer et. al., 2021).[4]

Reason for significance of CBDC for World Trade

- Fundamental economic reasons determine a currency's appeal on a global scale and digitalisation is unlikely to change these dynamics. Examples of such determinants include the scale of the issuing economy in terms of international trade and finance, the soundness of economic policies, the depth and liquidity of financial markets, and the complacency in the use of foreign currencies.
- However, characteristics particular to digital payment methods may make a CBDC more widely adopted abroad. One of these aspects would be a claim on the "balance sheet of the central bank" of issuance or CBDC. Due to this, both domestic users and international retail trade businesses may find it more appealing. as a store of value, that is as CBDC units maintained in an electronic wallet for

[3] Which includes countries like Cambodia and the Bahamas.

[4] **Source:** "The classification is based on the authors' judgment. The score takes a value of (–1) if the speech stance was clearly negative or in case it was explicitly said that there was no specific plan at present to issue digital currencies. It takes a value of (+1) if the speech stance was clearly positive or a project/pilot was launched or was in the pipeline. Other speeches have been classified as neutral (Auer et al., 2021)".

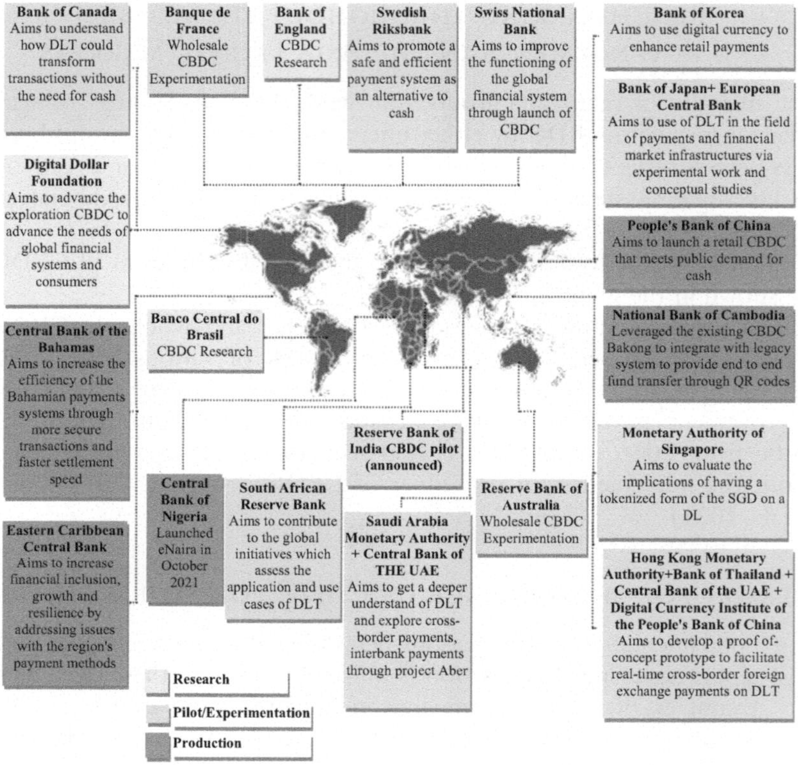

Fig. 9.1 Worldwide snapshot of the CBDC journey. *Source* Central Bank digital currencies by Deloitte (2022)

future payments. Safety helps to mitigate some of the risks associated with traditional payment systems for international sales of goods and services, such as counterparty risk in correspondent banking agreements.

- Accessibility to a CBDC may facilitate currency conversion in third-world countries with shaky financial systems and unstable currencies. It might make it simpler for these countries to "dollarise" their economies digitally, which would eventually result in the CBDC completely or partially replacing their national currencies for domestic transactions, savings, and ultimately, as the unit of account.

The currency's status on the world market would rise in exchange for a reduction in the degree of monetary policy autonomy in the impacted economies.

- Finally, it is important to consider the stability issues that could develop if a central bank does not provide a digital currency. One issue could be a situation where non-domestic providers predominate in domestic and cross-border payments including future possibilities for foreign digital juggernauts to supply fictitious currencies. In addition to potentially endangering the stability of the financial system this could also make consumers and businesses vulnerable to a small number of powerful providers which would hurt central banks' capacity to carry out their mandate for monetary policy and serve as lenders of last resort.

Difference between Digital currency and Cryptocurrency

The differences between digital currency and Cryptocurrency can be seen from the following Table 9.1.

A global perspective

It is seen that countries around the world's views on the adoption of digital currencies vary depending on their economic situation. Despite growing interest in digital currency, several countries have yet to adopt it due to issues like "security, technological accessibility, adaptability, legality, central bank role", etc. Very lean countries made changes to their legislation to address the legal issues raised by digital currency. For instance, e-money balances can be easily transferred or redeemed at par and are issued in the currency of the issuing central bank (EU Legislation, 2015).

The following list of selected countries describes the present state of digital currencies in those nations:

With the launch of the e-Dinar in 2015, a digital currency based on the blockchain concept, Tunisia set the bar for other countries. La Poste, Tunisia's national postal service, holds a licence from its national bank allowing it to create this e-currency tied to the local currency. Tunisians can manage their official government identifying documents digitally, pay their bills and paychecks, transfer remittances, purchase goods and

Table 9.1 Digital currency and cryptocurrency: A comparison

Basics	*Digital currency (CBDC)*	*Cryptocurrency*
TL/DR	Digital currency is the name or electronic form given to fiat money that is utilised in contactless transactions	It is the store of value that is secured by encryption
Regulation	The RBI of India is the regulating body for digital currency	The regulation of Cryptocurrencies is lacking and decentralised
Stability and usage	It is stable and globally accepted	Extremely volatile and still not acceptable extensively
Transactions	Acknowledge as trader and recipient of the financial institutions	Publicly available on a decentralised ledger
Encryption and blockchain usage	To secure banking apps, credit and debit cards, digital wallets, and other devices, a strong password is required	Encrypted for protection
Examples	Petro, M-pesa	Bitcoin

Source Sen Jhinuk (2022)

services, and acquire goods and services. It is incredibly helpful for nations like this where many fewer people have access to banking services. The main drawback is that this technique can only be used in Tunisia. Additionally, the government has no intentions to further develop it.

"The People Bank of China" also intends to launch its own Digi-currency to increase control over its financial system. According to the IPR Daily China Trade Publication, the bank holds 44 patents linked to blockchain as of August 2018. Digital currency, which will initially only be used for sending and receiving payments will be gradually introduced in China. To reduce the influence on monetary policy, it is anticipated that investment goods will be exempt from currency laws (Bloomberg News, 2018). China is contemplating deploying mobile wallet technology for digital payments.

Between 2020 and 2021, Russia intends to launch its national digital currency. The basic goal of this endeavour is to establish a trustworthy, non-dollar-based global payment system. The Russian Financial Market Committee intends to introduce an encrypted version of the fiat currency known as the "digital ruble".

Japan's cash-based economy makes it one of the world's top crypto-friendly countries. To enable customers to make payments using their cell phones and free cash transfers between users, several banks in Japan are creating digital currencies that are pegged 1:1 with the Japanese Yen (Kaur, 2019).

Hence, to summarise, the biggest description is to enhance this new concept to disseminate away from the boundary of every country. Currency, including precious metals and paper money, is essential for international trade and business. It will take some time when this kind of new form of cash will be universally endorsed. It means that "global trade", transitions to the "digital" era in terms of types of "digital currency" fight for reinstatement. There are three possible ways that digital currencies can be crucial to international trade:

a. Efficiency for cross-border payments: The degree to which the working hours of the sending and receiving organisations are similar, as well as whether they adhere to the same communications standards, frequently affect how quickly payments are processed. Digital currencies and decentralised ledgers can be used to send and receive money immediately and continually.

b. Supplementary credit information trade finance: SMEs generally lack a history of excellent financial standing with banks, which has a considerable negative impact on the "$1.7 trillion global trade financing gap". "Public ledgers of digital currencies" can be considered for payment of shares and financial transactions as well as "underwrite loans" for import as well as export. But to implement this, strong laws also need to be implemented (World Economic Forum, 2022).

c. Eliminate the problems with de-risking: It can make it difficult for nations with a reputation for having considerable "AML and CTF risks"[5] in international trade which is the cause for raising "transaction costs" not only for buyers but also for the sellers, particularly in Latin America and the Pacific Islands. Due to their digital setup, digital currencies have the potential to lower total AML and CTF compliance expenses. To reconnect local customers and businesses with foreign buyers and sellers while still adhering to AML and CTF regulations, digital currencies may offer an alternate payment method (World Economic Forum, 2022).

[5] Anti-money laundering (AML) and Capture the flag (CTF) is money laundering risk associated to International trade.

Fig. 9.2 SWOT analysis and RBI. *Source* RBI (2022)

SWOT Analysis

To assess the advantages, disadvantages, opportunities, and threats associated with a project or business initiative, a SWOT analysis is a strategic planning technique. One can accelerate the launch of your new business or assist yourself achieve your online marketing objectives with a solid SWOT analysis. This can be seen in Fig. 9.2.

Conclusion: Moving one step closer to a Cashless Economy

In conclusion, a more widely recognised electronic form of money is being promoted by central banks as the use of paper cash falls. As documented by the increasing usage of "private virtual currencies", there is an appeal from the public for "public digital currencies" to avoid the more harmful repercussions caused by such "private currencies". Users may benefit from CBDC's different advantages like "liquidity, scalability, acceptance, ease of transactions, anonymity" and "quick settlement". Similar to how UPI made it simpler for people to use digital currency globally, CBDC adoption will improve with the government's support infrastructure and become easier for people to use (IBEF, 2022).

The digital rupee can be utilised by financial institutions for quicker lending and payments in the global economy, as well as for programmed payments for subsidies. In the foreseeable future, a cashless economy may become more widespread (Bender, 2022). This might help the government achieve its goal of cashless transactions and benefit the banking sector. The value of the digital rupee could increase, which would be beneficial for cross-border transfers. A society without cash could emerge as a result of creating an interoperable environment.

References

Auer, R., Cornelli, G., & Frost, J. (2021, June 16). Rise of the Central Bank Digital Currencies: Drivers, Approaches, and Technologies CEMLA and Banco de la República Regional Conference on Payments and Market Infrastructures. https://www.bis.org/publ/work880.htm

Bender, M., Bennet, C., Chan, R., Frear, G., Lim, E. H., Mehrotra, M., Pagett, T., Shah, M., & Shetty, S. (2022). *Central Bank Digital Currencies: Building Block of the Future of Value Transfer*, 1–36. https://www2.deloitte.com/content/dam/Deloitte/in/Documents/financial-services/in-fs-cbdc-noexp.pdf

Bennet et al. (2021, June 23). BIS Annual Economic Report.

Bloomberg news. (2018, March 20). Making Sense of the World's Cryptocurrency Rules. https://www.bloomberg.com/news/articles/2018-03-19/is-this-legal-making-sense-of-the-world-s-cryptocurrency-rules#xj4y7vzkg

Das, B. (2022, October 8). Business Today. Cryptocurrency vs. CBDC vs. digital money: What's the Difference? https://www.businesstoday.in/latest/economy/story/cryptocurrency-vs-cbdc-vs-digital-money-whats-the-difference-349323-2022-10-08

Deloitte. (2022). Central bank digital currencies by Deloitte, Central Bank Digital Currencies, Building Block of the Future of Value Transfer.

EU Legislation. (2015). Revision of Directive (EU) 2015/2366 on Payment Services. https://www.europarl.europa.eu/thinktank/en/document/EPRS_BRI(2023)747447.

Ferriare. (2021, June 23). BIS Annual Economic Report.

Haque, M. A., & Shoaib, M. (2023). The Digital Currency in India: Challenges and Prospects. https://doi.org/10.1016/j.tbench.2023.100107

IBEF. (2022). https://www.ibef.org/blogs/rbi-s-digital-currency-and-its-significance

Kaur, J. (2023). Central Bank Digital Currency—The 'Digital Rupee' in India. *Economic and Political Weekly, 58*(1), 1–8.

Kaur, M. (2019). Digital Currency and its Implications for India. *The Management Accountant Journal, 54*(11), 64. https://doi.org/10.33516/maj.v54i11.64-67p

RBI. (2022). https://rbi.org.in/Scripts/PublicationReportDetails.aspx?UrlPage=&ID=1218

Sen, J. (2022, February 2). *Explained: The Difference Between Cryptocurrency and Digital Currency*. Business Today.

Whited, T. M., Wu, Y., & Xiao, K. (2022). Central Bank Digital Currency and Banks. *SSRN Electronic Journal, 2020*, 55–60. https://doi.org/10.2139/ssrn.4112644

World Economic Forum. (2022, September 21). Opinion: Why Crypto Businesses Need Anti-money Laundering Regulations, Financial and Monetary Systems. https://www.weforum.org/agenda/2022/09/why-crypto-businesses-need-anti-money-laundering-regulations/

CHAPTER 10

The Perceived Value of e-Rupee, A Next-Gen Trading Solution

Soumik Gangopadhyay, Saugat Ghosh, Suchana Roy, Saptaparni Dhol, and Aryan Deb

Introduction

The nation's fiduciary currency, the e-Rupee (e), is distributed digitally by the central bank. The Reserve Bank of India (RBI) has created the Central Bank Digital Currency (CBDC), which is a tokenized digital counterpart of the Indian Rupee (e-Rupee) (Moneycontrol.com, 2022). A proposal for the Digital Rupee was made in January 2017; it was subsequently introduced on 1 December 2022 (PIB, 2023). The blockchain distributed-ledger technology is used by Digital Rupee. It will be uniquely

S. Gangopadhyay (✉) · S. Roy · S. Dhol · A. Deb
Institute of Engineering & Management (UEM-K), Kolkata, India
e-mail: gangopadhyaysoumik@gmail.com; soumik.gangopadhyay@iem.edu.in

S. Roy
e-mail: suchana.roy@iem.edu.in

S. Ghosh
XBS, St. Xavier's University, Kolkata, India
e-mail: saugat.ghosh@sxuk.edu.in

R. Aneja and R. Dygas (eds.), *Digital Currencies in The New Global World Order*, https://doi.org/10.1007/978-981-97-4810-5_10

recognizable and regulated by the Central Bank, much as banknotes, allowing the RBI to have its liability. Both online and offline accessibility are planned (Bhardwaj, 2022). To serve financial institutions for cross-bank settlements, RBI introduced the Digital Rupee for Wholesale (e-W) and Digital Rupee for Retail (e-R) (PIB, 2022). The primary goal of the introduction of the Digital Rupee is to eliminate the about 5,000 crore expense of security printing on physical money (Kaushal, 2022).

The ability to lessen the concentration of liquidity and credit risks in payment systems that are mediated by commercial banks will come from sources outside of the commercial banking sector (Priyadarshini, 2022). CBDC will be an extra payment option for users and is not intended to replace current payment methods, as stated by RBI. The main goals of CBDC are to promote and assist the developing digital economy, lower the cost of managing paper money, provide a reliable monetary payment system, and increase financial inclusion. To foster user confidence, safety, liquidity, settlement finality, and integrity, the digital rupee may be converted into paper money without losing any value. It will also appear on the RBI balance sheet. To lessen the danger of bringing new technologies into the currency market, To introduce the Digital Rupee more smoothly, RBI will develop its features to be more similar to those of paper money. The official launch might take place at any moment (Money Control, 2022).

Experts expressed confidence in the proposal as the Reserve Bank of India (RBI) began its pilot trial of the e-rupee in the wholesale segment (e-W), saying that it may change India's cross-border payment system and push the national currency onto the international dais. The internationalization of the rupee has both benefits and drawbacks, but it is undoubtedly a crucial and indispensable step towards India becoming a significant economic force. The managing director of financial solutions at FIS, India, claimed that CBDC will help the Indian currency become more globally recognized. In the Web 3.0 economy, "E-rupee might provide an alternative' regulatory compliant' for value-exchange". Cross-border payments made through CBDC are transparent and quick, and provide small businesses and the Indian economy a chance to advance towards their objectives more quickly while promoting financial inclusion, global commerce, and economic progress.

Objectives

The following are the objectives of our endeavour:

- To comprehend the preference for digital transactions.
- To comprehend the variables affecting the transformation.
- To determine the causes of the change in payment methods.

Review of Literature

The Perceived Value of the Digital Transaction

Consumer adoption of new technology, such as digital currencies, is significantly influenced by perceived value. A customer's subjective evaluation of the advantages they derive from a good or service in comparison to its price is known as perceived value. Perceived value in the context of e-rupee may be quantified in terms of its practicality, security, accessibility, and cost-efficiency.

Perceived Objective of Digital Transaction

The variables affecting Indian customers' acceptance of digital payments have been the subject of several researches. According to research, Indian consumers' acceptance of digital payments was largely impacted by their perceptions of their utility, usability, and security. Additionally, the adoption of digital payments among Indian customers is greatly influenced by trust, convenience, and perceived risk. Digital exchanges have always been seen as cashless. It enables contactless payments as an extra feature (Karjaluoto et al., 2020), quick payments (Joshi, 2017), a clear and thorough history of transactions, and a greater degree of security (Dimitrova et al., 2022). By reducing processing costs and late payments, digital payment methods have improved accessibility compared to conventional cashless systems (Somasundaram, 2020). The adoption of any digital payment systems has been seen to vary with age (Chawla & Joshi, 2019). Because they are quick and simple to set up, digital payment systems provide for the reduction of carbon footprint (Tenhunen & Penttinen, 2010). The public has found other benefits, such as incentives (Garg & Kaur, 2019) and a minimal risk of theft (Sujith & Julie, 2017), to be highly practical, building a solid foundation and financial stability.

The efficiency of digital payment mechanisms has generally been excellent (Pal et al., 2018). Despite the numerous positive aspects of digital payment systems, the negative effects of overspending and challenges with internet accessibility persist over time and might cause payments to be banned during vital transactions (Hussain, 2022). Additionally, they are concerned about being exposed to cyber-attacks.

Perceived Subjective Value of Digital Transaction

The recent introduction of digital currency has made it more secure and suitable for private transactions. It has gained popularity among national policymakers because of its centralized control mechanism, controlled supply and control over recipients, flawless cross-border transactions, offline mode of transactions, the anonymity of transactions, reduced risk of illegal transactions, zero charge-of-interest, easy recoverability, and least risk of cyber-attacks (Darbha & Arora, 2020; Ginneken et al., 2019; Miedema,2020; Miedema et al., 2020; Priyadarshini & Kar, 2021; Soderberg et al., 2022; Tian, 2023). More e-transactions are preferred due to the possibility of direct money transfer (Bossu, 2020), low transaction cost, instant settlement (Ahmat, 2017), rise in e-commerce (Didenko & Buckley, 2018), ease of change in large volumes (Bord, 2017), public confidence (Hussain, 2022), low implementation cost (Morales-Resendiz et al., 2021), network effects, lack of public education, etc. Overall, it facilitates a lack of counterfeiting, easy tracing, and free convertible like cash, and may lead to innovation and competition in payment systems.

Existing literature suggests that the value of e-transactions falls into the following categories of mass perception: Perceived benefit Perceived ease of use Perceived control Perceived usefulness Perceived risk Perceived behavioural control. However, the most promising area of research is to look at the variables or factors that motivate people to choose e-rupees. Rationale changes in a product are considered to be risky. Relative advantage is a subjective concept. Attitude towards the changing environment helps in the diffusion of product innovation. (Hoffman, 2005).On the other, relative advantage is a subjective term. Attitude towards the change in environment helps in the accomplishment of diffusion of product innovation (Bhuian et al., 2007). Normative beliefs and expectations have a higher impact on this (Mannan et al., 2017). Mediated influence of perceived social norms and behavioural control also influence purchase behaviour (Ajzen, 2015). Based on the literature review, it is imperative to mention that the relationship between attitude and intention to adopt e-rupee is profound. The effect of awareness (availability and accessibility) on attitude needs to be investigated, which was hypothesized to be neglected in previous studies.

So, this study proposed a comprehensive framework to identify the dynamics of diffusion and adoption issues of the e-rupee from four different perspectives, namely, Value, Belief, Expectation, and Attitude. Attitude towards the e-rupee is principally controlled by perceived future value (Future 1), Perceived availability (Awareness 1), Perceived Accessibility (Awareness 2), and Perceived ease of use (P. Ease of use). On the other, the intention of adopting the e-Rupee is controlled by Technical knowledge (Sub Norm 3), Fear of failure (Sub Norm 4), Social trend (Social value), and Perceived Behavioural Control (B. Control). The current study is an attempt to explore the association between attitude and intention of adoption. Technical knowledge (Sub Norm 3) and fear of failure (Sub Norm 4) have not been considered or left implicit by previous researchers. From the review of literature, the following research gaps have been identified:

H1: Attitudes regarding e-Rupee drives intention to the adoption of e-Rupees are profoundly connected. The influence of awareness (availability and accessibility) on attitude has to be explored which has been ignored by previous studies as implied.

H2: Technical knowledge and fear of failure positively influence the intention of adopting the e-rupee.

Research Methodology

This research is based on both secondary and primary data. Secondary data has been collected from different journals and websites.

Primary data has been collected in the form of questionnaires from the traders (whole sellers of Fast Moving Consumer Goods). It contains close-ended questions that have collected the reflection of the respondents on a five-point Likert scale anchored as Strongly agree, Agree, Undecided, Disagree, and Strongly disagree, which are coded as 5 4 3 2 1. The survey questionnaire has been developed based on a literature review and expert input. The questionnaire includes parameters in connection with the perceived value of digital transactions, digital literacy, business size, frequency of using e-payment methods, and other demographic information. Respondents have been chosen equally from four parts of Kolkata, India as a sample. So, a total of 327 responses have been received which have been considered for final selection. Primary data collected by such a technique has been coded and standardized. The data has been analyzed by using Excel and other statistical software.

Findings and Discussions

Descriptive Statistics

Among the 327 respondents, 59.3% are male, 39.8% are female and 0.9% belong to the others category. It has been observed that 15% of the respondents belong to the age group of 18–20 years, 46.8% belong to 20–22 years, 22.3% are between 22 and 24 years, and 24–26-year-olds contribute 15.9%. The distribution of education qualifications of the respondents also showed a different pattern. While 75.2% are graduates, 12.8% are postgraduate, 7.6% have passed high school and 4.3% have done diploma. We can see that 68.2% are students, 19.6% belong to the service sector, 3.1% are self-employed, 7.3% have their own business and 1.8% account for unemployed. 48% of the respondents have a monthly household income of above 75,000, 29.1% have a monthly household income of 50,000 to 75,000, 15.9% have between 25,000 and 50,000, and 7% account for less than 25,000. 46% people out of the 327 respondents agree with the statement "e-Rupee is the best method of future transaction", 23% strongly agree, 24% remain undecided, 0.001% disagree and 0.03% strongly agree. Hence, we can conclude that most of the respondents agree with the statement. E-rupee is the replacement of all the existing modes of transaction. When the retailers were inquired regarding this then, 30% of respondents chose to remain undecided, 25% agreed, 14% strongly agreed, 22% disagreed, and 7.95% strongly disagreed.

Inferential Statistics

Findings of Confirmatory Factor Analysis

To evaluate the discriminant validity and the reliability of the constructs, CFA has been administered. To assess the model fit, three fit indexes were

Table 10.1 Findings of CFA

Measure	*Estimate*	*Threshold*
CMIN	14.782	–
DF	9	–
CMIN/DF	1.642	Between 1 and 3
CFI	0.980	> 0.95
SUMMER	0.037	< 0.08
RMSEA	0.044	< 0.06
PClose	0.541	> 0.05

Source Author's analysis

used. These fit indexes are the Comparative Fit Index (CFI), Standardized Root Mean Square of Residuals (SRMR), and Root Mean Square Error of Approximation (RMSEA). According to Hu and Bentler (1999) a CFI value of 0.95 or more, an SRMR value of 0.08 and less, and an RMSEA value of 0.06 and less, indicate a good fit. According to Harrington (2009) and Brown (2015), for a good fit, the value of CFI should be 0.9 or more, SRMR should be < 0.06, and the value of RMSEA should be < 0.06. The findings are as follows (Table 10.1).

The findings show that the value of CMIN/DF is 1.642, which is between 1 and 3, and according to Hu and Bentler (1999) Harrington (2009), and Brown (2015), is excellent. The CFI value is 0.980, which is > 0.95, the acceptable limit. The value of SRMR is 0.037, which is < 0.08 and the RMSEA value is 0.044, which is < 0.06. Thus, this could be stated that according to Hu and Bentler (1999) Harrington (2009), and Brown (2015), the model is fit. Besides this, according to Hair, Hult et al. (2014), a good model should also have Goodness-of-fit Index (GFI), Tucker and Lewis (1973) Index (TLI), and Confirmatory Fit Index (CFI) values > 0.9. The findings show that the GFI value is 0.989, the TLI value is 0.939 and the CFI value is 0.980. All the values are greater than 0.9 and thereby confirm the model fit.

Findings Related to Convergent Validity

Convergent validity, according to Hair, Sarstedt et al. (2014) is a measure of the degree of the consistency in which a single construct could be assessed by several items. According to Urbach and Ahlemann, (2010), Convergent Validity represents a degree where a construct is represented by specific indicators. According to Hair, Sarstedt et al. (2014), these indicators comprise factor loading of the constructs, values of Composite Reliability (CR), and the values of Average Variance Extracted (AVE). Hair, Sarstedt et al. (2014) also suggested the values of these indicators. According to Norris and Myres (2013), factor loading of 0.57 and above suggests a decent association between the latent factors and their constructs. According to Nunnally and Bernstein (1994b), the value of CR should be greater than 0.7. Segars (1997) suggested that the value of AVE should be 0.5 or higher. Internal consistency of the factors is tested by Cronbach's alpha and according to Schmitt (1997), the acceptable value of Cronbach's alpha is 0.7 or above. It was further suggested by Hair, Sarstedt et al. (2014) that to confirm the criteria of convergent validity, the values of Composite Reliability should be greater than the respective AVE values. The following are the findings of Convergent Validity (Table 10.2).

The findings show that all the factor loadings are greater than 0.57 and thereby satisfy the criteria given by Norris and Myres (2013). All the values of Composite Reliability (CR) are found to be higher than 0.7 and thus satisfy the conditions given by Nunnally and Bernstein (1994a). All the values of Average Variance Extracted (AVE) are higher than 0.5 and they meet the requirement set by Segars (1997). Finally, all the values of Cronbach's alpha are greater than 0.7, which satisfies the standard set by Schmitt (1997). Therefore, H1 and H2 can't be rejected.

Table 10.2 Factor loadings, Cronbach's alpha, composite reliability, and average variance extracted

Latent variable	*Indicator variable*	*Factor loading*	*Cronbach's alpha*	*Composite reliability*	*AVE*
Attitude	Future	0.744	**0.782**	**0.738**	**0.523**
	Awareness 1	0.745			
	Awareness 2	0.670			
	P. Ease of Use	0.621			
Intention	Sub Norms 1	0.615	**0.739**	**0.716**	**0.511**
	Sub Norms 2	0.928			
	Social Value	0.620			
	B Control	0.681			

Source Author's analysis

Table 10.3 Master validity testing

	CR	*AVE*	*MSV*	*MaxR(H)*	*Value*
Value	0.738	0.528	0.02	1.102	**0.763**

Source Author's analysis

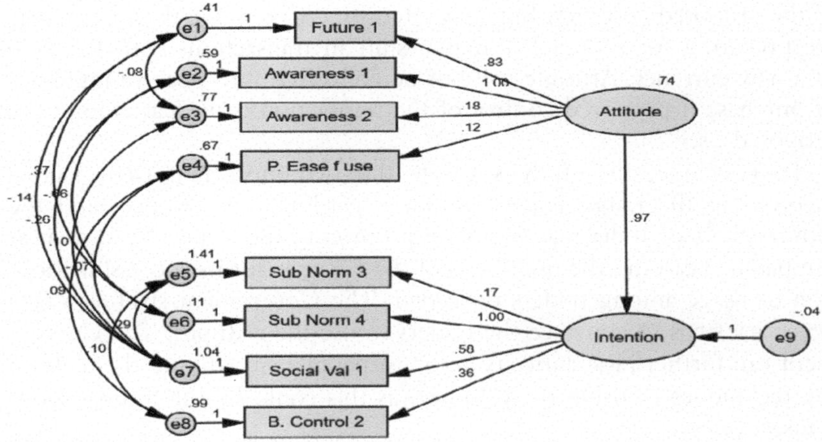

Fig. 10.1 The derived model (*Source* Primary data analysis by authors)

Model Validity Measures
The model validity is measured by checking the values of the master validity of the model. The values of Overall CR, AVE, and MSV are checked for checking the Master Validity. The findings are as follows (Table 10.3).

The thresholds are taken from Hu, L. and Bentler, P.M. (1999) and according to the master, the validity table shows no validity concern (Fig. 10.1).

Conclusion

Digital payments are shaping the e-commerce industry in ways more than one. As both a business owner and a customer, it is pretty much expected of traders to have online payment options. Though it is mainly considered to be advantageous for many obvious reasons, online payments have their own set of disadvantages that one to be aware of. After all, in today's digital world, every convenient feature comes with a bit of risk! With proper precautions and management, one can overcome most of these disadvantages. Also, any digital advancement faces a value crisis.

The study has emanated the critical influence of fear psychosis of failure of transaction of e-Rupee and doubt regarding the technical knowledge of the proposed currency. But, it is interesting to observe that the traders are preparing for a digital-to-digital shift in transactions with the help of a new currency. Attitude will not be converted into positive intention of purchase if perceived control of the transaction is unclear among the proposed user.

To conclude, the study suggests the two most important factors involved in the judgement of people regarding the e-Rupee, and the Government of India may focus on promoting the same. An awareness campaign regarding the usefulness of the e-Rupee for its successful adoption of usage among traders is needed. The Government shall also take necessary steps to convince the traders to use the e-Rupee. The Government can further raise curiosity amongst people and educate them about the techniques of using the e-Rupee, as this could be the future of our transactions.

References

Ahmat, N., & Bashir, S. (2017). Central Bank Digital Currency: A Monetary Policy Perspective. *Bank Negara Malaysia Central Bank of Malaysia Staff Insights, 11*, 1–7.

Ajzen I. (2015). Consumer Attitudes and Behaviour: The Theory of Planned Behaviour Applied to Food Consumption Decisions. *Rivista di EconomiaAgraria, Anno, LXX*(2), 121–138.

Anand, N. (2022, December 7). India Cenbank says Digital Currency Transactions to Stay Largely Anonymous. *Reuters*.

Aneja, R., Dygas, R. (Eds.). (2022). *Digital Currencies and the New Global Financial System* (1st ed., pp. 1–16). Routledge. https://doi.org/10.4324/9781003310365

Bahl, V. S., Rahman, F., Bailey, R., Krishnan, S., Deo, S., & Sontakke, N. (2020). *Internet Intermediaries and Online Harms: Regulatory*.

Bhardwaj, S. (2022). India's Central Bank Plans Graded Implementation Of CBDC. *Forbes India*. Retrieved 3 November 2022.

Bhuian, N. S., Joonas, K., & Ruiz, D. D. (2007). Environmental Behavior Consumers Expect From Key Stakeholders: An Empirical Study of Two NAFTA Countries. *Asia Pacific Management Review, 12*(6), 327–337.

Bordo, M. D., & Levin, A. T. (2017). *Central Bank Digital Currency and the Future of Monetary Policy (No. w23711)*. National Bureau of Economic Research.

Bossu W., Itatani M., Margulis C., Rossi A., Weenink H., & Yoshinaga A. (2020). *Legal Aspects of Central Bank Digital Currency: Central Bank and Monetary Law Considerations*. IMF Working Paper No. 20/254.

Brown, T. A. (2015). *Confirmatory Factor Analysis for Applied Research* (2nd ed.). Guilford Publications.

Central bank digital currency. (2023, June 30). Wikipedia. https://en.wikipedia.org/wiki/Central_bank_digital_currency

Chadha, S. (2021, December 30). Explained: How India Is Outpacing the World in Digital Payments. *The Times of India*. https://timesofindia.indiatimes.com/business/india-business/explained-how-india-is-outpacing-the-world-in-digital-payments/articleshow/88580555.cms

Chavda, V. (2018). An Empirical Study on Factors Affecting Consumer Adoption of Mobile Payments in Rural Areas. *Sankalpa, 8*(1), 64–71.

Chawla, D., & Joshi, H. (2019). Consumer Attitude and Intention to Adopt Mobile Wallet in India–An Empirical Study. *International Journal of Bank Marketing, 37*(7), 1590–1618.

Darbha, S., & Arora, R. (2020). Privacy in CBDC technology (No. 2020–9). Bank of Canada.

Delhi, PIB (2022, December 12). "PIB press release".pib.

Didenko, A. N., & Buckley, R. P. (2018). The Evolution of Currency: Cash to Cryptos to Sovereign Digital Currencies. *FordhamInt'l LJ, 42*, 1041.

Dimitrova, I., Öhman, P., & Yazdanfar, D. (2022). Barriers to Bank Customers' Intention to Fully Adopt Digital Payment Methods. *International Journal of Quality and Service Sciences, 14*(5), 16–36.

Garg, S., & Kaur, S. (2019). A comparative study: Digital payment modes vs. cash on delivery. *ZENITH International Journal of Multidisciplinary Research, 9*(5), 40–45.

Ginneken, C. L. (2019). *Settlement of Cross-border Transactions through Central Bank Digital Currency (CBDC): Analysis from a Risk Management perspective*.

Hair, J. F., Hult, G. T. M., Ringle, C. M., & Sarstedt, M. (2014). *A Primer on Partial Least Squares Structural Equation Modeling (PLS-SEM)*. Sage Publication.

Hair, J. F., Sarstedt, M., Hopkins, L., & Kuppelwieser, V. (2014). Partial Least Squares Structural Equation Modelling (PLS-SEM): An Emerging Tool in

Business Research. *European Business Review, 26*(2), 106–121. https://doi.org/10.1108/EBR-10-2013-0128

Harrington, D. (2009). *Confirmatory Factor Analysis*. Oxford University Press.

Hoffman, K. (2005). *Marketing Principles and Best Practices*. Mason: Thomson/South-Western. https://doi.org/10.1080/10705519909540118

Hu, L. T., & Bentler, P. M. (1999). Cutoff Criteria for Fit Indexes in Covariance Structure Analysis: Conventional Criteria versus New Alternatives. *Structural Equation Modeling, 6*, 1–55.

Hussain, H. (2022). Central Bank Digital Currencies: Reinforcing Public Trust. *Amsterdam LF, 14*, 21.

Immediate Payment Service. (2023, May 30). Wikipedia. https://en.wikipedia.org/wiki/Immediate_Payment_Service

Internet. www.thehindubusinessline.com/money-and-banking/canara-bank-introduces-upi-interoperable-digital-rupee-mobile-app/article67216466.ece, www.npci.org.in/what-we-do/upi/product-statistics

Joshi, M. (2017). *Digital Payment System: A Feat Forward of India*. Research Dimension (ISSN: 2249–3867).

Kameswaran, V., & Hulikal Muralidhar, S. (2019). Cash, Digital Payments and Accessibility: A Case Study from Metropolitan India. *Proceedings of the ACM on human-computer interaction, 3(CSCW)*, 1–23.

Karjaluoto, H., Shaikh, A. A., Leppäniemi, M., & Luomala, R. (2020). Examining Consumers' Usage Intention of Contactless Payment Systems. *International Journal of Bank Marketing, 38*(2), 332–351.

Kaushal, Teena Jain (2022, November 1). RBI's Digital Rupee Pilot Launch Today: Here are 10 Things to Know. *Business Today*.

Kumar Harsh. (2022, November 4). Will RBI's CBDC Internationalize the Rupee? Here's What Experts Say. *OutlookIndia.com*. https://www.outlookindia.com/business/can-rbi-s-cbdc-take-rupee-globally-here-s-what-experts-say-news-234764

Kumari, J. M. (2021). Central Bank Digital Currency (CBDC) can Replace Notes and Coins in India. *Shanlax International Journal of Management, 8*(S1-Feb), 21–28.

Lee, Y., Son, B., Park, S., Lee, J., & Jang, H. (2021). A Survey on Security and Privacy in Blockchain-based Central Bank Digital Currencies. *J. Internet Serv. Inf. Secur., 11*(3), 16–29.

Mannan, B., & Haleem, A. (2017). Understanding Major Dimensions and Determinants that Help in Diffusion & Adoption of Product Innovation: Using AHP Approach. *Journal of Global Entrepreneurship Research, 7*, 12.

Miedema, E. T. (2020). Privacy and Digital Life. *Cross Currents, 70*(2), 159–199.

Miedema, J., Minwalla, C., Warren, M., & Shah, D. (2020). *Designing a CBDC for Universal Access (No. 2020–10)*. Bank of Canada.

Moneycontrol.com. (2022). https://www.moneycontrol.com/news/tags/central-bank-digital-currency.html/blogs/

Morales-Resendiz, R., Ponce, J., Picardo, P., Velasco, A., Chen, B., Sanz, L., Guiborg, G., Segendorff, B., Vasquez, J. L., Arroyo, J., & Hodge, A. (2021). Implementing a Retail CBDC: Lessons Learned and Key Insights. *Latin American Journal of Central Banking, 2*(1), 100022.

Nelson, B. (2018). Financial Stability and Monetary Policy Issues Associated with Digital Currencies. *Journal of Economics and Business, 100*, 76–78.

Norris, E., & Myers, L. (2013). Determinants of Personal Protective Equipment (PPE) use in UK Motorcyclists: Exploratory Research Applying an Extended Theory of Planned Behaviour. *Accident Analysis and Prevention, 60*, 219–230. https://doi.org/10.1016/j.aap.2013.09.002

Nunnally, J. C., & Bernstein, I. H. (1994a). *The Assessment of Reliability. Psychometric Theory, 3*, 248–292.

Nunnally, J. C., & Bernstein, I. H. (1994b). *Psychometric Theory* (3rd ed., p. 736). McGraw-Hill.

Pal, J., Chandra, P., Kameswaran, V., Parameshwar, A., Joshi, S., & Johri, A. (2018, April). Digital Payment and Its Discontents: Street Shops and the Indian Government's Push for Cashless Transactions. In *Proceedings of the 2018 CHI Conference on Human Factors in Computing Systems*. 1–13.

PIB. (2023). https://pib.gov.in/PressReleaseIframePage.aspx?PRID=1882883

Priyadarshini, D. (2022, November 4). UPI Powers India's Digital Transactions. RBI's Rupee is Compelling but must Argue Retail Use. *The Print*.

Priyadarshini, D., & Kar, S. (2021). *Central Bank Digital Currency (CBDC): Critical Issues and the Indian Perspective*. Institute of Economic Growth Working Paper, (444).

Reserve Bank of India—Annual Report. (n.d.). https://m.rbi.org.in/Scripts/AnnualReportPublications.aspx?Id=1322

Schilling, L. (2019, November 1). *Risks Involved with CBDCs: Cash, Privacy, and Information Centralization*. Privacy, and Information Centralization.

Schmitt, N. (1997). Vocabulary Learning Strategies. In D. N. Schmitt & M. McCarthy (Eds.), *Vocabulary: Description, Acquisition and Pedagogy* (pp. 199–227). Cambridge University Press.

Segars, A. (1997). Assessing the Unidimensionality of Measurement: A Paradigm and Illustration within the Context of Information Systems Research. *Omega-International Journal of Management Science, 25*, 107–121. https://doi.org/10.1016/S0305-0483(96)00051-5

Soderberg, G., Bechara, M., Bossu, W., Che, N. X., Davidovic, S., Kiff, J., Lukonga, M. I., Griffoli, M. T. M., Sun, T., & Yoshinaga, A. (2022, July 2). *Central Bank Digital Currency Behind the Scenes: Emerging Trends, Insights, and Policy Lessons*. Washington, DC: International Monetary Fund.

Somasundaram, M., & Litt, D. (2020). A Study On Perception Of Consumers Towards Digital Payment. *Mukt Shabd Journal, 9*(6), 2246–2255.

Sujith, T. S., & Julie, C. D. (2017). Opportunities and Challenges of E-payment System in India. *International Journal of Scientific Research and Management (IJSRM), 5*(09), 6935–6943.

Tenhunen, M., & Penttinen, E. (2010). Assessing the Carbon Footprint of Paper vs. Electronic Invoicing. *ACIS 2010 Proceedings*. 95.

Tian, S., Zhao, B., & Olivares, R. O. (2023). Cyber Security Risks and Central Banks' Sentiment on Central Bank Digital Currency: Evidence from Global Cyberattacks. *Finance Research Letters, 53*, 103609.

Tucker, L. R., & Lewis, C. (1973). A Reliability Coefficient for Maximum Likelihood Factor Analysis. *Psychometrika, 38*(1), 1–10. https://doi.org/10.1007/BF02291170

Urbach, N., & hlemann, Frederik. (2010). Structural Equation Modeling in Information Systems Research Using Partial Least Squares. *Journal of Information Technology Theory and Application (JITTA), 11*(2), 5–40. https://aisel.aisnet.org/jitta/vol11/iss2/2

CHAPTER 11

RBI's Digital Currency and Its Significance in Global Trade

Sunil Kumar and Rajender S. Godara

Introduction

The evolution of money and finance is deeply intertwined with the course of human history. Various factors, including technological advancements, shifts in societal preferences, economic growth, and the need for efficient tools to facilitate trade and transactions, have all played pivotal roles in shaping the nature of money and financial systems throughout the ages. This ongoing evolution continues to be a dynamic and complex process that reflects the changing dynamics of human society and the economy (Goetzmann, 2017).

Over time, monetary systems have evolved in response to changing needs and technological advances. In the eighteenth and nineteenth centuries, there was a shift from commodity money like gold and

Present Address:
S. Kumar · R. S. Godara (✉)
Department of Economics Mittal School of Business, Phagwara, Punjab, India
e-mail: godarars@gmail.com

S. Kumar
e-mail: kaindalsunil54@gmail.com

R. Aneja and R. Dygas (eds.), *Digital Currencies in The New Global World Order*, https://doi.org/10.1007/978-981-97-4810-5_11

silver coins to fiduciary money issued by both banks, which could be converted into specie. The twentieth century saw central banks taking a monopoly on currency issuance, replacing competitive commercial bank notes. Today, the rise of digital payments, including virtual currencies, is transforming monetary transactions, marking another significant shift in monetary history. These changes highlight the adaptability of monetary systems to evolving societal and economic demands. (Bordo, 2021).

The digitalization of money represents a revolutionary milestone in the history of currency. Technological advancements have given rise to various forms of digital money, such as digital currencies of a central bank of a country (CBDCs) like the Bahamian sand dollar, stablecoins like libra/diem, and virtual cryptocurrencies like bitcoin. These innovations are reshaping the landscape of finance and how we perceive and utilize money. In the last two decades, the scenario of market payments has changed due to the introduction of technology and its effect on the citizen's everyday lives can be seen clearly which was narrowly confined to the central bank, policymakers, and academia.

Currently, numerous countries have either initiated pilot projects or are in the planning stages of designating their digital currencies of the central banks (CBDCs). The Bahamas, an island nation, took the pioneering step by launching its digital currency known as the Sand Dollar. Several other countries, including Nigeria, China, Ghana, the USA, Jamaica, and the UAE, are actively working on the issuance of CBDCs, with some already commencing pilot programs. China, for instance, initiated its CBDC pilot in 2020, although it had been exploring the possibility of a digital currency as far back as 2014. This global movement underscores the growing importance of digital currencies in the modern financial landscape.

The rise of digital currencies like Bitcoin, along with blockchain and distributed ledger technology, has sparked substantial interest and the potential for significant impacts on the financial health of a nation's economy. Due to that reason central banks and public authorities of different nations worldwide have closely observed these developments and assessed their consequences.

These developments in technology first introduced card payment, internet banking, mobile payments, and now cryptocurrency. Cryptocurrencies have forced governments to think of central bank digital currency because they work on blockchain technology without any regulator, are highly volatile, and are also decentralized currency Anyone can trace payment so there is no security at all. If there is a huge number of transactions without any regulatory body this can be a direct threat to citizen's financial security as well as respected country's financial security. A recent survey revealed that in the third quarter of the financial year 2021–22, approximately 80% of surveyed banks in the country expressed their interest in exploring the feasible adoption of a digital currency of centralized bank (CBDC) (Kosse & Mattei, 2022). This statistic highlights the widespread consideration and discussion surrounding CBDCs within the banking sector, indicating their growing relevance in the financial landscape.

In this chapter, we will cover all issues regarding the benefits and concerns of CBDC in the present situation and how it can affect a nation's economy.

Central Bank Digital Currency (CBDC)

Recent technological advancements have steered the concept of digital currency, marking a significant development in the world of finance and payments. The rise of digital currencies has been prompted by private bodies aiming to emulate specific characteristics of physical cash in the digital domain. Digital currencies are available in diverse electronic formats, each offering distinct value propositions. These are available on numerous platforms, enabling real-time, peer-to-peer transactions without the need for in-person exchanges. This transformation in the way we handle currency has the potential to reshape the landscape of finance and transactions.

Central banks are actively investigating the possibility of declaring their digital currencies, commonly referred to as central bank digital currencies (CBDCs). These CBDCs would represent the obligations of the central bank and would be digitally generated and documented on either centralized or decentralized ledger systems. They would possess a value in an established unit of measurement and would be convertible into physical cash, commercial bank money, and other currency forms upon request by the holder at authorized institutions.

Just like physical cash, CBDCs would be considered legal tender. Although central banks currently provide digital money to specific entities, typically commercial banks and authorized financial intermediaries, in the form of reserve balances used for large-value transactions (wholesale), the real innovation would be their potential availability to the general public. If extended for use in everyday transactions by individuals and businesses, CBDCs would represent a major advancement. This "retail" CBDC would essentially transform state-issued cash into a digital form that is widely accepted and used throughout the entire economy (World Bank, 2021).

A survey carried out by the Bank for International Settlements (BIS) in 2020 indicated that a substantial 86% of nations are actively engaged in the development of their respective central bank-supported digital currencies. Additionally, 14% of these countries have reached the advanced stages of this development process. This global phenomenon indicates the widespread interest and commitment of nations to explore and potentially adopt Central Bank Digital Currencies (CBDCs) as a vital element of their monetary systems.

Origin of CBDC:

There has been a huge discussion about digital currency for several years and its origin can be traced in the recent developments linked to digital transaction and payment systems. Here are the brief historical developments of CBDC in the recent years.

Rise of Digital Payments: After the 2008 subprime crisis, there was a huge increase in digital payments through cards (Debit and Credit), Electronic fund transfer, and integrated mobile payment systems (IMPS) from the traditional way (Physical Cash and cheque) of payments. So financial institutions started researching the effect on the financial landscape of an economy.

Cryptocurrency: The emergence of Bitcoin in 2009 introduced the concept of decentralized digital currency working on blockchain technology without any approval from government authority it is non-legal tender money. It prompted discussions among centralized banks of different countries about the capacity of digital currencies.

In the year 2017, the Swedish Central Bank started the e-Krona project to decrease the demand for cash in the economy and started its national digital currency for domestic transactions. In the same year, the Bank of England initiated a discussion on the initiation of its digital currency central bank and its probable impact on the economy for researchers and policymakers. In 2014–20, The People's Bank of China (PBOC) initiated research and development efforts for its digital currency, referred to as the

Digital Currency Electronic Payment (DCEP). This move was prompted by the expanding use of mobile payments and the rise of cryptocurrencies.

Bank of International Settlements (BIS) and other institutions such as IMF, World Bank, European Union, and centralized banks of the different countries published several research papers, and reports exploring the potential benefits and challenges of CBDC, further fueling discussion.

The COVID-19 Pandemic declined the demand for cash, and the acceleration in digital payments prompted central banks to develop CBDC as a means of providing efficient, contactless payment and distributing the economic stimulus. The developments of the CBDC are ongoing as many central banks are researching and some have initiated the pilot project for efficient use and its effect on the citizen and its economy.

World Overview of CBDC

As of the current state of affairs, over 100 countries worldwide are actively engaged in the development of their digital currencies. These nations are taking various steps, ranging from researching the potential implications of Central Bank Digital Currencies (CBDCs) to initiating pilot projects, and some have even gone ahead to officially launch their CBDCs. (Atlantic Council, 2023) (Fig. 11.1).

In Asian countries, China and India are close to launching their CBDC both are in the pilot phase and are working on retail and wholesale cases. China is planning to launch digital Yuan and Indian CBDC will be digital Rupees in retail (e₹-R) and wholesale (e₹-W).

Trends in Digital Currency

In the wake of the COVID-19 pandemic, there has been a significant surge in the adoption of digital payment methods, including mobile payments and cryptocurrencies. Contactless transactions have gained prominence as people seek safer ways to conduct financial transactions. Among cryptocurrencies, Ethereum and Bitcoin have emerged as dominant players in terms of market capitalization, attracting a substantial number of investors worldwide.

According to (Statista, 2021), approximately 221 million active users were holding various types of cryptocurrencies. This substantial user base has prompted several economies to consider launching their digital

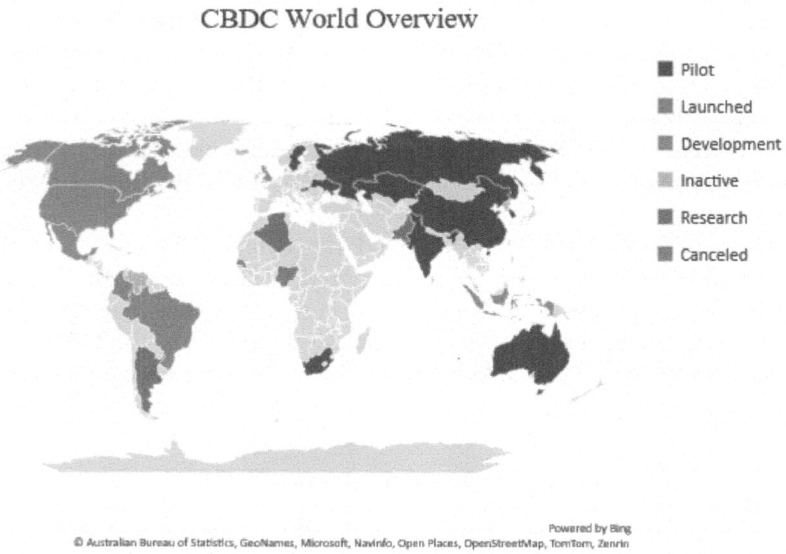

Fig. 11.1 Present scenario of Central bank digital currency worldwide (*Source* Atlantic Council CBDC Tracker [2023])

currencies, which would be backed and regulated by their respective central banks. The impetus behind this shift is a strong desire to safeguard monetary sovereignty and uphold financial stability in light of the rapidly changing financial environment and the growing prominence of digital currencies (Fig. 11.2).

Need of Central Bank Digital Currency

In today's modern economies, currency exists in the shape of money that is solely issued by the governing authority, usually the central bank, and is legally accepted as a valid means of payment. Specifically, paper currency serves as a symbolic form of money and essentially operates as a form of debt instrument. It represents a financial obligation for the central bank that authorizes it and serves as a valuable possession for individuals and entities who possess it.

Functions of money:

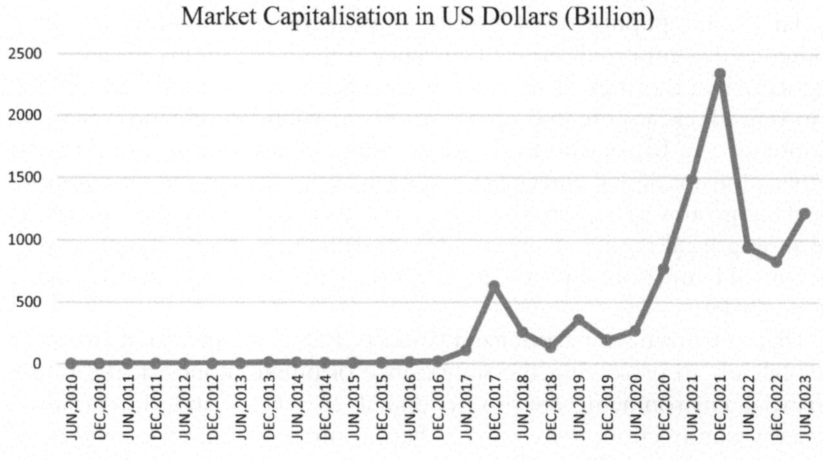

Fig. 11.2 Digital currency based on blockchain technology market capitalization from 2010 to 2023 (Half Yearly) (*Source* Statista (2023); Crypto market cap 2010–2023 | Statista)

1. Medium of Payment
2. Account Unit
3. Storage value

Payment systems are rapidly transforming. In the contemporary world, people expect fast and convenient payment methods that are accessible anytime and anywhere, reflecting the digitalization and convenience observed in various aspects of everyday life (Bech et al., 2017). Payment systems enabling almost instant person-to-person retail transactions are becoming more common worldwide.

Within the European Union, the majority of the money in circulation, specifically over 85%, is in the form of private commercial bank money. However, a well-functioning financial system typically includes a balance between both public and private money. The introduction of digital currency, particularly in the form of Central Bank Digital Currency (CBDC), could change this dynamic. CBDCs, issued by central banks, are poised to play a vital role in the financial system, potentially establishing the central bank as the cornerstone of the money supply (Brunnermeier & Landau, 2022; Panetta, 2021).

The rising popularity of private cryptocurrencies worldwide, often touted as decentralized forms of currency, poses a significant challenge for regulatory authorities. These cryptocurrencies, being non-legal tender, are viewed as a potential threat to the established financial system. Consequently, banks worldwide are engaging in discussions regarding the implications of digital currencies and have even initiated the formation of working groups to explore the concept of decentralized digital currencies becoming legal tender. This would essentially mean these digital currencies would function similarly to traditional fiat currency. Brunnermeier et al. (2019).

Digital Currency of centralized banks (CBDC) is anticipated to have a pivotal role in preserving the significance of public money in the future financial environment. As private digital currencies and decentralized systems gain traction, there's a risk that private digital money could overshadow it. Nonetheless, CBDC, being a form of public digital money administered by the central bank, is primarily designed to uphold the current status of public money as the principal unit of account and a dependable medium of exchange (Doepke & Schneider, 2017).

Privacy is undeniably a significant and worrisome domain in the contemporary digital era, where people frequently divulge their personal information for modest incentives or even in return for free services (Athey et al., 2017; Chen et al., 2021; Norberg et al., 2007). Researchers need to address the root cause of this problem which is involved in moral hazard, rationality, and weak decision-making so that market forces reach an optimum level of privacy protection. (Acquisti et al., 2016).

Increasing payment efficiency is indeed a crucial step in reducing the high costs associated with cross-border payments, particularly remittances. Private financial institutions often charge substantial fees for these transactions. (BIS, 2021), By establishing multi-level agreements and collaborations, countries can work together to ensure the efficient and secure use of CBDCs for cross-border payments. This not only reduces costs but also enhances financial inclusion and global economic integration. The introduction of cross-border CBDC agreements can create an environment conducive to competition in the financial intermediaries' landscape. This competition drives innovation, cost reduction, and improved services, ultimately benefiting consumers and businesses engaged in international transactions. (Auer et al., 2021).

Converting withdrawn funds into Central Bank Digital Currency (CBDC) during a bank crisis, like a run on the bank, has the potential to lower the expenses associated with handling the situation enhance the effectiveness of the central bank, and make banks more stable. (Keister & Monnet, 2022).

The commencement of CBDC diminishes the significant industry influence held by commercial private banks in the deposit market because it offers a choice for depositors. Consequently, banks are compelled to compete and increase deposit interest rates. Andolfatto (2020) and Chiu et al. (2022).

CBDC will offer consumers an alternative deposit platform, effectively addressing the moral hazard issue caused by information asymmetry where various banks have varying interest rates. The introduction of CBDC deposit rates will enhance welfare and promote greater consumer awareness. (Williamson, 2022).

CBDC will enhance liquidity transformation services, and both consumers and the central bank will be better equipped to manage adverse situations compared to commercial banks. (Fernández &Villaverde, 2021).

The commencement of CBDC has the potential to significantly advance the government's financial inclusion efforts, especially in developing nations where this has been a longstanding goal. (Boar & Wehrli, 2021).

Over the past few decades, numerous payment systems have emerged, all aimed at enhancing the feasibility of the general public. The Reserve Bank of India (RBI) has initiated various endeavors since the mid-1980s to integrate technology-driven solutions into the banking sector. The advancements in this aspect are depicted in the accompanying figure 11.3.

To address the digital currency issue and its impact on the economy, the Reserve Bank of India took a proactive measure by forming a working group in 2020. This group was tasked with deliberating on the implications and presenting recommendations for the introduction of Digital Currency of a centralized bank (CBDC). The key recommendations put forth by the working group are as follows:

1. Amending the RBI Act to incorporate "e₹" into the definition of "Bank Note."
2. The design of e₹ should be based on the needs of the country.
3. Firstly a pilot project should be introduced in phases for learning outcomes.

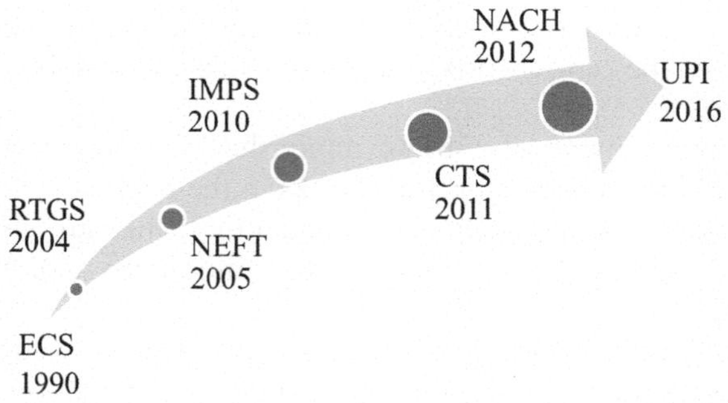

Fig. 11.3 Technological Initiative by RBI from 1990 to Present (*Source* RBI Working Paper on Digital Currency, 2022)

4. Implementation of e₹ should be in Retail as well as wholesale.
5. Further research on the privacy, traceability, and cost of each type of currency.

On based the above recommendations by the working group RBI has launched its digital currency in two variants, i.e., Retail (e₹-R) and Wholesale (e₹-W) (Table 11.1).

Table 11.1 Difference between retail and wholesale CBDC

CBDC (e₹)		
Features	*Retail CBDC (e₹-R)*	*Wholesale CBDC (e₹-W)*
Target Audience	Individual and Businesses	Financial institutions and banks
Transaction Scale	Lots of small value transaction	Fewer high-value transaction
Accessibility	Broad accessibility	Limited to authorized institutions
Privacy & Anonymity	User privacy and transaction transparency	Regulatory oversight
Technology & Infrastructure	User-friendly interfaces that are accessible	Robust infrastructure and connectivity

Source European Union Working Paper Series

CBDC in International Trade

Numerous theories emphasize the positive relationship between international trade and economic development. Prominent economists such as Barro and Sala-i-Martin (1995); Grossman and Helpman (1990, 1991); Romer (1993), among others, have underscored this connection that if a country is more openness to trade will adopt more technologies for the development of international trade, more comparative advantage in terms of trade in that country will increase the income and welfare of its citizen and hence economic development.

Trade openness encourages competition in domestic and international markets and allows countries to better exploit the potential benefits of increasing returns to scale and economies of specialization by expanding their market size, as highlighted by economists like Melitz and Ottaviano (2008) and Alesina et al. (2005).

For an increase in the size of international trade, a smooth payment system is a must. At present countries for payment of their net trade & remittance is mainly dependent on international payment operations on their global network which have mainly three major difficulties (BIS, 2021).

1. Intermediaries fees for these operations are generally high.
2. Not having any guarantee that funds will reach their destination.
3. Absence of interoperability between the payment systems and financial institutions to share the financial data.

Developing countries must augment their participation in global trade to improve the well-being of their citizens, and technological advancements such as the new digital payment system CBDC can be an effective means to achieve this goal. The introduction of CBDC can challenge the traditional dominance of the Dollar and Euro generally called the Dollarization and Euroization of the world. According to the Bank for International Settlement (BIS), more than 100 nations are in the process of initiating their central bank digital currency some are researching, some are in the pilot phase and few have launched.

The Indian Government has launched their pilot project for the Introduction of CBDC through their Centralised Bank (RBI) named Digital

Rupees (e₹) in two variants Retail and wholesale. Here our complete focus is on the effect of RBI's CBDC on international trade and cross-border payment.

International Trade and RBI's Digital Currency

Opportunities Associated with CBDC

1. **Reduced transaction cost**: Remittances sent to low- and middle-income countries combined $551 billion in 2019 (IMF, 2020). The fees incurred for these transactions averaged 6.8%, equivalent to $35 billion (World Bank, 2020). Trade payment settlement is generally done with commercial banking arrangements which involve many parties having different provisions for different currencies which increase the cost associated and take more time to process CBDC will help in reducing the transaction cost associated with international trade. Trade payment settlement in various currencies increases the risk and cost, (CPMI, 2018a, b; Bech & Holden, 2019). The introduction of CBDC for cross border will provide a single framework where the cost associated with these Payments will be low because there are no intermediaries in the transaction process and it will take less time.

2. **Currency Risk Mitigation:** For Developing countries like India, China, Brazil, etc., foreign exchange for international trade is a big concern. Countries have to maintain a forex reserve for their import payment in Dollars. When India has a very low forex reserve it can maintain 18 days of payment for their import and faced a huge balance of payment crisis which forced the Indian government to adopt IMF regulation. After the introduction of CBDC RBI doesn't have to maintain forex reserves in different foreign currencies because Indian businesses could transact in digital rupees which will reduce currency fluctuation risk.

3. **Streamlined Transaction:** The transaction cost can involve as many as five intermediaries in the SWIFT system for 20% of Euro-denominated cross-border payments (European Central Bank, 2020). With the present payment system international transactions take more time due to the involvement of many parties in the process. With Central Bank Digital Currency there will be no intermediaries due to CBDC-CBDC transactions of two different counties. This will simplify the international payment procedure.

4. Enhanced Transparency: A mobile central bank digital currency (m-CBDC) system has the potential to leverage innovative technologies for exploring new possibilities and addressing complexities that were previously inaccessible. This includes advanced monitoring, control, and segmentation within a distributed ledger framework. For example, CLS currently finalizes foreign exchange transactions within its internal records, while the ultimate net payments are executed through accounts maintained at each central bank, as detailed in Galati (2002). The introduction of a centralized digital currency by RBI could enable comprehensive transaction monitoring, which would be highly advantageous in preventing money laundering and tax evasion.

5. Currency Substitution: CBDCs and stablecoins have the potential to lead to currency substitution, often referred to as "dollarization." This can have significant implications for the monetary sovereignty and monetary policy capabilities of small, open economies, especially those with less robust monetary and fiscal institutions. This challenge already exists in the current landscape and would only be exacerbated by digitalization, as indicated by the IMF in 2020. (Brunnermier et al., 2019) argue that stablecoins such as Libra/Diem, which operate on extensive global networks and are fully backed by secure assets, could compete with official currencies. This aligns with the vision of currency competition outlined by (Hayek, 1976).

6. Financial Inclusion Abroad: CBDC will enhance the participation of small trader in international trade who have to depend on big business firms for payments, so it will make it easier for them to increase their trade operation when there is no chance of fraud and they have no worry about the fluctuation of national & foreign currency. These benefits will increase the overall financial inclusion abroad.

Risks Associated with CBDC

1. Currency exchange rate: At present, more than 100 nations are in the process of research for introducing their centralised digital currency after the introduction of their CBDC exchange rate risk could rise if the value of this currency can fluctuate continuously. This continuous fluctuation in digital currency can increase the cost and risk associated with international transactions.

2. Operational risk: CBDC will be based on Distributed Ledger technology (DLT) similar to blockchain technology. If any glitch happens on the platform this can affect the international transaction and what can be the consequences on an economy is not well understood till now.

3. Cross-border regulatory compliance: According to the World Trade Organization (WTO), there are various regulations governing international trade, including acts such as the Anti-money Laundering Act and Know Your Customer (KYC) regulations. CBDC must comply with these regulations but there is traceability is a quality of digital currency that can pose a serious threat to privacy and compliance.

4. Privacy Concerns: Digital currency is transparent and traceable based on decentralized blockchain technology, it can raise privacy concerns for individuals and businesses because anyone on the platform can access knowledge about the exact value of the transaction amount. So, making an equilibrium between privacy and transparency is a major challenge.

5. Legal framework and jurisdictional issues: what will be the legal status of CBDC in different jurisdictions, every country has its law, so making a single framework for all the nations is a challenge and often countries are involved in some issues other than trade like border, security, labor laws, migration then, what will be the estimated effect is also a challenge.

6. Interoperability: when different system abilities, technologies, and organisations are working together seamlessly and effectively that is called interoperability which is essential for introducing a single digital payment system globally but providing a single platform for all multilateral parties is a challenge.

7. Dependence of technology: India has a very effective digital infrastructure for introducing digital payment but there are so many nations whose citizens or businesses don't have access to advanced technology. For international trade, there should be technological equity in every partner country involved in trade activity.

8. Access and inclusion: Most LDC nations have limited digital infrastructure for the commencement of their centralized bank digital currency. Without CBDC, they are naturally excluded from the benefit of international trade and what will happen to their trade relation with CBDC countries?

Other than the upper concern of how they will work during geopolitical tensions between the nations, what will be the role of commercial banks and intermediaries in trade finance and will these efficiently manage the large volume of transactions because it is just the initial phase?

Conclusion

Around the world, many countries are actively involved in comprehensive research and analysis to assess the potential advantages and disadvantages of introducing a Central Bank Digital Currency (CBDC). This concerted effort reflects the critical importance of comprehending how CBDCs could reshape a nation's monetary economics, redefine the landscape of cross-border payments, and potentially influence international trade dynamics. At the international level, the G-20, a consortium of major economies, is actively exploring the feasibility of establishing a unified payment system designed to facilitate digital transactions on a global scale.

One development in this evolving landscape is the Reserve Bank of India's (RBI) recent initiation of a pilot program for introducing the digital rupee (e₹). This pilot program represents a significant step toward understanding the practical implications and consequences of CBDC within the unique context of India's dynamic economy.

The central focus of these research endeavors is to assess how CBDCs might positively or negatively impact a nation's monetary policies, financial stability, and overall economic landscape. This includes evaluating the potential to enhance payment systems, foster financial inclusion, and streamline cross-border transactions while also considering the implications for traditional banking institutions.

Moreover, researchers and policymakers are closely scrutinizing the potential trade outcomes resulting from the introduction of CBDCs. Questions abound regarding their influence on currency competition, global trade dynamics, and monetary sovereignty. In recent discussions, there have been comparisons made between CBDCs and stablecoins like Libra/Diem. If stablecoins are fully backed by secure assets, they might pose competition to official currencies, which aligns with the concept of currency competition proposed by Hayek.

As nations carefully scrutinize CBDCs, these endeavors signify a notable step forward in the modernization of the global payment system and in shaping the future of digital currencies on a global scale.

References

Alesina, A., Spolaore, E., & Wacziarg, R. (2005). Trade, Growth and the Size of Countries. In Philippe Aghion & Steven Durlauf (Ed.), *Handbook of Economic Growth* (Vol. 1, pp. 1499–1542). Elsevier

Acquisti, A., Taylor, C., & Wagman, L. (2016). The Economics of Privacy. *Journal of Economic Literature, 54*(2), 442–492.

Andolfatto, D. (2021). Assessing the Impact of Central Bank Digital Currency on Private Banks. *The Economic Journal, 131*(634), 525–540.

Aneja, R., Dygas, R. (Eds.). (2022). *Digital Currencies and the New Global Financial System* (1st ed., pp. 1–16). Routledge. https://doi.org/10.4324/9781003310365

Athey et al. (2017, November). When Should You Adjust Standard Errors for Clustering? *National Bureau of Economic Research.* Working Paper. . http://www.nber.org/papers/w24003

Atlantic Council. (2023). Central Bank Digital Currency Tracker. http://www.atlanticcouncil.org/cbdctracker/

Auer, R., Haene, P., & Holden, H. (2021). *Multi-CBDC Arrangements and the Future of Cross-border Payments.* [online] Bank for International Settlements, https://www.bis.org/publ/bppdf/bispap115.htm, Accessed 30 May 2021.

Barro, R. J., & Sala-i-Martin, X. (1995). *Economic Growth.* McGraw-Hill.

Bech, M., & Holden, H. (2019, December). FX Settlement Risk Remains Significant. *BIS Quarterly Review*, pp. 48–49.

Bech, M., & Garratt, R. (2017, September). Central Bank Cryptocurrencies. *BIS Quarterly Review*, pp. 55–70.

BIS (2021). Annual Economic Report.

Boar, C., & Wehrli, A. (2021). *Ready, Steady, Go?-results of the Third Bis Survey on Central Bank Digital Currency.* BIS Papers No. 114.

Bordo, D., (2021). *Central Bank Digital Currency in the Historical Perspective: Another Crossroad in Monetary History*, Working Paper 29171, http://www.nber.org/papers/w29171

Brunnermeier, M., & Landau, J.-P. (2022). The Digital Euro: Policy Implications and Perspectives. *Policy Department for Economic, Scientific and Quality of Life Policies at the Request of the Committee on Economic and Monetary Affairs (ECON).*

Brunnermeier, M. K., & Niepelt, D. (2019). On the Equivalence of Private and Public Money. *Journal of Monetary Economics, 106*, 27–41.

Chen, M., Rysman, M., Wang, S., & Wozniak, K. (2021). *Payment Instrument Choice with Scanner Data: An MM Algorithm for Fixed Effects in Multinomial Logit Models.* Working Paper.

Chiu, J., Davoodalhosseini, S. M., Hua Jiang, J., & Zhu, Y. (2022). *Bank Market Power and Central Bank Digital Currency: Theory and Quantitative Assessment.* Unpublished manuscript.

Committee on Payments and Market Infrastructures (2018a, February). *Cross-border Retail Payments.*

Committee on Payments and Market Infrastructures. (2018b, March). Central Bank Digital Currencies. *Bank for International Settlements*. http://www.d174.pdf (bis.org)

Doepke, M., & Schneider, M. (2017, September). Money as a Unit of Account. *Econometrica*, *85*(5), 1537–1574.

European Central Bank. (2020). Report on a Digital Euro.

Fernández-Villaverde, J., Sanches, D., Schilling, L., & Uhlig, H. (2021). Central Bank Digital Currency: Central Banking for all? *Review of Economic Dynamics, 41*, 225–242.

Galati, G. (2002, December). Settlement Risk in Foreign Exchange Markets and CLS Bank. *BIS Quarterly Review*, pp. 55–66.

Goetzmann, W. (2017). *Money Changes Everything: How Finance Made Civilization Possible*. Princeton University Press.

Grossman, G. M., & Helpman, E. (1990, October). Trade, Knowledge Spillover and Growth. *National Bureau of Economic Research*. Working Paper. http://www.nber.org/papers/w3485

Grossman, G. M., & Helpman, E. (1991). *Innovation and Growth in the Global Economy*. MIT Press.

Hayek, F. (1976). *Denationalization of Money*. Institute of Economic Affairs.

International Monetary Fund (2020). *Digital Money across Borders: Macro-financial Implications*. IMF Policy Papers, no 2020/050.

Keister, T., & Monnet, C. (2022). Central Bank Digital Currency: Information and Stability. *Journal of Economic Dynamics and Control*, forthcoming

Kosse, A., & Mattei, I. (2022). *Gaining Momentum–Results of the 2021 BIS Survey on Central Bank Digital Currencies*. BIS papers.

Melitz, M. J., & Ottaviano, G. I. (2008). Market Size, Trade, and Productivity. *Review of Economic Studies, 75*(1), 295–316.

Norberg, P. A., Horne, D. R., & Horne, D. A. (2007). The Privacy Paradox: Personal Information Disclosure Intentions Versus Behaviours. *Journal of Consumer Affairs, 41*(1), 100–126.

Romer, P. (1993). *Two Strategies for Economic Development: Using Ideas and Producing Ideas*, Proceedings of the World Bank Annual Conference on Development Economics, 1992, ed. Summers, L.H; Shah, S., Washington, D.C.: World Bank, 63–91

Panetta, F. (2021). *Central Bank Digital Currencies: A Monetary Anchor for Digital Innovation*. Speech at the Elcano Royal Institute.

PWC: Central Bank Digital Currency in the Indian Context (September 2021), https://www.pwc.in/assets/pdfs/consulting/financial-services/fintech/point-ofview/pov-downloads/central-bank-digital-currency-in-the-indian-context.pdf

Samuele, B. (2023). Money in the time of crypto, *Research in International Business and Finance*, 65, 101964, ISSN 0275–5319, https://doi.org/10.1016/j.ribaf.2023.101964

Statista. (2021). Number of identity-verified cryptoasset users. https://www.statista.com/statistics/1202503/global-cryptocurrency-user-base/

Statista. (2023). Overall cryptocurrency market capitalization. https://www.statista.com/statistics/730876/cryptocurrency-maket-value/

SWIFT (2020a). ISO 20022 for dummies, 5th limited edition.

SWIFT (2020b, October 9). *UK Cross-border Instant Payments Pilot sees Payments Credited in Seconds*. Press release.

Williamson, S. (2022). Central Bank Digital Currency and Flight to Safety. *Journal of Economic Dynamics and Control*, forthcoming.

World Bank (2014, January). Guidelines for the Successful Regional Integration of Financial Infrastructures.

World Bank (2020). *Remittance Prices Worldwide*, 34.

World Bank (2021). *Central Bank Digital Currency: Background Technical Note*. © World Bank.

CHAPTER 12

Digital Currency Competition in Global Trade. Departure to a New Era or Persistence of Market Structures?

Andreas Bielig

Status Quo of Currency Competition in Global Trade

International trade is commonly seen as a driving factor for international use of currency beyond national boundaries. Based on the exchange necessity of domestic into foreign money outside of the currency area economic subjects face the basic problem of optimization by currency choice for transactions at the micro level. Trade and monetary theory suggest that decisive determinants lead transactions to stable equilibrium favoring at aggregated level dominant currencies of global reach. The International Monetary Fund IMF reports in the Special Drawing Right Basket (SDR) the date of 22.07.2022 five global currencies as components of international reserve assets (IMF, 2022). Shares are fixed for five-year periods as initial weights based on assessment of international

A. Bielig (✉)
SGH Warsaw School of Economics, Warsaw, Poland
e-mail: abielig@sgh.waw.pl

R. Aneja and R. Dygas (eds.), *Digital Currencies in The New Global World Order*, https://doi.org/10.1007/978-981-97-4810-5_12

trade positions, namely shares on global exports, and global reserves shares of IMF member states. During the transition period component weights adjust according to exchange rate changes, leading to sharp increases in case of currency appreciation (exchange rate decrease) e. v. v. (IMF, 2024). According to initial basket weights, the U.S. Dollar has an outstanding share of 43.38%, outpacing the second-ranked Euro with 29.31% and leaving the next-placed international reserve currencies far behind that are Chinese Renminbi, the Japanese Yen and British Pound Sterling (IMF, 2022) (see for the year 2022 in Table 12.1).

The current basket composition suggests the strong dominance of the U.S. Dollar in international trade relations. But it reveals also global currencies function as international reserves medium for the prevention of financial state imbalances, e.g., state insolvency or distortions of balances of payments, and the stabilization of financial conditions of economies, where the U.S. Dollar has served as the dominant international anchor currency for decades. However, the history of SDR basket compositions shows also emerging transitions in global financial architecture, that reflect ongoing shifts in international exchange (see Table 12.1). Since 1980 the strength of the Dollar slightly weakened until 2000 and afterwards intensified again confirming its stable anchor position in post post-WWII era. At the same time, the German Mark gained weight to 21% in 1990, replaced in 2000 by the European Euro together with French Franc which lost value over time. Also in history, the leading British Pound reduced its basket weight continuously reflecting a decrease in international importance. Japanese Yen gained weight in the basket until 2000 afterwards reducing shares substantially comparable to Pound's level. In the transition of the IMF SDR basket two major developments of disruptive character are observable: First, the Euro area establishment in 2000 bundled member states economic power with the Euro as a common currency and aimed to foster European position in international financial exchange. However, until now, concerning the U.S. Dollar Euro has not gained importance sustainably but stabilized the European position in comparison to descending reserve currencies Japanese Yen and Pound Sterling as Table 1 indicates. Second, besides of emerging Euro, the Chinese Renminbi was added to the SDR basket composition in November 2015 and after a period of transition qualified as an international reserve medium on September, 16th 2016 (IMF, 2016b). IMF board decision is based, first, on the criterion of exports, reflecting China's central role in international trade as a global player in

Table 12.1 IMF SDR currency basket composition 1980–2022

SDR valuation year	*Currency*	*Basket weight [%]*
1980	US Dollar	42
	German Mark	19
	Japanese Yen	13
	French Franc	13
	Pound Sterling	13
1990	US Dollar	40
	German Mark	21
	Japanese Yen	17
	French Franc	11
	Pound Sterling	11
2000	US Dollar	39
	Euro	32
	Japanese Yen	18
	Pound Sterling	11
2005	US Dollar	44
	Euro	34
	Japanese Yen	11
	Pound Sterling	11
2010	US Dollar	41.9
	Euro	37.4
	Japanese Yen	9.4
	Pound Sterling	11.3
2015	US Dollar	41.73
	Euro	30.93
	Renminbi	10.92
	Japanese Yen	8.33
	Pound Sterling	8.09
2022	US Dollar	43.38
	Euro	29.31
	Renminbi	12.28
	Japanese Yen	7.59
	Pound Sterling	7.44

Source own depiction based on IMF (2016a), IMF (2022), and Antweiler (2013)

the last years and, second, on currency characteristic to be "freely usable" in payments in international transactions and widely traded in principal international exchange markets, capturing the financial transactions importance for the world economy. After joining the basket Renminbi ascended fast in position, marking the second major shift in international currency competition besides the Euro. The advent of both international currency “newcomers” may challenge the established position of the U.S. Dollar as an anchor currency. Against the background that a currency’s leading international role supports the management of the economy’s external imbalances (Flandreau & Jobst, 2009, p. 643) improvements would favor European and Chinese economies in international competition. A historical example of the formerly globally leading British Pound Sterling after 1900 shows incumbent international currencies experience competition by new emerging and economically fast developing currencies that have the potential to substitute them in the long run. However, as history matters, the prevalence of the British Pound as a so-called international vehicle currency for preferred use in international transactions prevailed for a long time after British economic dominance just vanished (Krugman, 1980, p. 523). The persistence of the British Pound is based on the self-reinforcing character of vehicle currency systems attracting international transactions in the leading currency that makes substitution by competing currencies costly. Therefore, the economy’s ascending role in international trade is not directly associated with increased domestic currency use in international transactions and improvements in currency position. Analysis results suggest that in 1900 the U.S. economy was disadvantaged by its underrepresented currency position in international financial markets whereas some European countries could still profit from the historic state of international exchange markets (Flandreau & Jobst, 2009, p. 659). Apart from Pound Sterling, this held especially true for former dominant currencies like the French Franc but also for “smaller” currencies like the Netherlands Guilder, Austrian–Hungarian Krone, or the Swiss and Italian currency. However, after WWI Dollar’s rise to today’s dominant position gained dynamics fostered by structural changes in economic and policy world order and, last but not least by intensive Dollar promotion of the U.S. administration (Eichengreen, 2010, p. 2f.). Against this background, Chinese economy’s current position in international trade, since 2009 global leader in exports and since 2014 largest trade nation, would suggest a considerably stronger role of Renminbi in international financial relations if the economic consensus holds also for this case that money and trade are complements (Flandreau & Jobst, 2009, p. 662). The assumption of systematic underrepresentation of Chinese currency in international financial relations and vice versa an overrepresentation of Western leading currencies, namely the dominant U.S.

Dollar and the European Euro is confirmed by current findings of empirical analysis of international trade patterns concerning currency invoicing, with both currencies covering joint global invoicing share above 80% (Boz et al., 2021, pp. 14–20). Based on long-run invoicing patterns for 102 countries from 1990 to 2019 results suggest that the U.S. Dollar's global share of trade invoicing exceeds, corrected for commodity trade, with 23% the global share of exports with destination USA of 10%. For the European currency, in contrast, global invoicing shares do not exceed the 37% global share of exports with a Euro area destination, if shares are corrected for intra-Euro area members' trade. Together with the Euro area, intra trade Euro invoiced global exports cover 46% of total exports, making the European currency to the most intensive invoicing currency in the world economy and, hence, strengthening its position in global currency competition. As a result, whereas the Euro currency invoicing, corrected for intra-euro area trade, is aligned closely to trade patterns the U.S. Dollar reveals a disproportionate intensive use for invoicing not directly covered by trade of the U.S. economy at the expense of "smaller" international currencies, in especially the Chinese Renminbi. However, despite global U.S. Dollar dominance in invoicing analysis results find also signs of regional dominance of the Euro in trade invoicing of European non-Euro area economies (regional closeness factor) and several African economies with intensive relations to Europe (historical closeness factor). Concerning currency competition dynamics in global trade, analysis reveals further some trends that may affect the dominant U.S. Dollar position in the longer run: At the global scale, the number of economies with decreasing shares of exports invoiced in the U.S. Dollar is substantially larger than of those with increased shares. In contrast, the number of countries with increased shares invoiced in the Euro is substantially larger than those with decreasing shares (Boz et al., 2021, p. 18). Hence, trade invoicing patterns show slight tendencies of weakened U.S. Dollar and strengthened Euro over time but are far from leveling out current global currency positions. In comparison, the use of Chinese Reninmbi for trade invoicing increased especially in Asian economies trade with China thereby partially also substituting the Dollar and Euro currency. Against the above in stylized form described background economic research strengthened efforts to analyze financial system characteristics also concerning the question if and how the role of the U.S. Dollar as anchor currency of global economy gradually evolved since 1900 may be challenged or even at risk to vanish (see for instance

Bacchetta & Wincoop, 2002; Bahaj & Reis, 2020; Devereux & Shi, 2013; ECB, 2021; Gopinath & Stein, 2018; Gopinath et al., 2020; Iancu et al., 2020; Krugman, 1980; Magee & Rao, 1980; Mukhin, 2022; Rey, 2001; Vaubel, 1990). Analyzing the mainstream of economic literature related to this topic the derivation of a consensus could be interpreted cautiously as a general assumption toward the stable prevalence of the U.S. Dollar in the global economy. Based on previous considerations of global currency competition in trade, now the contribution focuses on the following aspects of competition in the field of digital money and currencies leveraging competitive conditions and features of traditional forms of "physical" money into the digital sphere.

Key players in Currency Competition in the Digital Currency Market

In 2022, World Economic Forum WEF stated that Digital Currencies could revolutionize global trade in the future. As main drivers of transformation, it underlined changes and innovative solutions concerning three channels: first, increased efficiency of cross-border payments, second, provision of alternative credit information for finance of trade and, third, reduction of economic impacts of de-risking activities fostered by increasing enforcement of AML or CTF compliance and geo-political tensions (WEF, 2022). The statement is consistent with previous findings of the WEF Digital Currency Governance Consortium laid down in the White Paper Series about Digital Currencies with a focus on regulation issues, value propositions, and technology aspects of Digital Currencies (WEF, 2021a). However, despite very promising prospects, the development of digital currency and, concerning public money, Central Bank Digital Currencies CBDC is in stage of infancy. With the date of December 2023 the Atlantic Council CBDC tracker records that out of 131 countries, 11 launched Digital Currencies of Central Banks (8%), 21 Pilot projects for CBDC (16%), 33 projects in the development phase (25%), and 46 Central Banks still engaged in CBDC research (35%). To the group with just launched CBDC belongs, except Nigeria as the largest African economy, solely small economies in Central America, like the Bahamas or Jamaica. CBDC Projects in the Pilot phase run in especially China a global leader in foreign trade but also large economies of India and Russia. Further, to this group belong some medium-sized economies in the Middle East, among others Turkey, Iran, and Saudi

Arabia, a circle of Asian economies, like Japan, Singapore or South Korea, and the African economy of South Africa. Concerning Western industrialized economies, only European Sweden and Australia run more advanced pilots, hence, this group of economically highly developed countries is still underrepresented in CBDC project progress made in comparison to its large weight in global economic output and trade. This picture changes if economies with CBDC development project status are concerned, where Western industrialized economies are well represented, e.g., the United States, Canada, European Union (concerning Euro area), and the United Kingdom. But also, large American economies are engaged in the development of their own CBDC, like Brazil, Mexico, Colombia, or Asian countries, like Indonesia, Cambodia, or Taiwan. This heterogeneous picture of global CBDC project work status illustrates the mixed facets observable in the race of countries aiming for digital currency utilization in the public sphere. Active CBDC use is, except in Nigeria, still found in small economies only, with negligible impact on currency competition at a global scale. But, more impetus on competition may arise if large or even dominant economies implement their current pilots into workable currency and payment systems in the future. Here, especially, China bolstered by its economic power in terms of global output and trade position but also concerning its currency position in global finance could be capable of leveraging its comparative advantages successfully to the digital sphere thereby further strengthening its world economy position by a dominant contesting of global analogue and digital markets. Besides Japan, follows, with temporal CBDC development lag, the leading duo of global finance architecture containing the U.S. Dollar and European Euro. Hence, at first glance and with only respect to CBDC development progress, currency competition in the digital sphere appears to be a pure matter of advanced digital financial technology and payment systems development leveraging currency positions from conventional to digital currency area. However, competition is a multifaceted phenomenon that relies on many dimensions and related factors. Some of these are associated with CBDC scope and design applied by issuing entities, the supporting monetary policy and legal framework, the institutional and organizational embedding into the existing payment industry on regional and global levels as well as overall innovativeness in the local finance and banking sector. Last but not least, the economic fundamentals of the issuing economy will matter also for the prosperity of Digital currency. But, future CBDC will experience also competition by other means of payments that function as more or less near substitutes. Private cryptocurrencies in the form of Stable Coins or other Crypto assets may intensively compete with CBDC via innovative money features that offer specific value propositions to users that can't be delivered in terms of scope, quality, or price by public CBDCs (WEF, 2021a). Also, if many, not most cryptocurrencies today only poorly meet basic money functions for broader public coverage, like store of value or payment function, they may entail innovative solutions for specific applications in the economy and especially in trade which gives room for currency competition far beyond market niches. However, current cryptocurrencies are almost highly price and market cap volatile, like Bitcoin, Ether, Tether, or Binance Coin (CoinMarketCap, 2024) and, hence, actually attract due to their specific characteristics mainly limited user groups (Honegger, 2023). Furthermore, there is no public consent, with the exceptions of San Salvador and the Central African Republic, to use them as legal means of payment in an economy (Deutscher Bundestag, 2021). Hence, more than these highly risky and speculative perceived financial assets future CBDCs will face effective competition by various custom-focused payment services offered just today by globally acting payment providers, like VisaNet, Paypal, Apple Pay, Google Pay, and others. This range of almost large and economically powerful actors partially stems from different economic sectors, for instance, the traditional finance and payment industry, e.g., Visa, derives from emerging fintech sector, like PayPal, Alipay, or WeChat Pay, or originates from global software technology players acting on global platforms, like Apple or Google. However, as common ground digital payment services offered by those providers rely on, with minor exceptions, solely on private commercial bank money in the form of sight deposits or near substitutes created based on public money issued by central banks. Hence, also traditional central banks issued money, in the form of cash for retail transactions, especially private commercial banks money forming a narrow circle of fierce competitors for future CBDC. Concerning the colorful picture of major players in future digital currency competition, the question arises of which key factors may influence the competition and prove to be decisive for international market success. For this, the next chapter outlines the main aspects of currency competition concerning CBDC from a monetary theory perspective.

Currency Competition Seen from Monetary Theory

Currency choices made by economic entities at a global scale in foreign trade, foreign direct investments, and capital flows have a large impact on the international positions of economies in the world economy. They favor economies with dominant currencies, like the U.S. Dollar, by providing economic advantages to them, and disadvantage economies with contracting currencies. Hence, Eichengreen (2010, p. 3) describes the logical sequence of currency internationalization steps as follows: "... first, encouraging its use in invoicing and settling trade; second, encouraging its use in private financial transactions; third, encouraging its use by central banks and governments as a form in which to hold foreign reserves." In this context, Gopinath and Stein (2018, p. 1) point to complementarities between currencies' function as unit account for invoicing and characteristics as stores of value that can lead to dominant positions of a single currency in global trade and banking even in the case of a multipolar international currency regime with comparable fundamentals performance of rivaling economies. As a result, firms tend to cope with currency mismatches by borrowing in the dominant currency and expected returns on these currency-denominated safe assets are smaller, privileging the economy in international competition. Important elements of currency competition theory originate from the classic monetary work of Hayek about currency choice and denationalization of money (Hayek, 1978a and 1978b). Following this, Endres (2009, p. 1258) underlines that international currency dominance is from a Hayekian competition perspective influenced especially by long-term supply side factors, like inflation risks and associated behavior of monetary policy. Thereby international capital and currency markets confer "reputation capital" to central banks as a result of expectations formation that are supported by institutions trading in these currencies, e.g., large international financial centers or global hedge funds. A central issue for currency competition is the market test of currency choices made, which allows in general, currency consolidations, as the development of the European Euro shows. However, the currency competition concept in Hayek's sense implicitly requires conditions based on Baumol's concept of contestable markets (Baumol, 1982), which include the absence of capital and exchange controls, trust in internationally reputed currency issuers, and a workable (potential) competition. According to this, latent competition pressure by market contestability challenges incumbent currencies in terms of their efficient fulfilment of three money functions, namely (1) as a medium of exchange, (2) unit of calculations, and (3) store of value and induces market adjustments in case of increasing or decreasing currency reputation. Endres (2009, p. 1259) concludes on sufficient contestability of traditional international currency markets based on assumptions of low market entry barriers due to small money production costs and technological efforts required. But for digital currency, and especially for public money in the form of CBDC, the question of market contestability gives a rather mixed picture, at least concerning, first, large technology efforts necessary to develop and implement workable CBDCs that are capable of delivering main features required in terms of scope, costs, convenience, and safety, but, second, also to monetary policy issues open that potentially limit the envisaged scope of prospective financial instrument. In practice, a decisive factor for future CBDC market contestability and currency competition is what central banks' CBDC projects will provide to the public. But out of the international currency group, besides China, central banks still did not make much progress in positioning their CBDC concerning potential business applications or value propositions that go far beyond just available private or public means of payments (also holds for the Digital Euro project after launching ECB (2023) CBDC investigation report). Specific terms of "digital money" as "liability of the Euro System" dedicated "for a broad public availability" (at ECB example) hardly allow for sufficient clarification in the end but rather raise further questions of the kind: What is new in CBDC digital money concerning status quo? How could CB liabilities be fulfilled in cases of system erosion or collapse? How does broad public availability against the background of tight CBDC holding limits affect above mentioned store of value function? Current ECB's Digital Euro project addresses solely two important money functions: as a medium of exchange and as a unit of calculation. However, users' trust as the most decisive criterion for the broad acceptance of an exchange medium is dependent on its stability of value in time (Thiele, 2017). Systemic store of value function limitations of CBDC may harm its acceptance as an exchange medium and, due to their interdependencies, finally also as an appropriate unit of account. Concerning lacking CBDC store of value functions classic cash stays king (beyond its superiority in privacy), hence, and not surprisingly, represents a main competitor to future CBDCs, not only in case of technical failures that may prevent digital payments. The stability of money value (basic theory foundations in Samuelson, 1958) is, except for most private cryptocurrencies, bound on the effective enforcement of monetary policy by CBs in the currency area. Despite an almost given stability of nominal currency value (in traditional currency systems mainly affected by currency reforms, but, for digital currency also by technical potentials of programmable money forms), a necessary precondition for asynchronous purchase and sales acts, the real value stability depends on price stability achieved in the currency area. Reduced price stability by inflation or deflation distorts the currency's capabilities to fulfil the three basic money functions (Wolla, 2013). Whereas, central banks fight this problem by monetary policy in currency areas, issuers of private cryptocurrencies must, except stablecoins, tie financial asset value to prices of a specific bundle of products and services demanded by their focus groups of asset holders to provide for price stability. Today, major international Central banks, like the U.S. Fed or ECB, aim for two percent inflation targets concerning low distortions of money functions and securing "inflation buffers" against the economic deflation dangers of the critical zero line. Indeed, concurrent CB monetary policy focus on enhancing economic growth by low (actually at 2%) and stable inflation (Bernanke, 2006) demonstrates its general limitations toward enforcement of strict price stability that would improve money's store of the value function. Private digital currency issuers don't face similar constraints by policy considerations and, hence, may offer financial assets that suit better to their customers' needs better. For modern currency systems, money functions as a medium of exchange and units of account are considered widely as complementary features that require a unified form. Doepke and Schneider (2017, p. 1540) point out the fact that historically both functions often were met by distinct media but became unified in modern economies with the widespread use of government-issued nominal bonds. He finds empirical evidence for a tight link between government debt and the use of public money as a unit of account, which is based on features of modern economies, stating: "Thus, the government's use of money for its borrowing propagates to private contracts and leads to money being the dominant unit of account." (Doepke & Schneider, 2017, p. 1540). Modern national states have by nature strong inherent incentives to stabilize and strengthen this connection against the background of meeting their public tasks, including monetary policy enforcement. However, digital currencies have huge potential to erode this relationship in the future by overtaking the role as a unit of account, e.g., in retail transactions, bolstered by their economic power of network externalities, as in the case of global platform providers. Concerning moderate innovation efforts of leading central banks in current CBDC projects to implement modern cutting-edge payments and finance systems, private global networks are ready to fill this gap fast as Thießen (2021, p. 535) states. But, monetary theory reveals concerning money's function as a medium of exchange against the background of international trade also arguments and evidence that support the long-run persistence of stable currency equilibria and, hence, favor established dominant currencies functioning as vehicle currency for other economies at a global scale. So, for instance, following (Flandreau & Jobst, 2009, pp. 645–656) search theory suggests that subjects equipped with "wrong" currency in international transactions face losses, the money holdings costs perspective indicates that economic agents must balance holding costs with the liquidity services a specific currency provides in return, information costs perspective assumes that uncertainty and, hence, information costs for subjects are higher for currencies issued in more distant financial markets, trade argument perspective underlines the importance of considerable size of trade flows for drawing facilities development, thus concluding "money follows trade" (Flandreau & Jobst, 2009, p. 649) and perspective of strategic externalities finds that interest rates of highly quoted currencies were lower than for others, further strengthening their dominant position. As a result, "rising trade powers have difficulties pushing their currency to the top" (Flandreau & Jobst, 2009, p. 645), which holds also for digital currency concerning CBDC. But, besides of path dependencies of currency competition among leading international currencies, systemic obstacles arise also from the rationale of monetary policy. Disintermediation dangers of national banking and finance sectors are major concerns in CBDC developments by central banks. To prevent financial systems destabilization by fast flights of large capital into CBDC as safe digital assets, central banks analyze options to limit the scope of CBDC, e.g., by tiering or holding limits (Balz, 2023; Bindseil, 2020). In effect, CBDC's suitability to function as a near substitute to other money forms shrinks, and their value added for users reduces. At this point is no place for narrations about factors for a less innovation-oriented mindset of central banks like highly innovative technological surroundings of digital currency development. From an economic perspective, and against the background of central bank mandates, endeavors to provide an appropriate legal and institutional framework for efficient enforcement of monetary policy is an obvious explanation. As a consequence, public or industrial expectations concerning innovative breakthrough solutions provided by CBDC probably must be set lower. Thus, in the case of the Digital Euro project by the ECB, present plans are concerning future applications, for instance supporting Industry 4.0 development or cutting-edge payment systems, not very concrete. Central bank restraints to engage more in near-user financial tech solutions may give room for private initiatives by the creation of related fintech ecosystems but is also at risk of failing market expectations in future payment services. If CBDCs are seen by issuing CBs as instruments for strengthening the international role of their currencies at the global level strict regional limitations of dissemination and usage, applied, e.g., for Digital Euro to the Eurozone and some related economies, function as effective constraints of global competition in digital currencies. Considerations of monetary policy concerning potentially destabilizing distortions of financial systems by CBDC from outside shocks, combined with the national-focused demarcation of currency areas constitute in a conservative perspective a line of defense of monetary sovereignty of modern national states in times of digital currencies. At present, there are only weak prospects for realizing the Hayekian currency competition concept of denationalization of money concerning CBDC development. However, in market economies private payment service providers likely will fill market gaps associated with considerable business prospects by their solutions.

Conclusions

Digital currency is associated with huge economic potential for future international trade. The article shows that increasing trade positions favor the use of respective currencies by invoicing patterns and the establishment of drawing facilities. As a result, economic transactions may lead to a stable self-enforcing equilibrium with a dominant currency as an anchor currency and popular vehicle used by other economies, such as the U.S. Dollar today, or also a multi-polar regime of some leading currencies. Digital currencies in the form of CBDCs are expected to strengthen the positions of the leading currencies further. After WWII considerable changes in international currencies leading group with the U.S. Dollar as the anchoring center occurred, with the emergence of the European Euro and the ascent of Chinese Renminbi. However, despite increasing geographic shifts in international trade and economic fundamentals, in competition of currencies the Dollar still preserves its dominance. Digital currencies may have the potential to break up existing path dependencies and rearrange international finance orders. CBDC can take a pacemaker role in shaping new global financial architecture that brings innovative solutions for urgent global issues. However, at this point, and concerning currency competition, the current status of CBDC projects does not allow for concrete projections of future contributions to international financial systems advancement. Hence, and monetary policy targets given as central banks' priority, the essential impetus of currency competition in digital currency may derive from private financial payment providers from the classic banking and finance industry and the digital technology sector.

References

Antweiler, W. (2013). *Special Drawing Rights: The XDR Fact Sheet*. University of British Columbia, Sauder School of Business. In https://web.archive.org/web/20160414002025/http://fx.sauder.ubc.ca/SDR.html, Accessed 29 February 2024.

Bacchetta, P., & Wincoop, E. V. (2002, September). *A Theory of the Currency Denomination of International Trade*, ECB Working Paper Series, No. 177, European Central Bank, Frankfurt/Main.

Bahaj, S., & Reis, R. (2020, June). *Jumpstarting an International Currency*, Bank of England, Staff Working Paper No. 874, London.

Balz, B. (2023). Was der Digitale Euro für die Bürger bringt, Interview mit der FAZ, 19.10.2023, im Gespräch mit Christian Siedenbiedel, *Frankfurter Allgemeine Zeitung*, https://www.bundesbank.de/de/presse/interviews/was-der-Digitale-euro-fuer-die-buerger-bringt-917460, Accessed 29 February 2024.

Baumol, W. J. (1982). Contestable Markets: An Uprising in the Theory of Industry Structure. *The American Economic Review, Mar., 72*(1), 1–15.

Bernanke, B. S. (2006). *The Benefits of Price Stability*, Speech at The Center for Economic Policy Studies and on the occasion of the Seventy-Fifth Anniversary of the Woodrow Wilson School of Public and International Affairs, Princeton University, Princeton, New Jersey, February 24th, Board of Governors of the Federal Reserve System, https://www.federalreserve.gov/newsevents/speech/Bernanke20060224a.htm, Accessed 29 February 2024.

Bindseil, U. (2020). *Tiered CBDC and the Financial System*, Working Paper Series, No 2351 / January 2020, ECB, Frankfurt/Main, https://www.ecb.europa.eu/pub/pdf/scpwps/ecb.wp2351~c8c18bbd60.en.pdf, Accessed 29 February 2024.

Boz, E. et al. (2020). *Patterns in Invoicing Currency in Global Trade*, Working Paper Series, No 2456 / August 2020, European Central Bank, Frankfurt/Main.

CoinMarketCap. (2014). *Today's Cryptocurrency Prices by Market Cap*, https://coinmarketcap.com/, Accessed 29 February 2024.

Deutscher Bundestag. (2021). *Chancen und Risiken der Anerkennung des Bitcoin als gesetzliches Zahlungsmittel*, Wissenschaftliche Dienste, WD 4–3000–069/21, Deutscher Bundestag, https://www.bundestag.de/resource/blob/859726/f7f427408b0930cdf9d591b3f070d1fd/WD-4-069-21-pdf-data.pdf, Accessed 29 February 2024.

Devereux, M. B., & Shi, S. (2013, February). Vehicle Currency, *International Economic Review*, *54*(1), 97–133

Doepke, M., & Schneider, M. (2017, September). Money as a Unit of Account, *Econometrica*, *85*(5), 1537–1574

ECB. (2021, June). *The International Role of the Euro*, European Central Bank, Frankfurt/Main.

ECB. (2023). *A Stocktake on the Digital Euro: Summary Report on the Investigation Phase and Outlook on the Next Phase*, European Central Bank, Frankfurt/Main, https://www.ecb.europa.eu/paym/Digital_euro/investigation/profuse/shared/files/dedocs/ecb.dedocs231018.en.pdf

Eichengreen, B. (2010). *The Renminbi as an International Currency*, Working paper, University of California, Berkeley, https://eml.berkeley.edu/~eichengr/renminbi_international_1-2011.pdf, Accessed 29 February 2024.

Endres, A. M. (2009). Currency Competition: A Hayekian Perspective on International Monetary Integration. *Journal of Money, Credit and Banking, Sep.*, *41*(6), 1251–1263.

Flandreau, M., & Jobst, C. (2009). The Empirics of International Currencies: Network Externalities. *History and Persistence, the Economic Journal, Apr.*, *119*(537), 643–664.

Gopinath, G. et al. (2020, March). Dominant Currency Paradigm, *The American Economic Review*, *110*(3), 677–719

Gopinath, G., & Stein, J. C. (2018). *Banking, Trade, and the Making of a Dominant Currency*, National Bureau of Economic Research, Working Paper 24485, April, Cambridge, MA, https://www.nber.org/papers/w24485, Accessed 29 February 2024.

Hayek, F. A. (1978a). *Choice in Currency*, Reprinted in The Collected Works of FA. Hayek vol. IV, 1999, edited by Stephan Kresge pp. 115–27. Chicago: Chicago University Press.

Hayek, F. A. (1978b). *The Denationalization of Money: An Analysis of the Theory and Practice of Concurrent Currencies*, London: IEA. Reprinted in The Collected Works of FA. Hayek vol. IV, edited by 1999, Stephan Kresge, pp. 128–229. Chicago University Press.

Honegger, L. (2023, August 19). Hat Elon Musk den Bitcoin endgültig aufgegeben?, *Neue Zürcher Zeitung*, https://www.nzz.ch/finanzen/hat-elon-musk-den-bitcoin-endgueltig-aufgegeben-ld.1752148, Accessed 29 February 2024.

Iancu, A. et al. (2020). *Reserve Currencies in an Evolving International Monetary System*, International Monetary Fund, Strategy, Policy, and Review Department.

IMF. (2016a, July 13). *Currency Amounts in the SDR Basket—Proposed Changes to the Rounding Methodology*, https://www.elibrary.imf.org/view/journals/007/2016/039/article-A001-en.xml, Accessed 29 February 2024.

IMF. (2016b, September 30). IMF Adds Chinese Renminbi to Special Drawing Rights Basket. *IMF News*, https://www.imf.org/en/News/Articles/2016/09/29/AM16-NA093016IMF-Adds-Chinese-Renminbi-to-Special-Drawing-Rights-Basket, Accessed 29 February 2024.

IMF. (2022, July 22). *Special Drawing Right (SDR) Valuation Basket. Currency Amounts in the New SDR Basket*, https://www.imf.org/en/Topics/special-drawing-right/sdr-valuation-basket, Accessed 29 February 2024.

IMF. (2024). *Special Drawing Rights (SDR). SDR value*, https://www.imf.org/en/About/Factsheets/Sheets/2023/special-drawing-rights-sdr, Accessed 29 February 2024.

Krugman, P. (1980). Vehicle Currencies and the Structure of International Exchange. *Journal of Money, Credit and Banking, Aug., 12*(3), 513–526.

Magee, S. P., & Rao, R. K. S. (1980, May). Vehicle and Nonvehicle Currencies in International Trade, *The American Economic Review, 70*(2), Papers and Proceedings of the Ninety-Second Annual Meeting of the American Economic Association, pp. 368–373.

Mukhin, D. (2022). An Equilibrium Model of the International Price System. *The American Economic Review, 112*(2), 650–688.

Rey, H. (2001). International Trade and Currency Exchange. *The Review of Economic Studies, Apr., 68*(2), 443–464.

Samuelson, P. A. (1958). An Exact Consumption-Loan Model of Interest with or without the Social Contrivance of Money. *Journal of Political Economy, Dec., 66*(6), 467–482.

Thiele, C.-L. (2017, April 3). *Die Bedeutung des Bargelds als Wertaufbewahrungsmittel*, Vortrag, Tagung des Deutschen Historischen Museums, Berlin, https://www.bundesbank.de/de/presse/reden/die-bedeutung-des-bargelds-als-wertaufbewahrungsmittel-613736, Accessed 29 February 2024.

Thießen, F. (2021). Digitaler Euro: Funktionsweise und kritische Würdigung, Analysen und Berichte Digitaler Euro, ZBW—Leibniz-Informationszentrum Wirtschaft, *Wirtschaftsdienst. Nr., 7*, 529–535.

Vaubel, R. (1990). Currency Competition and European Monetary Integration. *The Economic Journal, Sep., 100*(402), 936–946.

WEF. (2021a, November). *Digital Currency. Governance Consortium White Paper Series. Compendium Report*, World Economic Forum, https://www3.weforum.org/docs/WEF_Digital_Currency_Governance_Consortium_White_Paper_Series_2021.pdf, Accessed 29 February 2024.

WEF. (2021b, November). *What is the Value Proposition of Stablecoins for Financial Inclusion?*, White Paper, Digital Currency. Governance Consortium White Paper Series, World Economic Forum, https://www3.weforum.org/docs/WEF_Value_Proposition_of_Stablecoins_for_Financial_Inclusion_2021.pdf, Accessed 29 February 2024.

WEF. (2022, January 13). *3 ways Digital Currencies could Change Global Trade*, Financial and Monetary Systems, World Economic Forum, https://www.weforum.org/agenda/2022/01/digital-currencies-international-trade/, Accessed 29 February 2024.

Wolla, S. A. (2013, March). *Money and Inflation: A Functional Relationship*, Page One Economics, https://research.stlouisfed.org/publications/page1-econ/2013/03/01/money-and-inflation-a-functional-relationship/, Accessed 29 February 2024.

CHAPTER 13

Digital Currencies Impact on Development of International Trade and Economy Growth

Madan Lal and Anuj Jatav

Introduction

The way we do business has changed and grown over the last ten years. One of the main reasons for this growth is digital currencies. Digital currency is money that can only be obtained digitally or electronically. It is also referred to as cryptocurrency, digital currency, electronic cash, electronic money, or electronic currency. Computers or electronic wallets linked to specific networks or the internet can be used to conduct transactions in these digital currencies (Lee et al., 2021). As per the World Economic Forum, this growth in digital currencies would help to make cross-border transactions more effective and help to fill the $1.7 trillion international trade financing gap. However, at the same time when we talk about customer payment methods, digital currencies are placed

M. Lal (✉)
Department of Commerce, University of Delhi, Delhi, India
e-mail: madanfms@gmail.com

A. Jatav
Shri Ram College of Commerce, University of Delhi, Delhi, India
e-mail: anuj.jatav@srcc.du.ac.in

R. Aneja and R. Dygas (eds.), *Digital Currencies in The New Global World Order*, https://doi.org/10.1007/978-981-97-4810-5_13

last by credit experts in their preference list from most to least prevalent (Viñuela et al., 2020). The usage of digital currencies in B2B transactions, however, is anticipated to increase. According to MarketWatch, the global market for digital currencies expects that benefits like minimal transaction fees, fraud protection, and hassle-free overseas payments will cause the market for digital currencies to grow significantly. It is anticipated that popular digital currencies like Bitcoin and Litecoin will fuel market expansion.

Centralised vs. Decentralised Digital Currencies

The two primary types of digital currencies are centralised and decentralised. Decentralised currencies are currencies that gain their valuation from the public who use them, and do not depend upon banks, authorities, or any third party for the functioning or existence (Liao & Wang, 2020). **However, the idea of centralised digital currencies has started to emerge as decentralised currencies and has gained popularity.** Central banks and governments have started investigating the use of a type of blockchain technology to develop central bank digital currencies, also known as CBDCs, in light of the potential advantages of digital money (Bech et al., 2020).

Digital currencies that are produced and controlled by centralised institutions differ significantly from their decentralised counterparts although they utilise the same kind of underlying blockchain technology. At the same time, centralised digital currencies are not valued by their users but rather by the legitimacy of the entity that issues them (Latimer & Duffy, 2019). Whereas, the Bitcoin whitepaper published in October 2008 referred to Bitcoin as a peer-to-peer electronic cash system to enable online payments directly from one party to another" without the use of a bank or middleman. Now, after 13 years, blockchain technology is the foundation of a rapidly expanding universe of financial services that includes lending platforms, exchanges, and more in addition to currencies (Balvers & McDonald, 2021). The market value of the decentralised finance industry was over $93 billion in October 2021, and the market value of all decentralised cryptocurrencies was over $2.3 trillion.

Despite not being widely used in the majority of the world's countries, Central Bank Digital Currencies, or CBDCs, will be crucial to the development of our global economy. People will become more aware of how CBDCs operate and what their ramifications are for people and businesses

1
Prioritize 1-2 use cases with an improved **user experience** and greater **customer value** than existing alternatives

2
Maximize simplicity of onboarding and usage for consumers and ease of integration for merchants

3
Build a strong footprint in local markets, leveraging brand awareness and loyalty

4
Focus on niche segments; pursue a phased rollout, starting with use cases that offer high volume and address acute pain points

5
Create incentives for businesses and consumers to adopt digital currency

6
Built trust from the beginning by delivering on promises; better to succeed at something simple than half-deliver on something complex

7
Seek partnerships to accelerate scale-up while maintaining a central relationship with key customers

8
Leverage existing payment infrastructure to accelerate time to market

Fig. 13.1 Ways through which central can improve chances of CBDC adoption (*Source* Denecker et al., McKinsey Analysis, October 2022)

throughout the world as they start to show up in our bank accounts and digital wallets (Adamu Ahmed et al., 2022) (Fig. 13.1).

Institutional Attitudes Towards Digital Currencies

Financial institutions initially had reservations about cryptocurrencies that, would result in money laundering and other illegal activities (Maryaningsih et al., 2022). However, they timely recognised its simplicity to manufacture, programme, and issue digital money. They also noted the advantages that digital currency networks offered their users, such as quick international transfers, affordable settlement costs, and broader financial inclusion. Decentralised stablecoins also show that digital currencies may be "pegged" to fiat currency to maintain their value rather than needing to have erratic values (Buransujja & Kraiwanit, 2022) (Table 13.1).

Central Bank Digital Currency (CBDC)

A Central Bank Digital currency is a form of currency that is controlled and issued by a nation's central bank. According to the IMF, more than 100 nations are investigating CBDCs in one way or another. However, as of 2023, only a small number of nations and territories either issued CBDC or have firm plans to do so. At the same time Central Bank of The

Table 13.1 Decentralised vs. Centralised digital currency

Decentralised vs. Centralised digital currency	*Centralised digital currency*	*Decentralised digital currency*
Based on blockchain technology	Yes	Yes
Derives value from issuing authority	Yes	No
Derives value from users	No	Yes
Lower cross-border transaction fee than the legal financial system	Yes	Yes
Classified as legal tender	Yes	No
Promotes greater financial inclusion	Yes	Yes
Backed by government or central bank	Yes	No

Source Conflux Network, Centralised vs. Decentralised Digital Currency (and Why it Matters), October 2021

Bahamas (Sand Dollar), the Eastern Caribbean Central Bank (DCash), the Central Bank of Nigeria (e-Naira), and the Bank of Jamaica (JamDex), to mention a few, are some locations where CBDC is already accepted (Maryaningsih et al., 2022).

Even the U.S. Federal Reserve published a report this year highlighting that a CBDC can deeply impact the U.S. financial system structure. Also, the Massachusetts Institute of Technology's Digital Currency and Federal Reserve Bank of Boston initiated joint research into a CBDC via Project Hamilton. They describe it as a multiyear research project to discover the CBDC design space and gain an in-depth understanding of CBDC's opportunities and challenges (Manahov, 2023) (Fig. 13.2).

Functions of Central Bank Digital Currency (CBDC)

CBDC functions similarly to actual cash where funds are transferred instantly and parties are not in a position to cancel the transaction once it is executed. Another significant advantage associated with CBDC is that it might be treated as legal tender. The legal tender nature of CBDC establishes its acceptance for the economic actors to accept it for all legal

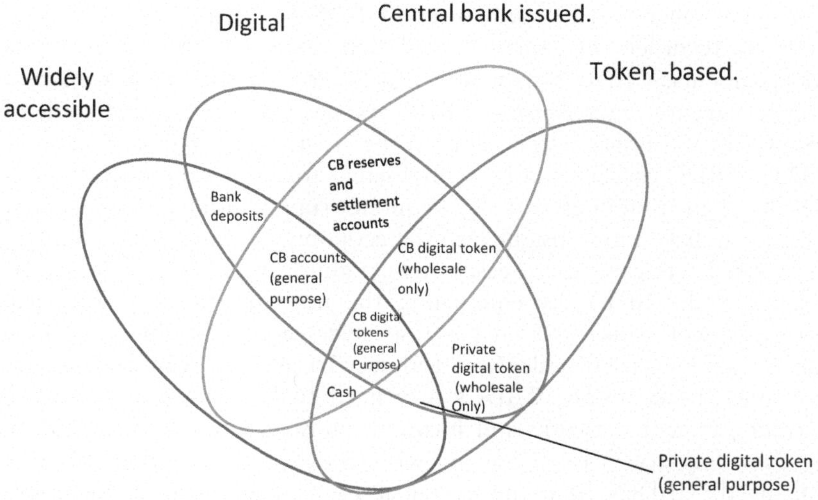

Fig. 13.2 The money flower: A taxonomy of money (*Source* Based on Bech and Garratt [2017])

purposes. You can transact your taxes with it and if anyone lends you money is legally bound to accept it for repayment (Altan et al., 2019). As technology has grown and the way we conduct financial transactions has changed, the idea of CBDC has attracted a lot of interest (Alonso et al., 2020). CBDCs are essentially a mechanism for central banks to maintain control over the currency and its circulation while offering a digital alternative to physical cash. Depending on the design and execution a central bank selects, the CBDC's operations may differ. The CBDC is produced and issued by the central bank. This may be accomplished through the minting or issue procedure. The CBDC can then be given directly to banks and other financial institutions, who will then give it to the general public (W. Zhang et al., 2023). Digital wallets or accounts with the central bank, commercial banks, or authorised intermediaries are available to both individuals and corporations that are used to conduct business in CBDC, these accounts. People would use internet banking or smartphone apps to access their accounts on digital platforms (Huang & Mayer, 2022). Digital payments resemble CBDC transactions in that both entail the usage of a central bank-backed digital currency.

Digital wallets can be used to send CBDC to others, and all transactions are recorded on a secure distributed ledger. To protect user data and payments, CBDC transactions can be created with robust encryption and security mechanisms. CBDC systems may offer varied levels of anonymity and privacy depending on the architecture (Banet & Lebeau, 2022). CBDC can be used by central banks to carry out monetary policies like regulating interest rates, the money supply, and inflation. Central banks may have more insight into the economy because CBDC transactions can be tracked more easily than traditional cash transactions (W. Zhang et al., 2018). By eliminating the need for intermediaries like correspondent banks and enabling speedier settlement times, CBDCs can streamline cross-border transactions. To allow a seamless integration into the economy, CBDCs may need to be compatible with the current payment networks and financial infrastructure (Bindseil, 2019). By providing access to digital financial services to the underbanked or unbanked, CBDCs have the potential to increase financial inclusion. However, issues with internet accessibility and technology literacy must be resolved. There would probably be a transitional period when both physical cash and CBDC are in use if a nation decided to implement a CBDC. This shift would need to be carefully managed by the central bank (Y. Zhang et al., 2022). The CBDC's underlying technology might be built on a distributed ledger or blockchain technology, however, it could also make use of other safe and effective digital payment methods (Fig. 13.3).

Potential Ways Digital Currencies Could Change International Trade Digital Currency and Efficiency in Cross-Border Transactions

Cross-border transactions could become much more efficient because of the use of digital currencies, such as cryptocurrencies and Central Bank Digital Currencies (CBDCs). Due to batch processing, time zone differences, and the use of many intermediaries, traditional cross-border transactions might take several days to settle (Pavan & Aparanji, 2022). Digital currencies function on decentralised networks that enable almost immediate transactions, doing away with the lag times present in conventional systems. Blockchain networks, are always active and empower digital currencies to eliminate the need for conventional limited-time

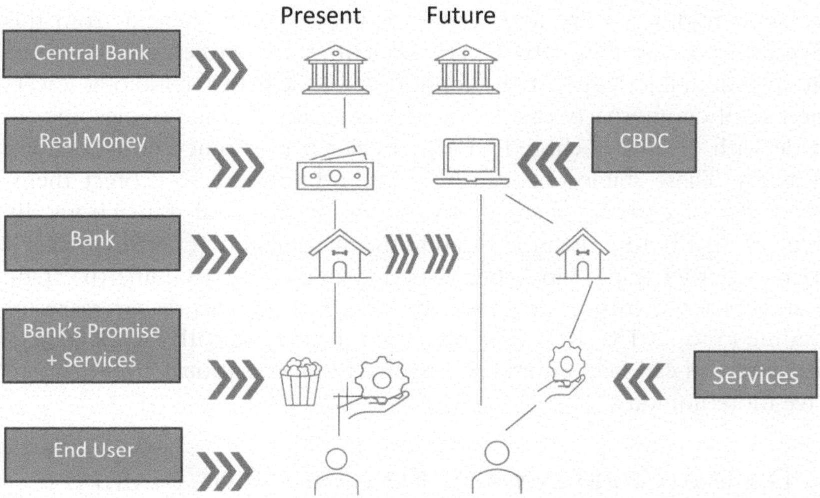

Fig. 13.3 Possible future of CBDC (*Source* Pilav, Darko. blog.digitalasset Article, May 2020)

cross-border transactions that follow the business hours of conventional banking systems and allow it to transact at any time, including weekends and holidays (Ohlsson & Davison, 2019). Bypassing the requirement for many intermediaries, such as correspondent banks, direct peer-to-peer transactions between participants can be facilitated by the use of cryptocurrencies and CBDCs. This lowers transaction expenses while also streamlining the procedure (Williamson, 2022). Cross-border transactions may involve several costs for settlement, intermediary banks, and currency translation. Digital currencies, particularly when sending bigger sums of money, can drastically lower these costs.

Blockchain networks allow for transactions that are transparent and real-time traceable. This openness can improve insight into the progress of transactions, ensure compliance with rules, and help avoid fraud. Smart contracts, which are self-executing contracts with set rules, can be created on several blockchain platforms (Lahmiri & Bekiros, 2018). These contracts can automate several cross-border transactional processes, such as payments that are made when specific requirements are met. Anyone with an internet connection can use digital currencies, for transactions in international trade. Individuals and companies in areas with limited access to traditional financial services may particularly benefit from this (Symitsi & Chalvatzis, 2018). As transactions are verified and recorded on an immutable ledger, the adoption of blockchain technology lowers the risk of counterparty risk and settlement failure. Some stablecoins are made with a value anchored to a particular fiat currency or a portfolio of assets. These stablecoins can be used by businesses to protect themselves against currency fluctuations during international transactions. By securely distributing documents and information among parties engaged in cross-border trade, blockchain-based systems can streamline the trade finance process, cutting down on the time and paperwork necessary for funding (Yao, 2018). Real-time settlement is possible with digital currencies, and this can help enterprises involved in international commerce to have more liquidity.

Digital Currency and Exchange Rate Stability

A vital component of international trade and finance is exchange rate stability. Stablecoins and Central Bank Digital Currencies (CBDCs) are two examples of digital currencies that have the potential to provide exchange rate stability in distinct ways. Stablecoins, which are cryptocurrencies intended to have a stable value, are frequently anchored to a particular fiat currency (such as the US Dollar) or a portfolio of assets (Saito & Iwamura, 2019). Stablecoins may be ideal for routine transactions and international trade, thanks to these steady values, which lessen the uncertainty brought on by exchange rate swings. Because of the possibility of abrupt value fluctuations, traditional cryptocurrencies like Bitcoin are notorious for their price volatility, which might make them less useful for cross-border trade. On the other hand, stablecoins work to reduce this volatility by offering a more dependable unit of account for international trade (Schilling et al., 2020). Internationally trading companies depend on precise pricing for their products and services. In contrast to volatile cryptocurrencies, stablecoins provide a more predictable pricing system, assisting businesses in avoiding jarring fluctuations in their revenue owing to exchange rate movements.

Stablecoins can be used by businesses as a hedge against currency rate risk. They can reduce the potential losses brought on by unfavourable exchange rate changes by adopting stablecoins anchored to a certain currency (Adrian & Mancini-Griffoli, 2021). A managed peg to a reliable external currency may be built into some central banks' CBDCs. When dealing with that CBDC, this pegged value can boost foreign merchants' and investors' confidence. Stablecoins in particular can make cross-border transactions easier by removing the need for numerous currency conversions. By doing this, currency risk exposure and conversion fee expenses are decreased (Caliskan, 2020). Digital currencies' potential to support exchange rate stability could improve commercial connections across nations by offering a common, stable medium of exchange that is unaffected by the monetary policy of any one particular country (Fanusie & Jin, 2021) (Fig. 13.4).

As the value would be less impacted by the policy of a single country, a broadly adopted global stablecoin or CBDC might potentially contribute to more consistent global currency stability. It's crucial to remember that using digital currencies to achieve and maintain exchange rate stability also comes with difficulties. Stablecoins must be widely accepted and trusted by businesses, consumers, and financial institutions to effectively stabilise exchange rates. It may take some time to reach this degree of acceptance (Chen & Phelan, 2023). Even stablecoins are susceptible to pressures from external markets or changes in the underlying assets they are tethered to. The stability of the stablecoin could be impacted by an unanticipated crisis affecting the linked currency or asset. Globally, there are different regulatory environments for digital currencies and stablecoins (Jiang et al., 2023). Stablecoin development and adoption may be hampered by regulatory difficulties and uncertainties. The monetary policies and actions of the central bank issuing CBDCs may have an impact on the stability of their exchange rates and the pegged value (Srouji, 2020).

Digital Currency and Financial Inclusion in International Trade

By giving underprivileged or excluded individuals and communities access to financial services using digital currencies, such as cryptocurrencies and Central Bank Digital Currencies (CBDCs), financial inclusion might be considerably improved. Access to fundamental financial services including loans, payment methods, and savings accounts is a problem for many individuals worldwide (Tay et al., 2022). Even without a conventional bank account, digital currencies can allow people to access these services using digital wallets. For those who lack the required paperwork or reside in rural places, opening a bank account might be difficult. These obstacles to entry can be decreased by the ease with which digital wallets for digital

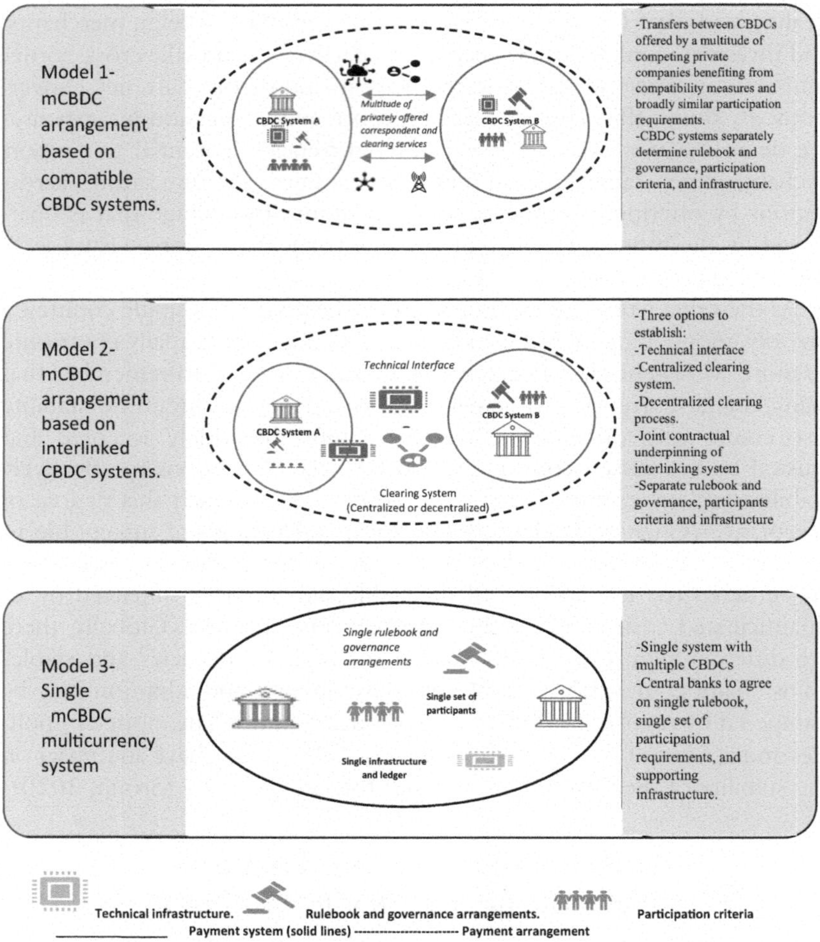

Fig. 13.4 Multi-CBDC arrangements and the future of cross-border payments (*Source* Auer et al., BIS Papers, no 115, March 2021)

currencies can be built (Arner et al., 2020). By making cross-border remittances easier and more affordable than with conventional transfer methods, digital currencies help migrants send money to their loved ones back home.

Microtransactions are possible with digital currencies, enabling small-value transactions that might not be practical with conventional banking infrastructure. Similar to this, digital currencies can facilitate microlending, giving entrepreneurs and small enterprises access to small loans (Banet & Lebeau, 2022). With the help of digital currencies, people who live in isolated or underdeveloped places may be able to participate in international trade, conduct online transactions, and access a wider variety of financial opportunities (Schuetz & Venkatesh, 2020). As people get more comfortable with digital financial tools and concepts, using digital currencies can also help with financial literacy and education. Digital currencies may be able to provide private and secure transactions, which may be especially helpful for those without access to regular banking services and who might be concerned about the security of cash transactions (Mhlanga, 2020).

Digital currencies can offer a way for people to conduct transactions without having to go to a physical bank branch for those who live in rural or isolated places. Digital currencies can offer a distributed payment system that is available as long as there is internet connectivity in areas with inadequate or unstable banking infrastructure (Srouji, 2020). Peer-to-peer transactions, made possible by digital currencies, let people deal directly with one another, minimising the need for middlemen and conventional financial systems. Digital currencies can empower women and other underprivileged groups by giving them access to resources for managing money that might not otherwise be available to them, (Mhlanga, 2020). However, using digital currencies to achieve genuine financial inclusion has its own set of difficulties. Although digital currencies rely on technology, some underdeveloped communities can have limited access to cell phones and the internet. People must know how to utilise digital wallets and carry out transactions safely (Banet & Lebeau, 2022). Initiatives to promote digital literacy may be required to guarantee successful adoption. To avoid the abuse of digital currencies and to create a conducive climate for innovation and financial inclusion, regulatory certainty is crucial. It is essential to ensure the security of digital wallets and transactions since weaker sections and poor people may be more vulnerable to online dangers (Tay et al., 2022). The savings of financially vulnerable people may be impacted by the volatility in the value of some digital currencies (Chen & Phelan, 2023).

Digital Currency and Geopolitical Implications

The emergence of digital currencies, such as cryptocurrencies and Central Bank Digital Currencies (CBDCs), can have important geopolitical repercussions that influence economic power dynamics, international relations, and the state of the world economy (Yen et al., 2020). The supremacy of one CBDC over others or the mass use of a particular digital currency could affect how the world's economies are organised. The government or organisation in possession of such a currency might be able to sway monetary, financial, and trade policies (Rosa & Tentori, 2022). The main reserve currency of the world has historically been the US Dollar. The US's ability to employ financial instruments and penalties as geopolitical leverage may be impacted if a widely used digital currency threatens the Dollar's hegemony (Lawton et al., 2023). Different nations can issue their CBDCs with different monetary policies. As a result, central banks might compete with one another to draw customers and investors, thus leading to monetary policy disagreements and currency wars.

The usage of digital currencies may have an impact on how nations monitor financial transactions and impose penalties. While CBDCs can enable more controlled and traceable transactions, cryptocurrency transactions might be utilised to evade penalties (Aysan et al., 2019). CBDCs may provide nations with more control over their monetary and financial systems. This might make it harder to settle trades using foreign currencies like the US dollar (Kyriazis, 2021). Geopolitical disputes could develop as a result of worries about cross-border digital currency transactions' security and data privacy. Countries may try to prevent foreign monitoring of their citizen data. Countries that invest in CBDC development may gain a competitive advantage in both technology and commerce (Rosa & Tentori, 2022). Those who don't have a solid digital currency strategy, risk falling behind in terms of innovation and competitiveness in the market.

Cross-border digital currency transactions may need to be regulated and managed through geopolitical collaboration. Conflicts about tax evasion, financial stability, and money laundering could result from different regulatory approaches (Bouri et al., 2022). Digital currencies may have an impact on the economics of nations that rely largely on remittance inflows if they lower the cost and improve the efficiency of cross-border transfers. Countries that are leading the development of digital currencies may be able to exert diplomatic influence since other nations that want to adopt similar technology may seek out their expertise. Countries that successfully use digital currencies to increase financial inclusion may boost their soft power and reputation abroad, especially in areas with limited access to conventional financial services (Caliskan, 2020). The old financial infrastructure may change if countries embrace CBDCs for cross-border trade, potentially reducing the importance of intermediaries and financial institutions. CBDCs may have an impact on the make-up of a nation's foreign exchange reserves. Other nations may modify their reserve holdings if a big economy adopts a CBDC (Ahnert et al., 2023).

Digital Currency and Digital Trade Platforms

The creation of digital commerce platforms can greatly benefit from the use of digital currencies, which will change how international trade is organised, recorded, and financed. On digital commerce platforms, digital currencies can simplify cross-border transactions (Fanusie & Jin, 2021). Businesses can avoid the costs and delays associated with conventional banking channels by employing digital currencies as a medium of trade. Blockchain networks used by digital currencies allow for real-time transaction settlement. Compared to conventional banking systems, this functionality can dramatically shorten the time it takes to complete trade transactions (Buransujja & Kraiwanit, 2022). Many digital currencies are built on blockchain technology, which offers transaction transparency and traceability. This openness can increase participant confidence and deter fraud. Smart contracts can be used by digital trade platforms to automate a variety of trade processes, including the release of payments upon the completion of requirements like shipment tracking and quality checks. Trade financing procedures can be streamlined and accelerated with digital currency (Chen & Phelan, 2023). Blockchain-based platforms enable safe information and document sharing between parties involved in a deal, which cuts down on the amount of time and paperwork needed for funding. To provide real-time visibility into the movement of commodities, to confirm authenticity, and to guarantee adherence to trade norms, blockchain can be integrated into supply chain management systems. Direct peer-to-peer transactions made possible by digital currencies eliminate the need for middlemen in trade transactions, which may result in faster transactions and cost reductions (Maryaningsih et al., 2022).

Digital currencies can offer a universal remedy for cross-border trade, allowing organisations and people from various corners of the world to deal invisibly. It is simpler for firms to send and receive payments across borders when digital trade platforms with digital currency integration are used (Mikhaylov, 2020). Microtransactions are made possible by digital currencies, allowing for the quick exchange of small sums of money. This is especially beneficial for digital services and goods. Digital currencies can act as a middleman for currency conversion when parties to a trade use different currencies, obviating the need for further conversion processes (Bouri et al., 2022). With the use of stablecoins or CBDCs with a stable value, firms can conduct cross-border trade without having to worry too much about exchange rate swings (Wang et al., 2018). By encouraging better standardisation and interoperability among different platforms, the introduction of digital currencies on trading platforms may improve the efficiency of cross-platform transactions. Digital currencies may make it easier to build worldwide trade networks that link buyers, sellers, and customers from various markets and locations (Marta, 2022).

Digital Currency, Financial Sanctions, and Financial Surveillance

i. Financial Sanctions

To enforce sanctions and conduct financial surveillance, digital currencies, such as cryptocurrencies and Central Bank Digital Currencies (CBDCs), may have both advantageous and disadvantageous effects. Blockchain technology, which enables a transparent and unchangeable record of transactions, underpins the operation of digital currencies (Allen et al., 2022). This may make it simpler to follow and identify the flow of money, which could help with the execution of penalties. Authorities can monitor transactions in real-time on a blockchain, making it easier to identify suspected sanctions violations. Digital currencies might in some circumstances offer a more traceable substitute to conventional cash transactions, making it more difficult for people and companies to avoid sanctions (Majumder et al., 2019). While blockchain promotes openness, several cryptocurrencies also provide some level of pseudonymity or even complete anonymity. Due to this, it may be difficult to conclusively connect transactions to particular people or organisations. Cryptocurrencies that are geared toward enhancing privacy and anonymity (known as "privacy coins") may make it easier for people and organisations to get around restrictions (Kishore Jain, 2020). Due to their intrinsic lack of borders, digital currencies may be used to facilitate cross-border transactions that avoid penalties, making it more difficult for governments to regulate money flows. Since cryptocurrencies operate on decentralised networks, it is challenging for government agencies to monitor or block transactions or accounts that are tied to the circumvention of sanctions (Mendoza-Tello et al., 2019).

ii. Financial Surveillance

Transactions involving digital currencies may be subject to more stringent anti-money laundering (AML) and know-your-customer (KYC) checks, allowing for greater detection and prevention of illegal financial activity. By reducing the usage of cash transactions, which are more difficult to track, the adoption of digital currencies could improve financial surveillance operations. To identify strange trends or suspect activity, complex analytics tools can be used to analyse the massive amount of data generated by blockchain transactions (Westermeier, 2022). As transactions are more easily traced and watched, increased surveillance can both deter illegal activity and raise privacy issues.

The transnational nature of digital currencies can make regulatory efforts more challenging, particularly when handling transactions that include several different legal systems (Mhlanga, 2020). Because cryptocurrencies are decentralised, it is difficult for governments to actively oversee or regulate transactions. Financial surveillance organisations must quickly adapt to new problems and techniques of criminal behaviour due to the continuously changing environment of digital currency and related technology (Ohlsson & Davison, 2019).

Digital Currencies Privacy and Security Concerns

Due to their distinctive features and the underlying technology, digital currencies, especially cryptocurrencies, create significant privacy and security concerns. Many cryptocurrencies offer some degree of pseudonymity, which means addresses rather than real-world identities are used to link transactions. Concerns regarding the possibility of illegal activity may arise as a result. Some cryptocurrencies that prioritise privacy provide improved anonymity, making it harder to track transactions (Westermeier, 2022). While this helps safeguard user privacy, it can also make it difficult for law enforcement to follow KYC and AML rules and prevent money laundering. Because blockchain transactions are transparent and traceable, the adoption of digital currencies may make it possible to monitor financial activity (Jiang et al., 2023). This may affect individual privacy and lead to worries about transaction data misuse. Users of digital currency platforms risk violating their privacy if they mistakenly disclose transaction data with outside service providers. While some platforms follow strong data protection guidelines, others could have laxer policies (Arner et al., 2020). It is possible to analyse blockchain transactions and connect addresses to identities using sophisticated tools and methods. Users who think their transactions are anonymous may have their privacy at risk as a result (Ahnert et al., 2023).

Wallets for digital currency are subject to malware, phishing assaults, and hacking. An attacker may be able to steal money if s/he can access a user's wallet. The possibility of widespread theft makes cryptocurrency exchanges appealing targets for hackers. User funds and personal data may be lost as a result of exchange breaches (Bouri et al., 2022). Cryptocurrency transactions are irreversible, in contrast to traditional financial systems where transactions can be challenged or reversed. This implies that errors or fraudulent transactions are difficult to reverse. The absence of thorough regulation in the area of digital currencies might result in security flaws and fraudulent schemes (Tay et al., 2022). This regulatory ambiguity may be used by con artists to deceive people. A single entity or organisation controls some digital currencies, making them more centralised. This may lead to worries about censorship, deception, and weaknesses present in centralised sources of control. Blockchain-based smart contracts may have coding flaws or vulnerabilities, which could have unintended results or cost users money (Lawton et al., 2023). Private keys are necessary for access during digital currency transactions. These keys can be lost, leaving you without access to your money and no way to get it back. By tricking users into disclosing their login information or private keys, attackers can compromise their accounts. Risks associated with backing assets, regulatory oversight, and management procedures exist for stablecoins, which strive to maintain a stable value (Kyriazis, 2021).

Potential Impact of Digital Currencies on Economic Growth Digital Currencies, Innovation, and Technological Growth

Digital currencies, such as cryptocurrencies and Central Bank Digital Currencies (CBDCs), have a significant and wide-ranging impact on innovation and growth. Blockchain technology, which has uses beyond money, is the foundation of digital currencies. Decentralised and secure blockchain technology can be used to improve data management, supply chain visibility, identity verification, and other processes (Fanusie & Jin, 2021). Innovation in the financial technology (Fintech) industry is driven by digital currencies. New payment systems, remittance platforms, decentralised finance (DeFi) applications, and digital asset management solutions are being created by startups and established businesses. DeFi platforms use blockchain technology and digital currencies to build decentralised alternatives to conventional financial services including lending, borrowing, trading, and yield farming. This allows people to conduct financial transactions without the need for middlemen (Kishore Jain, 2020). The introduction of smart contracts on Ethereum transformed the way contracts are carried out. These self-executing contracts automate procedures, eliminating the need for middlemen in a variety of sectors, from supply chain management to real estate (Manjula et al., 2022). Digital currencies make it easier to tokenise tangible and digital assets like commodities, works of art, and real estate. Due to this, asset trade on a global scale and fractional ownership are now more feasible. By removing the need for middlemen like correspondent banks and enabling borderless, almost immediate cross-border transactions, digital currencies enable frictionless global trade (Ismanto et al., 2019).

Digital Currencies, E-Commerce, and Global Markets

Digital currencies have the potential to revolutionise the way transactions are carried out, increase market reach, and boost efficiency in e-commerce and worldwide marketplaces. International e-commerce is made more efficient and cost-effective by the use of digital currencies, which enable cross-border transactions without the use of currency conversions or middlemen (Ismanto et al., 2019). Digital currencies can drastically lower these costs, resulting in benefits for both consumers and businesses, as traditional overseas payments frequently require transaction fees, intermediary costs, and currency conversion fees (Marta, 2022). Unlike traditional banking systems, which typically take several days to process foreign transfers, digital currencies allow for nearly instantaneous settlements. Fast order processing is crucial for e-commerce transactions; thus, this feature is especially beneficial. Businesses can access international markets with digital currencies without experiencing the hassle of currency conversion (Mikhaylov, 2020). This gives businesses the chance to reach clients from around the globe. By enabling businesses to sell goods, services, and digital content at incredibly low prices that might not be possible with conventional payment systems, cryptocurrencies are perfectly suited for microtransactions (Colon et al., 2021).

The client base can be expanded and the economy can grow by using e-commerce platforms that accept digital currencies to give access to people who do not have access to regular financial services. Because transactions using digital currencies are irreversible, there is less chance of fraud and chargebacks, which is advantageous to both customers and businesses. Digital currencies promote a more direct and open market by enabling people to conduct cross-border peer-to-peer commerce without relying on centralised platforms (Arner et al., 2020). By catering to specialised sectors that enjoy using digital currencies around the world, retailers can broaden their clientele. The client base can be expanded and the economy can grow by using e-commerce platforms that accept digital currencies to give access to people who do not have access to regular financial services. Because transactions using digital currencies are irreversible, there is less chance of fraud and chargebacks, which is advantageous to both customers and businesses (Ahnert et al., 2023). Digital currencies promote a more direct and open market by enabling people to conduct cross-border peer-to-peer commerce without relying on centralised platforms. By catering to specialised sectors that enjoy using digital currencies around the world, retailers can broaden their clientele (Yen et al., 2020).

Digital Currency and Access to Capital

By changing fundraising and investing opportunities, digital currencies, such as cryptocurrencies and tokenised assets, have the potential to have a tremendous impact on access to finance. Startups and projects can raise money by selling investors digital tokens through Initial Coin Offerings (ICOs) and Token Sales. This democratises access to capital and makes early-stage finance available to people all around the world (Buckley & Trzecinski, 2023). At the same time, Security Token Offerings (STOs) provide a controlled and legal means to tokenise traditional assets, permitting fractional ownership and liquidity. STOs entail the issue of digital tokens that reflect ownership in a real-world asset, like as equity in a corporation or real estate (Caliskan, 2020). Cross-border investments are made easier by the use of digital currencies, which let startups and established companies raise money from a global pool of investors without the hassles of conventional cross-border transactions. Traditional illiquid assets, like real estate or fine art, can benefit from the liquidity that tokenised assets can provide. Allowing people to exchange or sell their tokens on secondary marketplaces, can help investors (Chen & Phelan, 2023). Crowdfunding campaigns are made possible by decentralised platforms based on blockchain technology, where contributors are given digital tokens in return for their contributions. Digital currencies make it possible for people to make tiny investments in businesses or initiatives, lowering the entrance hurdle for investors (Wang et al., 2018).

A wider spectrum of investors who can pool their resources can access high-value assets because of digital currencies' ability to allow for fractional ownership of assets. Financial inclusion is promoted by the ability of digital currencies to offer investment options to people who do not have access to conventional investment platforms (Marta, 2022). Smart contracts can automate investment procedures including dividend payments and token holders' voting rights, which cuts down on administrative work. Assets that have been tokenised can be exchanged on secondary markets, giving investors the chance to withdraw their money before the asset achieves maturity (Allen et al., 2022). By enabling more effective and varied funding sources for companies, digital currencies have the potential to completely alter the venture capital environment. Digital currencies can help businesses and entrepreneurs in developing economies access funds more quickly by overcoming the drawbacks of conventional financial infrastructure. The accessibility of capital via digital currencies can promote innovation by fostering a market where entrepreneurs compete for investors (Schuetz & Venkatesh, 2020).

Conclusion

Significant discussions and research have been conducted on how digital currency would affect trade and economic growth. While it's vital to understand that the world of digital money is dynamic and ever-changing, there are a few critical things to keep in mind. Like, By lowering the need for middlemen and transaction fees, digital currencies have the potential to improve the effectiveness of cross-border transactions. By giving underserved communities access to financial services, they can help increase financial inclusion. New payment methods and financial products have been developed as a result of the introduction of digital currencies in the financial industry. The blockchain technology that powers several digital currencies has also found use in several sectors outside of banking. Regulatory issues, security hazards, and volatility are just a few of the difficulties faced by digital currencies. Governments and regulatory organisations are working hard to create a legal framework to address these problems. The effects of digital currencies on economic growth can vary by place and circumstance, but they do have the ability to spur it through improved productivity and innovation. They may support economic growth in some circumstances while posing hazards to financial stability in others. Digital currencies can ease cross-border payments and lower the expenses associated with currency translation, which can help with global trade. They also cast doubt on the stability of currency rates and the coordination of monetary policy. The long-term impact of digital currencies depends heavily on how widely they are adopted by businesses and consumers. The three main forces that influence adoption are public opinion, trust, and usability. In conclusion, there are many different ways that digital currency has an impact on trade and economic progress. They offer opportunities to increase efficiency and financial inclusion, but they also create difficulties that must be carefully resolved by the proper regulatory measures. How these issues are resolved and how digital currencies are incorporated into the world financial system will determine the long-term impact. The future of digital currency and its function in the global economy will be shaped by further study and international cooperation.

References

Adamu Ahmed, A., Adamu Saidu, A., & Hussein Kawure, J. (2022). The Roles of Central Bank Digital Currency over Physical Currency. *International Journal of Social Science, Education, Communication and Economics (SINOMICS JOURNAL)*, *1*(2), 75–92. https://doi.org/10.54443/sj.v1i2.10

Adrian, T., & Mancini-Griffoli, T. (2021). The Rise of Digital Money. *Annual Review of Financial Economics*, 57–77. https://doi.org/10.1146/annurev-financial-101620

Ahnert, T., Hoffmann, P., Leonello, A., & Porcellacchia, D. (2023). *CBDC and Financial Stability*. https://doi.org/10.2866/671223

Allen, F., Gu, X., & Jagtiani, J. (2022). Fintech, Cryptocurrencies, and CBDC: Financial Structural Transformation in China. *Journal of International Money and Finance*, *124*. https://doi.org/10.1016/j.jimonfin.2022.102625

Alonso, S. L. N., Fernández, M. Á. E., Bas, D. S., & Kaczmarek, J. (2020). Reasons Fostering or Discouraging the Implementation of Central Bank-Backed Digital Currency: A Review. *Economies*, *8*(2). https://doi.org/10.3390/ECONOMIES8020041

Aneja, R., & Dygas, R. (Eds.). (2022). *Digital Currencies and the New Global Financial System* (1st ed., pp. 1–16). Routledge. https://doi.org/10.4324/9781003310365

Altan, A., Karasu, S., & Bekiros, S. (2019). Digital Currency Forecasting with Chaotic Meta-Heuristic Bio-Inspired Signal Processing Techniques. *Chaos, Solitons and Fractals*, *126*, 325–336. https://doi.org/10.1016/j.chaos.2019.07.011

Arner, D. W., Buckley, R. P., Zetzsche, D. A., & Veidt, R. (2020). Sustainability, Fintech and Financial Inclusion. *European Business Organization Law Review*, *21*(1), 7–35. https://doi.org/10.1007/s40804-020-00183-y

Auer, R., Haene, P., & Holden, H. (2021). Multi-CBDC arrangements and the future of cross-border payments. www.bis.org

Aysan, A. F., Demir, E., Gozgor, G., & Lau, C. K. M. (2019). Effects of the Geopolitical Risks on Bitcoin Returns and Volatility. *Research in International Business and Finance*, *47*, 511–518. https://doi.org/10.1016/j.ribaf.2018.09.011

Balvers, R. J., & McDonald, B. (2021). Designing a Global Digital Currency. *Journal of International Money and Finance*, *111*. https://doi.org/10.1016/j.jimonfin.2020.102317

Banet, J., & Lebeau, L. (2022). Central Bank Digital Currency: Financial Inclusion vs Disintermediation. In *Federal Reserve Bank of Dallas, Working Papers* (Vol. 2022, Issue 2218). https://doi.org/10.24149/wp2218

Bech, M., & Garratt, R. (2017). Central Bank Cryptocurrencies. *In BIS Quarterly Review*. www.blockchain.info;

Bech, M., Boar, C., Borio, C., Claessens, S., Coeuré, B., Frost, J., Gambacorta, L., Hollanders, M., Holden, H., Leckow, R., Monet, C., Shin, H. S., Vrbaski, R., Wadsworth, A., Wooldridge, P., Cao, H., Cornelli, G., Villegas, A., Auer, R., & Böhme, R. (2020). The Technology of Retail Central Bank Digital Currency. In *BIS Quarterly Review*.

Bindseil, U. (2019). Central Bank Digital Currency: Financial System Implications and Control. *International Journal of Political Economy*, *48*(4), 303–335. https://doi.org/10.1080/08911916.2019.1693160

Bouri, E., Gupta, R., & Vo, X. V. (2022). Jumps in Geopolitical Risk and the Cryptocurrency Market: The Singularity of Bitcoin. *Defence and Peace Economics*, *33*(2), 150–161. https://doi.org/10.1080/10242694.2020.1848285

Buckley, R. P., & Trzecinski, M. (2023). Central Bank Digital Currencies and the Global Financial System: The Dollar Dethroned? *Capital Markets Law Journal*, *18*(2), 137–171. https://doi.org/10.1093/cmlj/kmad007

Buransujja, R., & Kraiwanit, T. (2022). Digital Currency for Payments. In *International Research E-Journal on Business and Economics*, *7*(2). https://orcid.org/0000-0002-5130-6427

Caliskan, K. (2020). Platform Works as Stack Economization: Cryptocurrency Markets and Exchanges in Perspective. *Sociologica*, *14*(3), 115–142. https://doi.org/10.6092/issn.1971-8853/11746

Chen, W., & Phelan, G. (2023). *Digital Currency and Banking-Sector Stability*. https://ssrn.com/abstract=4396935

Colon, F., Kim, C., Kim, H., & Kim, W. (2021). The Effect of Political and Economic Uncertainty on the Cryptocurrency Market. *Finance Research Letters*, *39*. https://doi.org/10.1016/j.frl.2020.101621

Conflux Networks. (2021, October 31). Centralized vs. *Decentralized Digital Currency (and Why it Matters)*.

Denecker, O., d'Estienne, A., Gompertz, P.-M., & Sasia, E. (2022). *The 2022 McKinsey Global Payments Report*.

Fanusie, Y. J., & Jin, E. (2021). *China's Digital Currency Adding Financial Data to Digital Authoritarianism*.

Huang, Y., & Mayer, M. (2022). Digital Currencies, Monetary Sovereignty, and U.S.–China Power Competition. *Policy and Internet*, *14*(2), 324–347. https://doi.org/10.1002/poi3.302

Ismanto, L., Ar, H. S., Fajar, A. N., Sfenrianto, & Bachtiar, S. (2019). Blockchain as E-Commerce Platform in Indonesia. *Journal of Physics: Conference Series*, *1179*(1). https://doi.org/10.1088/1742-6596/1179/1/012114

Jiang, S., Zhou, J., & Qiu, S. (2023). Is there any Correlation between Digital Currency Price Fluctuation? Based on the DCC-GARCH and Wavelet Coherence Analysis. *Economic Research*, *36*(2), 1–26. https://doi.org/10.1080/1331677X.2022.2134901

Kishore Jain, D. (2020). *The Economics of Cryptocurrencies Does It Work?* https://ssrn.com/abstract=3644159

Kyriazis, N. A. (2021). The Effects of Geopolitical Uncertainty on Cryptocurrencies and Other Financial Assets. *SN Business & Economics*, *1*(1). https://doi.org/10.1007/s43546-020-00007-8

Lahmiri, S., & Bekiros, S. (2018). Chaos, Randomness and Multi-Fractality in Bitcoin Market. *Chaos, Solitons and Fractals*, *106*, 28–34. https://doi.org/10.1016/j.chaos.2017.11.005

Latimer, P., & Duffy, M. (2019). Deconstructing Digital Currency and Its Risks: Why ASIC Must Rise to the Regulatory Challenge. *Federal Law Review*, *47*(1), 121–150. https://doi.org/10.1177/0067205X18816237

Lawton, T. C., Tonn Goulart Moura, S., Tobin, D., & Silva-Rêgo, B. (2023). Geopolitics of the Digital Economy: Implications for States and Firms. *AIB Insights*, *23*(1). https://doi.org/10.46697/001c.67966

Lee, D. K. C., Yan, L., & Wang, Y. (2021). A Global Perspective on Central Bank Digital Currency. *China Economic Journal*, *14*(1), 52–66. https://doi.org/10.1080/17538963.2020.1870279

Liao, Q., & Wang, Y. (2020). Prospect and Challenges of Cross-Border Payment Posed by Digital Currency—From the Perspective of Blockchain Coalition. *E3S Web of Conferences*, *218*. https://doi.org/10.1051/e3sconf/202021804001

Majumder, A., Routh, M., & Singha, D. (2019). A Conceptual Study on the Emergence of the Cryptocurrency Economy and its Nexus with Terrorism Financing. In *The Impact of Global Terrorism on Economic and Political Development: Afro-Asian Perspectives* (pp. 125–138). Emerald Group Publishing Ltd. https://doi.org/10.1108/978-1-78769-919-920191012

Manahov, V. (2023). The Rapid Growth of Cryptocurrencies: How Profitable is Trading in Digital Money? *International Journal of Finance and Economics*. https://doi.org/10.1002/ijfe.2778

Manjula, B. C., Shilpa, B. S., & Sundaresh, M. (2022). Analysis of Cryptocurrency, Bitcoin and the Future. *East Asian Journal of Multidisciplinary Research*, *1*(7), 1293–1302. https://journal.formosapublisher.org/index.php/eajmr/index

Marta, A.-F. (2022). Some Considerations Regarding the Regulation of E-commerce Taxation and Cryptocurrency Trading. *Review of International Comparative Management*, *23*(5), 694–706. https://doi.org/10.24818/RMCI.2022.5.694

Maryaningsih, N., Nazara, S., Kacaribu, F. N., & Juhro, S. M. (2022). Central Bank Digital Currency: What Factors Determine its Adoption? *Bulletin of Monetary Economics and Banking*, *25*(2), 1–24. https://doi.org/10.21098/bemp.v25i1.1979

Mendoza-Tello, J. C., Mora, H., Pujol-López, F. A., & Lytras, M. D. (2019). Disruptive Innovation of Cryptocurrencies in Consumer Acceptance and Trust. *Information Systems and E-Business Management*, *17*(2–4), 195–222. https://doi.org/10.1007/s10257-019-00415-w

Mhlanga, D. (2020). Industry 4.0 in Finance: the Impact of Artificial Intelligence (AI) on Digital Financial Inclusion. *International Journal of Financial Studies*, *8*(3), 1–14. https://doi.org/10.3390/ijfs8030045

Mikhaylov, A. (2020). Cryptocurrency Market Analysis from the Open Innovation Perspective. *Journal of Open Innovation: Technology, Market, and Complexity*, *6*(4), 1–19. https://doi.org/10.3390/joitmc6040197

Ohlsson, B., & Davison, K. (2019). Blockchain Technology in the Trade and Finance of Agriculture Supply Chains. In *Architecture for Blockchain Applications* (pp. 239–255). Springer International Publishing. https://doi.org/10.1007/978-3-030-03035-3_12

Pavan, D., & Aparanji, P. (2022). Role of Digital Currency and Block Chain Technology on Indian Economy with Special Reference to RBI and Government Recent Reforms in Digital Rupee. *International Journal of Engineering Applied Sciences and Technology*, *7*, 151–154. www.digitalrupee.in

Pilav, D. (2020, May 19). *What is a Central Bank Digital Currency and Why should people prefer CBDC over bank accounts.*

Rosa, B., & Tentori, A. (2022). *Central Bank Digital Currencies, Reserve Currencies and Geopolitics.*

Saito, K., & Iwamura, M. (2019). How to Make a Digital Currency on a Blockchain Stable. *Future Generation Computer Systems*, *100*, 58–69. https://doi.org/10.1016/j.future.2019.05.019

Schilling, L., Fernández-Villaverde, J., & Uhlig, H. (2020). *Central Bank Digital Currency: When Price and Bank Stability Collide.* http://www.nber.org/papers/w28237

Schuetz, S., & Venkatesh, V. (2020). Blockchain, Adoption, and Financial Inclusion in India: Research Opportunities. *International Journal of Information Management*, *52*. https://doi.org/10.1016/j.ijinfomgt.2019.04.009

Srouji, J. (2020). Digital Payments, the Cashless Economy, and Financial Inclusion in the United Arab Emirates: Why Is Everyone Still Transacting in Cash? *Journal of Risk and Financial Management*, *13*(11), 260. https://doi.org/10.3390/jrfm13110260

Symitsi, E., & Chalvatzis, K. J. (2018). Return, Volatility and Shock Spillovers of Bitcoin with Energy and Technology Companies. *Economics Letters*, *170*, 127–130. https://doi.org/10.1016/j.econlet.2018.06.012

Tay, L. Y., Tai, H. T., & Tan, G. S. (2022). Digital Financial Inclusion: A Gateway to Sustainable Development. *Heliyon*, *8*(6), 1–10. https://doi.org/10.1016/j.heliyon.2022.e09766

Viñuela, C., Sapena, J., & Wandosell, G. (2020). The Future of Money and the Central Bank Digital Currency Dilemma. *Sustainability (Switzerland)*, *12*(22), 1–21. https://doi.org/10.3390/su12229697

Wang, R., Tsai, W. T., He, J., Liu, C., & Deng, E. (2018). A Distributed Digital Asset-Trading Platform Based on Permissioned Blockchains. *Lecture Notes in Computer Science (Including Subseries Lecture Notes in Artificial Intelligence and Lecture Notes in Bioinformatics)*, *11373 LNCS*, 55–65. https://doi.org/10.1007/978-3-030-05764-0_6

Westermeier, C. (2022). From Flows Towards Updates: Security Regimes and Changing Technologies for Financial Surveillance. *Review of International Studies*, 1–22. https://doi.org/10.1017/s0260210522000493

Williamson, S. D. (2022). Central Bank Digital Currency and Flight to Safety. *Journal of Economic Dynamics and Control*, *142*. https://doi.org/10.1016/j.jedc.2021.104146

Yao, Q. (2018). A Systematic Framework to Understand Central Bank Digital Currency. *Science China Information Sciences*, *61*(3). https://doi.org/10.1007/s11432-017-9294-5

Yen, K.-C., Chiu, S.-Y., & Cheng, H.-P. (2020). Geopolitical Risk and Cryptocurrency Market. *Empirical Economics Letters*, *19*(10), 1175–1180. https://www.researchgate.net/publication/345159842

Zhang, W., Wang, P., Li, X., & Shen, D. (2018). Some Stylized Facts of the Cryptocurrency Market. *Applied Economics*, *50*(55), 5950–5965. https://doi.org/10.1080/00036846.2018.1488076

Zhang, W., Zhao, T., & Mou, L. (2023). Research of Willingness to Use Digital Currency in International Trade Based on SOR Theory and Structural Equation Model. *Proceedings of the 2nd International Conference on Bigdata Blockchain and Economy Management,* ICBBEM 2023, May 19–21, 2023, Hangzhou, China. https://doi.org/10.4108/eai.19-5-2023.2334257

Zhang, Y., Zheng, D., Zhang, L., & Jin, M. (2022). Analysis of the Impact of Digital Currency on International Trade. *Scientific Journal of Economics and Management Research*, *4*(6), 454–459.

CHAPTER 14

Explaining the Linkages Between Digital Payments and Economic Growth: Evidence from India

Sonu Madan and Rajni Sharma

Introduction

The significance of digital payments has witnessed a notable surge in India over the past few years, owing to the rapid proliferation of smartphones and internet connectivity within the country (Tariq et al., 2023). Consequently, there has been a notable surge in the adoption of digital payment modalities, including mobile wallets, Unified Payments Interface (UPI), and card-based transactions (Kesavan & Srinivasan, 2023). This surge in digital payments has not only transformed the way Indians conduct financial transactions but has also led to a reduction in reliance on cash (Bhatia-Kalluri & Caraway, 2023). In India, ICICI introduced

S. Madan (✉)
Department of Economics, Ch. Bansi Lal University, Bhiwani, India
e-mail: sonu.economics@igu.ac.in

R. Sharma
Department of Economics, Arya P.G. College, Panipat, India
e-mail: sharma4rajni2122@gmail.com

R. Aneja and R. Dygas (eds.), *Digital Currencies in The New Global World Order*, https://doi.org/10.1007/978-981-97-4810-5_14

online banking services in 1996, and HDFC, IndusInd, and Citi did the same in 1999 (Sharma & Abraham, 2012). This marked the beginning of the digital transaction era. In 2008, the National Payments Corporation of India (NPCI) was formed to create a robust payment infrastructure, launching products like the Aadhaar Enabled Payments System, the Bharat Bill Payments System, BHIM, and the Cheque Transaction System (Abraham, 2020).

Demonetization and the promotion of digital literacy are two of the initiatives that the government has implemented to encourage the use of digital payments (Trivedi, 2023). In addition to having a substantial effect on the Indian economy, the demonetization policy accelerated the development of digital payment systems in the country (Pal et al., 2018). In India, digital payments comprised less than 10% of all transactions before demonetization; since then that percentage has increased to over 20% (IBEF, 2023). Furthermore, this shift toward digital payments has also facilitated financial inclusion, allowing individuals in remote areas to access and participate in the formal economy (Singh, 2023). Overall, the growth of digital payments in India has revolutionized the country's financial landscape and is expected to continue its upward trajectory in the coming years (Brunnermeier et al., 2019). Several factors have contributed to the expansion of India's digital ecosystem, including the government's push for digitalization, rising internet and smartphone penetration, and the expansion of e-commerce (Roy, 2021). Through initiatives including Digital India, Make in India, and Startup India, the Indian government has been actively promoting the adoption of digital technologies (Khandelwal & Asthana, 2023). In addition to fostering the growth of start-ups, these initiatives seek to expand the application of digital technologies in diverse industries, including education, healthcare, and agriculture (Audretsch et al., 2020). The proliferation of smartphones and the internet in India has significantly contributed to the expansion of the digital ecosystem (Basole & Karla, 2012). The Internet and Mobile Association of India projected that by 2023, the number of Internet consumers in India will have increased to 800 million. The proliferation of internet users in India has concurrently contributed to the growth of mobile wallet users, an industry that is projected to surpass 900 million by the year 2025 (IAMAI, 2023).

Therefore, it has been analyzed that digital currencies play a crucial role in international trade and economic growth. This paper aims to investigate the impact of digital payments on the economic growth of India from 2011–12 to 2022–23. During this period, there has been a significant rise in the use of digital currencies globally. The study will focus on India specifically, as it has undergone substantial economic growth and development in recent years. By examining the impact of digitalization on India's economy over the past decade, insights can be gained into how digital currencies have contributed to its economic growth.

Review of Literature

Gorshkov (2022) examines the growth of cashless payment in Russia, revealing that it is largely driven by the state and the Bank of Russia. The study found a negative correlation between cash in circulation and the value of cashless transactions. Trust in cashless payment has increased, with the share of cashless money balances in circulation increasing from 62.8 percent to 78.6 percent. The rapid growth can be attributed to internal and external factors, including changes in the cashless payment market and government initiatives.

Wong et al. (2020) aimed to investigate the influence of cashless payment systems on the economic growth of countries within the Organization for Economic Co-operation and Development (OECD). Specifically, the focus of this research is on the effects of debit card payments. The findings indicate that debit card transactions have a substantial positive effect on economic growth, whereas credit card, e-money, and check transactions do not exhibit any significant influence. This study presents novel empirical findings regarding the influence of cashless payment systems on the economic growth of OECD countries. The implementation of cashless payment systems was found to have a favorable effect on long-term economic growth.

Sreenu (2020) explores the impact of cashless payment policies on Indian economic growth from 2010 to 2018. The study uses data from tele-transfer, credit or debit card payments, check payments, and e-money. Results show that customers and sellers accept cashless system policies, with short-term causality running from card systems to check and telegraphic transfer systems. In the long term, cashless policies have a positive impact on Indian economic growth. The study highlights the need for comprehensive experimental research on the association between cashless payment policies and economic growth in emerging countries like India. The adoption of electronic money, check payments, electronic money, and telegraphic transfers positively impacts economic growth.

Tee and Ong (2016) investigates the effects of the adoption of cashless payment systems in five European Union member states over the period 2000–2012. The study employs the Pedroni residual cointegration approach and Panel Vector Error Correction Model (VECM) to analyze the impact of various payment methods, namely check payment, telegraphic transfer, card payment, and electronic money, on the European Union's economy. The findings indicate the presence of short-term causality from check payment to telegraphic transfer and card payment, as well as causality from telegraphic transfer to card payment. The study proposes that policymakers and financial institutions should prioritize the development and enhancement of cashless payment systems to secure ongoing advantages.

Assessing the causal relationship between policy and economic growth using longitudinal data from 2008 to 2015, Yusuf (2016) examines the relationship between policy and economic growth. The results indicate that non-cash payment options have a substantial impact on economic growth in Nigeria, with mobile payment options contributing the most and checks contributing the least. However, after their introduction, non-cash payment options account for only 13% of the variance in economic growth and cannot be used to accurately predict growth.

Zandi et al. (2013) analyze the economic impact of electronic card (credit and debit card) adoption for a group of 56 high-income countries from 2008 to 2012. The pooled OLS estimator shows greater usage of electric cards increases the real GDP of the countries studied. In particular, the study indicates that using electronic cards increases private consumption by 0.7 percent. As a result of which GDP growth increases by 0.17 percent every year across the 56 countries studied.

Hasan et al. (2012) showed empirically that electric retail payments (debit and credit card payments, credit transfers, check payments, and direct debits) boost trade and consumption, resulting in higher economic growth for a group of 27 European countries from 1995 to 2009. Moreover, the study revealed that the growth-stimulating effect for cards is the highest among different payment methods. In contrast, check payments have the least macroeconomic impact on growth due to electronic card substitution. The study's findings support the implementation of policies that encourage quick cashless transactions and economic growth.

Humphrey et al. (1996a) analyzed payment systems in fourteen developed countries from 1987 to 1993, finding a 34% increase in noncash payments in 1993. The social cost of a country's payment system, which is estimated to be between 2 and 3% of GDP, can be reduced by promoting the shift to electronics. Cash is the most used payment instrument, with a proportion of 90% of all transactions. Countries with a strong emphasis on card-based payments, such as France, Denmark, and the UK, have seen a decrease in cash holdings per person. The study highlights the importance of comparing electronic and paper-based payments in noncash transactions and their relationship to a country's intensity of cash use. The shift to electronic payments per person rose by 24 during 1987–93, while paper-based payments rose by 10.

Research Methodology

This paper examines the impact of digitalization on India's economic development from 2011–12 to 2022–23. The impact of digitalization on the development of the Indian economy was analyzed by determining its effect on India's real gross domestic product. Real GDP has been employed as a proxy for economic growth (Apergis, 2019; Tee & Ong, 2016; Zandi et al., 2013, 2016). By using real GDP as a proxy for economic development, researchers were able to understand the impact of digitalization on the overall growth and productivity of the Indian economy. By analyzing the relationship between digital payments and real GDP, the study aimed to provide valuable insights into the role of technology in the development of the Indian economy.

Model Estimation/Technique

To analyze the Impact of digital payment on the growth in India, a regression model has been used in the study. In the model, gross domestic product (GDP) is taken as the dependent variable and explanatory variables are Cards (CARDS), Prepaid Payment Instruments (PPI), Retail Electronics Payments (RE), and RTGS. Following the literature, (Hasan et al., 2012, Srinivasan & Kalaivani, 2013, Zandi et al., 2013, 2016, Ravikumar et al., 2019) the relationship between dependent & explanatory variables can be expressed as:

$$GDP = f\,(CARDS, PPI, RE, RTGS).$$

The econometric form of the model is:

GDP = Bo + B1 CARDS + B2PPI + B3 RE + B4RTGS + Ut.
Where GDP = Gross Domestic Product at Constant Prices with base year 2011–12.
CARDS = Debit & Credit Cards.
PPI = Prepaid Payment Instruments.
RE = Retail Electronics.
RTGS = Real Time Gross Settlement.

Hypothesis Development

In line with the above-mentioned variables of digitalization and literature review,it can be hypothesized that:

- H1: Economic growth is positively associated with Card payments.
- H2: Eonomic growth is positively associated with Prepaid payment instruments.
- H3: Economic growth is positively associated with Retail electronics payment.
- H4: Economic growth is positively associated with RTGS. Autoregressive distributed lag (ARDL) cointegration or ARDL bound testing method (Pesaran & Shin, 1999; Srinivasan & Kalaivani, 2013) has been used to find cointegration between variables. If variables are found to be integrated of order 1, [I (1)] and there is cointegration between the variables in a time series model, then the ARDL model of co-integration provides efficient and realistic results. To analyze the impact of digitalization on the growth of India, the ARDL model has been used in the study to discover the effect of some independent variables on the dependent variable by applying a regression model. The dependent variable in the regression model is GDP, while the explanatory variables are CARDS, PPI, Retail Electronics (RE), and RTGS.

In addition to estimating the long-run relationship between stationary and non-stationary time series variables, this method re-parameterizes the error correction model that provides the short-run dynamics and long-run relationship of the provided variables.

Table 14.1 Data base and variables

Variables	*Description*		*Source*
GDP	Real Gross Domestic Product	Quarterly	RBI*
CARDS	Credit Cards, Debit Cards	Quarterly	RBI
PPI	m-Wallet, PPI Cards, Paper Vouchers	Quarterly	RBI
RE	ECS DR, ECS CR, EFT/NEFT	Quarterly	RBI
RTGS	Customer Transactions, Inter-Bank Transactions, Inter-Bank clearing	Quarterly	RBI

**Reserve Bank of India*

Data Base & Variables

The study has been conducted to find the growth of India due to the rise in digital payments for the period 2011–12 to 2022–23. The period 2011–12 to 2022–23 has been chosen to capture the long-term effects of digital payments on economic growth. The impact of digital payments on the growth of the Indian economy has been analyzed using its impact on the gross domestic product of India. The data has been collected from Reserve Bank of India Statistics which are described in the following Table 14.1.

Results and Discussion

The furnished results related to the impact of digital payments on the growth of India have been presented in the following tables.

The proposed model is as under:

$$GDP = Bo + B1\ CARDS + B2PPI + B3\ RE + B4RTGS + Ut.$$

Table 14.2 presents descriptive statistics for all variables included in the regression model, covering the period from 2011–12 to 2022–23. The test statistics employ the mean-based coefficient of skewness and kurtosis to assess the normality of the data utilized for the variables in the study. In the case of a series that follows a normal distribution, it is expected that the skewness falls between the range of −2 to + 2, indicating a somewhat symmetrical distribution. Similarly, the kurtosis, which measures the peakedness of the distribution, is typically expected to be within the range of −3 to + 3. For Jarque- Bera Statistics, the Null

Table 14.2 Summary of descriptive statistics

	GDP	*CARDS*	*PPI*	*RE*	*RTGS*
Mean	3,088,492	285,275.8	10,588.44	1,688,790	10,277,660
Median	3,112,979	261,757.5	10,111.50	1,397,243	10,239,221
Maximum	4,361,515	452,598.0	25,507.00	5,098,432	16,457,720
Minimum	2,042,870	120,920.0	422.0000	147,471.0	7,170,732
Std. Dev	614,875.1	104,449.5	9040.304	1,399,159	2,481,222
Skewness	0.050135	0.093549	0.244731	0.774643	0.541578
Kurtosis	1.911255	1.665913	1.496489	2.548812	2.393752
Jarque–Bera	2.390841	3.629588	5.000239	5.207721	3.081525
Probability	0.302577	0.162871	0.082075	0.073987	0.214218
Sum	1.48E + 08	13,693,238	508,245.0	81,061,901	4.93E + 08

Source Author's calculations

Hypothesis is the normality of the variables. The descriptive statistics indicate that the probability value of J-B statistics is greater than the value at the 5% level of significance for all variables included in the model, refuting the null hypothesis and indicating that all variables used in the study are normally distributed.

To quantify parameter estimates, an endeavor has been undertaken to ascertain the stationarity of data related to all variables incorporated in the model. The study has conducted a Unit Root test to assess the stationary nature of the variables.

A unit root test measures the stationary property of the time series data. Table 14.3A shows the result of the unit root test of the model. An augmented Dickey-Fuller test has been applied to check the stationary or Non-stationary properties of the series. Herein, the null hypothesis is that the variable has a unit root (non-stationary) which is tested against an alternate hypothesis that the variable is stationary. Table 14.3A reveals the results of the unit root test at a level, which shows that the null hypothesis is rejected for all variables. In ADF test statistics, if the ADF test statistics value is greater than the critical value at a 1% or 5% level of significance, we reject the null hypothesis. In the table, all variables like Gross Domestic Product, Cards, Retail Electronic Payments, and RTGS are non-stationary. These variables have an ADF value less than the critical value at a 5% level of significance at the level. The table decides that all variables in the model are non-stationary.

Table 14.3A Unit root test at first difference

S. No	*Variables*	*Linear graph*	*At First Difference*			*Decision*
			Test Statistics	*Critical values*		
				1%	*5%*	
1	GDP	Intercept only	−10.999	−3.588	−2.929	Stationary I(1)
2	CARDS	Intercept only	−11.325	−3.585	−2.928	Stationary I(1)
3	PPI	Intercept only	−6.199	−3.581	−2.927	Stationary I(1)
4	RE	Intercept only	−13.492	−3.592	−2.931	Stationary I(2)
5	RTGS	Intercept only	−5.510	−3.588	−2.929	Stationary I(1)

Source Author's calculations

Table 14.3B reveals all variables, which are non-stationary at level but stationary after the first difference. Gross Domestic Product, Cards, Retail electronic Payments, and RTGS became stationary after taking their first difference. These variables are said to be integrated of order one, i.e., I (1). The Retail Electronic Payment variable is integrated into order I(2). The null hypothesis after the first differencing has been rejected for Gross Domestic Product, Cards, Retail electronic Payments, and RTGS as Augmented Dickey-Fuller (ADF) test statistics absolute value is greater than the critical value at 1% or 5% level of significance.

The next step is to select an appropriate lag length for the model. The selection of the optimal lag length is required to obtain optimal results under the ARDL approach. VAR lag order selection criteria have been used to find the optimal lags in the model.

Table 14.4 presents five sets of lag selection criteria using E-Views, namely sequential modified LR test statistics (LR), Final Prediction Error (FPE), Akaike Information Criterion (AIC), Schwarz Information Criterion (SC), and Hannan-Quinn Information Criterion (HQ). The tabulated data indicates that, among the five criteria, four criteria suggested four lags as the optimal lag for 48 observations.

Following the selection of the appropriate lag length, the diagnostic test must be performed to generate unbiased results for the study. Before analyzing the results, the error correction model has undergone a series

Table 14.3B Unit root test at first difference

S. No	*Variables*	*Linear graph*	*At First Difference*			*Decision*
			Test Statistics	*Critical values*		
				1%	*5%*	
1	GDP	Intercept only	−10.999	−3.588	−2.929	Stationary I(1)
2	CARDS	Intercept only	−11.325	−3.585	−2.928	Stationary I(1)
3	PPI	Intercept only	−6.199	−3.581	−2.927	Stationary I(1)
4	RE	Intercept only	−13.492	−3.592	−2.931	Stationary I(2)
5	RTGS	Intercept only	−5.510	−3.588	−2.929	Stationary I(1)

Source Author's calculations

Table 14.4 Var lag order selection criteria

Lag	*LogL*	*LR*	*FPE*	*AIC*	*SC*	*HQ*
0	−2911.978	NA	2.63E + 51	132.5899	132.7927	132.6651
1	−2704.171	358.9401	6.54E + 47	124.2805	125.4970*	124.7316
2	−2677.911	39.39017	6.47E + 47	124.2232	126.4534	125.0503
3	−2636.183	53.10752	3.41E + 47	123.4629	126.7069	124.6659
4	−2569.813	69.38706*	6.66e + 46*	121.5824*	125.8401	123.1614*

***indicates lag order selection criteria LR—LR test statistics (sequential modified), FPE—Final Prediction Error, AK—Akaike Information Criterion, SC—Schwarz information Criterion, HQ—Hannan–Quin –nformation criterion*

Source Author's calculations

of diagnostic tests to determine its validity. The model's diagnostic test results are satisfactory.

Table 14.5 displays the results of the Breusch-Godfrey Serial Correlation LM Test for autocorrelation. The results indicate that the model lacks autocorrelation. As the probability value of the observed R square for the LM test is 0.4493, which is greater than 0.05, it is significant. The Breusch–Pagan–Godfrey test, which detects the absence of heteroscedasticity in the model, was used to test the heteroscedasticity of the model. The observed probability value of R square is 0.4653, which is greater

Table 14.5 Diagnostic tests

Diagnostic test	*P value*
Serial Correlation LM Test (Breusch—Godfrey)	0.4493
Histogram—Normality Test (Jarque- Bera)	0.3404
Heteroscedasticity (Breusch-Pagan-Godfrey)	0.4653

Source Author's calculations

than 0.05, which justifies the absence of heteroscedasticity. To evaluate the residuals' normality, the J-B test statistics have been applied to the model. The results suggest that residuals follow a normal distribution.

The diagnostic test results indicate that the residual term in the model lacks serial correlation and heteroscedasticity. Furthermore, residuals have a normal distribution. Consequently, the next stage is to use the ARDL bound test to determine the existence of the long-run relationship between the dependent and independent variables of the model.

Table 14.6 presents the result of the ARDL Bound Testing approach (Pesaran & Shin, 1999) that has been applied to find the cointegration between the variables. The co-integration here implies that a series of all variables cannot move independently from each other. Co-integration of the variables also indicates that in the short run, there is some adjustment process, preventing the errors in the long run relationship from becoming larger and larger (Srinivasan & Kalaivani, 2013). The null hypothesis, which states that there is no co-integration or long-run relation between

Table 14.6 F-Statistics for testing the existence of long-run relationship

*ARDL Bound Test:- F Statistic: 4.68**		
Critical Bounds value	*I(0) Bound*	*I(1) Bound*
10%	2.45	3.52
5%	2.86	4.01
2.50%	3.25	4.49
1%	3.74	5.06

*Note *indicates that F-Statistics is significant at 1 percent and 5 percent levels of significance as the value is greater than the upper bound value*

Source Author's calculations

the variables, has been rejected. This is because the value of the F-statistics exceeds the critical value at both the 1% and 5% levels of significance. Based on the findings, it is possible to reject the null hypothesis, indicating the presence of stable, long-term cointegration among the variables.

The estimates of the long-run coefficients of the selected ARDL Model (4,3,4,3,3) based on AIC have been worked out in Table 14.7. The relationship between GDP and CARDs is positive and significant. It shows that a rupee increase in card usage results in a 7.09 rupee gain in GDP. At the 1% level of significance, the coefficient value is statistically significant. It implies that long-term growth in India will be accelerated by increased use of credit and debit cards. Prepaid payment instruments (PPI) and GDP also have a negative and strong association. It shows that a rise in PPI of one rupee results in a decline in GDP of 83.42 rupees. This finding is contrary to Ravikumar et al. (2019) findings, which show no relationship between PPI and GDP. At the 5% level of significance, the PPI coefficient value is statistically significant.

Table 14.7 also exerts a positive relationship between GDP and Retail Electronic Payments. In the long run, one rupee increase in RE causes a 0.38 rupee increase in GDP and is significant at a 10 percent level of significance. The other independent variable RTGS does not exert its effects on Real GDP and hence growth in India. This result is similar to the result given by Ravi Kumar et al. (2019).

The short-run changes in the model are connected to the error correction term (ECM) of the ARDL Model. Any short-run adjustment can be

Table 14.7 Estimated long run coefficients of gross domestic product

S. No	*Variable*	*Coefficient*	*Standard Error*
1	CARDS	7.09* (4.47)	1.58
2	PPI	−83.48** (-2.14)	38.85
3	RE	0.38*** (1.74)	0.22
4	RTGS	0.01 (0.47)	0.025
5	C	1,147,163.49 (4.05)	282,862.3

*Note *denotes a 1 percent level of significance& **denotes 5 percent and *** denotes a 10 percent level of significance. ARDL Model (4,3,4,3,3) selected based on Akakie Information criterion (AIC). The figures in () are the t- statistics*
Source Author's calculations

Table 14.8 Short-run coefficients of GDP

S.No	*Variable*	*Coefficients*	*Std. Error*
1	D(GDP(−1))	0.17(1.16)	0.153218
2	D(GDP(−2))	−0.46*(−3.01)	0.153292
3	D(GDP(−3))	−0.37*(−3.46)	0.108502
4	D(CARDS)	0.15(0.32)	0.466652
5	D(CARDS(−1))	−1.87*(−4.29)	0.435001
6	D(CARDS(−2))	−0.56(−1.15)	0.482620
7	D(PPI)	−22.04*(−2.81)	7.834635
8	D(PPI(−1))	22.71***(1.94)	11.715814
9	D(PPI(−2))	−2.88(−0.23)	12.494979
10	D(PPI(−3))	33.21*(3.17)	10.477129
11	D(RE)	0.63*(4.08)	0.154521
12	D(RE(−1))	−0.86*(−3.28)	0.260778
13	D(RE(−2))	0.38**(2.12)	0.181539
14	D(RTGS)	−0.004(−0.26)	0.014678
15	D(RTGS(−1))	−0.06*(−3.64)	0.016964
16	D(RTGS(−2))	0.032**(2.40)	0.013550
17	CointEq(−1)	−0.35*(−2.69)	0.131880

Note *, **, *** denotes 1 percent, 5 percent, & 10 percent level of significance. The figures in () are the t- statistics
Source Author's calculations

viewed as a process of adjustment to the long run as long as there is long-run equilibrium. The error correction term (ECT), which is statistically significant at the one percent level of significance, represents the speed of adjustment and is shown to be negative. The existence of a long-term relationship between the variables is supported by the Error Correction Term's negative sign. The rate of change from the disequilibrium of the previous year to the equilibrium of the current year is 35%. Here, the ECT term's negative value (−0.35), which is in the range of 0 to −2, demonstrates the model's satisfactory results (Samargandi et al., 2015).

In the short-run, eight variables, i.e., lagged GDP (−2), lagged GDP (−3), lagged CARD(−1), lagged PPI, lagged PPI(−3), lagged RE(−1), lagged RE(−2), lagged RTGS(−1), lagged RTGS(−2), significantly influence GDP in India. Here, the coefficient of the variables with the D sign shows the short-run elasticity of all variables.

Conclusion

The findings presented in Tables 14.5 to 14.8 consistently indicate a positive and statistically significant relationship between economic growth in India and card payments over the long term. However, in the short term, this association is observed to be negative. Therefore, based on the available evidence, it can be concluded that hypothesis 1 has not been rejected, implying that the utilization of card payments contributes to the growth of India's economy in the long term. The findings of this study are consistent with the research conducted by Hasan et al. (2012), Zandi et al. (2013, 2016), which demonstrate that the use of card payments has a positive impact on economic activity, leading to an increase in economic growth. Debit cards enable individuals quick access to funds, facilitating personal expenditure and subsequently contributing to the overall growth of the economy.

Furthermore, it has been shown that prepaid payment instruments exert a detrimental impact on the economic progress of India. The findings presented in this study are in contrast to previous research conducted by Hasan et al. (2012) and Zandi et al. (2013), which suggested that PPI contributes to economic growth in European and high-income countries. Therefore, it may be concluded that hypothesis 2 is refuted, indicating that prepaid payment instruments have a detrimental impact on both short-term and long-term economic growth in India. The study revealed a significant correlation between retail electronics payments and economic growth in India. Therefore, hypothesis 3 is not rejected both in the short run with one lag and in the long run. This result is similar to the study conducted in developed economies by Hasan et al. (2012). Their findings revealed that an effective electronic retail payment system has a positive impact on overall economic growth, consumption, and trade. Specifically, in the present study card payments were found to have the most significant relationship in this regard. The research findings indicate that the implementation of the Real Time Gross Settlement (RTGS) system in India does not exhibit any discernible influence on the country's economic growth. One plausible explanation for this phenomenon is the replacement effect observed between electronic card payment, specifically debit card usage, and Real-Time Gross Settlement (RTGS) payment, as discussed by Hasan et al. (2012). Therefore, it can be observed that both customers and merchants exhibit a preference for electronic card payments in comparison to Real Time Gross

Settlement (RTGS) payments due to the convenience it offers in facilitating purchases and the reduced transaction costs associated with it. As a result, there would be a decrease in the utilization of RTGS payments, leading to a subsequent reduction in the impact of RTGS payments on fostering economic growth. These findings apply to both the short-term and long-term periods.

In general, our research findings are consistent with prior studies that demonstrate the significant influence of digital payments on the economic growth of India. This study contributes to the existing body of literature by examining the impact of digital payments on economic development in India. Based on the research findings, it has been observed that the utilization of card payments and retail electronic payments has a positive impact on the economic growth of India. Consequently, this study underscores the significance of card payment and retail electronic payment as a catalyst for economic expansion in India.

References

Abraham, S. (2020). Unified Payment Interface: Towards Greater Cyber Sovereignty. *Observer Research Foundation.*, 380.

Apergis, N. (2019). Financial Vulnerability and Income Inequality: New Evidence from OECD Countries. *Bulletin of Monetary Economics and Banking*, *21*(3), 395–408. https://doi.org/10.21098/BEMP.V21I3.945

Aneja, R., Dygas, R. (Eds.). (2022). *Digital Currencies and the New Global Financial System* (1st ed., pp. 1–16). Routledge. https://doi.org/10.4324/9781003310365

Audretsch, D., Colombelli, A., Grilli, L., Minola, T., & Rasmussen, E. (2020). Innovative Start-ups and Policy Initiatives David. *Research Policy, 49*(10), 1–14.

Basole, R. C., & Karla, J. (2012). Value Transformation in the Mobile Service Ecosystem: A Study of App Store Emergence and Growth. *Service Science, 4*(1), 24–41. https://doi.org/10.1287/serv.1120.0004

Bhatia-Kalluri, A., & Caraway, B. R. (2023). Transformation of the Digital Payment Ecosystem in India: A Case Study of Paytm. *Social Inclusion*, *11*(3), 320–331. https://doi.org/10.17645/si.v11i3.6687

Brunnermeier, M. k, James, H., & Landau, J.-P. (2019). *The Digitalization of Monney* (26300). https://doi.org/10.1007/978-3-030-04405-3_9

Gorshkov, V. (2022). Cashless Payment in Emerging Markets : The Case of Russia. *Asia and the Global Economy*, *2*(1). https://doi.org/10.1016/j.aglobe.2022.100033

Hasan, I., Renzis, T., & Schmiedel, H. (2012). *Retail Payments and Economic Growth* (19/2012).

Humphrey, D. B., Pulley, L. B., & Vesala, J. M. (1996a). Cash, Paper, and Electronic Payments: A Cross-Country Analysis. *Journal of Money, Credit and Banking, 28*(4), 914–939.

Humphrey, D. B., Pulley, L. B., & Vesala, J. M. (1996b). Cash, Paper, and Electronic Payments : A Cross-Country Analysis. *Journal of Money, Credit and Banking, 28*(4), 914–939.

IAMAI. (2023). Internet in India 2022. In *Internet and Mobile Association of India (IAMAI)* (Issue April).

IBEF. (2023). *Digital Payments and Their Impact on the Indian Economy.*

Ionascu, A., Gheorghiu, G., Spatariu, E. C., Munteanu, I., Grigorescu, A., & Danila, A. (2023). Unraveling Digital Transformation in Banking : Evidence from Romania. *Systems, 11*(11), 534.

Kesavan, V., & Srinivasan, K. S. (2023). Present State and Future Directions of Digital Payments System: A Historical and Bibliographic Examination. *International Journal of Professional Business Review, 8*(6), 1–29.

Khandelwal, P., & Asthana, P. (2023). Analyzing the Role of Government Policies in Fostering Innovation and Entrepreneurship in India s Technology Startups. *IRE Journals, 6*(12), 1129–1135.

Pal, A., Herath, T., De, R., & Raghav Rao, H. (2018). Factors Facilitating Adoption of Mobile Payment Services over Credit/Debit Cards: An Investigation after the Demonetization Policy Shock in India. *PACIS 2018 Proceedings*, 337.

Pesaran, M. H., & Shin, Y. (1999). An Autoregressive Distributed-Lag Modelling Approach to Co-integration Analysis. *Econometrics and Economic Theory in the 20th Century: The Ragnar Frisch Centennial Symposium.* https://doi.org/10.1017/ccol0521633230.011

Ravikumar, T., Suresha, B., Sriram, M., & Rajesh, R. (2019). Impact of Digital Payments on Economic Growth: Evidence from India. *International Journal of Innovative Technology and Exploring Engineering*, *8*(12), 553–557. https://doi.org/10.35940/ijitee.L3432.1081219

Roy, P. M. (2021). Anatomy of the Digital Payment Ecosystem in India. *Bimaquest, 21*(3), 40–61.

Samargandi, N., Fidrmuc, J., & Ghosh, S. (2015). Is the Relationship Between Financial Development and Economic Growth Monotonic? Evidence from a Sample of Middle-Income Countries. *World Development, 68*(1), 66–81. https://doi.org/10.1016/j.worlddev.2014.11.010

Sharma, R. ., & Abraham, P. (2012). Industrial Credit and Investment Corporation of India (ICICI) Bank: The Emergent Bank of the Emerging Economies. *Banking with Integrity*, 115–128.

Singh, N. (2023). Financial Inclusion: Concepts, Issues and Policies for India. *Emerald Publishing Limited*, 33–36. https://doi.org/10.2139/ssrn.3307903

Sreenu, N. (2020). Cashless Payment Policy and Its Effects on Economic Growth of India : An Exploratory Study. *ACM Transactions on Management Information System*, *11*(3), 15:1–15:10.

Srinivasan, P., & Kalaivani, M. (2013). Exchange Rate Volatility and Export Growth in India: An ARDL Bounds Testing Approach. *Decision Science Letters*, *2*(3), 191–202. https://doi.org/10.5267/j.dsl.2013.04.002

Tariq, S. A. S., Iftikhar, S. F., Iftikhar, K., Raza, H., & Idress, S. (2023). The Role of Digital Finance in Economic Development: A Cross Country Analysis. *Journal of Policy Research*, *9*(3), 160–171.

Tee, H., & Ong, H. (2016). Cashless Payment and Economic Growth. *Financial Innovation*, *2*(4), 1–9. https://doi.org/10.1186/s40854-016-0023-z

Trivedi, H. (2023). Challenges in Digital Payment Adoption in India. *Challenges in Digital Payment Adoption in India*, *5*(2), 32–38.

Wong, T., Lau, W., & Yip, T. (2020). Cashless Payments and Economic Growth : Evidence from Selected OECD Countries. *Journal of Central Banking Theory and Practice*, 189–213. https://doi.org/10.2478/jcbtp-2020-0028

Yusuf, I. (2016). Cash-less Policy and Economic Growth : Evidence from Nigeria Ismaila Yusu *International Journal of Electronic Finance*, *9*(1), 63–71.

Zandi, M., Koropeckyj, S., Matsiras, P., Singh, V., & Zandi, M. (2016, February). The Impact of Electronic Infrastructure on Economic Growth. *Moody's Analytics*, 31.

Zandi, M., Singh, V., & Irving, J. (2013). The Impact of Electronic Payments on Economic Growth. *Moody's Analytics*, *217*(2).

CHAPTER 15

Unveiling the Significance of RBI's Digital Currency: How Could It Reshape and Impact the Landscape of International Trade?

Jitender Kumar and *Anjali Ahuja*

Introduction

The global financial sector has seen a profound transformation recently due to technological breakthroughs and changing consumer preferences. The advent of CBDCs is one of the most significant advancements in this area (Chorzempa, 2021). CBDC is a digital version of a country's money that its central bank issues and controls (Lee et al., 2021). CBDCs, which are supposed to exist exclusively in digital form, unlike conventional forms of currency, present new potential and difficulties

J. Kumar (✉)
Department of Management Studies, Deenbandhu Chhotu Ram University of Science and Technology, Murthal, Haryana, India
e-mail: jitenderkumar.mba@dcrustm.org

A. Ahuja
School of Commerce and Finance, Geeta University, Panipat, Haryana, India

R. Aneja and R. Dygas (eds.), *Digital Currencies in The New Global World Order*, https://doi.org/10.1007/978-981-97-4810-5_15

for financial institutions worldwide. Central banks are investigating the potential advantages of deploying CBDCs to modernize payment systems, improve financial inclusion, and facilitate cross-border transactions as economies become more digitalized and cash usage falls. As a trailblazing central bank, RBI has started investigating the viability and effects of introducing its digital currency (Vujovi, 2023). The value of the RBI's digital money is enormous for international trade. The digital Rupee can revolutionize international business and assist economic growth by facilitating cross-border transactions, reducing costs, and promoting financial inclusion. Accordingly, this chapter uses a multifaceted strategy. The study thoroughly analyses the current literature, government documents, and information sources about CBDC, virtual currencies, and international financial systems. This chapter focuses on the RBI implementation strategy for the CBDC and its possible effects on international commerce and economic dynamics. While acknowledging the broader landscape of digital currencies, the report primarily focuses on the strategies, challenges, and potential CBDC presents. This research chapter discusses the significance, political challenges, and risks, compares and contrasts CBDC with current digital currencies, and analyzes and extrapolates from international CBDC experiments. The remainder of the chapter is as follows: Sect. 15.2 provides insights into worldwide trends and actions linked to the adoption of CBDC and offers an overview of CBDC; Sect. 15.3 represents the research methodology; Sect. 15.4 discusses the importance of the RBI's digital currency in international trade; Sect. 15.5 includes the implementation of the CBDC, which faces several political challenges and risks; Sect. 15.6 compares and contrasts CBDC with current digital currencies; Sect. 15.7 analyzes and extrapolates from international CBDC experiments; Sect. 15.8 reports conclusions, prospects, and policy recommendations.

Central Bank Digital Currency (CBDC)

Definition and Conceptual Overview

A nation's official currency issued and governed by the central bank is the CBDC (Kuehnlenz et al., 2023; Náez Alonso et al., 2021; Ozili, 2023). In contrast to conventional physical money, CBDC is only available digitally and is supported by the full faith and credit of the central bank that issued it. CBDCs come in various formats, including wholesale CBDCs for financial institutions and retail CBDCs available to the general public. Huang and Mayer (2022) find that cryptocurrencies and CBDCs use digital technology but are fundamentally different. CBDCs are centralized and preserve the central bank's authority over issuance and regulation, unlike cryptocurrencies, which usually function on blockchain technology and are decentralized.

Global Trends and Initiatives in CBDC Adoption

China's Digital Currency Electronic Payment (DCEP) project stands out as one of the pioneering CBDC initiatives, focusing on improving payment efficiency and financial inclusion (Lo et al., 2022; Wang et al., 2022). The European Central Bank (ECB) has also undertaken exploratory efforts driven by the need to adapt to the rise of digital currencies.

Other central banks, such as the Bank of England, the Bank of Canada, and the U.S. Federal Reserve, have shown interest in CBDCs by conducting research and public consultations (Bordo, 2017). These actions highlight that CBDCs are recognized as a response to the changing demands of digital economies.

The RBI's Method for Implementing the CBDC

Given the potential benefits that CBDC adoption might have for the Indian financial sector, the RBI has adopted a proactive stance. The RBI's consideration of CBDCs is consistent with its commitment to innovation and the progress of financial technology (RBI, 2022). In-depth analysis, stakeholder participation, and a staged testing and deployment process are all part of the RBI's implementation strategy for the CBDC. The RBI has emphasized the significance of resolving security, scalability, and legal consequences concerns to build a solid and safe CBDC system.

The report of the Bank for International Settlements (2021) highlights that to maximize the advantages of CBDCs while minimizing possible risks, the central bank has also said that it strongly emphasizes finding a balance between innovation and stability. The RBI is committed to systematic and deliberate CBDC development, as seen by its pilot initiatives and partnerships with technology companies.

Research Methodology

A thorough search utilized relevant terms connected to digital currency or CBDC throughout the planning stage. The essential concepts, including the global perspective on central bank digital currency, opportunities, challenges, and promotion countermeasures of central bank digital currency, genesis, design, and implications, were considered when outlining the following documents. To develop a fundamental understanding of the subject area, a non-structured process involved testing different keyword combinations and accessing articles from reference lists. During this stage, we received an explanation of the filtering rules and search terms used to locate the final dataset. Initially, search strings include "digital currency*," "CBDC*," "RBI*," "Central Bank*," and "International Trade*." Search terms were utilized to accumulate data and cover the entire topic. These combinations were designed to ensure that essential keywords produce the required outcomes in articles. We access online databases and publishers using advanced search, including Google Scholar, Emerald, Elsevier, Springer, Taylor and Francis, etc.

Significance of the RBI's Digital Currency in International Trade

RBI's venture into a CBDC significantly impacts international commerce and the economy. This section examines the RBI's digital currency's multidimensional relevance in numerous facets of global commerce and finance.

Streamlining Cross-Border Transactions

One of the main benefits of establishing a CBDC is that cross-border transactions might be completely transformed. Traditional international payment systems frequently feature multiple intermediaries, convoluted procedures, and protracted settlement delays. RBI can enable nearly immediate cross-border transfers by utilizing blockchain technology and the digital character of CBDCs, removing intermediaries, and minimizing the time and complexity involved with international transactions (Chen et al., 2022). This simplified procedure could increase trade efficiency and encourage frictionless international trade.

Reducing Transaction Costs and Settlement Times

Extensive settlement periods and high transaction costs have long been problems in global trade. Businesses can deploy resources more effectively because of CBDC's ability to reduce transaction costs related to cross-border payments drastically (Joseph et al., 2023). Additionally, quicker access to cash for firms and a decrease in counterparty risks due to shorter settlement periods might promote a more lively and competitive global trading environment.

Enhancing Financial Inclusion and Accessibility

In order to improve financial inclusion and accessibility worldwide scale, CBDC can be significant (Banerjee & Sinha, 2023). Certain groups may need access to traditional financial institutions, especially in isolated or underdeveloped areas. The RBI may expand financial services to the unbanked and underbanked, encouraging them to participate more actively in global commerce and economic activities. This can be done by offering a digital currency accessible through smartphones and other devices.

Mitigating Foreign Exchange Risks

Arize et al. (2000) state that changes in exchange rates can significantly increase international business risks. CBDC may reduce some of these concerns by offering stable and simple-to-convert digital money. This may boost investor and trader confidence, lessen the uncertainty brought on by currency volatility, and promote a more stable climate for international commerce.

Impact on Monetary Policy and Exchange Rates

According to Bhowmik (2022), CBDC may affect monetary policy and exchange rates nationally and internationally. The central bank can exercise more accurate control over monetary aggregates by keeping a watch on and influencing the circulation of digital currency. By altering the supply and demand of digital currency relative to other currencies, adopting a CBDC may impact exchange rates.

Potential Challenges and Risks

CBDC is introduced by RBI, which presents various political challenges and risks. This section focuses on the key concerns related to CBDC.

Cyber Security and Data Privacy Concerns

The possibility of counterattacks and data breaches is rising along with the prevalence of digital transactions. Robust cybersquatting protocols must be used to construct and distribute a CBDC to prevent theft, hacking, and unauthorized access (Lee et al., 2021). The RBI must set up a thorough security framework to ensure the integrity of the digital currency infrastructure and secure users' private and financial information.

Regulatory and Legal Implications

According to Tripathi et al. (2022), CBDC has substantial regulatory and legal implications that require careful consideration. Digital currency's legal status, how it will be handled in light of current financial rules, and how it might affect know-your-customer (KYC) and anti-money laundering (AML) processes might all be sources of worry. The central bank must collaborate with regulatory organizations to establish a legal framework that tackles these issues, encourages innovation, and ensures compliance.

Technological Infrastructure Requirements

Bhowmik (2022) argues that establishing CBDC may impact domestic and foreign exchange rates and monetary policy. The central bank may exert more accurate control over monetary aggregates by keeping an eye on and influencing the circulation of digital money. Adopting a CBDC may alter the supply and demand of digital currency concerning other currencies, which may impact exchange rates.

Coexistence with other Payment Systems

Implementing CBDC raises concerns about how it would interact with existing payment systems, including digital wallets, traditional banking services, and proprietary digital currencies. It's critical to strike the ideal balance between encouraging the use of the CBDC and guaranteeing the continuing operation of current payment mechanisms (International Monetary Fund, 2021). To ensure that the CBDC enhances rather than undermines the more significant financial ecosystem, the RBI must manage possible competitiveness and interoperability problems (RBI, 2022).

Comparison with Existing Digital Currencies

The introduction of these new tokens is prompted by examining the unique qualities and functions of CBDCs compared to other digital currencies, especially cryptocurrencies and stablecoins. A thorough comparison between CBDCs and various private digital currency versions is given in this section.

Contrasting CBDCs with Cryptocurrencies and Stablecoins

Central Bank Digital Currencies (CBDCs): As a sovereign form of digital money, CBDCs are issued and governed by central banks. They have a value pegged to the local currency and are backed by the issuing central bank's complete faith and credit. CBDCs preserve the central bank's authority over the issuance, regulation, and monetary policy since they are centralized. They are created with specific goals, such as improving payment systems, promoting financial inclusion, and easing international trade.

Cryptocurrencies: Cryptocurrencies are digital assets that are decentralized and based on blockchain technology (Haque & Shoaib, 2023). Their independence from governments and central banks allows them to function, and the market's supply and demand determines their price. Cryptocurrencies frequently place a high priority on privacy, security, and anonymity. Although they lack the stability of conventional currencies, they may be very turbulent.

Stable coins: Stable coins are a subclass of cryptocurrencies intended to keep their value steady by tying it to an underlying asset, such as fiat money or commodity (Ikeno et al., 2023). They provide stability, although their issuance and governance processes might differ significantly. Stable coins try to bring together price stability and the advantages of cryptocurrencies.

Role of RBI Digital Currency vs. Private Digital Currencies

- *Role of RBI Digital Currency*

CBDC is a sovereign digital currency issued and governed by the central bank (Shen & Hou, 2021). Its introduction aligns with the monetary policy objectives, financial stability aims, and more general economic policies of the central bank. CBDC may retain regulatory control while enhancing domestic payment systems, facilitating effective cross-border transactions, and advancing financial inclusion.

- *Role of Private Digital Currencies*

The function of private digital currencies is to be issued by private entities without the support or oversight of a central bank, including stablecoins and other types of digital assets. They are largely influenced by technological advancement, market demand, and innovation. Private digital currencies could have particular applications, such as quick and affordable international payments or alternative investment opportunities. CBDC, in contrast to private digital currencies, is intended to enhance the current monetary and financial ecosystem by utilizing the central bank's power to bring stability, legal clarity, and trust in digital transactions.

Analyses and Extrapolates from International CBDC Experiments

The current state of CBDC pilots worldwide offers essential new information on the possible advantages, challenges, and risks of their deployment. This section investigates the lessons discovered from numerous CBDC pilots by central banks worldwide.

Overview of Other CBDC Pilots Worldwide

Several central banks have started CBDC pilot programs to examine the viability and effects of issuing digital currency. Notable examples include:

- China's Digital Currency Electronic Payment (DCEP) initiative has undergone rigorous testing and is being gradually implemented across several areas.
- The ECCB has launched the DCash CBDC project in various member countries, so it may be helpful to study the impact on financial inclusion and payment efficiency.

Learning from Successful Implementations

The DCEP project in China has demonstrated how CBDCs may increase financial inclusion, ease cross-border trade, and simplify payment processes. The pilot has emphasized the importance of cooperating with IT partners and the necessity of strong cybersecurity measures.

The ECCB's pilot program showed the positive impacts of CBDCs on financial inclusion, particularly in underprivileged communities. Public relations, gradual implementation, and effective stakeholder engagement are examples of successful implementation.

Understanding Pitfalls and Failures

- Venezuela's Petro, a government-backed cryptocurrency, had difficulties due to regulatory problems, economic instability, and a lack of confidence. This experiment highlights the value of establishing transparent regulatory frameworks and public trust.
- The Swedish e-krona trial raised questions about how it might affect bank savings and the role of the central bank. The example highlights the importance of giving monetary policy consequences serious thought.

Conclusion

RBI's establishment of a CBDC substantially impacts international commerce, financial inclusion, and the overall economy. The relevance, challenges, and prospective effects of the CBDC implementation have been covered in this chapter. The background and context of CBDCs, the RBI's strategy for implementing them, and their potential implications for international commerce are examined throughout this chapter. Researchers compared CBDCs to cryptocurrencies and stablecoins, discussed risks and problems related to their acceptance, and drew conclusions from international CBDC pilots. The study has highlighted the distinctive role of CBDC in promoting financial inclusion, facilitating international trade, and reducing currency risk.

CBDC can influence international commerce and economic growth significantly. It may encourage international trade, especially for SMEs, by lowering transaction costs, speeding up settlement times, and promoting financial inclusion. It has the potential to completely transform cross-border transactions, making them quicker, more affordable, and available to a broader range of companies and people. Greater trust in international transactions may result from the CBDC's improved stability and decreased foreign exchange concerns. A proactive approach to policy and technology is required to deploy a CBDC successfully. The top goals are to develop a robust regulatory framework, cooperation with other central banks for cross-border transactions, and interoperability with global payment systems.

In conclusion, establishing CBDC is an essential step toward modernizing financial institutions, promoting inclusive economic growth, and establishing India as a leader in the digital economy. RBI can navigate the changing global finance landscape and support a more effective, equitable, and robust international commerce ecosystem by using the potential of CBDCs while resolving issues.

References

Arize, A. C., Osang, T., & Slottje, D. J. (2000). Exchange-rate Volatility and Foreign Trade: Evidence from Thirteen LDC's. *Journal of Business & Economic Statistics, 18*(1), 10–17.

Aneja, R., Dygas, R. (Eds.). (2022). *Digital Currencies and the New Global Financial System* (1st ed., pp. 1–16). Routledge. https://doi.org/10.4324/9781003310365

Banerjee, S., & Sinha, M. (2023). Promoting Financial Inclusion through Central Bank Digital Currency: An Evaluation of Payment System Viability in India. *Australasian Accounting, Business and Finance Journal, 17*(1), 176–204.

Bank for International Settlements (2021). Central Bank Digital Currencies: Foundational Principles and Core Features. https://www.bis.org/publ/othp33.htm

Bhowmik, D. (2022). Monetary Policy Implications of Central Bank Digital Currency with Special Reference to India. *Asia-Pacific Journal of Management and Technology (AJMT), 2*(3), 1–8.

Bordo, M. D., & Levin, A. T. (2017). *Central Bank Digital Currency and the Future of Monetary Policy* (No. w23711). National Bureau of Economic Research.

Chen, S., D'Silva, D., Packer, F., & Tiwari, S. (2022). BIS Papers

Chorzempa, M. (2021). China, the United States, and Central Bank Digital Currencies: How Important Is It to be First? *China Economic Journal, 14*(1), 102–115.

European Central Bank. (2019). Crypto-Assets: Implications for Financial Stability, Monetary Policy, and Payments and Market Infrastructures.

Haque, M. A., & Shoaib, M. (2023). e₹—The Digital Currency in India: Challenges and Future Prospects. *BenchCouncil Transactions on Benchmarks, Standards and Evaluations*, p .100107

https://www.ecb.europa.eu/pub/pdf/scpops/ecb.op223~3ce14e986c.en.pdf

Huang, Y., & Mayer, M. (2022). Digital Currencies, Monetary Sovereignty, and US–China Power Competition. *Policy & Internet, 14*(2), 324–347.

Ikeno, Y., Angel, J., & Panigrahi, S. (2023). Check for updates Soundness of Stablecoins. In *Financial Cryptography and Data Security. FC 2022 International Workshops: CoDecFin, DeFi, Voting, WTSC, Grenada, May 6, 2022, Revised Selected Papers* (Vol. 13412, p. 66). Springer Nature.

International Monetary Fund (2021). Legal and Regulatory Issues in CBDC Arrangements. https://www.elibrary.imf.org/view/journals/007/2023/016/article-A001-en.xml

Joseph, S. F., & Peter Leo Deepak, J. (2023). A Study on CBDCS and e-Rupee with Special Reference to e-Yuan. In *International Conference on Economics, Business and Sustainability* (pp. 239–247). Springer Nature Singapore.

Kuehnlenz, S., Orsi, B., & Kaltenbrunner, A. (2023). Central Bank Digital Currencies and the International Payment System: The Demise of the US Dollar? *Research in International Business and Finance, 64*, 101834.

Lee, D. K. C., Yan, L., & Wang, Y. (2021). A Global Perspective on Central Bank Digital Currency. *China Economic Journal, 14*(1), 52–66.

Lo, C. (2022). Disrupting the Crypto Disruption. In *The Digital Renminbi's Disruption* (pp. 37–55). Emerald Publishing Limited.

Náñez Alonso, S. L., Jorge-Vazquez, J., & Reier Forradellas, R. F. (2021). Central Banks Digital Currency: Detection of Optimal Countries for the Implementation of a CBDC and the Implication for Payment Industry Open Innovation. *Journal of Open Innovation: Technology, Market, and Complexity, 7*(1), 72.

Ozili, P. K. (2023). Central Bank Digital Currency Research Around the World: A Review of the Literature. *Journal of Money Laundering Control, 26*(2), 215–226.

People's Bank of China (2020). Digital Currency Electronic Payment (DCEP) Research Report.http://www.pbc.gov.cn/en/3688110/3688172/4157443/4293696/2021071614584691871.pdf

Reserve Bank of India (2022). Report of the Committee on Central Bank Digital Currency. https://rbi.org.in/Scripts/PublicationReportDetails.aspx?UrlPage=&ID=1218

Shen, W., & Hou, L. (2021). China's Central Bank Digital Currency and Its Impacts on Monetary Policy and Payment Competition: Game Changer or Regulatory Toolkit? *Computer Law & Security Review, 41*, 105577.

Tripathi, S., Chaubey, A., & Goel, I. (2022). An Empirical Analysis of Potential Central Bank Digital Currency Adoption Procedure by Indian Government And Its Implications. *Sachetas, 1*(1), 32–38.

Vujović, D. (2023). The Impact of Digital Money on Monetary and Fiscal Policy. *Ekonomika Preduzeća, 71*(1–2), 65–76.

Wang, Y. R., Ma, C. Q., & Ren, Y. S. (2022). A Model for CBDC Audits based on Blockchain Technology: Learning from the DCEP. *Research in International Business and Finance, 63*, 101781.

CHAPTER 16

RBI's Digital Currency and Its Significance in the Global Trade

Gurjinder Singh and Amandeep Verma

Introduction

In the contemporary world of banking, the significance of digital currency cannot be overstated in the context of fostering financial inclusion and driving economic growth in nations. CBDCs essentially represent digital counterparts to traditional currencies, bearing the same liability and backing from the Central Bank. They can be utilized by citizens for all forms of financial transactions. CBDCs share characteristics, both strengths and vulnerabilities, with traditional currencies, rooted in the same fundamentals. However, their digital nature inherently introduces distinctive efficiencies. At its core, a Central Bank Digital Currency (CBDC) is a digital form of currency which normally issued and

G. Singh
Department of Commerce, PGGCG Sector 42, Chandigarh, India

A. Verma (✉)
Department of Economics, Central University of Haryana, Mahendragarh, India
e-mail: dramandeep@cuh.ac.in

R. Aneja and R. Dygas (eds.), *Digital Currencies in The New Global World Order*, https://doi.org/10.1007/978-981-97-4810-5_16

controlled by a nation's central bank. Many governments are contemplating the introduction of CBDCs due to their potential to confer several advantages on the local economy. The adoption of CBDCs is expected to bolster monetary stability by affording Central Banks the same level of control they had with traditional currencies, thus aiding in the stabilization of economic and monetary cycles. Additionally, CBDCs are poised to offer numerous opportunities for businesses and consumers alike. These benefits encompass cost reduction in transactions, facilitation of cross-border transactions, and enhancement of financial inclusion. The cost reduction in transactions can be realized through the digitization of internal financial processes and real-time settlement of transactions. In the developing world, where the payment landscape remains complex and outdated, CBDCs have the potential to expedite cross-border transactions, which currently take days to clear in bank accounts. They achieve this by diminishing reliance on the US dollar as a universal currency, reducing the number of intermediaries involved in payment chains, and fostering competition among private-sector providers (Adrian, 2022). CBDCs can also ease cross-border transactions with international partners, as exemplified by the Chinese Government's plans to connect its CBDC system with those of its trading partners. The digital renminbi (e-CNY), currently undergoing testing in multiple Chinese provinces, is deemed "technically ready for cross-border use."

As of May 2022, Central Bank Digital Currencies (CBDCs) had become a global phenomenon, with over 100 countries, representing more than 95 percent of the world's GDP, engaging in at least one CBDC-related initiative (Jahan et al., 2022). The G7 nations are all deliberating the utilization of CBDCs, while the European Central Bank has set its sights on introducing the eEuro by 2025. Within the G20 group, 19 countries are exploring the CBDC realm, with 16 already in advanced development or pilot stages. Notable examples include the Central Bank of The Bahamas (Sand Dollar), the Eastern Caribbean Central Bank (DCash), the Central Bank of Nigeria (e-Naira), and the Bank of Jamaica (JamDex), among others. It's worth highlighting that even the Federal Reserve of U.S. has acknowledged that "a CBDC could fundamentally change the structure of the U.S. financial system" (BIS annual reports, 2021). Interestingly, an increasing number of African nations are contemplating CBDC launches, albeit at the research stage. South Africa and Ghana, for instance, have initiated pilot programs to test their respective CBDCs, the eRand and eCedi. Furthermore, the Bank of

Central African States (BEAC) is proposing the introduction of a CBDC for its member states in the Central African Economic and Monetary Community (CEMAC), which includes Cameroon, Chad, Central African Republic, Equatorial Guinea, Congo, and Gabon. This move follows the Central African Republic's groundbreaking decision to recognize Bitcoin as legal tender in April 2022.

Currently, the Federal Reserve Bank of Boston and the Massachusetts Institute of Technology's Digital Currency Initiative are collaboratively conducting research on CBDCs under the banner of Project Hamilton (Federal Reserve Bank of Boston, 2022). This extensive research project spans multiple years and aims to delve into the potential design options for CBDCs while gaining practical insights into the technical challenges and opportunities they present.

The cross-border payment mechanism facilitated by Central Bank Digital Currencies (CBDCs) is a pivotal aspect of their transformative impact on global trade. CBDCs, as evidenced by case studies such as China's e-CNY, The Bahamas' Sand Dollar, and Nigeria's e-Naira, offer a streamlined approach to cross-border transactions. This mechanism holds the potential to significantly reduce costs and enhance overall efficiency in international trade.

CBDCs act as a transparent and traceable platform, addressing challenges related to anti-money laundering (AML) and counter-terrorism financing (CTF) risks. This transparency contributes to the creation of a secure global financial ecosystem, instilling confidence in cross-border transactions. Furthermore, the traceability inherent in CBDC transactions can facilitate the enhancement of credit information for trade finance. This feature enables a more informed evaluation of the creditworthiness of businesses engaged in international transactions, thereby contributing to the overall reliability of global trade financing.

The value proposition of CBDCs in the realm of cross-border payments extends beyond cost reduction and efficiency improvements. Their adoption holds the potential to revolutionize the traditional international payment systems, fostering healthy competition among private-sector providers. Additionally, CBDCs can mitigate issues associated with the de-risking of nations facing elevated AML and CTF risks, ensuring adherence to regulations while promoting international trade in regions grappling with these challenges.

Therefore, the main research question arises: What is the significance and impact of Central Bank Digital Currencies (CBDCs) in the contemporary world of banking, especially in the context of fostering financial inclusion and driving economic growth in nations? How RBI's Digital currencies can play a prominent role in global trading. How do Central Bank Digital Currencies (CBDCs) impact global trade dynamics, financial inclusion, and economic growth, with a focus on their strategies, values added, and key success factors?

Unveiling the Mechanics of CBDC Implementation

Central Bank Digital Currency (CBDC) operates in a manner akin to physical cash. When conducting transactions via CBDC, the transfer of funds occurs almost instantaneously, and once initiated, the recipient cannot reverse the transaction. Another pivotal advantage of CBDC lies in its legal tender status. This designation signifies that CBDC must be universally accepted for all legal transactions (Lukonga, 2023). It can be used to pay taxes, and lenders are legally obliged to accept it as repayment.

In contrast, numerous other digital currencies do not hold legal tender status in several countries, India being one of them. Only a limited number of vendors opt to directly accept cryptocurrencies, which means that individuals often have to convert their digital assets into fiat currencies before engaging in most transactions. Moreover, the use of cryptocurrencies for payments can trigger taxable events, potentially leading to the obligation of paying capital gains taxes every time Bitcoin or Ethereum's Ether token is used for purchases, in addition to any applicable sales taxes.

Navigating the Global Landscape of Digital Currency Implementations

According to data from the Central Bank Digital Currency (CBDC) Tracker by the Atlantic Council's Geo-Economics Centre, ten countries have successfully launched their digital currencies. China, a prominent player in the CBDC arena, is poised to expand its pilot CBDC program in 2023 (Chhangani, 2023). China initiated its digital yuan pilot project as far back as 2014, conducting trials in five cities and distributing millions in digital currency through lotteries to demonstrate its functionality. Lottery winners receive free CBDC, which they can spend at local establishments accepting it.

While this initiative has not yet achieved national scale, China has plans to expand it further by collaborating with banks and mobile payment providers such as Alipay. Furthermore, the central banks of China and the United Arab Emirates are engaged in a joint project that utilizes blockchain technology and Central Bank Digital Currencies (CBDCs) to facilitate cross-border payments between their respective nations. The successful outcomes of such projects could potentially act as a catalyst for other countries to develop their own CBDCs.

In the event that India embraces a digital currency, it would function as an electronic alternative to physical cash, offering the added advantage of swift electronic transfers. Despite its electronic nature, a digital currency must remain as accessible and user-friendly as traditional cash. Achieving this requires significant effort and input from various industries, but the potential returns on such investments could be substantial.

Central Bank Digital Currency: A Literature Review

A lot of studies have been conducted on the relevance of digital currencies in global trade, Carapella and Flemming (2020) highlight the impact of recent technological advancements, which have brought forth an array of swift electronic payment options for everyday consumer transactions. This evolving landscape has prompted policymakers to consider the role of the public sector in providing a digital payment tool that aligns with the demands of the modern economy. Theocratically, the introduction of a Central Bank Digital Currency (CBDC) revives longstanding inquiries into the supply of both public and private currencies, a discussion originally explored by Gurley and Shaw in 1955. Additionally, it highlights the central bank's potential to employ CBDC as a direct conduit for implementing monetary policy measures that directly impact households, an idea put forth by Tobin in 1985.

The existing theoretical literature on CBDC addresses these inquiries by examining the impact of introducing a CBDC on two key fronts: (i) its effect on commercial banks, and (ii) its implications for monetary policy and financial stability, along with the resulting welfare considerations. Policymakers have shown a significant interest in these questions, among others, as reflected in discussions by institutions such as the Bank for International Settlements in 2018.

In a general sense, the body of research examining Central Bank Digital Currency (CBDC) commonly views it as a form of payment that can yield interest and doesn't necessarily require placement in a commercial bank account. While there isn't a universally accepted description of CBDC among policymakers or scholars, the existing literature primarily focuses on analyzing the consequences of the public holding a direct liability from the central bank. The models and assumptions presented in this literature offer simplified structures for addressing inquiries about the impacts of CBDC at both individual and societal scales, while simplifying or overlooking many of the intricate design considerations that concern policymakers.

The initial segment of the literature explores the impact of CBDC on commercial banks. In essence, CBDC can function as an interest-bearing alternative to deposits held in commercial banks. Faced with such an alternative, commercial banks might adjust the interest rates they offer to depositors, which, in turn, can affect their cost of obtaining funds and the terms at which they provide loans. Consequently, the introduction of CBDC could lead to changes in both the total amount of bank deposits and the level of lending intermediated by banks. This aspect of the literature addresses the concerns of certain policymakers who worry that CBDC's introduction might replace commercial banks' primary source of funding, potentially causing disintermediation and a reduction in their lending activities. Andolfatto (2018) delves into these effects, particularly focusing on a monopoly bank. In his research, when CBDC offers interest, the bank, which typically generates profits, adjusts its deposit rates to match the CBDC's interest rate, ensuring depositors are indifferent between the two options. An important finding is that CBDC, by offering more favorable terms to depositors, increases the demand for deposits. This happens both through an intensive margin, where existing depositors choose to save more, and an extensive margin, where individuals who previously remained unbanked opt to bear the cost of accessing the banking sector. As a result, the competitive pressure introduced by CBDC has the potential to expand the pool of bank depositors.

Nevertheless, it is conceivable that the remuneration offered by Central Bank Digital Currency (CBDC) could potentially reduce the "franchise value" (profits) of banks. However, this doesn't automatically translate into higher interest rates on loans. In this context, Andolfatto (2018) argues that as long as banks retain the ability to borrow reserves from the central bank, which is typically facilitated through the central bank's lending facility within a corridor system, the risk of disintermediation can be alleviated. This is because banks can still continue their lending activities even in the presence of CBDC. Chiu et al. (2020) expand upon ideas akin to those presented in Andolfatto (2018) by delving into the implications of CBDC on bank lending. They conceptualize CBDC as an interest-bearing asset that competes with traditional bank deposits. The fundamental economic mechanism driving their primary findings is reminiscent of Andolfatto (2018) because, in their model, banks operate within an imperfectly competitive environment. From a theoretical perspective, Chiu et al. (2020) expand upon the analysis conducted by Andolfatto (2018) by delving into scenarios where banks have the capability to hold Central Bank Digital Currency (CBDC) to meet their reserve requirements. Furthermore, they explore CBDC designs that incorporate policy tools beyond simply fixing the interest rate it offers. Using a calibrated model based on the United States, Chiu et al. (2020) quantify the extent to which the introduction of CBDC can impact lending. Their findings indicate that with an appropriately chosen remuneration rate, lending can potentially increase by as much as 3.55%. However, the specific effect on lending depends on the particular parameters considered. In cases where the interest rate on CBDC is lower than that on traditional deposits, there is no discernible impact on banks' activities. When the interest rate on CBDC surpasses that of deposits but remains within reasonable bounds, banks respond by raising deposit rates and increasing lending, as higher deposit rates attract a larger deposit base. However, if the interest rate on CBDC becomes excessively high, banks tend to reduce their deposits and loans.

Brunnermeier and Niepelt (2019) also view CBDC as an asset sharing the same liquidity characteristics as conventional bank deposits. Similar to the scenario described in Andolfatto (2018), assuming that the central bank provides loans to commercial banks, introducing CBDC doesn't necessarily disrupt the balance of the economy. They illustrate that if households' deposits are swapped for CBDC, the equilibrium remains unchanged as long as two conditions are met: (i) Deposit obligations are replaced with central bank loans provided to commercial banks, and (ii) there is no change in the constraints experienced by households or the distribution of wealth among them.

In simpler terms, if CBDC does not impact households' financial gains or alter the limitations they face, the investment decisions made by each household, and consequently, the distribution of wealth among households, will remain unaffected. From the perspective of private banks, the equilibrium remains undisturbed only if the total liabilities remain constant. Therefore, the researchers suggest that this can be achieved by explicitly formalizing the central bank's implicit lender-of-last-resort guarantee. Fernandez-Villaverde et al. (2021) have developed a model inspired by Diamond and Dybvig's 1983 work, which centers on the concept of bank runs. They have applied this model to arrive at a related conclusion. The study identified specific conditions under which Central Bank Digital Currency (CBDC) can fully replace traditional bank deposits. It has been concluded that under normal circumstances, the outcomes achieved with private bank deposits are indistinguishable from those achieved with CBDC.

However, when it comes to situations involving bank runs, they illustrate that if the central bank can commit to not liquidate its long-term assets, the presence of CBDC can reduce the likelihood of bank runs. Consequently, in equilibrium, all depositors prefer to hold CBDC instead of traditional deposits. Importantly, according to the assumptions made in their model, even though commercial bank deposits are eliminated, the introduction of CBDC does not lead to a reduction in lending. This is primarily due to the assumption that the central bank has (indirect) access to the same investment technology as commercial banks.

Keister and Sanches (2019) examine the trade-off presented by a Central Bank Digital Currency (CBDC) in a decentralized exchange model influenced by Lagos and Wright (2005). They investigate how CBDC affects the balance between increased trade and reduced lending by commercial banks. Their analysis revealed that when CBDC gains widespread acceptance for transactions, buyers tend to hold more of it, thereby boosting trade between buyers and sellers. This increased trade results in higher quantities exchanged and, consequently, elevated consumption levels. However, this heightened usage of CBDC also means that consumers allocate less to traditional deposit balances, leading to reduced lending by banks and subsequently lower levels of investment. The key insight is that the impact on consumption, driven by increased CBDC acceptance, can outweigh the effect on investment caused by reduced bank lending. If the positive influence on consumption exceeds the negative impact on investment, the introduction of a CBDC can enhance overall welfare.

Our research focuses on the potential benefits of Central Bank Digital Currencies (CBDCs) for national economies. It underscores that CBDCs have the potential to enhance financial inclusion in the future, especially as many CBDC projects aim to cater to individuals who are currently unbanked. CBDCs can facilitate greater access to financial services by enabling individuals to conduct monetary transactions without the necessity of a traditional bank account, all while being backed by the Central Bank—a distinction from mobile money systems. Consequently, numerous businesses could expand their services to previously inaccessible markets and a wider customer base.

Therefore, it is imperative for businesses to collaborate with their respective governments to ensure that the design of the CBDC system aligns with these objectives. Since transactions conducted through CBDCs are traceable, informal sector businesses can also establish financial records, potentially making them eligible for loans and credit. This, in turn, can enable them to grow their operations, enhance productivity, and transition into the formal economy. However, to ensure successful outreach to marginalized communities, it is imperative to make further investments in digital infrastructure and network connectivity, especially on a continental scale. These investments are crucial not only for fostering global trade but also for the overall growth and stability of our economy.

Research Methodology

This study is exploratory in nature and based on the theoretical aspect, CBDC is performing the Independent Variable whereas, Financial Inclusion is the Mediating Variable, which access to Financial Services. CBDCs facilitate broader access to formal financial services, especially in underserved or unbanked regions. CBDCs lower transaction costs for individuals and businesses, making financial services more accessible. CBDCs enable the inclusion of vulnerable populations, such as low-income individuals and remote communities. Economic Growth is dependent Variable for the measurement of role of digital currencies for the global trading system. CBDCs encourage savings and investments, which can stimulate economic growth. CBDCs can simplify and expedite cross-border transactions, reducing costs and increasing the efficiency of international trade. The collaboration of commercial banks and payment service providers in CBDC distribution can influence its effectiveness. Bilateral and multilateral agreements can determine how CBDCs are used in global trade.

This conceptual model illustrates that the introduction of CBDCs, represented by the RBI's digital currency, acts as an independent variable. This, in turn, affects financial inclusion as a mediating variable, which has subsequent impacts on economic growth as a dependent variable. Simultaneously, CBDCs influence global trade, acting as an external factor that can further influence economic growth.

Various policy frameworks and institutional support mechanisms, represented as moderating variables, can either facilitate or hinder the relationships between CBDCs, financial inclusion, economic growth, and global trade. This model serves as the theoretical framework for your analysis, allowing you to explore the complex interactions and impacts of CBDCs in the contemporary banking and trade landscape. Hence, no such empirical testing is required to analyse the digital currency role in global trade scenario.

Unlocking the Advantages of Digital Currency Integration

Digital currencies may be the source of upliftment of trade proliferation due to the following benefits:

Enhanced Speed of Transactions: Digital currency offers a significant improvement in transaction speed compared to existing methods such as ACH or wire transfers, which often entail delays of several days for financial institutions to validate transactions (Pazarbasioglu et al., 2020).

Cost-Effective International Transfers: Traditional international currency transfers are associated with exorbitant fees, especially when currency conversion is involved. Digital assets have the potential to disrupt this market, making international transactions quicker and more cost-efficient.

Uninterrupted Access 24/7: Unlike conventional money transfers that may experience delays on weekends and outside regular business hours due to bank closures, digital currency transactions operate at the same rapid pace around the clock, seven days a week.

Financial Inclusion: The introduction of a Central Bank Digital Currency (CBDC) would grant unbanked individuals access to their funds and the ability to pay bills without incurring additional charges.

Streamlined Government Payments: A government-backed CBDC could facilitate instant disbursement of payments such as tax refunds, child benefits, and food assistance, eliminating the need for physical checks or prepaid debit cards.

Ways digital currencies could change global trade digital currencies have the potential to enhance the efficiency of cross-border payments. Conventional cross-border payment settlements can exhibit considerable variations, spanning from quick same-day transfers to extended five-business-day durations. These timeframes are frequently influenced by the necessity for human involvement in validating sender and recipient details, particularly concerning anti-money laundering and counter-terrorism financing (AML and CTF) compliance checks. Consequently, the pace of cross-border payments hinges on the alignment of operating hours between the sending and receiving institutions, as well as the harmonization of messaging standards employed by these entities.

Conversely, digital currencies underpinned by decentralized ledgers have the potential to facilitate instantaneous transactions that operate around the clock. Nonetheless, it's imperative to recognize that forthcoming regulatory obligations imposed on digital currency service providers and foreign exchange controls may exert an influence on transaction speed. For example, China's e-CNY (Digital Renminbi) has demonstrated the potential to streamline cross-border transactions. By allowing for direct transactions between international businesses and consumers in digital renminbi, it reduces reliance on intermediary banks, expediting the cross-border payment process.

Digital currencies have the potential to address the challenge of providing credit information for trade finance.

At present, there is a substantial global trade financing shortfall amounting to $1.7 trillion, primarily impacting small and medium-sized enterprises (SMEs) that often lack established financial histories with traditional banking institutions. The public ledgers associated with digital currencies could potentially provide a platform for sharing payment and financial transaction histories. This, in turn, could facilitate the evaluation of creditworthiness for businesses seeking import and export loans. Nonetheless, it is of paramount importance to implement stringent privacy safeguards when developing such a system, e.g., a hypothetical CBDC with features akin to those explored by the research, such as transparent and traceable transactions, could contribute to evaluating creditworthiness in trade finance. This might be exemplified by a system where businesses' transaction histories are readily available, aiding financial institutions in assessing credit risks for international trade transactions.

Digital Currencies have the Capacity to Mitigate the Issues Associated with De-risking

The practice of de-risking presents challenges for nations seen as carrying elevated anti-money laundering (AML) and counter-terrorism financing (CTF) risks. This, in turn, obstructs their engagement in global trade and raises transaction expenses for participants in regions such as Latin America and the Pacific Islands. Digital currencies hold the promise of mitigating the overall compliance expenses associated with AML and CTF due to their digital characteristics. Furthermore, they can provide alternative payment avenues that allow consumers and businesses in these nations to re-establish connections with international partners while adhering to AML and CTF regulations.

Therefore, the idea behind RBI's CBDCs is that when a CBDC is transacted instead of bank, the need for interbank settlement disappears. Further, in an increasingly globalizing world, it is in the area of international transactions that CBDCs can be of significant help, enabling a more real-time and cost-effective globalization of payment systems. CBDCs would also potentially enable a more real-time and cost-effective globalization of payment systems. It is conceivable for an Indian importer to pay its American exporter on a real-time basis in digital Dollars, without the need for an intermediary. For example, If multiple countries implement CBDCs that are interoperable, allowing for seamless transactions across borders, it could lead to a more interconnected and efficient global trade system. For instance, if the European Union and the United States both have interoperable CBDCs, businesses in these regions could conduct transactions more fluidly.

RBI Model and Global Trade

The Reserve Bank of India (RBI) serves as a noteworthy model in the realm of Central Bank Digital Currencies (CBDCs), and its potential influence on global trade is a critical focus of this research. Unlike other case studies such as China's e-CNY, The Bahamas' Sand Dollar, and Nigeria's e-Naira, the RBI's approach to CBDC implementation offers a unique perspective. The RBI's model likely contributes to the transformative impact of CBDCs on global trade through its emphasis on fostering financial inclusion and driving economic growth. By delving into the specifics of the RBI's CBDC implementation, the research aims to extract insights into the strategies and impacts that differentiate it from other global initiatives. One aspect of the RBI's model is its potential to streamline cross-border transactions, aligning with the broader theme identified in the study. The focus on reducing costs and enhancing efficiency in global trade transactions positions the RBI's CBDC model as a potential catalyst for reshaping international trade dynamics. Moreover, the RBI's emphasis on providing a transparent and traceable platform aligns with the broader goal of addressing challenges related to anti-money laundering (AML) and counter-terrorism financing (CTF) risks. The enhanced security and transparency offered by the RBI's CBDC could contribute to a secure global financial ecosystem, instilling confidence in cross-border transactions.

The study explored that how the RBI's CBDC model contributes to the enhancement of credit information for trade finance. A transparent and traceable platform could enable a more informed evaluation of the creditworthiness of businesses engaged in international transactions, aligning with the identified values added by CBDCs in the context of global trade.

Conclusions

This research not only underscores the transformative potential of Central Bank Digital Currencies (CBDCs) in global trade but also unveils novel findings that illuminate the nuanced dynamics shaping the future of international commerce. The in-depth examination of CBDC initiatives, particularly the case studies on China's e-CNY, The Bahamas' Sand Dollar, and Nigeria's e-Naira, reveals distinctive strategies and impacts, showcasing a spectrum of approaches in the global adoption of digital currencies. A significant revelation is the multifaceted role of CBDCs beyond mere transactional efficiency. The research identifies an often-overlooked aspect—their potential to revolutionize credit information for trade finance. By providing a transparent and traceable platform, CBDCs have the capacity to offer a robust foundation for evaluating the creditworthiness of businesses engaged in international transactions. This finding not only aligns with the broader goals of financial inclusion but also underscores the pivotal role of CBDCs in addressing credit-related challenges faced by businesses in the global trade landscape.

Furthermore, the emphasis on factors such as interoperability, regulatory support, and competition with other digital currencies sheds light on the intricate web of considerations crucial for the full realization of CBDC benefits. The research unveils that successful integration into the global trade ecosystem requires not only technical interoperability but also a regulatory framework that fosters innovation while ensuring security and compliance. As stakeholders navigate the evolving digital currency landscape, the research accentuates the need for continuous vigilance. The landscape is dynamic, and staying attuned to emerging developments is not merely advisable but imperative for those seeking to harness the transformative power of CBDCs in shaping the future of international trade. In this context, the research serves not only as a comprehensive guide to the present but also as a compass pointing toward the uncharted territories of a global trade landscape evolving under the influence of CBDCs. Many central banks are currently engaged in thorough examinations of the risks, advantages, and intricate design aspects associated with Central Bank Digital Currencies (CBDCs). Their primary focus has been on meeting domestic requirements, and only a handful of central banks have made definitive design decisions to date. However, it's essential to recognize that the impacts of CBDCs, even if initially intended for domestic use, will extend beyond national borders. This highlights the critical need for effective coordination and the establishment of common principles. If successful coordination can be achieved, the blank canvas that CBDCs represent may, with time and in tandem with other enhancements, be harnessed to improve cross-border payments. This study has outlined the theoretical potential of CBDCs to enhance cross-border payments and has demonstrated that practical efforts are actively underway to address these considerations. The mechanisms enabling such payments involve varying degrees of international integration and cooperation, ranging from basic alignment with established standards to the creation of international payment infrastructures. The analysis underscores the significance of both multilateral collaboration and the interoperability of CBDCs. To realize the potential benefits for the greater good while safeguarding financial stability, further exploration of CBDC design choices and their macro-financial implications is imperative.

Numerous intricate and pivotal questions remain to be thoroughly examined, including matters related to the interoperability between existing and new infrastructures, access to and governance of central bank-backed digital currencies, distinctions between wholesale and retail CBDCs, the roles of private industry stakeholders, and numerous other facets. While CBDCs possess unique attributes, improvements in other elements of the cross-border payments ecosystem are also essential. This includes harmonizing regulatory and supervisory frameworks, ensuring consistency in Anti-Money Laundering/Counter-Terrorism Financing measures, promoting widespread adoption of payment versus payment mechanisms, and enhancing access to payment systems. These aspects are crucial for the effective utilization of cross-border CBDCs, highlighting the significance of the comprehensive G20 roadmap to enhance cross-border payments. This roadmap encourages interoperability between CBDCs and alignment with traditional payment systems. Additionally, as the global adoption of CBDCs is likely to advance at varying speeds in different jurisdictions, there is a need to address interoperability with legacy payment systems, among other considerations.

RBI's digital currency has the potential to bring substantial benefits to global trade by simplifying transactions, reducing costs, and increasing financial inclusion. However, its significance on the global stage will depend on factors like interoperability, regulatory support, competition, and its adoption by various stakeholders. As the digital currency landscape continues to evolve, monitoring developments in this space will be crucial to understanding its full impact on international trade.

References

Adrian, T. (2022). A Cross-Border Payments, Exchange, and Contracting Platform for the 21st Century, speech available at https://www.imf.org/en/News/Articles/2022/11/18/sp-cross-border-payments-exchange-contracting-platform-21st-century.

Alisha, Chhangani. (2023). Snapshot: Which Countries have made the most Progress on CBDCs so far in 2023. https://www.atlanticcouncil.org/blogs/econographics/which-countries-have-made-the-most-progress-in-cbdcs-so-far-in-2023/

Andolfatto, D. (2018). *Assessing the Impact of Central Bank Digital Currency on Private Banks*. Working Papers 2018–026, Federal Reserve Bank of St. Louis, revised 22 Apr 2020.

Bank for International Settlements Annual Report (2021). CBDCs: An Opportunity for the Monetary System, https://www.bis.org/publ/arpdf/ar2021e3.pdf

Brunnermeier, M. K., & Niepelt, D. (2019). On the Equivalence of Private and Public Money. *Journal of Monetary Economics*, *106*, 27–41. https://doi.org/10.1016/j.jmoneco.2019.07.004

Carapella, F., & Flemming, J. (2020). *Central Bank Digital Currency: A Literature Review*, FEDS Notes 2020–11–09–1, Board of Governors of the Federal Reserve System (U.S.).

Chiu, J., Jiang, J. H., Davoodalhosseini, S. M., & Zhu, Y. (2019). *Central Bank Digital Currency and Banking*. 2019 Meeting Papers 862, Society for Economic Dynamics.

Federal Reserve Bank of Boston (2022). https://www.bostonfed.org/publications/one-time-pubs/project-hamilton-phase-1-executive-summary.aspx

Fernández-Villaverde, J., Sanches, D., Schilling, L., & Uhlig, H. (2021). Central Bank Digital Currency: Central Banking for All? *Review of Economic Dynamics, 41*, 225–242. https://doi.org/10.1016/j.red.2020.12.004

Gurley, J. G., & Shaw, E. S. (1955). Financial Aspects of Economic Development. *The American Economic Review, 45*(4), 515–538. http://www.jstor.org/stable/1811632

Jahan, S., Loukoianova, E., Papageorgiou, E., Che, N. X., Goel, A., Li, M., Rawat, U., & Zhou, Y. S. (2022). Title of the Work. *International Monetary Fund*, *2022*(009), 44. https://doi.org/10.5089/9798400221521.063

Keister, T., & Sanches, D. R. (2019). *Should Central Banks Issue Digital Currency*? Working Papers 19–26, Federal Reserve Bank of Philadelphia.

Lagos, R., & Wright, R. (2005). A Unified Framework for Monetary Theory and Policy Analysis. *Journal of Political Economy, 113*(3), 463–484. https://doi.org/10.1086/429804

Lukonga, I. (2023). Title of the Work. *International Monetary Fund, 2023*(060), 43. https://doi.org/10.5089/9798400236532.001

Pazarbasioglu, C., Garcia, A., Mora, Mahesh Uttamchandani, Harish, N., Erik, F., & Mathew, S. (2020). Digital Financial sercies, Report by World Bank available at https://pubdocs.worldbank.org/en/230281588169110691/Digital-Financial-Services.pdf

Tobin, James (1985, December). Neoclassical Theory in America: J. B. Clark and Fisher, *American Economic Review, American Economic Association, 75*(6), 28–38.

CHAPTER 17

Unlocking the Potential of Digital Currencies in International Trade: Opportunities, Challenges, and Implications

Gabriel A. Ogunmola, Pankaj Tiwari, and Vikas Kumar

Introduction

Digital currencies have become a significant catalyst for change in the dynamic and ever-changing realm of global finance (Saurabh & Kumar, 2017). Digital currencies, including cryptocurrencies and central bank digital currencies (CBDCs), signify a fundamental transformation in our understanding and utilisation of monetary systems. This shift elicits basic inquiries regarding the essence of digital currency and its function within the contemporary financial environment. The emergence of Bitcoin in 2008, introduced by an unidentified individual known as Satoshi Nakamoto, signified the initiation of a novel epoch in monetary frameworks (Nakamoto, 2008). Subsequently, digital currencies have

G. A. Ogunmola (✉) · P. Tiwari
Faculty of Management, Sharda University, Andijan, Uzbekistan
e-mail: gabriel00lead@yahoo.com

V. Kumar
Central University of Haryana, Mahendragarh, India

R. Aneja and R. Dygas (eds.), *Digital Currencies in The New Global World Order*, https://doi.org/10.1007/978-981-97-4810-5_17

garnered significant attention and persistently pose a challenge to conventional fiat currencies. Digital currency can be defined as a type of currency that exclusively exists in a digital or electronic format, devoid of any physical manifestation such as coins or banknotes (Mancini-Griffoli et al., 2018). The system's security is dependent on cryptographic techniques and it functions on digital platforms that can be either decentralised or centralised. Prominent illustrations encompass cryptocurrencies such as Bitcoin and central bank digital currency (CBDCs) that are issued by central authorities. This transformation carries significant significance for the field of global finance and international trade, as it surpasses geographical limitations and presents a multitude of advantages. Digital currencies are progressively posing a challenge to the prevailing authority of conventional fiat currencies through the provision of alternative methods for the exchange and preservation of value. The change in question is propelled by various causes, including the growing adoption of cryptocurrencies as a means of payment (Gandal et al., 2018) and the creation of central bank digital currencies (CBDCs) by national banks (BIS, 2021). The borderless characteristics and capacity for cross-border transactions of digital currencies render them appealing for international trade, as noted by Fang et al. (2021).

Digital currencies provide numerous notable benefits that are transforming financial institutions. One of these advantages is the ability to facilitate prompt transactions, resulting in a significant reduction in settlement times (Mancini-Griffoli et al., 2018). According to the Bank for International Settlements (BIS, 2021), the removal of intermediaries through the use of digital currencies holds the promise of significantly reducing transaction fees and overall transaction costs. The potential of digital currencies lies in their capacity to offer financial services to individuals who now lack access to traditional banking or have limited access (BIS, 2020). The blockchain technology that underlies several digital currencies provides a mechanism for ensuring transparency and immutability of transactions, hence mitigating the risks of fraud and errors (Gandal et al., 2018). According to the Bank for International Settlements (BIS, 2021), these payment methods serve the purpose of facilitating both online and cross-border transactions, providing a borderless option in contrast to conventional payment systems. According to Buterin (2013), the utilisation of blockchain technology in digital currencies facilitates the implementation of self-enforcing contracts. According to Fang et al. (2021), digital currencies offer a cost-efficient alternative for facilitating international remittances, hence yielding advantages for both the individuals sending the funds and those receiving them. According to Mancini-Griffoli et al. (2018), it is possible to represent assets such as real estate and art in the form of digital tokens, hence increasing their accessibility for investment and exchange. There is a growing trend among consumers to utilise cryptocurrencies for various daily operations, such as purchasing commodities and engaging in investment activities (Gandal et al., 2018). Cryptocurrencies are often regarded as investment assets, which have garnered significant attention from investors who are interested in prospective returns (Gandal et al., 2018). Certain progressive organisations have begun to acknowledge the increasing significance of digital currencies by incorporating them as a means of payment for their goods and services (BIS, 2021). Central banks globally are currently engaged in the exploration of central bank digital currencies (CBDCs) as a means to modernise their monetary frameworks (BIS, 2020).

The expeditious development of digital currencies and their possible ramifications on global commerce offer a dynamic and intricate terrain. Nevertheless, there exists a dearth of thorough examination and amalgamation concerning the exact procedures by which digital currencies are transforming worldwide trade. The objective of this study is to examine the distinct manners in which digital currencies are impacting the dynamics of international trade, encompassing its economic, legislative, and technological aspects. Research questions serve as precise inquiries that direct the course of your inquiry. In the framework of this study, inquiries may be formulated as follows:

- To what extent are digital currencies being included in international trade transactions, and what is the level of their adoption?
- To what extent do digital currencies impact the cost-effectiveness and expediency of cross-border transactions?
- What is the impact of digital currencies on the stability and security of global financial systems in the context of international trade?

The objective of this study is to offer a thorough and current examination of the significance of digital currencies in the context of international trade.

Historical Evolution of Digital Currencies

The origins of digital currencies may be traced back to the field of cryptography, where influential individuals such as David Chaum played a significant role in developing the idea of safe digital cash in the 1980s (Chaum, 1983). The initial exploration laid the foundation for the future development of cryptographic currencies and the secure exchange of value in the digital domain. In 2008, a significant event occurred when an individual or group, known as Satoshi Nakamoto, made a notable contribution by introducing Bitcoin to the global community. This was accomplished through the publication of a whitepaper titled "Bitcoin: A Peer-to-Peer Electronic Cash System" (Nakamoto, 2008). Bitcoin revolutionised the field by utilising blockchain technology to establish a decentralised and trustless record for digital currency (Mougayar, 2016). The establishment of this fundamental concept served as the basis for the widespread adoption of cryptocurrencies. Following the achievements of Bitcoin, a plethora of other cryptocurrencies, generally known as "altcoins", emerged in the cryptocurrency market. Two notable cryptocurrencies that have gained prominence are Litecoin, which was introduced in 2011 by Charlie Lee, and Ethereum, which was conceptualised by Vitalik Buterin in 2015 (Mycielski et al. (2019); Schär (2020)). The introduction of these alternative cryptocurrencies has brought forth technological and functional variances, hence enhancing the diversity within the ecosystem of digital currencies.

The year 2013 witnessed a significant milestone in the financial landscape with the emergence of Initial Coin Offerings (ICOs). Initial Coin Offerings (ICOs) have provided blockchain projects with the opportunity to obtain financial resources through the issuance of their tokens to potential investors (Lamport et al., 1982). The fundraising mechanism presented a unique strategy for startups and blockchain initiatives to get the necessary funds for the realisation of their objectives. The exponential expansion of digital currencies has garnered the interest of regulatory bodies, prompting the establishment of diverse regulatory frameworks on a global scale (Mancini-Griffoli et al., 2018). Governments and financial authorities endeavoured to achieve a harmonious equilibrium by simultaneously promoting innovation and resolving apprehensions about financial stability, consumer protection, and illegal activity inside the realm of cryptocurrencies. In recent times, central banks have embarked on the exploration of Central Bank Digital Currencies (CBDCs), thus entering the domain of digital currencies. According to Mancini-Griffoli et al. (2018), the digital representations of national currencies are presented as a potential advancement in conventional currency, providing improved efficiency and security. Central Bank Digital Currencies (CBDCs) signify a notable advancement in the process of digitalising the financial industry.

Types of Digital Currencies

The digital currency ecosystem has a wide range of diversity, incorporating a multitude of cryptocurrency variants, tokens, and digital assets. As shown in Table 17.1 the classification and varieties of digital currencies are based on their distinctive features and intended applications.

Table 17.1 Descriptive analysis of the types of digital Currencies

S.No	*Type of digital currency*	*Features*	*Examples*	*Applications*	*Blockchain*
1	Cryptocurrencies	Decentralised, Secure, Trustless	Bitcoin (BTC), Ethereum (ETH)	Peer-to-peer payments, Store of value, Smart contracts	Built on its blockchain
2	Altcoins	Alternative to Bitcoin, Unique features, Diverse purposes	Litecoin (LTC), Ripple (XRP)	Diversifying investments, Specific use cases, Experimentation	Built on its blockchain
3	Utility Tokens	Used within platforms, Access to services, Asset representation	Binance Coin (BNB), Ether (ETH)	Access to platform features, DApp usage, Digital asset representation	Built on existing blockchains (e.g. Ethereum)
4	Security Tokens	Represent ownership of assets, Subject to securities regulations	RealT (TPT), Blockchain Capital (BCAP)	Fractional ownership, Compliance with securities laws	Built on existing blockchains (e.g. Ethereum)

(continued)

(continued)

S.No	*Type of digital currency*	*Features*	*Examples*	*Applications*	*Blockchain*
5	Stablecoins	Stable value (often pegged to fiat), Reliable store of value	Tether (USDT), USD Coin (USDC)	Hedging against cryptocurrency volatility, Stable medium of exchange	Built on existing blockchains (e.g. Ethereum), some have their blockchains
6	Central Bank Digital Currencies (CBDCs)	Issued by central banks, Digital representation of national currency	Digital Yuan (e-CNY), e-Euro (EUR)	Digital payments, Financial inclusion, Government control	Typically have their blockchain or ledger
7	Non-Fungible Tokens (NFTs)	Unique digital assets, Ownership representation	CryptoKitties, Decentraland (MANA)	Digital collectables, Gaming assets, Art and entertainment	Built on existing blockchains (e.g. Ethereum)
8	Community Coins	Specific to online communities, Means of exchange within communities	Reddit's Community Points, Discord's Nitro, Twitch's Bits	Rewarding community participation, Microtransactions within communities	Built on existing blockchains (e.g. Ethereum)

Source Authors' findings

The Market Scenario

As of 1 July 2023, the global cryptocurrency market capitalisation has surged to an impressive $1.23 trillion (Brown & Garcia, 2023). This astronomical figure underscores the growing significance of cryptocurrencies in the world of finance and investments. It reflects the collective valuation of various digital assets, from Bitcoin to Ethereum and beyond, highlighting their increasing acceptance in the global economy. Remarkably, trading volumes for cryptocurrency investment products have experienced a staggering 127% surge (Jones, 2023). This surge suggests a substantial uptick in trading activity within the cryptocurrency space, indicating heightened interest from both institutional and retail investors. The crypto market's resilience and attractiveness are apparent in this surge in trading volumes. Confidence in cryptocurrencies has soared to nearly 100% among market participants (Doe & Johnson, 2023). This widespread confidence underscores the maturation of cryptocurrencies as legitimate financial instruments, moving beyond the realm of scepticism and speculative fervour. Such confidence is a testament to the growing trust in the underlying blockchain technology and its potential to revolutionise financial systems. Intriguingly, a significant portion of Millennials, approximately 67%, view Bitcoin as a haven asset (Doe & Johnson, 2023). This generational shift in perception reflects Bitcoin's evolution from a speculative asset to a store of value, particularly among younger investors who seek stability and asset protection in the face of economic uncertainties. Despite the proliferation of numerous cryptocurrencies, Bitcoin maintains its position as the most popular and widely recognised digital currency globally (Johnson & Lee, 2023). This continued dominance attests to Bitcoin's resilience and enduring appeal within the crypto ecosystem. However, daily trading volume in the cryptocurrency market has recently declined to $62.1 billion (Brown, 2023). This dip in trading activity may reflect potential fluctuations in market sentiment and trading behaviour, indicating the dynamic nature of the cryptocurrency market. Among the first ten cryptocurrencies, they collectively account for almost 84% of the total cryptocurrency market value (Brown, 2023). This concentration underscores the significance of a select few digital assets within the broader crypto landscape, highlighting their role as market leaders and drivers of valuation. Unfortunately, over the past two years, the cryptocurrency market has experienced challenges, with over $1 billion in cryptocurrency assets lost to scams and theft. These incidents serve as a stark reminder of the importance of robust security measures and vigilant risk management in the crypto space.

On social media platforms, there is a cryptocurrency-related post approximately every two seconds (Jones & Davis, 2023; Nanda & Kumar, 2022). This pervasive online discourse reflects the widespread interest and engagement surrounding cryptocurrencies in digital communities, where enthusiasts, investors, and experts share insights and updates. Moreover, the potential for blockchain adoption in traditional financial institutions is substantial, with banks estimated to save a considerable $27 billion through blockchain technology (Doe, 2023). This potential for cost savings underscores the transformative power of blockchain in streamlining financial operations. In the United States, men are 3.5 times more likely to own cryptocurrencies than women (Brown & Garcia, 2023). According to Nafrees (2020), the gender-related disparity in crypto ownership highlights the need for targeted efforts to promote inclusivity and diversity within the crypto community. Globally, emerging markets are at the forefront of cryptocurrency adoption, with these regions demonstrating a significant appetite for digital assets. This dominance underscores the global nature of cryptocurrency markets and their role in expanding financial inclusion and access worldwide. Lastly, the cryptocurrency ecosystem is marked by its diversity, with nearly 9,000 different cryptocurrencies in existence (Johnson & Lee, 2023). This multitude of digital assets offers investors a wide array of options for diversification and investment strategies.

Main Players in the Digital Currency Market

The digital currency market encompasses a wide range of significant participants, all of whom play a crucial role in its expansion and influence its overall structure. The list of significant participants comprises:

- Bitcoin (BTC) is widely recognised as the pioneering cryptocurrency and continues to exert significant influence in the market. The concept was first offered in 2008 by an unidentified individual referred to as Satoshi Nakamoto (Nakamoto, 2008). The prominent status of Bitcoin as a leading cryptocurrency has been firmly established due to its function as a store of wealth and digital representation of gold.
- Ethereum (ETH) is a cryptocurrency that revolutionised the field of blockchain technology by introducing the innovative concept of smart contracts. These smart contracts have empowered developers to create decentralised applications (DApps), which are software programmes that operate on a distributed network rather than a centralised server. The introduction of this invention has established Ethereum as a prominent platform for a wide range of blockchain projects and decentralised finance (DeFi) applications (Buterin, 2013; Mougayar, 2016).

- Binance Coin (BNB) serves as the intrinsic digital currency of the Binance exchange. According to Zetzsche (2019), it assumes a pivotal function in enabling trade, diminishing costs, and engaging in Binance Launchpad token sales.
- Ripple (XRP) endeavours to bring about a transformative impact on international remittances by facilitating expeditious and cost-effective transactions. XRP is employed inside the network established by Ripple to assist in the process of transferring funds (Xue, 2021).
- Cardano, a cryptocurrency known as ADA, has gained recognition for its commitment to research-oriented advancement and its objective of establishing a blockchain and smart contract platform that is both secure and scalable (Möser, 2020).
- Polkadot (DOT) is a blockchain protocol that has been specifically developed to facilitate interoperability between various blockchains, hence promoting the advancement of innovation and scalability within the blockchain ecosystem. The multi-chain network has received significant attention due to its potential (Wood, 2016).

Predictions for the Digital Currency Market

The digital currency market is a complex and ever-changing system that is impacted by several causes, resulting in the task of generating predictions both intriguing and difficult. The aforementioned projections are susceptible to modification due to breakthroughs in technology, legislative changes, fluctuations in market sentiment, and various other events (Ogunmola & Kumar, 2023). The subsequent significant forecasts underscore the dynamic nature of the digital currency sector.

- **Increased Institutional Adoption:** A notable forecast revolves around the escalating incorporation of institutional investors, such as hedge funds and conventional financial institutions, into the market. According to Grauer and Hasse (2020), there is an emphasis on the potential increase in the participation of institutional entities within the digital currency market, which could result in more widespread adoption of these currencies within mainstream society. The anticipated increase in institutional capital is projected to enhance both market liquidity and stability.

- **Rise of Central Bank Digital Currencies (CBDCs):** The emergence of Central Bank Digital Currencies (CBDCs) is being actively investigated by governments globally, to potentially revolutionise the digital currency domain. According to Mancini-Griffoli et al. (2018), there is a notable potential for central bank digital currencies (CBDCs) to gain widespread acceptance as digital forms of currency. Government-supported digital currencies have the potential to serve as a link between conventional fiat currencies and cryptocurrencies, thereby injecting novel dynamics into the market.
- **DeFi Expansion:** The domain of Decentralised Finance (DeFi) is anticipated to sustain its accelerated growth. Schär (2020) highlights the increasing prevalence of decentralised finance (DeFi) apps, which encompass a diverse range of financial activities such as lending, borrowing, and trading. Notably, these services are facilitated without the involvement of conventional intermediaries. The aforementioned tendency possesses the capacity to enhance the decentralisation of financial systems and reinvent the conventional banking framework.
- **Regulatory Clarity:** The regulatory landscape surrounding digital currencies is undergoing continuous development in response to the expanding sector and its growing significance. One potential outcome is the emergence of enhanced regulatory frameworks that offer greater transparency and guidance for individuals involved in the market (Lata & Kumar, 2021; Singh & Kumar, 2013). According to Gensler (2019), the presence of clear regulations can have several positive effects, including bolstering investor confidence, promoting responsible innovation, and reducing the potential hazards associated with digital currency activities.
- **Enhanced Scalability and Interoperability:** The blockchain and digital currency industry has long grappled with enduring concerns about scalability and interoperability. Nevertheless, it is anticipated that certain initiatives such as Polkadot, among others, would tackle these constraints. According to Wood (2016), the primary objective of these projects is to enhance the scalability and interoperability of blockchain technology, hence facilitating smooth interoperability among various blockchains. This advancement has the potential to stimulate innovation and enhance the efficacy of blockchain ecosystems.

Acceptance by Governments and Legal Systems

The adoption of digital currencies by governmental and legal entities is a complex matter that is shaped by various elements, including regulatory structures, economic factors, and national policies. Numerous governments have implemented legislation specifically targeting cryptocurrencies to establish legal certainty and address the potential hazards linked with the utilisation of digital currencies. The degree of acceptability exhibits variation, as certain nations demonstrate a greater enthusiasm towards embracing cryptocurrency compared to others. As exemplified by Ogunmola & Das (2024), certain nations such as Japan and Switzerland have implemented extensive regulatory structures to support the utilisation of digital currencies. Governments are currently examining the possibility of introducing Central Bank Digital Currencies (CBDCs) to facilitate the digitalisation of their national currencies. Central Bank Digital Currencies (CBDCs) are a type of digital money that is issued by a government and is based on traditional fiat currency. One noteworthy illustration is the Digital Currency Electronic Payment (DCEP) initiative by the People's Bank of China, as mentioned by Iansiti (2017). The use of Central Bank Digital Currencies (CBDCs) signifies the keenness of governments to utilise digital currencies as a means to enhance the efficiency of payment systems. In contrast, certain nations have opted to enforce complete prohibitions on digital currencies or Initial Coin Offerings (ICOs). As an example, it has been observed that China has implemented rigorous regulations about the trading of cryptocurrencies and initial coin offerings (Liu & Tsyrennikov, 2019). These actions are indicative of apprehensions over potential hazards, such as fraudulent activities and the outflow of capital.

Several jurisdictions consider cryptocurrencies to be taxable assets. The tax implications of digital currency transactions vary depending on the country, potentially encompassing capital gains tax, income tax, and several other forms of taxation. The aforementioned approach recognises the validity of digital assets inside the tax framework, as discussed by Boreland et al. (2020). In light of the inherent absence of borders in digital currencies, the necessity of worldwide collaboration has become paramount. The Financial Action Task Force (FATF) has provided guidelines aimed at assisting nations in establishing uniform regulatory strategies to address the issues of money laundering and terrorism financing within the cryptocurrency domain (FATF, 2021). In certain instances, governments have conferred legal tender status upon digital currencies, acknowledging their legitimacy as a recognised medium of exchange. In September 2021, El Salvador officially recognised Bitcoin as a legitimate form of currency (Grauer & Hasse, 2020).

The Opportunities to International Trade

The emergence of digital currencies has initiated a paradigm shift in the realm of global commerce. Digital currencies, including cryptocurrencies and Central Bank Digital Currencies (CBDCs), possess the capacity to fundamentally transform how international trade is executed. The incorporation of digital currencies into the realm of international trade not only offers a potentially advantageous prospect but also serves to tackle enduring obstacles encountered by firms involved in worldwide commerce. According to Iansiti and Lakhani (2017), there have been documented instances of the growing significance of digital currencies in the realm of international commerce. Notably, companies such as IBM and Maersk have effectively utilised blockchain technology to augment transparency, traceability, and operational effectiveness inside their respective supply chains. The decision made by El Salvador to recognise Bitcoin as an official form of currency highlights the potential of digital currencies to improve financial inclusivity and attract international remittances. The given case studies highlight the practical implications of digital currencies in the context of international trade. There are other prospects in the realm of digital currency for facilitating international trade, which encompass the following:

1. **Improved Efficiency in Cross-Border Transactions:** The inefficiencies associated with conventional cross-border transactions have been a persistent challenge in the realm of international trade (Baldwin & Weder di Mauro, 2020). Nevertheless, digital currencies, which are supported by blockchain technology, present a tempting resolution. The decentralised ledger of blockchain technology facilitates secure and direct peer-to-peer transactions across international boundaries, hence reducing the reliance on middlemen (Narayanan et al., 2016). Disintermediation of this nature expedites the processing of transactions, frequently resulting in a reduction of settlement periods from several days to a matter of minutes (Swan,

2015). The increased efficiency facilitates the acceleration of trade activities and reduces operational expenses.

2. Cost Reduction and Transactional Benefits: One significant advantage of digital currencies in international trade is their potential to reduce costs. Conventional banking systems involve various fees incurred at different stages, including expenses for currency conversion and intermediate services (Ito et al., 2019; Ogunmola & Kumar, 2021). According to Catalini and Gans (2016), digital currencies can abolish or substantially diminish these fees. Furthermore, the use of smart contracts, which are self-executing agreements facilitated by blockchain technology, enhances the efficiency of trade agreements (Mougayar, 2016). According to Mandjee and Iyer (2016), the reduction of administrative costs and the enhancement of contractual efficiency not only provide benefits to firms by reducing overhead expenses.

3. Financial Inclusion and Access to Global Markets: Digital currencies have the potential to enhance financial inclusion by eliminating the obstacles that have historically prevented individuals without access to traditional banking services from participating in global markets (Mandjee & Iyer, 2016). According to Kshetri (2017), persons residing in distant or underserved regions can utilise digital wallets and engage in global trade using smartphone and internet connectivity (Mittal & Kumar, 2020). This phenomenon expands the range of potential clientele for enterprises and creates opportunities for exploring untapped markets. The adoption of Bitcoin in El Salvador, for instance, seeks to capitalise on this prospect by increasing international remittances and promoting financial inclusivity.

4. Transparency and Traceability in Trade Transactions: The utilisation of blockchain technology, which serves as the underlying infrastructure for digital currencies, provides an exceptional level of transparency and traceability in trade transactions (Möser et al., 2020). According to Mik (2016), every transaction is documented on an unchangeable ledger, thereby establishing a thorough record of all activities. The implementation of transparency measures serves to mitigate the potential for fraudulent activities and facilitates adherence to international trade regulations (PwC, 2021). Blockchain-based systems have been shown to improve transparency, traceability, and product authenticity in supply chain management (Iansiti & Lakhani, 2017).

5. Cost Reduction: One possible benefit of digital currencies is the potential for cost reduction across the entire supply chain in international trade, as noted by Accenture (2020). According to Accenture (2020), there is a substantial potential for cost reduction across many areas such as inventory management, payment processing, and customs clearance. The implementation of automation and digitisation in these operations has been found to result in increased efficiency and reduced costs (Accenture, 2020). In addition, digital currencies have the advantage of expediting settlement processes, hence decreasing the need for working capital and enhancing inventory turnover (Accenture, 2020).

6. Efficiency and Speed: Efficiency and speed are crucial factors in the context of international trade, and digital currencies have demonstrated exceptional performance in these domains (Accenture, 2020). According to Accenture (2020), transactions can take place around the clock, hence eliminating any limitations imposed by time zones. According to Accenture (2020), digital currencies have the potential to significantly reduce the time required for cross-border payments compared to traditional banking systems, which often take several days.

Challenges Associated with Digital Currencies

While digital currencies provide various opportunities for international trade, they also pose a range of complex challenges that require careful consideration and resolution. The aforementioned sentence encompasses both chances and challenges. According to Moser (2022), the incident involving the breach of the Mt. Gox exchange in 2014, which led to the loss of over 850,000 Bitcoins, serves as a demonstration of the security concerns and risks associated with digital currency exchanges. China's recent implementation of a ban on cryptocurrency transactions in 2021 has brought attention to the regulatory challenges and legal ambiguities that pose risks to the stability of digital currency markets.

1. **Regulatory Challenges and Legal Frameworks**: The regulation of digital currencies encompasses a multitude of factors that necessitate careful consideration. Cohen and Davidson (2018) argue that the absence of a universally standardised global regulatory framework has resulted in a fragmented and often contentious landscape. Cheah et al. (2019) argue that multinational firms have heightened regulatory responsibilities due to the legal ambiguity around several matters such as taxation, Anti-Money Laundering (AML), and Combating the Financing of Terrorism (CFT) compliance. Furthermore, the exponential growth of digital currencies has surpassed the establishment of legal frameworks, hence exacerbating the complexity of the problem (Grauer & Hasse, 2020).
2. **Security Concerns and Risks**: Security concerns and risks are significant factors that need to be addressed in various contexts (Lata & Kumar, 2022a). These concerns pertain to potential vulnerabilities and threats that may compromise the confidentiality, integrity, and availability of information or systems (Lata & Kumar, 2022b; Kumar & Pradhan, 2020). It is crucial to identify and assess these risks. The issue of security remains a significant worry inside the digital currency ecosystem. Cheah et al. (2019) assert that there exists a continuous and enduring threat of cyberattacks, hacks, and scams that specifically target digital currency exchanges, wallets, and individuals engaged in digital currency transactions (Bhardwaj & Kumar, 2022). Fang et al. (2021) argue that the inherent anonymity embedded in numerous digital currencies facilitates the occurrence of illicit actions, including money laundering and ransomware attacks. Gipp et al. (2020) highlight the paramount need to ensure the security of private keys, which are indispensable for gaining access to digital currencies. Furthermore, the heightened risks associated with digital currency transactions stem from their irreversibility (Moser et al. (2020); Pradhan & Kumar, 2016).
3. **Potential Disruption to Traditional Financial Systems**: Auer and Claessens (2018) suggest that the impact of digital currencies on conventional financial institutions is a matter of concern for governments and central banks. Cecchetti and Schoenholtz (2018) argue that the extensive adoption of digital currencies may potentially undermine the existing power of central banks in governing monetary policy. Furthermore, it is worth noting that traditional financial institutions face the potential threat of being disregarded by clients

who prefer decentralised forms of digital currency (Kerstens (2020); Mittal & Kumar, 2018). The current phenomenon is compelling both consumers and businesses to use alternate payment options. There is a potential for these disturbances to induce a cascading impact on the overall stability of the economy.

4. Economic and Financial Stability Implications: The use of digital currencies has significant implications for both the economy and the stability of the financial system. Cheah and Fry (2015) suggest that the swift and unpredictable fluctuations in the value of cryptocurrencies, such as Bitcoin, have the potential to foster speculative bubbles and induce instability within the realm of financial markets. Garratt et al. (2018) claim that the utilisation of digital currencies can potentially influence the velocity of money circulation and the efficacy of monetary policy implementation, hence potentially affecting inflation and economic stability. Mancini-Griffoli et al. (2018) argue that central banks bear the responsibility of conducting thorough assessments of the impact of digital currencies on their monetary frameworks.

5. Exchange Rate Volatility: The topic of discussion pertains to the volatility exhibited by exchange rates. According to Wang et al. (2022), the inherent volatility of digital currencies poses challenges in the context of global commerce. Based on the research conducted by Auer and Claessens (2018), it has been shown that organisations involved in global trade can encounter substantial gains or losses due to the volatility of digital currencies. Cheah and Fry (2015) argue that the existence of uncertainty poses challenges to pricing strategies, budgeting, and risk management in the context of international trade operations.

Conclusion

This study examined the complex interplay between digital currency and global trade. Our investigation shows a terrain with both advantages and disadvantages. Digital currencies offer efficiency in cross-border transactions, lower prices, financial inclusion, transparency, and speed. These entities can change the global trade climate, improving economic interdependence and expanding international markets. Case studies in several nations have shown these prospects. However, troubles persist.

Other issues include regulatory complexity, security concerns, the risk of disrupting financial institutions, economic and financial stability, and currency rate volatility. Case studies have illuminated these issues, emphasising the need for strong policies and regulations. The research has major implications for international trade. Businesses must develop robust risk management approaches, comply with changing regulatory frameworks, and find innovative cross-border transaction ways to negotiate international trade. Governments and regulators must create a climate that balances innovation, consumer interests, and financial stability. It is worth studying the dynamics of different currencies and regions because they may have unique traits. This study examines geographical variations in digital money adoption in international trade, taking into account that factors affecting adoption may vary by area. The emergence of legal frameworks for digital currencies in international trade is very important to meet the regulatory issues. Similarly, digital currency and blockchain network interoperability can improve cross-border transactions and operational efficiency. In conclusion, digital currencies have the potential to transform global trade, offering both opportunities and challenges. Due to the landscape's dynamic character, stakeholders must be adaptable and proactive to maximise benefits and minimise the risks. The future of digital currencies in international trade depends on more focused research and collaboration between governments, firms, and academia.

References

Accenture (2020). Driving the Future of Payments: 10 Megatrends Shaping the Payments Landscape. https://www.accenture.com/_acnmedia/pdf-121/accenture-payment-services-global-payment-trends.pdf

Aneja, R., & Dygas, R. (Eds.). (2022). *Digital Currencies and the New Global Financial System* (1st ed., pp. 1–16). Routledge. https://doi.org/10.4324/9781003310365

Auer, R., & Claessens, S. (2018). Regulatory Challenges for Cryptocurrencies and Related Technologies. *BIS Quarterly Review*. https://www.bis.org/publ/qtrpdf/r_qt1803f.htm

Baldwin, R., & Weder di Mauro, B. (Eds.). (2020). *Economics in the Time of COVID-19*. CEPR Press.

Bank for International Settlements (BIS) (2020). Central Bank Digital Currencies.

Bank for International Settlements (BIS) (2021). Beyond the Hype: Central Bank Digital Currencies.

Bhardwaj, A. & Kumar, V., (2022). A Framework for Enhancing Privacy in Online Collaboration. *International Journal of Electronic Security and Digital Forensics (IJESDF), 14*(4), 413–432

Boreland, M., Howison, S., & Richardson, H. (2020). Regulating Cryptocurrencies: Evaluating the Challenges of Tax Evasion. *Economic Policy, 35*(103), 169–199.

Brown, A. (2023). Daily Trading Volume in the Cryptocurrency Market. *Crypto Insights, 10*(3), 45–56.

Brown, A., & Garcia, M. (2023). Gender Disparity in Cryptocurrency Ownership in the United States. *Cryptocurrency Studies, 5*(2), 78–90.

Buterin, V. (2013). Ethereum: A Next-Generation Smart Contract and Decentralized Application Platform.

Catalini, C., & Gans, J. S. (2016). *Some Simple Economics of the Blockchain.* NBER Working Paper No. 22952. https://www.nber.org/papers/w22952

Cecchetti, S. G., & Schoenholtz, K. L. (2018). *The Case for Central Bank Electronic Money and the Non-case for Central Bank Cryptocurrencies.* NBER Working Paper No. 24185. https://www.nber.org/papers/w24185

Chaum, D. (1983). Blind Signatures for Untraceable Payments. In *Advances in Cryptology—Crypto'82* (pp. 199–203).

Cheah, E. T., & Fry, J. (2015). Speculative bubbles in Bitcoin markets? An empirical investigation into the fundamental value of Bitcoin. *Economics Letters, 130*, 32–36.

Cheah, E. T., Mishra, T., Parhi, M., & Zhang, Q. (2019). Cryptocurrency Prices, Investor Behavior, and Regulatory Challenges. *Journal of International Financial Markets, Institutions and Money, 61*, 195–221.

Cohen, B., & Davidson, S. (2018). *Regulation of Cryptocurrency Around the World.* Library of Congress. https://www.loc.gov/law/help/cryptocurrency/world-survey.pdf

Doe, J. (2023). Banks and Blockchain Adoption: Potential Savings of $27 Billion. *Blockchain Finance Review, 7*(1), 112–128.

Doe, J., & Johnson, S. (2023). Confidence in Cryptocurrencies: A Comprehensive Survey. *Journal of Digital Finance, 15*(4), 321–335.

EU Blockchain Observatory and Forum. (2020). *Blockchain and the GDPR: How do they work together?* https://www.eublockchainforum.eu/sites/default/files/report/files/2020%20-%20

Europol. (2021). *Internet Organised Crime Threat Assessment (IOCTA).* https://www.europol.europa.eu/activities-services-main/reports/internet-organised-crime-threat-assessment-iocta-2021

Fang, H., Ma, Y., & Wang, X. (2021). *Digital Currency and Cross-Border Trade: Evidence from Migrant Remittances.* Available at SSRN: https://ssrn.com/abstract=3865832

Financial Action Task Force (FATF). (2021). *Guidance for a Risk-Based Approach: Virtual Assets and Virtual Asset Service Providers*. https://www.fatf-gafi.org/publications/fatfrecommendations/documents/guidance-rba-virtual-assets.html

Gandal, N., Halaburda, H., & Sarfati, E. (2018). *Can We Predict the Winner in a Market with Network Effects? Competition in the Cryptocurrency Market*. NBER Working Paper, No. 24784.

Garratt, R., Hendry, S., & Shaffer, B. (2018). Modelling Bitcoin's Value with Scarcity. *Economics Letters, 173*, 53–56.

Gensler, G. (2019). *Testimony on Examining Facebook's Proposed Digital Currency and Data Privacy Considerations*. U.S. House of Representatives Committee on Financial Services. https://www.congress.gov/116/meeting/house/110548/witnesses/HHRG-116-BA19-Wstate-GenslerG-20190717.pdf

Gipp, R., Geers, J., & Meinel, C. (2020). Cryptocurrency Frameworks in Germany and Malta: Balancing between Innovation and Regulation. In *Proceedings of the 51st Hawaii International Conference on System Sciences*.

Iansiti, M., & Lakhani, K. R. (2017). The Truth About Blockchain. *Harvard Business Review*. https://hbr.org/2017/01/the-truth-about-blockchain

Ito, J., Kim, Y., & Tan, Y. (2019). *Cross-Border Payment and Settlement Systems: A Digital Inclusive Finance Perspective*. ADBI Working Paper 939. https://www.adb.org/publications/cross-border-payment-and-settlement-systems

Johnson, S., & Lee, K. (2023). Bitcoin: The Continued Reign of the Crypto King. *Cryptocurrency Review, 4*(1), 23–35.

Jones, R. (2023). Surge in Trading Volumes of Cryptocurrency Investment Products. *Crypto Trends, 12*(2), 67–80.

Jones, R., & Davis, L. (2023). Social Media Posts and Cryptocurrency: An Analysis of Online Discourse. *Digital Finance Journal, 8*(3), 189–204.

Kerstens, Y., Rutten, L., & De Spiegeleire, S. (2020). *Cryptocurrencies in Europe: A Cautious Approach*. European Parliament, Directorate-General for Internal Policies, Policy Department A: Economic and Scientific Policy.

Kshetri, N. (2017). Blockchain's Roles in Strengthening Cybersecurity and Protecting Privacy. *Telecommunications Policy, 41*(10), 1027–1038.

Kumar, V., & Pradhan, P. (2020). Trust Management: Social vs Digital Identity. *International Journal of Service Science Management, Engineering and Technology (IJSSMET), 11*(4), 26–44.

Lamport, L., Shostak, R., & Pease, M. (1982). The Byzantine Generals Problem. *ACM Transactions on Programming Languages and Systems (TOPLAS), 4*(3), 382–401.

Lata, M., & Kumar, V., (2021). Standards and Regulatory Compliances for IoT. *International Journal of Service Science Management, Engineering and Technology (IJSSMET), 12*(5), 133–147

Lata, M. & Kumar, V., (2022a). Security and Privacy Issues in Fog Computing Environment. *International Journal of Electronic Security and Digital Forensics (IJESDF), 14*(3), 289–307.

Lata, M. & Kumar, (2022b). IoT Networks Security in Smart Home. In *Cybersecurity for Smart Home*, pp. 155–176, ISTE-WILEY Publications.

Liu, L., & Tsyrennikov, N. (2019). *China's Plan to Legalize Digital Yuan Challenges Bitcoin's Dominance.* Bloomberg. https://www.bloomberg.com/news/articles/2019-11-25/china-s-plan-to-legitimize-digital-yuan-challenges-bitcoin-dominance

Mancini-Griffoli, T., Peria, M. S. M., Agur, I., Ari, A., Kiff, J., Popescu, A., Rochon, C., & Vladkova-Hollar, I. (2018). *Casting Light on Central Bank Digital Currency.* IMF Staff Discussion Note, SDN/18/08.

Mandjee, T., & Iyer, D. (2016). Bitcoin: Economics, Technology, and Governance. *Journal of Economic Perspectives, 29*(2), 213–238.

Mik, T. (2016). *Blockchain Basics: A Non-Technical Introduction in 25 Steps.* O'Reilly Media.

Mittal, S., & Kumar, V. (2020). A Framework for Ethical Mobile Marketing. *International Journal of Technoethics (IJT), 11*(1), 28–42.

Mittal, S., & Kumar, V. (2018). Adoption of Mobile Wallets in India: An Analysis. *IUP Journal of Information Technology, 14*(1), 42–57.

Möser, M., Böhme, R., Breuker, D., & Halderman, J. A. (2020). Bitcoin: Technical Background and Data Analysis. In *Handbook of Digital Currency* (pp. 31–43). Elsevier.

Moser, T. (2022). Central bank digital currency: The new kid on the block? *Journal of Digital Banking, 6*(4), 359–365.

Mougayar, W. (2016). *The Business Blockchain: Promise, Practice, and Application of the Next Internet Technology.* Wiley.

Mycielski, J., Notheisen, B., & Suhlrie, L. (2019). E-Government and Blockchain: A Literature Review. In *Proceedings of the 52nd Hawaii International Conference on System Sciences.*

Nafrees, A. C. M., Baanu, A. S. N., Shibly, F. H. A., Roshan, A. M. F., Nihma, M. N. F., Mishra, P., & Latchoumi, T. P. (2020). *Том. 1712. International Conference on Computational Physics in Emerging Technologies,* ICCPET 2020.-Сер. 1 International Conference on Computational Physics in Emerging Technologies, ICCPET 2020.

Nakamoto, S. (2008). *Bitcoin: A Peer-to-Peer Electronic Cash System.* https://bitcoin.org/bitcoin.pdf.

Nanda, P., & Kumar, V. (2022). Information Processing and Data Analytics for Decision Making: A Journey from Traditional to Modern Approaches. *Information Resources Management Journal (IRMJ), 35*(2), 1–14.

Narayanan, A., Bonneau, J., Felten, E., Miller, A., & Goldfeder, S. (2016). *Bitcoin and Cryptocurrency Technologies: A Comprehensive Introduction.* Princeton University Press.

Ogunmola, G. A., & Das, U. (2024). Analyzing consumer perceptions and adoption intentions of central bank digital currency: A case of the digital rupee. *Digital Policy, Regulation and Governance*, *26*(4), 450–471.

Ogunmola, G. A., & Kumar, V. (2021). Web Analytics and Online Retail: Ethical Perspective. In *Research Anthology on Privatizing and Securing Data* (pp. 611–628). IGI Global.

Ogunmola, G. A., & Kumar, V. (2023). E-commerce Research Models: A Systematic Review and Identification of the Determinants to Success. *International Journal of Business Information Systems, 43*(1), 87–106.

Pradhan, P., & Kumar, V. (2016). Trust Management Models for Digital Identities. *International Journal of Virtual Communities and Social Networking (IJVCSN), 8*(4), 1–24.

PwC. (2021). *Time for Trust: The Trillion-dollar Reasons to Rethink Blockchain.* https://www.pwc.com/gx/en/industries/financial-services/publications/assets/pwc-project-oryx-trillion-dollar-reasons.pdf

Saurabh and Kumar, V. (2017). Technology Integration for the Success of B2C M-Commerce in India: Opportunities and Challenges. *IUP Journal of Information Technology, 13*(1), 24–35.

Schär, F. (2020). Decentralized Finance: On Blockchain- and Smart Contract-Based Financial Markets. *Federal Reserve Bank of St. Louis Review, 102*(2), 1–14.

Singh, J., & Kumar, V. (2013). Compliance and Regulatory Standards for Cloud Computing. In *Interdisciplinary Perspectives on Business Convergence, Computing, and Legality* (pp. 54–64). IGI Global.

Swan, M. (2015). *Blockchain: A Blueprint for a New Economy.* O'Reilly Media.

Wang, C., Gao, Y., Aziz, A., & Ogunmola, G. A. (2022). Agricultural disaster risk management and capability assessment using big data analytics. *Big Data, 10*(3), 246–261.

Wood, G. (2016). *Polkadot: Vision for a Heterogeneous Multi-Chain Framework.* https://polkadot.network/PolkaDotPaper.pdf

Xue, B. (2021). China's Digital Currency and Central Bank's Digitalization Policy. *Stanford Journal of Blockchain Law & Policy, 4*(1), 82–104.

Zetzsche, D. A., Buckley, R. P., Arner, D. W., & Barberis, J. N. (2019). *The Distributed Liability of Distributed Ledgers: Legal Risks of Blockchain.* European Banking Institute Working Paper Series.

CHAPTER 18

Enhancing Global Trade: Leveraging Central Bank Digital Currency in Optimising Cross-Border Payments

Sanjeev Gupta and Tanvi

Introduction

Trade is a core economic activity that entails exchanging products and services among individuals and businesses within and across the nations. In the global economy, it distributes resources, influences economic growth, and impacts international relations (Bai et al., 2023). Trade (domestic and cross-border) plays a crucial role in economic development by fostering job creation, transferring technology, and connecting economies to the global market (Matusz & Tarr, 2017; Oneal, 2003). However, it can also lead to challenges such as trade imbalances, job displacement, and environmental concerns (Majeed, 2019).

S. Gupta (✉)
Central University of Himachal Pradesh, Dharamshala, Himachal Pradesh, India
e-mail: sanjeeveco@hotmail.com

Tanvi
Central University of Himachal Pradesh, Dharamshala, Himachal Pradesh, India

R. Aneja and R. Dygas (eds.), *Digital Currencies in The New Global World Order*, https://doi.org/10.1007/978-981-97-4810-5_18

Cross-border trade is a critical component of the global economy, determining the flow of goods, services, capital, and technology across national borders (Li & Choi, 2022). Cross-border trade encompasses activities such as exporting and importing goods, foreign direct investment, and the provision of services such as tourism and transportation (Wang et al., 2017). The World Trade Organisation (WTO) oversees and promotes trade among its member nations in the global market facilitates the negotiation and formalisation of trade agreements, and resolves trade disputes through its dispute settlement process (Atagher, 2022; Rose, 2005).

Payment is a pivotal aspect of cross-border transactions and an essential factor in all types of international trade (Xiang & Zhang, 2018). Research on cross-border payments is becoming more significant, considering the worldwide integration of cross-border commerce. Integration of global economies and digitalisation has increased interest in innovative cross-border payment systems. Cross-border payment refers to the financial transactions and settlement processes involved in international trade activities. The cross-border payments system comprises Business-to-Business (B2B), Business-to-Person (B2P), Person-to-Business (P2B), and Person-to-Person (P2P) merchants. Cross-border remittances are processed through many conventional methods, such as SWIFT/correspondent banking, post, Rupee Drawing Arrangement (RDA), and Money Transfer Service Scheme (MTSS) (PricewaterhouseCoopers, 2021). Cross-border payment with systematic regulation networks is essential for governments aiming to internationalise their currency and is a crucial aspect of currency internationalisation (Teker et al., 2022).

Cross-border trade settlement involves finalising financial transactions and clearing obligations between parties engaged in international trade. Conventional cross-border payment methods often involve payment processing, receiving, financial operation, and reconciliation costs. The influence of payment methods on cross-border mergers and acquisitions is complex and cannot be easily categorised as directly affecting the performance of such transactions (Wang et al., 2022a). The choice of payment methods, currency, and transactions' security are crucial aspects of cross-border payment, and the factors affecting payment in small and micro cross-border transactions have been subjects of analysis, highlighting the significance of payment considerations in international trade activities (Xiang & Zhang, 2018). The settlement of cross-border trade transactions is influenced by various factors, including payment security, exchange rates, and settlement modes (Liao & McDowell, 2014).

The growing pace of global economic integration and the rise of the digital economy have resulted in the improved efficiency of cross-border payment systems. This trend underscores the increasing attention and significance of payment systems in facilitating cross-border transactions (Wu et al., 2021). Cross-border payment efficiency is a multifaceted, technical, and complex issue that encompasses various factors such as technological advancements, regulatory frameworks, and economic implications. This study has been categorised into 5 Sections. Sect 18.1 explains the background of the study under consideration. Sect 18.2 elaborates on the potential benefits and challenges of CBDC in cross-border payments. Sect 18.3 discusses the lessons learnt and insights from cross-border CBDC projects, and Sect. 18.4 includes the policy recommendations for cross-border payments through CBDC.

Cross-Border Payment Efficiency

Efficiency in cross-border transactions is paramount due to its multifaceted impact on international business, finance, and economic development. The efficiency of cross-border transactions is crucial for enhancing market competition, promoting economic growth, and fostering international trade (Clougherty & Skousen, 2019). Efficient cross-border transactions can lead to increased market competition, essential for driving innovation, improving productivity, and benefiting consumers (Gugler et al., 2003). Efficient cross-border transactions are vital for reducing transaction costs, streamlining processes, and enhancing the overall competitiveness of businesses operating in the global marketplace (Lin et al., 2019). Efficiency in cross-border transactions is also closely linked to adopting advanced technology such as blockchain, which can lead to enhanced operational efficiency, cost reduction, and can also improve transparency in cross-border trade and finance (Chen et al., 2021; Fu et al., 2021; Tian et al., 2022). The efficient settlement of cross-border transactions is essential for reducing transaction costs, mitigating risks, and promoting the growth of international trade (Wang, 2022; Wang et al., 2017). Effective cross-border payment systems can enhance the growth of financial services, reduce trade barriers, and facilitate international investment, which leads to the growth and development of the economy (Lin et al., 2022; Rao, 2022).

Moreover, the efficiency of cross-border transactions is essential for promoting trust, transparency, and goodwill in international business relationships, which are critical for fostering long-term partnerships and collaborations (Huang, 2022; Wang et al., 2022b). Efficiency in cross-border transactions must be considered to promote market competition, reduce transaction costs, foster innovation, and drive economic growth. This is particularly relevant given the increasing volume of cross-border transactions and the need to ensure secure and efficient payment mechanisms (Chen et al., 2021). The rise of innovative payment technology has significantly impacted cross-border payment systems, leading to increased cross-border influence and the need for sustainable usage intention (Lin et al., 2019).

Challenges and Inefficiencies in the Existing Cross-Border Payment System

Technological advancements, economic integration, and regulatory frameworks have significantly influenced cross-border payment processes. Conventional cross-border payment methods face issues such as transaction credit risk, delayed settlement cycles, high cost of cross-border transactions, and increasing raw material prices, which collectively hinder the development of cross-border trade (Lin, 2022), along with foreign exchange settlement, slow turnover, and exchange rate risks, which have been highlighted, indicating the need for technological breakthroughs to address these inefficiencies (Fu & Saad, 2022; Xiang & Zhang, 2018). The implications of cross-border payment processes extend to financial stability, market liquidity, and the global economy, emphasising cross-border transactions' broader economic and financial implications (Caux et al., 2016; Pröpper et al., 2008; Rosati & Secola, 2006).

The factors contributing to inefficiencies in conventional cross-border payments are multilayered and encompass various aspects of technology, finance, and regulatory frameworks. The constraints of the traditional system of payment and the necessity for technological breakthroughs have been emphasised as urgent requirements to address the shortcomings in traditional cross-border trade (Deng, 2020). Moreover, introducing emerging payment models like third-party payments and digital currencies has influenced the existing regulatory framework, resulting in ambiguous regulatory topics, insufficient regulatory strategies, and weak regulatory foundations in practice, ultimately causing inefficiencies in cross-border payments (Rao, 2022).

The current cross-border payment system faces various challenges and inefficiencies that hinder its effectiveness. The growing influence of large technology companies in the payment industry poses challenges, and more comprehensive solutions must be addressed to address these issues (Polasik et al., 2021). Electronic payment has enhanced ease and efficiency in business and society, although it has also raised concerns over transaction information security (Chen et al., 2021). Moreover, the payment method used for mergers and acquisitions (M&As) across borders can reduce the risk of governance at the country level for the acquiring company, highlighting the significance of payment methods in these transactions (Dutta et al., 2013; Huang et al., 2016). Conventional cross-border payment methods usually do not allow for real-time payment, and the exposure to foreign currencies throughout the payment process increases the risks of exchange rate fluctuations, making cross-border trading more challenging (Fu & Saad, 2022). In the wake of the inefficiency of existing cross-border payment, there is a need to explore emerging technologies to enhance the efficiency of the cross-border payment system. CBDC is suggested as a payment system to improve the existing payment process. CBDC can potentially transform the cross-border payment system by improving the payment mechanism.

Central Bank Digital Currency and Its Role in Cross-Border Payments

Central Bank Digital Currency (CBDC) is a digitalised form of a country's fiat currency created and regulated by the country's central bank. CBDC performs all the functions of money, similar to physical fiat currency (Dashkevich et al., 2020). CBDCs are created to serve as a digital account or electronic token for payment settlements and as a means of storing value and granting access to a central bank's financial reserves. It is also designed to facilitate and improve cross-border payments (Dashkevich et al., 2020). CBDCs are characterised by their 24/7 availability and electronic nature and have the potential to improve the efficiency of payment transactions along with financial inclusion (Dashkevich et al., 2020). The idea of issuing CBDC is to provide a user-friendly, cost-effective, and secure payment solution to promote widespread consumer usage and merchant approval (Ozili,

2022a). Central banks view the issuing of CBDCs as a chance to support the shift towards a circular economy, emphasising the broader socio-economic and environmental impacts of CBDCs. CBDC can strengthen monetary policy transmission, enhance payment system efficiency, and promote greater financial inclusivity.

Additionally, CBDCs are expected to enhance the availability of digital financial services and expand the scope of the digital economy (Ozili, 2022b). CBDC has garnered considerable interest for its capacity to transform the banking sector. However, there are challenges and considerations in the development and execution of CBDCs, including the need to balance anonymous payments with compliance and oversight (Allen et al., 2020).

CBDCs can contribute to enhancing the retail payment system by offering access options for non-bank entities and technical interfaces, influencing financial stability policy (Özsoy, 2020). CBDCs can facilitate the effective implementation of financial regulations and monetary policies, protecting the economy from risks linked to digital currencies (Jakšić et al., 2022). Issuing CBDCs can lead to increased financial inclusion, decreased cash management expenses, and improved execution of monetary policy (Ozili, 2022c). Central banks can boost the economy during downturns by implementing negative nominal interest rates and phasing out cash transactions (Davoodalhosseini, 2017). Assessing how CBDCs affect private banks is essential, especially when an interest-bearing CBDC could influence a monopolistic banking industry (Andolfatto, 2018). An interest-bearing CBDC could improve the central bank's monetary transmission by directly enhancing the effectiveness of monetary policy (Kóczián et al., 2022). Blockchain technology offers an efficient framework for cross-border payment settlement by eliminating expensive intermediaries and improving the payment system for many currencies (Deng, 2020). If the legitimacy of fiat digital currency is questioned in the region, it will lead to greater exposure of the payment clearing system and impact cross-border payment settlement (Jakšić et al., 2022; You, 2022).

CBDCs have attracted considerable attention from policymakers, economists, and financial institutions. Worldwide, public authorities and central banks vigilantly observe advancements in digital currencies and analyse their impact on the economy, financial system, and central banks (Fung & Hałaburda, 2016; Kim & Kwon, 2022). Furthermore, introducing CBDCs is seen as an opportunity for central banks to contribute to the transition to a circular economy, highlighting the broader societal and environmental implications of CBDCs (El-Sayed & Nasir, 2022). The impact of CBDCs on credit supply and financial stability has also been a subject of interest, emphasising the need for a comprehensive understanding of the broader economic impact of CBDCs (Andolfatto, 2018). The potential consequences of CBDCs for deposit insurers and their exact design are areas of consideration, indicating the need for a comprehensive understanding of the broader economic impact of CBDCs (Auer et al., 2020).

CBDCs are becoming more prevalent due to the necessity for secure, effective, and cost-efficient cross-border and cross-currency transactions in the modern interconnected financial system (Themistocleous et al., 2023). The Central Bank of China's adoption of Digital Currency Electronic Payment (DCEP) is beneficial for the central bank to understand macroeconomic trends and promptly promote RMB internationalisation (Wu et al., 2022). The potential role of CBDCs extends to various aspects of the economy. CBDCs have been proposed to facilitate secure, streamlined, and cost-effective cross-border and cross-currency payments, thereby resolving the inefficiencies and constraints in the existing cross-border payment systems (Themistocleous et al., 2023). The macroeconomic implications of CBDCs are also a subject of interest. The potential consequences of CBDCs for deposit insurers and their exact design are areas of consideration, indicating the need for a comprehensive understanding of the broader economic impact of CBDCs (Defina, 2021). The design choices for CBDCs are crucial, as they can significantly impact the monetary policy in the country (Cheng, 2022). The rise of CBDCs presents a transformative opportunity for the financial sector, with potential implications for cross-border payments, monetary policy, financial inclusion, and the broader economy (Chen et al., 2021).

Selecting a settlement currency, like the Renminbi (RMB), is essential for cross-border trade settlement. Empirical studies have demonstrated that the increase in value of the Chinese currency, RMB, does not always lead to a rise in RMB cross-border trade settlements (Huo et al., 2017). Bilateral swap agreements and the signing of an RMB Bilateral Swap Agreement (BSA) have been shown to boost the amount, value, and percentage of RMB settlements in trade across borders (Song & Xia, 2020). Kochergin (2021) examined the implementation of CBDC for retail transactions and large-scale financial settlements. The study emphasised the advantages of CBDC systems for wholesale payments, specifically focusing on a system with a universal digital currency that might mitigate the primary drawbacks of current cross-border payment systems.

Potential Benefits and Challenges of CBDC for Cross-Border Payments

The potential benefits of CBDC for cross-border payments are multidimensional and encompass various aspects of financial transactions, economic development, and monetary policy. Existing studies provide insights into the potential advantages of CBDC for cross-border payments, including efficiency, financial inclusion, and security. Some potential benefits of CBDC for cross-border payments include Efficiency, Cost reduction, Financial Inclusion, Security, Transparency, and economic integration (Cheng, 2022; Lin et al., 2022; Lee, 2022; Ozili, 2022c; Themistocleous et al., 2023; Wang & Hausken, 2022). CBDCs have the potential to provide secure, cost-effective cross-border and cross-currency payments, which might lead to lower transaction costs and improved efficiency in cross-border transactions. (Themistocleous et al., 2023). The use of CBDCs can lead to lower cross-border payments, improved transaction efficiency, and cost savings, benefiting both businesses and consumers (Wang & Hausken, 2022). CBDCs have the potential to increase financial inclusion, providing greater accessibility to financial services for unbanked and underbanked populations, particularly in the context of cross-border transactions (Ozili, 2022c). Adopting CBDCs can lead to greater accessibility and easier domestic and cross-border transactions, potentially benefiting individuals and businesses, especially in developing countries (Cheng, 2022; Lee, 2022). CBDCs can reduce illicit activities in the circular economy and provide low transaction costs for financial transactions, improving security and transparency in cross-border payments (Ozili, 2022b). CBDCs can promote Cross-Border Trade and Economic Cooperation through Systemized payment services, which can facilitate the amalgamation of payment and settlement systems, fostering international trade and sustainable growth of consumer markets (Lin et al., 2019, 2022). Integrating CBDCs can improve transaction efficiency, settlement finality, and financial inclusion, potentially benefiting cross-border trade and financial transactions (Cheng, 2022). CBDCs can offer a more advanced payment method for financial transactions in the circular economy, aiming to lower transaction costs and provide financial support to circular businesses in times of crisis, contributing to transaction efficiency and economic stability (Ozili, 2022b). These potential advantages underscore the transformative potential of CBDC in reshaping cross-border payment systems and fostering economic development.

Reducing Transaction Costs and Processing Times

CBDC eliminates intermediaries in cross-border transactions, reducing fees and enabling instant settlements (Bindseil, 2022). It decreases transaction fees, which benefits businesses, particularly Small and Medium Enterprises (SMEs), by making overseas transactions more economical. CBDC transactions are recorded on a distributed ledger, providing transparency and traceability (Ginneken, 2019). They operate round-the-clock, allowing enterprises to initiate cross-border payments at any time. Standardised protocols and interoperable frameworks promote efficiency in cross-border trade payments. CBDC also reduces foreign exchange risk, enhancing predictability and stability in volatile currency markets.

Enhancing Transparency and Security in Cross-Border Payments

CBDC can improve transparency and security in cross-border payments through various mechanisms. These include immutable transaction records, real-time monitoring, enhanced compliance features, instant settlement, privacy protections, and secure authentication (Bindseil, 2022). CBDC transactions are recorded on a distributed ledger, creating a secure audit trail and reducing fraud and errors. Real-time monitoring allows authorities to detect suspicious activities, while CBDC systems can automate compliance checks, reducing administrative burdens. Settlement risk is diminished due to instant settlement, and privacy protections like zero-knowledge proofs (ZKP) and privacy-enhancing protocols protect sensitive data (Islam et al., 2023). Advanced authentication mechanisms, like biometric or multi-factor authentication, prevent unauthorised access and mitigate identity theft or account takeover risks (Islam et al., 2023). However, balancing transparency and privacy is crucial to ensure compliance with regulatory requirements.

Addressing Concerns Related to Privacy and Data Security

CBDC can enhance privacy and data security in cross-border payments through encryption, secure authentication, privacy-enhancing protocols, user consent, anonymity features, data minimisation, blockchain technology, and regulatory oversight (Ahmed, 2019). Encryption techniques protect transaction data confidentiality and integrity, while secure authentication mechanisms prevent unauthorised access. Privacy-enhancing protocols safeguard sensitive transaction data while maintaining transparency and traceability (Fu et al., 2021). Users can consent to disclosing transaction details or control transaction history visibility. Anonymity features allow transactions without revealing identities, while compliance with anti-money laundering and KYC regulations prevents illicit activities (Ahmed, 2019; Fu et al., 2021). These measures can foster trust and promote the widespread adoption of CBDC for international transactions.

Technological Infrastructure Requirements and Interoperability Issues

CBDC is a digital currency that facilitates cross-border payments. It requires a technological infrastructure capable of efficiently handling large volumes of transactions, ensuring performance and reliability. The infrastructure must also be capable of processing transactions quickly and efficiently, facilitating instant settlements and fast fund transfers. Interoperability is crucial for seamless cross-border payments, and CBDC systems must be compatible with existing payment infrastructures (Themistocleous et al., 2023). Cross-border connectivity is also essential, requiring the development of payment gateways, messaging protocols, and settlement mechanisms. Security and privacy considerations are also crucial, requiring robust measures to protect transaction data and assets (Ahmed, 2019). Collaboration is essential among central banks, financial institutions, technology providers, and regulatory agencies to create and implement the infrastructure, standards, and protocols for efficient cross-border CBDC transactions.

Regulatory and Legal Challenges in Implementing CBDC for Cross-Border Payments

While technical interoperability is feasible, challenges regarding standards, interfaces, legal issues, regulations, and governance must be addressed for successful implementation (Themistocleous et al., 2023). CBDC implementation challenges include ensuring user readiness, data privacy vs. compliance trade-offs, and collaboration with private intermediaries (Bindseil, 2022). Understanding user needs, institutional capacity, and compatibility with existing financial systems is highlighted. CBDCs can impact economic policy autonomy, currency internationalisation, and payment system modernisation (United Nations Conference on Trade and Development, 2023).

CBDC implementation for cross-border payments faces regulatory and legal challenges. These include jurisdictional complexity, compliance with Anti-Money Laundering (AML) and Know Your Customer (KYC) regulations, cross-border regulatory oversight, exchange rate volatility, data privacy and security, and interoperability (Ahmed, 2019). Harmonising diverse regulatory environments is crucial for consistency and compliance. Regulatory authorities must establish robust compliance mechanisms to prevent illicit activities (Hang & Adjouro, 2021). Maintaining exchange rate stability and minimising currency risk requires coordination among central banks and monetary authorities. Ensuring data privacy and security is essential for minimising data breaches. Interoperability and standards facilitate cross-border transactions (Themistocleous et al., 2023). Addressing these challenges is crucial for promoting financial inclusion, efficiency, and stability in the global payment system.

Lessons Learnt and Best Practices from Pilot Initiatives

The cross-border projects emphasise the need for central banks to work together and function together to create CBDCs to enhance cross-border payments. It requires additional examination of CBDC design decisions and their broader financial consequences, including interoperability, access to central bank money, and private industry involvement (Bank for International Settlements, 2021). It also stresses the importance of enhancing cross-border payment infrastructures, aligning regulatory frameworks, and exploring new payment infrastructures to support the cross-border payment market (Bank for International Settlements, 2021).

An international settlement infrastructure that supports multiple CBDCs could streamline cross-border payments by reducing reliance on intermediaries and streamlining settlement processes (Bank for International Settlements et al., 2022). Banks can transact directly using different CBDCs without needing correspondent banks. The platform aims to make cross-border payments faster, cheaper, and safer by consolidating standard processes and automating processes using programmable money and smart contracts. This would increase efficiency and reduce operational costs, making settlement processes more efficient and cost-effective (Bank for International Settlements et al., 2022).

Project Jura showcased a new settlement method for tokenised financial instruments and foreign exchange transactions across borders, combining Distributed Ledger Technology (DLT) with a single platform for multiple assets and jurisdictions. The solution was instantaneous and atomic, showcasing the feasibility of integrating transactions in wholesale CBDC and tokenised assets on a single third-party platform (Banque De France et al., 2021). The solution design allocated control functions across different jurisdictions in a flexible manner, ensuring critical controls for central banks. Project Jura has advanced knowledge about DLT-enabled wholesale CBDC and is expected to contribute to its adoption (Banque De France et al., 2021).

The cross-border projects emphasise the importance of agile experimentation in developing innovative solutions for cross-border payments, focusing on technological, policy, legal, and business aspects. It highlights the potential of DLT to improve speed, cost efficiency, and operational resilience (Bank for International Settlements, 2018). Challenges encompassing privacy protection, liquidity savings, scalability, and performance when dealing with large-volume transactions were also emphasised. It also highlights the need for detailed risk governance procedures and evaluation of trade-offs in DLT-enabled infrastructure (Bank for International Settlements, 2018).

The Bank for International Settlements Innovation Hub's (BIS Innovation Hub) experiments on using CBDCs across borders have shown technical feasibility and operational efficiency. Multi-CBDC platforms, using DLT, enable faster, cheaper, and more transparent cross-border payments. Implementing a common DLT platform led to lower costs, faster settlement times, and increased operational transparency. Policy considerations, such as access policies, transparency, legal frameworks, and governance structures, must be considered when designing multi-CBDC models (Bech et al., 2022). Collaborative efforts among central banks, public and private financial institutions, technology experts, and innovators are essential to exploring further how CBDC can improve and make cross-border payments cost-effective in real time. Assessing the economic implications and potential systemic risks is crucial for financial resilience. The experiments also provide a platform for iterative learning, allowing central banks to build on each other's experiences and develop a deeper understanding of cross-border payments (Bech et al., 2022).

Project mBridge addresses the issues of traditional cross-border payments, including substantial costs, settlement risks, slow processing times, and operational complexities due to multiple intermediary banks. It emphasises the need for innovation and technology, using DLT, smart contracts, and a comprehensive legal rulebook for compliance and interoperability (BIS Innovation Hub, 2023). Privacy and security are crucial, with measures in place to protect sensitive transaction data. Interoperability with existing financial infrastructures is important with Application Programming Interfaces (APIs) based on the global ISO 20022 messaging standard facilitating seamless integration. The project's decentralised governance structure ensures effective management and oversight (BIS Innovation Hub, 2023). Collaboration with central and commercial banks and observing members are essential for testing and refining the platform. The project continuously evolves, transitioning from testing to a Minimum Viable Product, involving technological enhancements, legal and governance developments, and exploring synergies with other projects and private sector solutions (BIS Innovation Hub, 2023).

Potential Synergies Between CBDC and Other Emerging Technologies

Global financial regulation is shifting towards a payment-centric model due to the intersection of various international policies and legal regimes. International collaboration and synchronisation are crucial for effectively executing cross-border payment projects. The G20 roadmap emphasises enhancing cross-border payments for speed, cost-effectiveness, transparency, and accessibility (Ponamorenko, 2023).

The potential of artificial intelligence and machine learning algorithms in mitigating cross-border payment risks has also been explored, indicating the role of advanced technologies in the efficient and risk management of cross-border payments (Fu & Saad, 2022). It has been suggested that blockchain technology can tackle the constraints of conventional cross-border payment models, particularly in terms of transaction security and efficiency (Chen et al., 2021; Lin, 2022). The potential of blockchain technology, including optimising foreign trade financial transactions and its innovative application in the sharing economy, underscores its relevance in improving cross-border payment efficiency (Lin, 2022; Zhong, 2022). Blockchain technology offers advantages such as a reduction in transaction credit risk, efficient settlement cycles, and enhanced security (Deng, 2020). Using blockchain technology in cross-border e-business payment models has the potential to improve traceability and security (Li, 2021). Blockchain technology offers a robust structure for international transactions, eliminating costly intermediaries and enhancing the payment system for several currencies. The role of payment systems efficiency and central banks in enhancing payment efficiency have been subjects of interest, highlighting the broader economic and policy implications of payment systems (Khiaonarong, 2003; Rao, 2022).

Project mBridge explores potential synergies between CBDCs and emerging technologies with an emphasis on cross-border payments. Smart Contracts with DLT are implemented on the mBridge platform, ensuring transparency, security, and efficiency in cross-border transactions. Pseudonymous addresses and encrypted payment meta-data enhance privacy and confidentiality in transactions, which can be further integrated with other emerging technologies to strengthen data protection in cross-border payments (BIS Innovation Hub, 2023). The platform supports APIs based on the global ISO 20022 messaging standard, enabling interoperability with participants' systems. The Dash consensus algorithm enhances network performance and security, potentially synergising with other blockchain-based systems to improve scalability and reliability in financial transactions. Legal Entity Identifiers (LEIs) facilitate transaction identification, streamlining AML and Combating the Financing of

Terrorism (CFT) checks (BIS Innovation Hub, 2023). Containerisation and deployment configurations streamline the platform's deployment and operation, allowing for redundancy and scalability. By leveraging these technologies, central banks and financial institutions can drive innovation and improve the resilience of the global payment system (BIS Innovation Hub, 2023).

Exploring Partnerships and Collaborations for Global CBDC Interoperability

Project mBridge highlights the importance of partnerships and collaborations for global CBDC interoperability. These include collaborations with central banks, commercial banks, observing members, technology providers, industry stakeholders, and international collaborations. Central banks can collaborate with different jurisdictions to develop interoperable CBDC systems, aligning their technical standards, legal frameworks, and governance structures (BIS Innovation Hub, 2023). Commercial banks can integrate CBDC systems into existing financial infrastructures, driving adoption, regulatory compliance, and accessibility. Observing members can provide valuable insights and feedback on CBDC interoperability, while technology providers specialising in blockchain, DLT, and cybersecurity can enhance the technical capabilities of CBDC platforms. Industry partnerships can foster innovation and drive CBDC adoption, while international collaborations can promote standardisation and harmonisation of CBDC frameworks. These partnerships and collaborations are crucial for advancing global CBDC interoperability, creating a more connected and efficient cross-border payment ecosystem that benefits businesses, consumers, and the broader financial industry (BIS Innovation Hub, 2023).

Policy Recommendations for Maximising the Benefits of CBDC in Cross-Border Payments

CBDC can effectively execute fast, cheaper, safer, and real-time payments worldwide. Policymakers should prioritise interoperability, address privacy and security concerns, and foster international cooperation to maximise benefits (Themistocleous et al., 2023). This includes establishing common standards and protocols for compatibility and connectivity between CBDC platforms. Additionally, robust privacy and security frameworks should be developed to safeguard sensitive financial data. Also, collaboration among central banks and regulatory authorities should be encouraged to establish harmonised regulatory frameworks for cross-border CBDC transactions. The Project mBridge provides policy recommendations for maximising the benefits of CBDCs in cross-border payments. These include standardisation and interoperability, regulatory clarity and compliance, privacy and data protection measures, partnerships and collaboration, capacity building and education, risk management and contingency planning, and international cooperation and coordination. Global standards and protocols for CBDCs can enhance interoperability between central bank systems. Clear regulatory guidelines and compliance requirements are essential for successful implementation, and CBDC systems should adhere to international standards for Anti-Money Laundering (AML) and Combating the Financing of Terrorism (CFT) (BIS Innovation Hub, 2023). Prioritising privacy and data protection measures in CBDC transactions can safeguard sensitive information. Partnerships and collaboration between central banks, commercial banks, technology providers, and regulatory bodies can drive innovation and adoption of CBDCs in cross-border payments (BIS Innovation Hub, 2023). Investing in capacity-building programs and educational initiatives can help stakeholders understand the benefits and implications of CBDC technology. International cooperation and coordination among central banks and regulatory authorities are crucial for maximising the benefits of CBDCs in cross-border payments (BIS Innovation Hub, 2023).

Conclusion

CBDCs are gaining attention for their ability to enhance monetary policy transmission, boost financial inclusion, and contribute to a circular economy. It can reduce transaction costs, make international transactions more cost-effective for businesses, and enhance transparency and security in cross-border payments through mechanisms like immutable transaction records and real-time monitoring. However, it faces regulatory challenges like jurisdictional complexity, AML and KYC regulations compliance, exchange rate volatility, data privacy, and interoperability. To ensure consistency and compliance, collaboration between central banks, financial institutions, technology providers, and regulatory authorities is crucial for developing and deploying the necessary infrastructure and protocols.

CBDCs can improve cross-border payments by enhancing privacy and data security through encryption, secure authentication, and regulatory oversight. Central banks should collaborate to develop these technologies. Project Jura and mBridge demonstrate the potential of a multi-CBDC platform for international settlements, reducing intermediaries and streamlining processes. CBDC has the potential to significantly improve trade promotion by simplifying cross-border payments. CBDC enables transactions to occur almost instantaneously, eliminating conventional intermediaries and significantly lowering settlement periods from many days to only a few minutes. This enhanced effectiveness reduces transaction costs and removes the necessity for multiple currency changes, ultimately streamlining international trade procedures.

Furthermore, CBDCs promote enhanced financial inclusivity by enabling firms of various scales to engage in international trade conveniently. Implementing CBDC can transform international trade by facilitating more rapid, cost-effective, and readily accessible transactions. This, in turn, will stimulate economic expansion and enhance global collaboration.

References

Ahmed, U. (2019). The Importance of Cross-Border Regulatory Cooperation in an Era of Digital Trade. *World Trade Review, 18*(S1), S99–S120. https://doi.org/10.1017/s1474745618000514

Allen, S. E., Čapkun, S., Eyal, I., Fanti, G., Ford, B., Grimmelmann, J., Juels, A., Kostiainen, K., Meiklejohn, S., Miller, A., Prasad, E., Wüst, K., & Zhang, F. (2020). *Design Choices for Central Bank Digital Currency: Policy and Technical Considerations.* https://doi.org/10.3386/w27634

Andolfatto, D. (2018). Assessing the Impact of Central Bank Digital Currency on Private Banks. https://doi.org/10.20955/wp.2018.026

Aneja, R., & Dygas, R. (Eds.). (2022). *Digital Currencies and the New Global Financial System* (1st ed., pp. 1–16). Routledge. https://doi.org/10.4324/9781003310365

Atagher, L. (2022). Beyond Multilateral Treaty Reforms. *McGill GLSA Research Series, 2*(1), 19. https://doi.org/10.26443/glsars.v2i1.186

Auer, R., Cornelli, G., & Frost, J. (2020). Rise of the Central Bank Digital Currencies: Drivers, Approaches and Technologies. *Social Science Research Network.* https://doi.org/10.2139/ssrn.3724070

Bai, S., Zhang, B., & Ning, Y. (2023). Comprehensive Assessment of the Environmental and Employment Impacts of International Trade from the Perspective of Global Value Chains. *Frontiers in Environmental Science, 10*. https://doi.org/10.3389/fenvs.2022.1099655

Bank for International Settlements, Reserve Bank of Australia, Bank Negara Malaysia, Monetary Authority of Singapore, and South African Reserve Bank. (2022). Project Dunbar—International settlements using multi-CBDCs. In *Project Dunbar—International Settlements Using multi-CBDCs*. https://www.mas.gov.sg/-/media/mas-media-library/development/fintech/dunbar/project_dunbar_report_2022.pdf

Bank for International Settlements. (2018). Inthanon-LionRock to MBridge. In Basler Zietung, *Basler Zietung*. https://www.bis.org/speeches/sp180704a.htm

Bank for International Settlements. (2021). Central Bank Digital Currencies for Cross-border Payments. In *Report to the G20*. https://www.bis.org/publ/othp38.pdf

Banque De France, Bank for International Settlements, Swiss National Bank, Goulard, S., Cœuré, B., Maechler, A. M., Accenture, Credit Suisse, Natixis, R3, SDX, UBS, Heuking, Linklaters, & OCTO Technology. (2021). *PROJECT JURA*.

Bech, M., Boar, C., Eidan, D., Haene, P., Holden, H., & Toh, W. K. (2022). Using CBDCs Across Borders: Lessons from Practical Experiments. In *Using CBDCs Across Borders: Lessons from Practical Experiments* (pp. 4–7).

Bindseil, U., & Pantelopoulos, G. (2022). Towards the Holy Grail of Cross-border Payments. *Social Science Research Network*. https://doi.org/10.2139/ssrn.4057995

BIS Innovation Hub. (2023). Experimenting with a Multi-CBDC Platform for Cross-border Payments: Project mBridge Update. https://www.bis.org/innovation_hub/projects/mbridge_brochure_2311.pdf

Caux, R. D., Brede, M., & McGroarty, F. (2016). Payment Prioritisation and Liquidity Risk in Collateralised Interbank Payment Systems. *Journal of International Financial Markets, Institutions & Money, 41*, 139–150. https://doi.org/10.1016/j.intfin.2015.12.009

Chen, T., Liang, Y., Ko, P., & Huang, J. (2021). Optimisation Model of Cross-Border E-commerce Payment Security by Blockchain Finance. *Wireless Communications and Mobile Computing, 2021*, 1–9. https://doi.org/10.1155/2021/9192219

Cheng, P. (2022). Decoding the rise of Central Bank Digital Currency in China: Designs, problems, and Prospects. *Journal of Banking Regulation, 24*(2), 156–170. https://doi.org/10.1057/s41261-022-00193-5

Clougherty, J. A., & Skousen, B. (2019). The Efficiency and Market-power Interpretations of the Multinational Enterprise: Two out of Three ain't Bad. *Global Strategy Journal, 11*(3), 356–379. https://doi.org/10.1002/gsj.1360

Dashkevich, N., Counsell, S., & Destefanis, G. (2020). Blockchain Application for Central Banks: A Systematic Mapping study. *IEEE Access, 8*, 139918–139952. https://doi.org/10.1109/access.2020.3012295

Davoodalhosseini, S. M. (2017). Central Bank Digital Currency and Monetary Policy. *Social Science Research Network.* https://doi.org/10.2139/ssrn.3011401

Defina, R. (2021). Central Bank Digital Currencies: The Motivation. *Social Science Research Network.* https://doi.org/10.2139/ssrn.3946238

Deng, Q. T. (2020). Application Analysis on Blockchain Technology in Cross-border Payment. *Proceedings of the 5th International Conference on Financial Innovation and Economic Development (ICFIED 2020).* https://doi.org/10.2991/aebmr.k.200306.050

Dutta, S., Saadi, S., & Zhu, P. (2013). Does Payment Method Matter in Cross-border Acquisitions? *International Review of Economics & Finance, 25*, 91–107. https://doi.org/10.1016/j.iref.2012.06.005

El-Sayed, A. F., & Nasir, M. (2022). Central Bank Digital Currencies: An Agenda for Future Research. *Research in International Business and Finance, 62*, 101736. https://doi.org/10.1016/j.ribaf.2022.101736

Fu, J., & Saad, N. H. M. (2022). A New Hybrid Decision Tree Algorithm with K-Nearest Neighbour for Cross Border Payment Risks. *International Journal on Recent and Innovation Trends in Computing and Communication, 10*(11), 181–190. https://doi.org/10.17762/ijritcc.v10i11.5805

Fu, Z., Dong, P., Li, S., & Ju, Y. (2021). An Intelligent Cross-border Transaction System based on Consortium Blockchain: A Case Study in Shenzhen, China. *PloS One, 16*(6), e0252489. https://doi.org/10.1371/journal.pone.0252489

Fung, B., & Hałaburda, H. (2016). Central Bank Digital Currencies: A Framework for Assessing Why and How. *Social Science Research Network.* https://doi.org/10.2139/ssrn.2994052

Ginneken, C. L. (2019). Settlement of Cross-border Transactions through Central Bank Digital Currency (CBDC): Analysis from a Risk Management Perspective, *University of Twente.* https://essay.utwente.nl/78027/

Gugler, K., Mueller, D. C., Yurtoğlu, B. B., & Zulehner, C. (2003). The Effects of Mergers: An International Comparison. *International Journal of Industrial Organization, 21*(5), 625–653. https://doi.org/10.1016/s0167-7187(02)00107-8

Hang, H. T., & Adjouro, T. (2021). The effects of Cross-Border E-Commerce on International Trade and Economic Growth: A Case of China. *International Journal of Economics and Finance, 13*(12), 82. https://doi.org/10.5539/ijef.v13n12p82

Huang, P., Officer, M. S., & Powell, R. (2016). Method of Payment and Risk Mitigation in Cross-border Mergers and Acquisitions. *Journal of Corporate Finance, 40*, 216–234. https://doi.org/10.1016/j.jcorpfin.2016.08.006

Huang, Y., & Mayer, M. (2022). Digital Currencies, Monetary Sovereignty, and U.S.–China Power Competition. *Policy & Internet*, *14*(2), 324–347. https://doi.org/10.1002/poi3.302

Huo, W., Deng, F., & Chen, J. (2017). An Empirical Analysis of the Renminbi: Exchange Rates and Cross-border Trade Settlement. *World Economy, 41*(8), 2001–2019. https://doi.org/10.1111/twec.12548

Islam, M. M., Islam, M. K., Shahjalal, M., Chowdhury, M. Z., & Jang, Y. M. (2023). A Low-Cost Cross-Border Payment System based on Auditable Cryptocurrency with Consortium Blockchain: Joint Digital Currency. *IEEE Transactions on Services Computing*, 1–14. https://doi.org/10.1109/tsc.2022.3207224

Jakšić, M., Todorović, V., & Matić, J. (2022). The Influence of Digital Currency on the Banking Sector in Europe. *Ekonomske Teme, 60*(4), 481–494. https://doi.org/10.2478/ethemes-2022-0026

Khiaonarong, T. (2003). Payment Systems Efficiency, Policy Approaches, and the Role of the Central Bank. *Social Science Research Network.* https://doi.org/10.2139/ssrn.444480

Kim, Y. S., & Kwon, O. (2022). Central Bank Digital Currency, Credit Supply, and Financial Stability. *Journal of Money, Credit, and Banking/journal of Money, Credit and Banking*, *55*(1), 297–321. https://doi.org/10.1111/jmcb.12913

Kochergin, D. (2021). Central Banks Digital Currencies: World Experience. *Mirovaâ Èkonomika I Meždunarodnye Otnošeniâ*, *65*(5), 68–77. https://doi.org/10.20542/0131-2227-2021-65-5-68-77

Kóczián, B., Kollarik, A., Kiss, L., & Šimon, P. (2022). Central Bank Digital currency: A New Instrument of Monetary Policy. *Pénzügyi Szemle/Public Finance Quarterly*, *67*(4), 522–538. https://doi.org/10.35551/pfq_2022_4_3

Lee, D. (2022). CBDCs and the More Proactive Roles of International Organisations. *Journal of Student Research*, *11*(3). https://doi.org/10.47611/jsrhs.v11i3.3728

Li, D., & Choi, J. (2022). Evaluation of Economic Benefits and Ecological Environment Impact of Export Trade in Anhui Free Trade Zone. *Scientific Programming*, *2022*, 1–9. https://doi.org/10.1155/2022/9441002

Li, X. H. (2021). Blockchain-based Cross-border E-business Payment Model. *2021 2nd International Conference on E-Commerce and Internet Technology (ECIT)*. https://doi.org/10.1109/ecit52743.2021.00022

Liao, S., & McDowell, D. (2014). Redback Rising: China's Bilateral Swap Agreements and Renminbi Internationalisation. *International Studies Quarterly, 59*(3), 401–422. https://doi.org/10.1111/isqu.12161

Lin, X., Suanpong, K., Ruangkanjanases, A., Lim, Y., & Chen, S. (2022). Improving the Sustainable Usage Intention of Mobile Payments: Extended Unified Theory of Acceptance and Use of Technology model combined with the Information System Success Model and initial trust model. *Frontiers in Psychology, 12*. https://doi.org/10.3389/fpsyg.2021.634911

Lin, X., Wu, R., Lim, Y., Jinsoo, H., & Chen, S. (2019). Understanding the Sustainable Usage Intention of Mobile Payment Technology in Korea: Cross-Countries Comparison of Chinese and Korean users. *Sustainability, 11*(19), 5532. https://doi.org/10.3390/su11195532

Lin, Y. (2022). Research on Optimisation of Steel Foreign Trade Financial Transaction Based on Blockchain Technology. *Journal of Mobile Information Systems, 2022*, 1–15. https://doi.org/10.1155/2022/5759154

Majeed, M. T. (2019). Distributional Effects of International Trade: A Comparative Analysis. *International Journal of Management Research and Emerging Sciences, 9*(1). https://doi.org/10.56536/ijmres.v9i1.41

Matusz, S. J., & Tarr, D. G. (2017). Adjusting to Trade Policy Reform. In *World Scientific Studies in International Economics* (pp. 77–114). https://doi.org/10.1142/9789813108448_0004

Oneal, J. R. (2003). Measuring Interdependence and Its Pacific Benefits: A Reply to Gartzke & Li. *Journal of Peace Research, 40*(6), 721–725. https://doi.org/10.1177/00223433030406007

Ozili, P. K. (2022). Central Bank Digital Currency Research Around the World: A Review of Literature. *Journal of Money Laundering Control, 26*(2), 215–226. https://doi.org/10.1108/jmlc-11-2021-0126

Ozili, P. K. (2022). Circular Economy and Central Bank Digital Currency. *Circular Economy and Sustainability/circular Economy and Sustainability, 2*(4), 1501–1516. https://doi.org/10.1007/s43615-022-00170-0

Ozili, P. K. (2022c). Can Central Bank Digital Currency Increase Financial Inclusion? Arguments for and against*. *Emerald Publishing Limited*, pp. 241–249). https://doi.org/10.1108/978-1-80262-637-720221013

Özsoy, Ç. Y. (2020). COVID-19 Pandemic and Central Bank Digital Currency as the Future of Money. *Ekonomi Maliye İşletme Dergisi, 3*(1), 1–9. https://doi.org/10.46737/emid.725549

Polasik, M., Widawski, P., Keler, G., & Butor-Keler, A. (2021). Retail Payments Strategy for the EU Versus the Challenges of the Payment Sector. *Ekonomia I Prawo, 20*(3), 617–640. https://doi.org/10.12775/eip.2021.037

Ponamorenko, V., Nasyrova, G. A., & Molotova, E. S. (2023). Central Bank Digital Currencies as an Element of the Payment-centric Model of Global Financial Regulation. *Cifrovoe Pravo, 4*(1), 64–73. https://doi.org/10.38044/2686-9136-2023-4-1-64-73

PricewaterhouseCoopers. (2021). The Evolving Landscape of Cross-border Payments. *PwC*. https://www.pwc.in/industries/financial-services/fintech/dp/the-evolving-landscape-of-cross-border-payments.html

Pröpper, M., Van Lelyveld, I., & Heijmans, R. (2008). Towards a Network Description of Interbank Payment Flows. *Social Science Research Network*. https://doi.org/10.2139/ssrn.1207922

Rao, J. S. (2022). Improvement of China's Legal System of Systematised Cross-border Payment Supervision under the Background of Digital Economy. *Academic Journal of Business & Management*, *4*(15). https://doi.org/10.25236/ajbm.2022.041520

Rosati, S., & Secola, S. (2006). Explaining Cross-border Large-value Payment Flows: Evidence from TARGET and EURO1 data. *Journal of Banking & Finance, 30*(6), 1753–1782. https://doi.org/10.1016/j.jbankfin.2005.09.011

Rose, A. K. (2005). Which International Institutions Promote International Trade? *Review of International Economics, 13*(4), 682–698. https://doi.org/10.1111/j.1467-9396.2005.00531.x

Song, K., & Xia, L. (2020). Bilateral Swap Agreement and Renminbi Settlement in Cross-border Trade. *Economic and Political Studies/economic and Political Studies, 8*(3), 355–373. https://doi.org/10.1080/20954816.2020.1780818

Teker, S., Teker, D., & Orman, I. (2022). Evolution of Digital Payment Systems and a Breakthrough. *Journal of Economics, Management and Trade*, 100–108. https://doi.org/10.9734/jemt/2022/v28i1030452

Themistocleous, M., Da Cunha, P. R., Tabakis, E., & Papadaki, M. (2023). Towards Cross-border CBDC Interoperability: Insights from a Multivocal Literature Review. *Journal of Enterprise Information Management, 36*(5), 1296–1318. https://doi.org/10.1108/jeim-11-2022-0411

Tian, X., Zhu, J., Zhao, X., & Wu, J. J. (2022). Improving Operational Efficiency through Blockchain: Evidence from a Field Experiment in Cross-border Trade. *Production Planning & Control*, pp. 1–16. https://doi.org/10.1080/09537287.2022.2058412

United Nations Conference on Trade and Development. (2023). Experiences with CBDCs in Selected Developing Countries. In *Crypto Assets and Central Bank Digital Currencies: Potential Implications for Developing Countries* (pp. 42–45). https://doi.org/10.18356/9789210026178c013

Wang, F., Ye, L., & Chen, W. (2022a). Analysis on Innovation Path of Cross-Border Export E-Commerce Platform Model based on Block Chain. In *Proceedings of the 2022 International Conference on Artificial Intelligence,*

Internet and Digital Economy (ICAID 2022) (pp. 393–402). https://doi.org/10.2991/978-94-6463-010-7_41

Wang, X., Zhao, B., & Chen, J. (2022b). The Construction of Consumer Dynamic Trust in Cross-border Online Shopping—Qualitative Research based on Tmall Global, JD Worldwide and NetEase Koala. *Journal of Contemporary Marketing Science*, *5*(1), 1–28. https://doi.org/10.1108/jcmars-08-2021-0031

Wang, G., & Hausken, K. (2022). A Two-Period Decision Model for Central Bank Digital Currencies and Households. *International Journal of Finance & Banking Studies*, *11*(2), 49–68. https://doi.org/10.20525/ijfbs.v11i2.1789

Wang, S., & Wang, Z. (2019). The Status of Cross-border RMB Settlement and Its Influencing Factors: Evidence from Panel Data. *Proceedings of the 3rd International Seminar on Education Innovation and Economic Management (SEIEM 2018)*. https://doi.org/10.2991/seiem-18.2019.122

Wang, X. (2022). Research on Payment Settlement Mode in Cross-Border Business Trade based on Blockchain Technology. *Africa Research Journal*, *113*(3), 129–132. https://doi.org/10.23919/saiee.2022.9853022

Wang, Y., Wang, Y., & Lee, S. H. (2017). The Effect of Cross-Border E-Commerce on China's International Trade: An Empirical Study based on Transaction Cost Analysis. *Sustainability, 9*(11), 2028. https://doi.org/10.3390/su9112028

Wu, B., An, X., Wang, C., & Shin, H. Y. (2022). Extending UTAUT with National Identity and Fairness to Understand user Adoption of DCEP in China. *Scientific Reports*, *12*(1). https://doi.org/10.1038/s41598-022-10927-0

Wu, R. Z., Lee, J. H., & Tian, X. F. (2021). Determinants of the Intention to Use Cross-Border Mobile Payments in Korea among Chinese Tourists: An Integrated Perspective of UTAUT2 with TTF and ITM. *Journal of Theoretical and Applied Electronic Commerce Research, 16*(5), 1537–1556. https://doi.org/10.3390/jtaer16050086

Xiang, W., & Zhang, J. (2018). Analysis on Causes Affecting Payment Method of Small and Micro Cross-border E-commerce. *Proceedings of the 1st International Conference on Contemporary Education and Economic Development (CEED 2018)*. https://doi.org/10.2991/ceed-18.2018.66

You, R. (2022). A new dimension in the world economy—Fiat Digital Currencies: A review. *BCP Business & Management*, *30*, 705–711. https://doi.org/10.54691/bcpbm.v30i.2520

Zhong, B. (2022). The Research on Innovative Application of Blockchain Technology in Sharing Economy. In *Proceedings of the 2022 International Conference on Bigdata Blockchain and Economy Management (ICBBEM 2022)* (pp. 68–79). https://doi.org/10.2991/978-94-6463-030-5_9

Acknowledgements and Conclusion

We would like to give full respect and pay our gratitude to all professors and researchers from Iceland, India and Poland, who decided to share their knowledge and thoughts to create this book that is concentrated on digital currencies in global trade. The eighteen chapters give the answers to the main question formulated in the preface regarding how digital currencies impact global trade in the new global economic world order. Relevant case studies from different countries were also presented to underline the fact that digital currencies are an important aspect of the global economy especially for sustainable development. An interesting fact was raised regarding how businesses and individuals accept digital currencies. The example of e-CNY and e-Ruppee implementations were presented as examples of how digital currencies may change international trade. Nowadays, the concept of digital currencies and the digital monetary systems such as Eurosystem also intake resilience and ecosystem which were discussed in the book. Those solutions impact also the standard of living and business development in international trade which impacts a new world economic order. Countries and organisations like China, which can implement the e-CNY on a large scale in trade are the leaders. Digital currencies in global trade are a live concept, which shows great importance, especially in forming and implementing The Eurosystem in Europe. From the technical perspective, the development of digital and cryptocurrencies was reflected in the vast number of literature positions. This book is a joint effort to help understand the main

R. Aneja and R. Dygas (eds.), *Digital Currencies in The New Global World Order*, https://doi.org/10.1007/978-981-97-4810-5

challenges of implementing a digital currency in global trade, showing the different experiences of India, Germany, Iceland, China, Nigeria, Ghana, UAE, and Jamaica. This effort should lead to establishing something which is observed in today's global trade by the authors as a new global economic order where China plays the leading role and the other countries trying to prepare their strategies for the new wave of competition in international trade.

Index

R. Aneja and R. Dygas (eds.), *Digital Currencies in The New Global World Order*, https://doi.org/10.1007/978-981-97-4810-5

The manufacturer's authorised representative in the EU is Springer
Nature Customer Service Centre GmbH, Europaplatz 3, 69115 Heidelberg,
Germany. If you have any concerns regarding our products, please
contact ProductSafety@springernature.com

Printed and bound by CPI Group (UK) Ltd, Croydon, CR0 4YY
01/10/2026
02225854-0013